LAN SLUDER'S
GUIDE
TO THE
CAYES, COAST
AND BEACHES OF
BELIZE

COPYRIGHT

Lan Sluder's Guide to the Cayes, Coast and Beaches of Belize
By Lan Sluder

equator

ISBN-13: 978-0692675571
ISBN-10: 0692675574
Published by Equator, Asheville, NC.
First Edition, 2016.

Photographs by Rose Lambert-Sluder, except where noted.

All possible efforts have been made to ensure that the information in this travel guide is accurate and up-to-date. However, things change. If you feel we have left something out or got something wrong, please notify us. We are not liable for delays or losses caused by errors or omissions.

E-mail: lansluder@gmail.com
Website: www.belizefirst.com

Front Cover Photograph: Beach on offshore Belize island, Shutterstock
Back Cover Photographs: Author photo by Sheila M. Lambert; Ambergris Caye beach by James Bommarito/Shutterstock

TABLE OF CONTENTS

Copyright..2

Table of Contents 3

WHY BELIZE? **8**

PLANNING YOUR TRIP......................................**13**
    Overview of Destinations **13**
    Belize City...**14**
    Northern Cayes...**14**
    Offshore Cayes and Atolls **14**
    Northern Belize: Sugar Coast.................................**15**
    Southern Belize: Mainland Beaches **15**
    Itineraries: Where to Go in Belize? **17**

KNOW BEFORE YOU GO **25**
    Where Is Belize? 25
    Entry and Exit Requirements....................................26
    Air Travel to Belize..27
    Climate 27
    Crime and Safety...28
    Practicalities and Emergencies 29

Accommodations.. 30
In-Season and Off-Season.. 32
Best Times to Visit Belize... 33
Food and Dining in Belize 33
Beer, Booze and Other Drinks.. 36
Nightlife.. 39
Holidays 39
Price Levels.. 40
Banks and ATMs... 40
Money and Credit Cards 42
How to Stretch Your Money 43
What to Pack.. 45
Maps... 46
GPS in Belize... 47
Satellite Radio 47
Population of Belize... 47
People of Belize 48
Languages... 49
Taxes 50
Shopping 51
Best Souvenirs 51
Internet... 53
Cell Phones.. 53
Media 54
LGBT 56
Women Traveling Alone.. 56
Travelers with Disabilities 57
Green Belize 58
Churches and Religion.. 59
Kids 59
Pets 60
Drugs 62
Health... 62
Hospitals and Clinics.. 65
Politics and Government... 67
Economy 68
Brief History of Belize 70
Visiting Belize on a Cruise Ship 73
Visitor Information 75

TRANSPORTATION 77
Getting to Belize 77

Arriving by Air 78
Arriving by Sea 81
Arriving by Bus 82
Arriving by Car 83
Traveling Around Belize **87**
Travel by Air 87
Travel by Bus 88
Travel by Rental Car or Golf Cart 90
Travel by Shuttle 93
Travel by Water Taxis 94

BELIZE IN DEPTH **96**
Marine Reserves and National Parks **96**
Art & Craft Galleries **103**
Great Outdoors: Sports & Activities **108**
Festivals and Events **114**
Wild Belize **119**
Tourism Industry in Belize **134**

TOP 10 EVERYTHING **139**
Top 10 Marine Attractions **139**
Top 10 Beach Resorts **142**
Top 10 Budget/Value Hotels **143**
Top 10 Restaurants **144**
Top 10 Watering Holes **145**
Top 10 Sea Adventures **146**
Top 10 Off-the-Beaten-Path Spots **147**
Top 10 Beaches in Belize **148**

DESTINATIONS **149**

Belize City and Environs **150**
Belize City Ratings 150
Belize City Overview 151
Getting to Belize City 154
What to See and Do in Belize City 154
Belize City Lodging 159
Belize City Dining 161
Around Belize City **163**

Northern Belize **168**
Corozal District **168**
Corozal Ratings 168
Corozal Overview 168

Getting to Corozal.. 172
What to See and Do in Corozal............................... 174
Corozal Lodging.. 176
Corozal Dining.. 178

Cayes and Atolls **182**
Ambergris Caye.. **182**
Ambergris Caye Ratings 183
Ambergris Caye Overview 183
Getting to Ambergris Caye 187
What to See and Do on Ambergris Caye................. 191
Ambergris Caye Lodging 195
Ambergris Caye Dining 219
Caye Caulker **227**
Caye Caulker Ratings 227
Caye Caulker Overview 228
Getting to Caye Caulker 230
What to See and Do on Caye Caulker..................... 231
Caye Caulker Lodging 233
Caye Caulker Dining 237
Offshore Cayes & Atolls **240**
Offshore Cayes & Atolls Ratings............................. 240
Offshore Cayes & Atolls Overview 241
Getting to Offshore Cayes & Atolls......................... 241
What to See and Do on Offshore Cayes & Atolls 242
Offshore Cayes Lodging and Dining 242
The Atolls Lodging and Dining 250

Southern Belize **255**
Dangriga and Hopkins **256**
Dangriga and Hopkins Ratings............................... 256
Dangriga and Hopkins Overview 257
Getting to Dangriga and Hopkins........................... 259
What to See and Do in Dangriga and Hopkins 260
Dangriga and Hopkins Lodging............................... 262
Dangriga and Hopkins Dining................................. 266
Placencia Peninsula **269**
Placencia Ratings 269
Placencia Overview 270
Getting to Placencia 274
What to See and Do in Placencia 276
Placencia Lodging 280
Placencia Dining.. 287

Punta Gorda **290**
    Punta Gorda/Toledo Ratings 290
    Punta Gorda/Toledo Overview..............................291
    Getting to Punta Gorda..293
    What to See and Do in Punta Gorda/Toledo 294
    Punta Gorda/Toledo Lodging..................................299
    Punta Gorda/Toledo Dining 303

Appendixes..**305**
   Best Belize Websites **305**
   Kriol & Spanish Phrases...**308**

About Lan Sluder **314**

Best of two worlds: Belize over and under water   Photo licensed from Adobe

WHY BELIZE?

You have a whole world of vacation destinations. Why should you consider Belize? What's special about it? What's different or unique? Will you like it? Here are some of the reasons we believe that you will have a great time in Belize.

BELIZE BARRIER REEF

The Belize Barrier Reef and Belize's atolls became a UNESCO World Heritage site in 1996. Belize's reef, part of the Mesoamerican Barrier Reef system, is the longest reef in the Western and Northern Hemispheres. Belize's reef is only a few hundred yards offshore in the north of Belize and 25 miles out in the far south.

Although it faces challenges from human pollution and global climate change, the Belize Barrier Reef and its related marine environments remain home to a stunning variety of sea life, from hammerhead sharks and eagle rays to permit, bonefish, tarpon and other game fish to beautiful living coral and tropical fish.

Belize's reef is one of the most diverse ecosystems in the world, with more than 500 species of fish, more than 100 types of hard and soft corals and hundreds of species of invertebrates.

The Belize Barrier Reef system and the atolls offer visitors some of the world's best diving, snorkeling and fishing.

Also good news is that Belize is taking positive steps to protect its reef system. Belize has established seven marine reserves and marine national parks. In 2010, Belize became the first country in the world to completely ban bottom trawling and in 2015 the government banned offshore oil drilling within one kilometer of the reef.

ISLAND AND ATOLL HOPPING

In Belize's Caribbean are some 1,000 cayes (islands) and three atolls. The Northern Cayes, Ambergris Caye and Caye Caulker, have regular water taxi and air service. A few other cayes, such as Tobacco, have boats going out regularly. It's not easy, or cheap, to get out to most other islands, or from one island to another. The atolls, 30 to 50 miles offshore, are even tougher. But the payoff for your time and money is the awesome beauty of these islands in the blue Caribbean. Few other places in the world have remote islands like these where you can swim, snorkel, dive, fish and just relax in total peace and calm.

CARIBBEAN BEACHES

Belize has nearly 200 miles of coastline on the Caribbean Sea. And that doesn't count all the miles of beaches on the islands and atolls off the Belize mainland.

Are the beaches in Belize the best in the world? Candidly, no. The Belize Barrier Reef along the coast of Belize creates an ecology that's a nursery for marine life. This means that even the most pristine of beaches in

Belize, despite the crystal clear Caribbean waters and clean white or khaki-colored sand, may have seagrass or may not be ideal for swimming.

Still, until you've relaxed under a cocopalm on a sandy beach, looking out over the emerald green, turquoise blue and deep purple Caribbean and see the white waves on the reef, you've never been on a Belize beach.

OUTDOOR ADVENTURES

Belize's coast and cayes are all about outdoor fun. Hard, soft and in-between. World-class diving and snorkeling. Swimming with nurse sharks, stingrays and whale sharks. Windsurfing. Kitesurfing. Paddleboarding. Sport fishing for bonefish, permit, snook and tarpon, trolling for jack, grouper and barracuda or blue water fishing for tuna, sailfish and wahoo. Canoeing and kayaking, on lagoons, rivers and sea.

Of course it's easier if you're 23 and a triathlete, but even we who are not young and fit anymore can participate in many of the outdoor adventures Belize offers.

SUNNY WARM WEATHER

Belize has weather similar to that of Central and South Florida, depending on where you are in Belize. The mean average temperature is 81°F along the coast and on the cayes, although prevailing breezes from the sea nearly year-round make it feel cooler. The water temperature stays in the low to mid-80s. The coldest month is January while the highest temperatures are during the month of May.

Cloud cover can be significant, especially in the summer, but generally Belize has warm, sunny weather year round.

CULTURAL DIVERSITY

Belize is a tropical gumbo of cultures, races and ethnicities. Talk about diversity! There are Creoles, a mixture of African, European and indigenous genes, once the dominant culture in Belize and still so in Belize City and a few other places. The Bileez Kriol language (to use the proper spelling) still is the *lingua franca* in Belize. However, Mestizos from Mexico and elsewhere in Latin America, often referred to in Belize as "Spanish," are now the largest ethnic group, about one-half of the population. Some are long-time Belizeans who came to south to escape the Caste Wars in Mexico in the 19th century and others are recent migrants from Guatemala, El Salvador and Honduras. There are Maya – Mopan, Yucatec and other – and Garifuna, plus East Indians, Middle Easterners ("Lebanese"), Chinese from Hong Kong and Mainland China, Mennonites, Old School and progressive, and a good number of expat U.S., Canadian, British and European folks.

GREAT FOOD & DRINK

You might have heard that Belizean food is nothing special. You heard wrong! Belize today has some wonderful food, from basic Belizean dishes like stew chicken with beans and rice or *garnaches* and *empanadas* to amazing pork and delicious lobster, conch, snapper and other seafood. You can eat a filling meal for a few dollars in a local restaurant or enjoy a sophisticated dinner in San Pedro, Placencia, Hopkins or Caye Caulker. That special dinner won't be cheap, but it probably will cost two-thirds less than you'd pay in Miami, San Francisco, New Orleans or New York. In most cases, you'll enjoy the seaside ambiance even more.

SPEAK ENGLISH

English is the official language of Belize. Government documents and signs are in English. Police and immigration officials speak English. Tour guides, hotel employees and restaurant staffs speak English. It makes traveling in Belize really easy. You can have real discussions with Belizeans you meet.

On the other hand, if you want to practice your Spanish – or Kriol, Garifuna, German, one of the Maya languages or even Mandarin – you'll have a chance to do so in Belize. Many Belizeans are fluent in two, three or four languages.

GET A FRIENDLY WELCOME

Every country brags that it is friendly and welcoming. In Belize, they really mean it. Belizeans, by and large, are among the friendliest people you'll ever meet. A few are out to hustle you, but most are just interested in you, what you have to say and want to pass the time with you. Begging is rare, except here and there in Belize City. Relax, keep your guard down (but use common sense), and you'll meet some wonderful people in Belize.

SAVE MONEY

Whoever told you Belize was expensive was right. And wrong.

Sure, you can drop US$400 a night, or more, at some fancy beach resorts. One private island resort goes for over US$2,000 a night, although that rate includes everything from cocktails to your personal butler.

But you can also stay at a delightful seaside cabaña for under US$100 or stay in a charming guesthouse for under US$50 or in a hostel for US$15. You can get a filling lunch of stew chicken and beans and rice for US$5, drink local rum or beer in a nice bar for US$2 or $3 and have an amazing lobster dinner with all the trimmings for US$25.

Belize may be a little more expensive than much of the rest of Central America, but in Belize you can drink the water, eat salads and wander about most places without fearing for your life. By comparison with the islands in the main Caribbean, Belize is a bargain, baby.

GO FOR IT!

Belize is only two or three hours by air from many gateways in the U.S. You can leave home in the morning and be on the beach by mid-afternoon. What are you waiting for?

Success! Fly fisherman lands a bonefish   Photo by Matt Jeppson/Shutterstock

PLANNING YOUR TRIP

Rolling on the Rio Grande, Toledo   Photo by Sheila M. Lambert

OVERVIEW OF DESTINATIONS

This guidebook focuses on the islands, atolls and coastal beach resort areas of Belize. The country has wonderful inland destinations as well, with rainforests, Maya ruins, jungle lodges and adventures like jungle trekking, caving and cave tubing, hiking, horseback riding, mountain biking, birding and wildlife spotting. For more information about that amazing part of Belize, see *Lan Sluder's Guide to Belize* or *Lan Sluder's Guide to Mainland Belize*.

Here, in thumbnail sketches, are your main choices of places to visit and stay on the cayes, atolls and coastal beach areas of Belize. In the chapters that follow, we'll explore in more detail the options in each of these areas, including a general overview of each destination, its rating (based on a scale of A+ to F, just like on your old school report card) on key factors likely important to you, how to get to the destination, what to do and see there, your lodging choices and the best places to eat and drink there.

BELIZE CITY

We're including Belize City not because it is a destination of much interest to those visiting Belize for activities on the water but because it is where most visitors arrive, and it also is the transportation, commercial and cultural hub of the country.

NORTHERN CAYES

The two largest of Belize's Northern Cayes are Ambergris Caye (pronounced Am-BUR-griss Key) and Caye Caulker, sometimes known as Caye Corker.

Ambergris Caye

Ambergris Caye is the most popular destination for visitors to Belize (and also for expats), for many good reasons. It offers the beauty of the Caribbean in a compact, accessible and friendly package. The island is roughly one-half the size of Barbados. You can dive, snorkel, swim and fish to your heart's content.

San Pedro, Ambergris Caye's only town, has Belize's biggest and arguably best selection of resorts, restaurants and nightlife. While San Pedro is no Cancún by any means, it is much more developed than it used to be, with many of the old hard-packed sand street now paved. Even the old golf cart path up North Ambergris Caye is being paved. Quite a few residents now have cars instead of golf carts or bicycles, occasionally creating mini-traffic jams. While there are no highrises as in the mass tourism destinations in Mexico and the main Caribbean, a few buildings are now taller than coconut palms.

Caye Caulker

Ambergris Caye's sister island is smaller and, if anything, even friendlier. Caye Caulker still has the old Caribbean island atmosphere, with sandy streets, just one small village and almost no cars. You can enjoy the diving, snorkeling, swimming and other water sports on Caulker at lower cost than on Ambergris Caye. While it has a number of good restaurants and some nice hotels, the choice is smaller than San Pedro's. It's definitely more of a budget destination.

OFFSHORE CAYES AND ATOLLS

Although most of Belize's island visitors don't stray much beyond Ambergris Caye and Caye Caulker, Belize has about 1,000 other cayes (some just a few square yards in size) in the Caribbean. A couple dozen of these islands have diving and fishing lodges. Belize also has three Pacific-style atolls – Lighthouse, Glover's and Turneffe – with coral islands around a central lagoon. The atolls, sometimes called Belize's Outer Reef in contrast with the Inner Reef, the Belize Barrier Reef, are almost unique in the Americas. There is only one other atoll, Banco Chinchorro Atoll, a bit north of Belize off the Yucatán on Mexico's Gulf Coast.

NORTHERN BELIZE: SUGAR COAST

Most visitors to Belize either never get to Corozal or pass through quickly en route somewhere else. But Corozal Town and nearby villages, not to mention the Cerros area and Sarteneja, a quaint fishing village, offer a lot for those lingering awhile: low prices, friendly people, a generally low-crime environment, the beautiful blue waters of Corozal Bay and even, in the Corozal Free Zone, casinos. Then there's the bonus of having Mexico next door for shopping, dining and fun. Chetumal, capital of Quintana Roo, is the gateway to Mexico's Costa Maya and the tourism hotspots of Tulum, Playa del Carmen, Cancún and Cozumel.

Corozal is one of the undiscovered jewels of Belize. There's not a lot to do, but it's a great place to do it.

The Sugar Coast – sugarcane is a main agricultural crop in Corozal as it is in the adjoining Orange Walk District – is a place to slow down, relax and enjoy life. The climate is appealing, with less rain than almost anywhere else in Belize, and fishing is good. The sunny disposition of residents – Mestizos, Creoles, Maya, Chinese, East Indians and even North Americans – is infectious.

SOUTHERN BELIZE: MAINLAND BEACHES

Dangriga

Most visitors bypass Dangriga, except as a jumping off spot for Tobacco Caye, Southwater Caye and other offshore cayes. While the Garifuna town is a bit scruffy, it has a lively attitude and a thriving art and crafts community, and there are a few beach areas. It is also the hometown of what is probably Belize's best-known export, Marie Sharp's hot sauce.

Hopkins

On the southern coast of Belize in Stann Creek District between Dangriga and Placencia, Hopkins today is what nearby Placencia was like 15 years ago. Hopkins is a friendly Garifuna village that got its first telephones only in the mid-1990s.

New small seaside resorts and luxury condo developments are going up in Hopkins and Sittee Point. Although at times the sand flies can eat you alive here, you can get in some excellent fishing and beach time, with Barrier Reef and atoll diving and snorkeling a boat ride away.

Placencia

The Placencia peninsula boasts the longest and best beaches on the mainland, and it's an appealing seaside alternative to the bustle of Ambergris Caye. The paving of the Placencia Road, the main road down the peninsula, completed in 2012, has made access much easier.

This peninsula has some 16 miles of beachfront along the Caribbean, a backside lagoon where manatees are frequently seen, two small, colorful villages, more than 125 hotels, several dozen restaurants and an increasing number of expatriates and foreign-owned homes. In recent years, the Placencia peninsula has been undergoing a boom, a boom that was slowed only temporarily by Hurricane Iris in 2001 and the Great Recession of 2008-2011. Building lots by the score have been sold to foreigners who think they'd someday like to live by the sea.

Besides beaches, Placencia offers fine diving and snorkeling (including with whale sharks in the late spring and early summer) on patch reefs, the Belize Barrier Reef about 20 miles offshore and two of Belize's three atolls. Sport fishing is good here, too.

The unknown kicker here is the scheduled opening in late 2016 of the Norwegian Cruise Lines cruise port on an island just off Placencia. Who knows what the impact will be of tens of thousands of cruise daytrippers waddling around Placencia and environs?

Punta Gorda

Rainy, beautiful and remote, Punta Gorda in far Southern Belize is the base for you to visit unspoiled southern cayes and reefs, with a break to see ancient Maya sites, contemporary Maya villages and lush rainforest, and for onward travel to Guatemala and Honduras. The completion of the Southern Highway, now the best major road in Belize, has made access to the Deep South a lot easier, and work is far along on a new paved road connecting the Southern Highway to Guatemala, with a planned new border crossing at Jalacte.

PG, as it's known in Belize, is Toledo's only real town, with about 6,000 people, mostly Garifuna, Maya and immigrants from Guatemala. It enjoys a picturesque setting on the Bay of Honduras. While there are no real beaches around the town, there are beaches elsewhere in Toledo, around Monkey River and Punta Negra as well as on the offshore cayes. These beaches are accessible in most cases only by boat.

ITINERARIES: WHERE TO GO IN BELIZE?

See the wonders of Belize   Map courtesy of Belize Tourism Board

Here are several possible itineraries for your Belize visit or visits. We've outlined four different itineraries, of different lengths from one to two weeks and for those with varying interests. Note that on a one-week trip you really need to plan a total time of at least eight days to allow for travel time coming and going plus short arrival and departure days. Of course, there are many other ways to see Belize. Consider these just starting points.

ONE-WEEK NORTHERN CAYES
Day 1: Arrive at **Philip S. W. Goldson International Airport** near Belize City. Board Tropic Air or Maya Island Air for a 20-minute flight to **San Pedro, Ambergris Caye**. On arrival at San Pedro, get settled into your resort hotel (**The Phoenix Resort, Xanadu, Victoria House** or **Pelican Reef Villas Resort** are top choices, but there are also budget and mid-level options). Do a walking tour of San Pedro Town. Have dinner at **Casa Picasso, El Fogón** or another restaurant in town.

Day 2: After breakfast at your hotel or at **Estel's Dine by the Sea,** take a morning snorkel trip to **Hol Chan Marine Reserve.** Snorkel with nurse sharks and stingrays at **Shark-Ray Alley.** Back on the island, relax on a beach, grab a light lunch at **Robin's Kitchen** or do some shopping in town. Have dinner at **Elvi's Kitchen** or **Blue Water Grill.** Top off the evening with rum drinks or beers at one of the bars and clubs such as **Wayos, Wahoo's** or **Jaguars**.

Day 3: Get some breakfast at **The Baker**. Take a golf cart or bike ride up **North Ambergris** on the newly paved road (or go by **Coastal Xpress** ferry.) Stop along the way at a beach bar such as **Rojo Beach Bar** or the roadside **Truck Stop** for a cold Belikin or two. Alternatively, tour the **Marco Gonzalez Maya site** at the south end of the island. Walk on the beach. Have a nice dinner at **Black Orchid** or **Palmilla** at Victoria House or at a restaurant in town.

Day 4: After an early breakfast at your hotel or one of the local eateries, take a boat tour to **Bacalar Chico National Park and Marine Reserve on North Ambergris** with a stop at **Mexico Rocks** for great snorkeling. After a day in the sun, cool down and relax with something cold at one of the beach bars. Have dinner at **Wild Mango's** or **Red Ginger** or another restaurant.

Day 5: Say your goodbyes to San Pedro and take a water taxi (30 minutes) to Caye Caulker. On Caulker, check into your hotel. **Iguana Reef, CayeReef, Seaside Cabañas, Seadreams, Tree Tops** and **Maxhapan** are good choices in a variety of price ranges. After checking in, walk Front Street and take in the island atmosphere. Go to **The Split** and the **Lazy Lizard** for a swim, a cold beer and a peek at the sunset over the back side of the island. Have dinner at **Habaneros,** perhaps with a nightcap at **I&I bar.**

Day 6: Take the full-day dive or snorkel trip by fast boat to the **Blue Hole** and **Half Moon Caye** at **Lighthouse Reef Atoll.** You'll be tired after a full day on and in the water, so have a casual dinner at **Wish-Willy** or at one of the fish and lobster grills set up on Front Street.

Day 7: Go **fishing for bonefish** on the flats, or if you're up for more snorkeling, do a boat trip to the Belize Barrier Reef in the **Caye Caulker Marine Reserve,** combined with **manatee spotting** at **Swallow Cave Reserve.** Have an Italian meal with a Belizean touch at **Il Pellicano Cucina Italiana** or **Pasta Per Caso.**

Day 8: Take a puddle-jumper (about 15 minutes) direct to the international airport or a water taxi (45 minutes) and then a cab (25 minutes) for your **departure flight.**

ONE-WEEK ISLAND OR ATOLL LODGE

For a totally relaxed, no-worry, no-decision vacation, choose a weeklong stay at an offshore island or atoll dive or fishing lodge. If you don't want to dive, snorkel or fish, you can just chill in a hammock, soak up the rays or beachcomb. Most remote lodges offer all-inclusive packages that include transportation in Belize to the lodge, a set schedule of daily diving or fishing, along with accommodations and meals. Some offer a complete AI package including drinks, taxes and tips. The options for a week on an island are many, ranging from the US$2,000+ night at Cayo Espanto to US$200-a-week camping at Glover's Atoll Resort. An alternative for divers is a week on one of the live aboard dive boat in the Aggressor fleet, with up to five dives a day. *See the Remote Cayes and Atolls section for options.*

Day 1: Arrive at **Philip S. W. Goldson International Airport** near Belize City. In most cases, you'll be met at the airport for transportation by boat or air to your lodge.

Days 2-7: Dive, snorkel, fish or laze around to your heart's content. Everything is yours with no hassle – meals, snacks, drinks and activities.

Day 8: **Return to the international airport** for your flight home.

10-DAY BELIZE BEACH TRIP

Day 1: Arrive at **Philip S. W. Goldson International Airport** near Belize City. Board Tropic Air or Maya Island Air for the 15-minute flight to **Caye Caulker,** or cab into Belize City and take a water taxi. Alternatively, you could start your beach trip in **San Pedro, Ambergris**

Caye *(see One-Week Northern Cayes itinerary above for ideas on Ambergris Caye.)* On Caulker, check into your hotel. **Iguana Reef, CayeReef, Seaside Cabañas, Seadreams, Tree Tops** and **Maxhapan** are good choices in a variety of price ranges. After checking in, go to **The Split** and the **Lazy Lizard** for a beer and a peek at the sunset over the west side of the island. Have dinner at **Habaneros.**

Day 2: Do a snorkel trip to the **Caye Caulker Marine Reserve** before continuing on to **Hol Chan Marine Reserve** to swim and snorkel with nurse sharks and stingrays. Depending on which tour operator you choose, a full-day snorkel trip may include other stops such as **San Pedro.** After returning to Caulker and setting up your next day's dive or snorkel trip to Lighthouse Reef, have authentic Italian prepared the a Belizean touch with dinner at **Il Pellicano Cucina Italiana** or **Pasta Per Caso.** End the evening with drinks in a swing at **I&I Bar.**

Day 3: Take a full-day trip by fast boat to the **Blue Hole** and **Half Moon Caye at Lighthouse Reef Atoll.** You'll be tired after a full day on the water, so have a casual dinner at **Syd's, Wish-Willy** or at one of the fish and lobster grills set up on Front Street.

Day 4: After an early breakfast at **Amor y Café** or **Glenda's,** take a water taxi to Belize City. Then hop a Tropic Air or Maya Island Air flight from **Belize Municipal Airport** to **Dangriga,** or go by pre-arranged shuttle or, for a true Belizean experience, take a bus via Belmopan and down the scenic Hummingbird Highway to Dangriga. From Dangriga, you have several options for the next stage in your beach vacation. You could go from the Dangriga airstrip by taxi to Hopkins and stay at least two or three days at **Hamanasi Adventure & Dive Resort** if it's in your budget or at **Hopkins Inn** or **Jungle Jeanie's** or **Coconut Row** if not. Another option is to head out to one of private island resorts off Dangriga. A top choice is **Pelican Beach Resort** on **Southwater Caye**. You will probably need to overnight at the Pelican Beach in Dangriga first. Another choice is to do a three- or four-night stay at one of the dive and fishing lodges on **Turneffe** or **Glover's atoll** such as **Turneffe Flats** at Turneffe Atoll or **Off-the-Wall Dive Center & Resort at Glover's.** Finally, if you're more of a budget traveler, you can take a boat from Dangriga to **Tobacco Caye.** Again, depending on arrival time in Dangriga, you may need to overnight. **Chaleanor** is a good low-end choice.

Days 5, 6, 7: Dive, snorkel and fish to your heart's content at Hopkins, Southwater Caye, Tobacco Caye or Turneffe or Glover's atoll. You'll be eating and drinking at your lodge, with no decision except what pair of shorts and tee shirt to wear.

Day 8: Return to Dangriga and **move on to Placencia** by bus, shuttle or taxi. (You may also be able to rent a car in Dangriga or have one delivered from Placencia, if you want the extra freedom of your own transportation.) If you have time, make a quick stop at the **Pen Cayetano Studio** and **Gulisi Garifuna Museum** in Dangriga. In Placencia, among the great lodging options are **Chabil Mar Villas, Maya Beach Hotel, Laru Beya** and Frances Ford Coppola's **Turtle Inn.** For your first night, you'll probably want to eat at your hotel, and if it's Maya Beach Hotel you'll be steps from the **Maya Beach Hotel Bistro,** the best restaurant in Southern Belize. Note: It is also possible to go from Caye Caulker to Placencia on a three-day Raggamuffin or Blackhawk boat trip, with a camping stopover on Tobacco Caye, but let's not complicate the itinerary any more than we have to.

Day 9: Since you've been diving and snorkeling your eyes out the past few days, take a break and just explore the Placencia peninsula. You'll want to see **Maya Beach, Seine Bight**, the Garifuna village, and of course **Placencia village.** Traveling up and down the peninsula is best done with a rental car, but it can also be done by taxi or rental golf cart, scooter or, if you're up for sweating in the heat and humidity, by bicycle. Relax on the breezy shore at Maya Beach or in Placencia village. Be sure to take a walk on the Placencia sidewalk. Have a local lunch at **Dawn's Grill 'n Go** and by all means don't miss the gelato at **Tutti-Frutti.** It's authentically Italian with a tropical twist. Arrange your next day's dive, snorkel or fishing trip – if it's whale shark time you usually need to do the arrangements further ahead, as space on the trips is limited -- and then have dinner at **Maya Beach Hotel Bistro, The Secret Garden, Rumfish y Vino** or via a quick boat shuttle at **Tranquilo** on an island just off Point Placencia. End the evening at **Barefoot Beach Bar.**

Day 10: If it's whale shark season (usually April through June) and the timing is right, take a **whale shark dive or snorkel trip to Gladden Spit.** Otherwise, do a dive or snorkel trip to **Laughing Bird Caye National Park** or to **Glover's** or **Turneffe atoll.** If you're an angler, fishing for bonefish, permit and tarpon also is great from Placencia. End your evening with a big dinner at your favorite restaurant, but leave room for more gelato from **Tutti-Frutti.**

Day 11: Take a Tropic Air flight back to the **Philip S. W. Goldson International Airport** in Ladyville to connect with your flight home.

TWO-WEEK OFF-THE-BEATEN PATH TRIP

This itinerary gets you to lightly visited areas of Belize, both in the far north and far south of the country. It also provides for beach time on

Tobacco Caye and Hopkins. Although you will miss some of the highlights of Belize, you'll see a side of Belize that many tourists don't see. Another advantage is that generally this is a fairly inexpensive way to see Belize (except for renting a car), and you won't have difficulty getting reservations in Corozal and Toledo even at peak times like Christmas and Easter. Of course, you can adapt this itinerary to visit just the northern or the southern destinations and plug in what interests you from other itineraries, such as Ambergris Caye, Caye Caulker or Placencia. This itinerary can be done by bus or shuttle, and partly by air, but the first few days of it is most easily done by rental car, which is what we recommend.

Day 1: Arrive at **Philip S. W. Goldson International Airport** near Belize City. Pick up a rental car at the airport – we like Budget Belize or Crystal – and drive to **Corozal Town.** Spend the night at one of the inexpensive to moderate inns, such as **Serenity Sands B&B** near Consejo village, **Coco Banana** or **Tony's Inn.** The top end in Corozal, yet still quite affordable, is **Almond Tree Resort.** All these lodging choices are on or very near Corozal Bay. Have an inexpensive dinner at **Patty's Bistro** or pizza and drinks at **Corozo Blue.**

Day 2: Spend the morning exploring the bayside town of Corozal, including the **Hoare Market,** where you can get a cheap breakfast or lunch or buy fruit for almost nothing. See **Corozal House of Culture** and the murals at the **Corozal Town Hall.** In the afternoon, take a quick look at the **Santa Rita** Maya ruins at the north end of town and then drive the 8 miles to the **Consejo village** area where a lot of U.S. and other expats live. Have dinner at **Smuggler's Den** on the water near Consejo or at the **Y Not Bar & Grill** by the bay at Tony's Inn back in Corozal Town.

Day 3: After breakfast at **Miss June's Kitchen,** drive to **Cerros Maya** site in the Cerros area near Copper Bank. You'll cross the New River on a hand-pulled vehicle ferry. Be prepared for mosquitos at the ruins, which are on Corozal Bay. Have lunch at the small, delightful **Cerros Beach Resort.** You may like it so much you'll decide to spend the night here, in which case you could do the following the next day. If you don't stay at Cerros, drive a little further, crossing Laguna Seca on another hand-pulled vehicle ferry, to **Orchid Bay.** It is a real estate development selling primarily to foreigners, but it has a decent restaurant, **Tradewinds,** and an inn, **Crimson Orchid B&B.** Stay the night at this B&B and see what you think about living in a place like this.

Day 4: From Cerros or Orchid Bay, drive on to **Sarteneja village.** If you have time in the afternoon, visit **Shipstern Nature Reserve** and do a short self-guided walk. Spend the night in Sarteneja, a quaint little fishing and boat-building village. **Oasis Guest House** and **Fernando's**

Seaside Guesthouse are your best bets, both inexpensive. Have dinner at **Nathalie's Restaurant** at Backpacker's Paradise hostel.

Day 5: Get a cheap early breakfast at **Liz's Fast Food** in Sarteneja, then head out for your **drive back to Belize City,** where you'll turn in your rental car. Go to the **Belize Municipal Airport** for a 45-minute Tropic Air or flight to Dangriga. If you arrive in Dangriga early enough, you can get a boat to **Tobacco Caye**, a tiny, somewhat funky island directly on the reef, with snorkeling from shore. Stay and eat at **Paradise Caye Lodge, Tobacco Caye Lodge** or **Reef's End Lodge**. For the boat transport, check at the Riverside Café, where boat captains hang out, or arrange in advance to be met by a boat from your lodge.

Day 6: Chill out on the island and go snorkeling. Eat and drink at your hotel or at one of the other little lodges on the caye.

Day 7: Use the Reef's End Lodge dive shop for a **dive or snorkel trip to Glover's Reef atoll or Southwater Caye walls.**

Alternative: If money is less of an issue, choose **Pelican Beach Resort at beautiful Southwater Caye** instead of going to Tobacco Caye.

Day 8: Boat back to Dangriga and bus or taxi to Hopkins village about 15 miles from Dangriga, just off the Southern Highway, for a beach break. Check in at **Hopkins Inn** or **Jungle Jeanie's.** Both are on the beach. Another good choice is **Coconut Row.** Take a swim in the Caribbean and top off the day with a delicious meal at **Chef Rob's.**

Day 9: Take a **day dive or snorkel trip to Turneffe or Glover's atoll.** Have dinner at the **Barracuda Grill at Beaches and Dreams** or at another restaurant in Hopkins.

Day 10: Taxi the 4 miles to the Southern Highway and flag down a James Line bus heading south to **Punta Gorda.** If you'd rather, taxi back to Dangriga and take a Tropic Air or Maya Island Air flight to PG. Check in at a small moderately priced inn in PG, such as **Coral House, Hickatee Cottages** or **Blue Belize.** Explore the town a little and have dinner at **Asha's Culture Kitchen,** which is in a shack over the waters of the Gulf of Honduras, or at another inexpensive local eatery.

Day 11: Take a full-day snorkel/dive trip to the **Port Honduras Marine Reserve** or, farther out, to **Sapodilla Caye Marine Reserve**. You'll likely stop at a small caye or two, such as **West Snake Caye** or **Hunting Caye,** for swimming and picnicking.

Day 12: Arrange a **fishing trip to try your luck on permit, tarpon or bonefish.** Off Toledo is one of the world's best permit fishing grounds.

Day 13: For something a little different to end your trip, bus, taxi or take a tour to the **Mopan and Kekchi Maya villages** in rural Toledo, such as **San Antonio, San Pedro Columbia, Santa Cruz, Laguna** and **San Miguel.** The **Toledo Cultural Trail** is being developed to showcase Maya, Garifuna, Creole, Mestizo and East Indian cultures in Toledo. Try to work in time to visit **Blue Creek Cave** near Blue Creek village, tour a **cacao farm** and possibly see the Garifuna village of **Barranco,** birthplace of the late Andy Palacio, the famed punta rock musician. Alternatively, you could visit one of the Maya sites in Toledo, **Lubaantun** or **Nim Li Punit.** A good place for lunch off the newly paved San Antonio Road is **The Farm Inn.** For an upscale final repast, have drinks and a good meal at **Belcampo Belize** lodge, where you can take the tram down to the Rio Grande River and look for crocs or watch the jungle for a passing troop of howler monkeys. *Alternative:* If you have still not had enough marine time, skip the land tours and **head back to one of the pristine cayes off PG for a day of swimming, snorkeling and diving.**

Day 14: Take a Maya Island Air or Tropic Air flight back to **Philip S. W. Goldson International Airport** for your flight home.

Lobster traps on Caye Caulker

KNOW BEFORE YOU GO

Belize is on the Caribbean south of Mexico and east of Guatemala

WHERE IS BELIZE?

Belize is on the Caribbean Coast of Central America, bordered by Mexico to the north and Guatemala to the west and south. To the east is the Caribbean Sea. In Belize waters are as many as 1,000 islands, most

25

unpopulated specks of sand, coral or mangrove. Belize's land area is about the size of the U.S. state of Massachusetts or the country of Wales in the U.K. — 8,867 square miles — with a population estimated at around 368,000 in mid-2015, about as many people as live in metro Savannah, Ga. In addition, Belize's marine area, assuming its territory stretches out 20 kilometers or a little over 12 miles from shore, adds another 9,133 square miles, for a total land and sea area of about 18,000 square miles. From north to south Belize is less than 200 miles in length, and at its widest point it is less than 70 miles across. From popular air gateways in the U.S. including Atlanta, Charlotte, Dallas, Houston and Miami, Belize is only two to three hours.

ENTRY AND EXIT REQUIREMENTS

You must have a valid passport to enter Belize, valid at least during the period of your stay, according to the U.S. Embassy in Belize. However, some airlines flying to Belize, and Belize Immigration, go beyond this and say your passport should have at least six months before expiration. As a precaution, follow the latter rule. **Visas are not required for citizens of the U.S., Canada, the U.K., Mexico, Guatemala, Costa Rica, British Commonwealth, Caribbean Community (CARICOM), European Union (EU)** and a number of other countries. Check the Belize Immigration website (www.belize-immigration.org) for the latest visa requirements.

You should also have an **onward or return ticket.** Immigration in Belize won't ask for it, but the airline you fly in on may.

Entry is granted for up to 30 days at no cost. Note that says *up to 30 days*. The immigration officer can choose to stamp a shorter date in your passport but usually will stamp 30 days. If asked how long you are staying, say "30 days" or "about a month" even if you think you will only be in Belize for a week. Your plans might change.

Renewals of your tourist permit are permitted. Renewals cost US$25 per month per person for the first six months, then US$50 a month. You must apply for a permit at the nearest Immigration office or in remote areas at a police station. After six months, you may need to demonstrate to Belize Immigration why you need or want to stay. Overstaying your permit may incur a fine of US$500, although it usually will be less, or possibly nothing. You are also supposed to have funds sufficient to cover your length of stay (currently put at US$60 a day), but it is highly unlikely that you will be asked to prove this, and in the rare cases of being asked a credit card should be sufficient proof.

When leaving Belize by air, there is a **US$39.25 exit fee.** Citizens and official residents of Belize pay a lower rate. Many airlines include the fee in the ticket price. When leaving Belize by land, at either the Mexico or Guatemala borders, there is a US$15 border fee, plus a $3.75 conservation fee, for a total of **US$18.75 exit fee.** Currently, those leaving by water taxi/ferry pay US3.75. Children under 12 accompanied by parents are exempt from all exit fees.

No vaccinations are required unless coming from a yellow fever endemic area. Check with the U.S. Centers for Disease Control (www.cdc.gov) for any recommended immunizations. On Belize entry or departure, currency in excess of US$5,000 or BZ$10,000 must be declared; if not declared it can and likely will be confiscated.

Cruise ship passengers do not need to go through Belize immigration or show a passport on stops in Belize, but cruise passengers need a valid passport in order to board the ship at their initial port of departure.

AIR TRAVEL TO BELIZE

At present, six major airlines fly to Belize: **American** (which recently merged with US Airways), **Avianca** (formerly TACA), **Copa** (which in late 2015 began offering two weekly flights to Belize from Panama), **Delta, United Airlines** (which merged with Continental) and **Southwest Airlines** (which began service to Belize in late 2015). The gateways for nonstop flights from the U.S. include Atlanta, Charlotte, Dallas, Houston, Los Angeles, Miami and Newark. Avianca has service from San Salvador, and Copa has service from Panama City. In addition, Belize-based **Tropic Air** has service between Belize City and Cancún, Mérida, Flores, Guatemala City, Roatán, San Pedro Sula and Tegucigalpa. *For more information on transportation to and in Belize, see the Transportation section of this guide, below.*

CLIMATE

The climate of Belize has two seasons: a rainy and a dry season. Most of the year's rainfall occurs during the period **June to November, the rainy season,** with the **driest months being February to May.** The transition from dry to the rainy is usually very sharp. Mean annual rainfall across Belize ranges from 60 inches in the north to 160 inches or more in the south. Except for the southern regions, the rainfall varies a good deal from year to year.

Most of Belize has a sub-tropical climate similar to that of Central and South Florida. Belize usually has lows in the 60s to 70s F., with highs in the 80s to low 90s. Occasionally during the winter cold fronts from the north will drop temperatures into the 50s at night, and even into the 40s at the higher elevations. The entire country is frost-free, and snow has never been reported in modern times.

January sees the coolest temperatures of the year, while May has the hottest. In general, daytime temps are higher inland, due to the influence of prevailing winds from the sea on the cayes and coast. The humidity is high year round in all parts of the country.

Belize National Meteorological Service (www.hydromet.gov.bz) is a good source of information both on short-term weather forecasts and longer-term climatic data.

CRIME AND SAFETY

Like many developing countries in the region, Belize has a relatively high crime rate. For example, the homicide rate in Belize was around 33 per 100,000 population in 2014 and 2015. That compares with about 4.5 per 100,000 in the U.S. and 1.4 per 100,000 in Canada for the same period. Other serious crimes such as rape, robbery, burglary and theft in Belize are also generally higher than in the U.S. or Canada, although the difference is not as dramatic in most categories.

However, to put this in context, keep in mind:

First, a **large percentage of serious crimes including murder take place in just one city – Belize City – and within Belize City a large percentage of crimes take place in a fairly small area of the South Side.** Much of this crime is due to extreme poverty in the South Side and to drug and gang activity there. Outside of this "inner city" area of Belize City, the crime rate is much lower.

Second, most violent crimes in Belize involve drugs, gang activity and family or personal feuds. Most visitors to Belize spend little time in Belize City, except in transit, and most are not exposed to the drug-, gang- and feud-related situations. Therefore, tourists in Belize are much less exposed to violent crime risk than the average Belizean resident.

Theft of personal property is a risk in Belize, as it is for most travelers anywhere in the world, **but beyond that most visitors to Belize say they feel safe and express little serious worry about being the victim of crime**. The author of this book has been traveling to every area of Belize for more than 25 years and has never been the victim of any violent crime and only on two occasions experienced minor thefts, totaling less than US$50.

When in Belize, as when you travel anywhere, you should take the standard traveler's precautions: Use common sense – if something seems sketchy, it may well be; ask locally, at your hotel or elsewhere, about neighborhoods and areas that are best avoided; don't wander into unlit, unpopulated areas at night, whether it's at the beach or in a city; keep an eye on your personal possessions; don't flaunt your wealth (and by comparison with the average Belizean you are definitely wealthy) by wearing expensive jewelry or exposing wads of cash; be careful of friends you make in bars – Belizeans are very friendly, but a few are too friendly; and of course don't put yourself in situations, such as buying drugs or drinking to excess, when bad things can easily happen. In Belize City in particular, don't walk alone or even as a couple or group after dark and always take a licensed taxi (they have green license tags) anywhere you go at night.

U.S. citizens and official residents should consider enrolling in **STEP, Smart Traveler Enrollment Program** (https://step.state.gov/step/), a service of the U.S. Department of State. It provides important emergency information on your foreign destinations, helps the U.S. Embassy get in touch with you and gives family and friends a way to contact you when abroad.

PRACTICALITIES AND EMERGENCIES

Belize telephone country code: 501

Belize Tourism Board: 64 Regent Street, Belize City, 501-227-2420 or 800-624-0686, www.travelbelize.org

Calling from U.S. or Canada to Belize: When calling from the U.S. or Canada to any Belize landline or mobile number dial 011 plus the Belize country code (501) and then the seven-digit Belize number.

Calling from Belize to U.S. or Canada: Calling from Belize, dial 001 plus the area code plus seven-digit number.

Calling from United Kingdom to Belize: Dial 00 plus the country code (501) and then the seven-digit Belize number.

Calling from Belize to the United Kingdom: Dial 00 plus U.K country code (44) plus city code if any (e.g., London 22) plus telephone number.

Electricity: Standard electric current in Belize is the same as in the U.S., 110 volts AC, 60 cycles, and the regular two-prong U.S.-style plug is used. Some outlets may not have the third opening for a ground. Remote jungle lodges may have direct current (DC) from batteries, especially at night but still use the two-prong U.S.-style plug.

Police, fire and ambulance emergencies in Belize: 911

Public telephones: Public telephones are available all over the country but do not accept coins or currency. You will need a pre-paid Belize Telemedia Ltd. (BTL) phone card, available at BTL offices and in many shops around the country.

Time in Belize: The entire country of Belize is on the same time as U.S. Central Standard Time. Belize does not observe Daylight Savings Time.

Telephone operator assistance in Belize: Dial 114 or 115.

U.S. Embassy in Belize: Floral Park Road, Belmopan City, Cayo. Belize. During business hours, call 501-822-4011. For emergencies after business hours, call 501-822-4012. Website is http://belize.usembassy.gov, email embbelize@state.gov. The current U.S. ambassador to Belize, appointed in 2014, is **Carlos R. Moreno**, a graduate of Yale and Stanford School of Law and a former associate justice of the California Supreme Court.

Canadian Honorary Consulate in Belize: Mr. Patrick Andrews, 80 Princess Margaret Drive, Belize City, Belize, 501-223-1050, email cdncon.belize@btl.net. Canada does not have a regular embassy in Belize. The Canadian Embassy in Guatemala (13 Calle 8-44, Zone 10, Edificio Edyma Plaza, Guatemala City, Guatemala, C.A., 502-2363-4348, www.canadainternational.gc.ca/) handles diplomatic matters relating to Belize.

British High Commission in Belize: North Ring Road/Belhado Parade, Belmopan City, Belize, 501-822-2146, email brithicom@btl.net.

ACCOMMODATIONS

Belize has some 800 lodging places (not including some vacation home rentals), with about 7,400 total rooms. Most of these hotels, inns, lodges and guesthouses are small, owner-operated places -- about 70% have 10 or fewer rooms. Only four hotels in the country have 100 rooms or more: the 180-room Ramada Princess Hotel & Casino in Belize City, the 106-room Las Vegas Hotel in the Free Zone at the Mexican border in Corozal (plus additional rooms and suites in an older hotel), the 102-room Radisson Fort George in Belize City and The Placencia Hotel & Residences on the Placencia peninsula, which has about 100 condo apartments.

Travelers to Belize today can expect to find a variety of accommodations to fit almost any budget or preference.

A delightful type of lodging in Belize is the **seaside resort.** At the top end, places like Victoria House, El Pescador and The Phoenix on Ambergris Caye or Hamanasi in Hopkins have rooms and amenities that could earn a spot in *Architectural Digest*, with rates from US$200 to $500+ a night. But seaside resorts also come in more affordable categories. The best of these are sandy barefoot spots, such as Maya Beach Hotel on the Placencia peninsula, Jungle Jeanie's or Hopkins Inn in Hopkins or Tree Tops and OASI on Caye Caulker. Here, a couple can spend a night at the beach for as little as US$60 to US$100.

The small private cayes have **lodges,** often focused on diving and fishing but sometimes just on getting away from it all, that are expensive but beautiful. Think of places like Turneffe Flats, Turneffe Lodge, Cayo Espanto, St. George's Caye Lodge, Pelican Beach on Southwater Caye, Coco Plum Caye and Thatch Caye. Due to their locations, most of these are all-inclusive, or at least include transportation, lodging and meals.

All around Belize you can find **small guesthouses and inns** with clean, safe rooms at budget prices. Look at places like Tree Tops or Maxhapan on Caye Caulker, Sea Breeze in Corozal Town or Serenity B&B in Consejo near Corozal Town, Oasis Guesthouse in Sarteneja, Tipple Tree Beya Inn in Hopkins and Coral House Inn or Blue Belize in Punta Gorda. At these places you can get a nice little room for around US$75 double or less, sometimes much less. For just a tiny step up in price, you can enjoy a delightful stay at a very reasonable price.

In a few areas, mainly San Pedro, you can enjoy the extra space of a condo-style unit at a regular hotel-style price. These are called **condotels.** Grand Caribe, Grand Colony, Coco Beach and Pelican Reef, all on Ambergris, are great examples. Especially on Ambergris Caye, Caye Caulker and Placencia, you also have the option of vacation home rentals, ranging from basic cottages to deluxe villas with private pools.

Do You Need to Book Ahead?

Can you wing it in Belize? Or do you need to book hotels in advance? The answer, except around busy holidays such as Christmas and Easter, used to be that you could just wing it. Rooms in all price levels were plentiful most of the time. However, beginning in the early 2000s tourism reached record levels. Despite a large increase in the number of hotel rooms, annual occupancy has reached 47% for the latest year for which data are available, and on Ambergris Caye and Belize City annual occupancy rates are over 50%. Quite a few hotels, especially those offering the best value or top service and location, are heavily booked in-season. When visiting Belize in-season, roughly mid-December through Easter, it's a good idea to book ahead for at least the first night or two. And at resort areas definitely book in advance for Christmas/New Year's and Easter. This doesn't mean that if you arrive without reservations you'll have to sleep on the beach with the sandflies, but your first choices may well be booked and you may have to spend valuable vacation time hunting for a room. Tours and dive trips can usually be booked after you arrive, except for high-demand tours such as whale watching.

Using the Internet to Find and Book Rooms

Belize is wired. Nearly all hotels in Belize have websites (or at least Facebook pages) and email. You can use their web sites (listings in this book include internet addresses) to help you choose your accommodations, but remember that these sites are advertising and naturally put the best face on things. Nearly all hotels in Belize are small, and though many won't admit it for fear of alienating travel agents and travel wholesalers they would prefer you book direct, preferably via the internet. That saves them 10 to 25% in agent commissions, plus the cost and trouble of faxing, mailing brochures and telephoning back and forth. Some, but not all, hotels offer discounts for direct bookings via the internet. Many don't advertise this, but it won't hurt to ask.

However, it pays to compare direct rates with online lodging booking companies such as **Hotels.com** (www.hotels.com), **TripAdvisor** (www.tripadvisor.com), **Expedia** (www.expedia.com), **Priceline** (www.priceline.com), **Travelocity** (www.travelocity.com), **Vacation Rentals By Owner** (www.vrbo.com) and others.

The cheapest way to communicate with hotels in Belize is via email. Unfortunately, not all hotels in Belize check their email regularly and respond to messages in a timely way. In addition, many hotels have to deal with spam email seeking bookings, with the scam coming after the booker sends a deposit with a bogus credit card number. Also, email in Belize may be down, sometimes for several days at a time. If you don't hear back after sending an email, follow up with a second email or with a telephone call or fax.

IN-SEASON AND OFF-SEASON

Like the Caribbean islands, Mexico and some other warm-weather destinations in the region, Belize has two main visitor seasons: winter, considered *in-season*, and summer, considered *off-season*. The actual dates vary, but as a rule of thumb in-season is from around U.S. Thanksgiving week to mid-December through Easter week, while off-season is the rest of the year. Many, though not all, hotels, car rental companies and other tourism operators, reduce their rates off-season by 10 to 40%. Budget hotels and guesthouses tend to have year-round rates, although they may offer some short-term specials during slow periods. Some operators have a shoulder season, again varying in dates, but typically is from just after Easter to early June and also November through mid-December. During shoulder season rates may be reduced somewhere between the in-season and off-season levels. Nearly all hotels in Belize have a peak season, Christmas and New Year's holidays, and sometimes also the Easter holidays, when rates are at their highest, higher even than the in-season rates. Check hotel and other tourism operator websites to determine exactly when various rate levels apply over the year.

BEST TIMES TO VISIT BELIZE

Anytime is a good time to visit, but here are the "best times" for different activities and budgets:

Best time to avoid tourists: September-October

Best time to avoid rain: February-April

Best time for underwater visibility: March-June

Best time for lowest hotel prices: After Easter to mid-December

Best time to visit Toledo District: February-May

Best time to visit Placencia: January-May

Best time to visit cayes and atolls: December-June

Best time to avoid hurricanes and tropical storms: December-June

FOOD AND DINING IN BELIZE

We don't know who started the rumor that you can't get a good meal in Belize. The fact is, you can eat gloriously well, at modest prices.

Rice and beans is the quintessential Belizean dish, but this is not the rice and beans your momma used to fix — unless she's from Belize or perhaps New Orleans. Rice and beans (or beans and rice, which is slightly different, means spicy and smoky, with plenty of **recado** (also known as achiote) and other seasonings, perhaps flavored with salt pork and some onions and peppers and cooked in coconut milk. Usually these are served with a chunk of stew chicken, fish or pork. The whole thing might cost just US$5 or $6 in a pleasant restaurant. If you're not happy in Belize, you're probably not getting enough rice and beans. You'll find **Marie Sharp's hot sauces** everywhere. There are now more than a dozen different varieties. You can tour Marie Sharp's small factory near Dangriga and perhaps meet Marie herself.

Along the coast and on the cayes, **seafood** is as fresh as the salt air. In-season (mid-June to mid-February) **spiny lobster**, which is a Caribbean lobster without large claws and nearly all the edible meat in the tail — grilled, broiled, steamed, even fried — is fairly inexpensive and very good. But a big filet of **snapper or grouper,** prepared over a grill with lime juice, is just as tasty and cheaper. Belizeans love **barracuda,** and the more-local seafood restaurants serve it. **Conch**, in season October to June, is delicious grilled or stewed in lime juice as ceviche, but we like it best in fritters, chopped and fried in a light batter. **Shrimp** in Belize are farm-raised in the country, not harvested from the sea. There are no local oysters in Belize, because the water is too warm.

Lobster as served in an Ambergris Caye restaurant

Every ethnic group in multicultural Belize has its own taste treats. Among them: ***Hudut,*** the best-known **Garifuna** dish, is fish usually cooked in coconut milk with mashed plantains. ***Sere*** is another Garifuna fish soup dish similar to *hudut*. Each of these classic dishes has several variations. **Cassava bread,** made with the starchy tuber that is common across Africa, the Caribbean and Latin America, is another common Garifuna item.

Boil-up is a **Creole** favorite, fish boiled with plantains, yams and potatoes and served with tomato sauce and bread. **Cow-foot soup** is another Creole dish, and yes it is made with a real cow's hoof. **Stew chicken with rice and beans** is served in nearly every Belizean restaurant and eaten by Belizeans of all backgrounds, although the origin probably was Creole. You can also get stew pork, stew fish and other stewed meats with rice and beans. **Fryjacks** (in the Kriol language you often drop the plural, so a Belizean might just order fryjack) are fried pieces of dough, a kind of beignet without the powdered sugar or a version of Mexican *sopapillas*. They are served at breakfast instead of toast. **Journeycakes**, also called Johnnycakes, are another breakfast bread, although they can be eaten at other meals. They are like a somewhat hard biscuit, traditionally cooked over an open-hearth fire but now more often baked in an oven. **Creole buns** are sweet breads made with coconut milk, flour, yeast, butter, brown sugar, raisins and spices such as cinnamon and nutmeg.

The **Maya** dish most popular with visitors and most often found in restaurants is *pibil,* pork and other meats seasoned, wrapped in banana leaf and cooked slowly in an underground oven. **Pok chuk** is a Maya-style dish with strips of grilled pork, onions, green peppers, pureed beans, *pico de gallo salsa* and corn tortillas.

Of course, with Mexico next door, and with **Mestizos** making up about one-half of Belize's population, Belize has a wide variety of Mexican-derived dishes, including ***tamales, tacos, burritos, garnaches*** (corn tortillas fried and topped with beans, salsa and cheese) and ***panades*** (deep-fried tortillas often filled with fish). ***Escabeche*** is a traditional Mexican soup with chicken, onions, vinegar and tortillas.

Chicken is by far the number one meat in Belize, and you will find it served nearly every way possible – in Mexican-style dishes, soups, stewed with rice and beans and also fried. Fried chicken is a special favorite and is found on the menus of nearly all Belizean restaurants. At fried chicken stands it is still sometimes referred to as "dollah chicken," even though it costs more than that today. Expat Belizeans returning home to visit family often seek out their personal favorite fried chicken shack or stand.

We find most of the **beef** in Belize to be poor, although you can get a tasty steak in Belize if you look hard enough. If you have the choice, take a filet, which tends to be less tough. By the way, hamburgers in Belize are called, appropriately enough, beefburgers.

The **pork** is heavenly. Belizean pork chops are tender and flavorful, the best we've ever tasted.

Belizean bacon is a little different from most we've had but delicious with fresh farm eggs. Only brown eggs are legal in Belize, by the way, to protect Belize's chicken farmers — if you see a white egg it's an illegal alien. For breakfast, or almost anytime for that matter, fruit is the thing — fresh pineapple, mango, papaya, watermelon, banana, star fruit and orange. With fryjacks and a cup of rich Guatemalan or Gallon Jug Estates or other locally grown Belizean coffee, we're set for the day.

Speaking of fruit, Belize offers a virtual cornucopia of tropical and semi-tropical fruits, some native to the region and many imported to Belize and thriving here. Among them: **mangos,** in dozens of different varieties, **soursop, papaya, sapote** (or mamey), **craboo, custard apple, star fruit, ambarella** (also known as golden plum), **breadfruit, guava, sorrel, Malay apple, dragon fruit, sea grape, tamarind, pineapple, sapodilla, cashew fruit and apple banana,** a delicious variety of banana not found in U.S., Canadian or European stores because it does not ship well.

Cacao farming and **chocolate** making are growing industries in Belize. The **Toledo Cacao Growers Association** (Main Street, Punta Gorda, 501-722-2992, www.tcgabelize.com) is an organization of hundreds of small farmers, 95% of which are indigenous Maya. The TCGA helps farmers market their organic product to chocolate makers in Belize and around the world. One of the major buyers of Toledo cacao is Green & Black in the U.K. **Maya Mountain Cacao** in Punta Gorda also sources Belizean-grown cacao from Toledo and Stann Creek districts for sale to ultra-premium chocolate makers.

In Belize, there are a number of small chocolate makers, including **Goss Chocolate** on the Placencia peninsula, **Cotton Tree Chocolate** in Punta Gorda, **Ixcacao Maya Belizean Chocolate** (formerly Cirila's) in San Felipe village, Toledo and **Belize Chocolate Company** in San Pedro, Ambergris Caye.

For the most part, Belize dining isn't fancy, but Belize is branching out in some of the newer worlds of cuisine – Thai, North and South Indian, Vietnamese, Japanese, French, Italian and more. Among our favorite restaurants in Belize – in a variety of price ranges and ambiances -- are the Bistro at Maya Beach Hotel on the Placencia peninsula, Chef Rob's in Hopkins, Asha's Culture Kitchen in Punta Gorda and Casa Picasso and El Fogón in San Pedro. The extraordinary and totally authentic Italian gelato at Tutti-Frutti in Placencia village is amazing and in a class of its own.

BEER, BOOZE AND OTHER DRINKS

Non-Alcoholic Drinks: To drink, there's nothing more refreshing than a fresh lime juice, watermelon juice, pineapple juice, tamarind juice or other freshly made fruit juice drinks. Try a half and half watermelon and lime juice. In Belize, it's usually just the natural juice, perhaps mixed with water and without extra sugar added. For soft drink drinkers, brands bottled in Belize, including regular Coca-Cola, as in Mexico use at least part cane sugar instead of all corn syrup for sweetening. Fans claim local Coke tastes different, and better, too. Belize produces a number of brands of bottled water, with Crystal from Bowen and Bowen Ltd. *(see below)* being the most popular. Bowen sells soda water and tonic water (in both bitters pink and regular clear versions), too. Red Fanta, sometimes called the "national drink of Belize," Orange Fanta and other Fanta flavors, plus Sprite are also made locally by the Bowen company.

Coffee: Gallon Jug Estates Coffee is the only commercially produced coffee in Belize. Some jungle lodges and farmers grow small amounts of coffee, dry and prepare it and roast it in small batches for local use. Gallon Jug Estates Coffee is grown, harvested, processed and roasted at Bowen and Bowen Ltd.'s Gallon Jug farm in Orange Walk District. The

Gallon Jug coffee is from plants imported from Costa Rica in the 1980s and shade-grown on the Bowen farm. Belize is not a major coffee producer because the best Arabica coffees are grown at 4,000 to 6,000 feet in tropical highlands areas such as those in Guatemala, Costa Rica, Nicaragua and Mexico. The highest mountains in Belize are only around 3,700 feet. Much of the coffee sold in restaurants in Belize is instant. Some Belizeans just order a "Nescafé" instead of asking for coffee.

A generic brand of purified water costs in shops or stores goes for about BS$1 (50 U.S. cents) for a half-liter plastic bottle. A 600 ml bottle of Coke in stores is around US$1. In restaurants, a lime juice or other juice costs US$1 to $2.

Beer: There's a special situation with beer in Belize. The country has passed laws to protect its local beer brewers, specifically Bowen & Bowen Ltd. (1 King Street, Belize City, 501-227-7031, www.bowenbz.com). The company was established in 1969 as a joint effort of Cerveceria Hondureña, S.A, the majority shareholder, Barry M. Bowen and Barry's father, Eric W. M. Bowen, splitting the minority stake.

Following Sir Barry Bowen's death in an airplane accident in 2010, the company is run by family members and long-time executives. As a result of the Belize protective laws, for several decades only Bowen beers had any real distribution in Belize. It was, and is, illegal to bring in beer from Mexico next door, for example. Today, the situation is slightly different, in that beers brewed in Caribbean Community (CARICOM) countries, of which Belize is one, may be imported. This means **Red Stripe** from Jamaica, **Carib** from Trinidad & Tobago, **Heineken** brewed in St. Kitts, **Kubuli Gold** from Dominica and others are sold in Belize. However, **Belikin** (www.belikin.com) is still by far the dominant brand in the country.

Besides regular **Belikin** and **Belikin Premium** (also called export) lagers, Bowen at its brewery in Ladyville near Belize City brews **Lighthouse Lager, Belikin Stout, Guinness Stout** under license and seasonal beers such as **Sorrel Stout** and a Christmas **Chocolate Stout**. Regular Belikin is 4.8% alcohol and comes in a 284 ml bottle, approximately 10 oz. (redesigned in 2014) while Lighthouse is 4.2% alcohol and comes in an 8-oz. bottle. The stouts have a higher level of alcohol: The Belikin stouts are 6.5% alcohol and Guinness is 7.5%. The name Belikin comes from a Maya word meaning "Road to the East" and the label includes a graphic of a Maya temple at Altun Ha. Regular Belikin generally costs from US$2 to $3 in bars, with Premium going for US$4 or $5. By the case from a local distributor, Belikin is about US$1 a bottle, plus bottle deposit.

Although there have been efforts to start competitive national beers, Belikin's long-established distribution system keeps it far ahead of the pack. Due to Belize laws it has so far proved difficult to open, or to keep open, craft breweries or brewpubs in Belize.

Rum: Belizean-made rums are cheap and tasty. In stores and bars, you'll see a variety of local rums, chiefly made by Travellers Liquors Ltd., headquartered in Belize City and the dominant distiller in Belize, and Cuello's, based near Orange Walk Town.

Cuello's makes an inexpensive light rum, **Caribbean White,** which is widely used in mixed drinks in bars. It also produces **Caribbean Gold** and several other rums, including **Caribbean Coconut Rum.**

The most famous rum in Belize is **One-Barrel,** made by Travellers. First introduced in 1990, One-Barrel has won a number of awards, and visitors seem to love it. It is aged one year and has a burnt caramel taste. Travellers also offers more expensive **Three-Barrel (Parrot)** and **Five-Barrel** versions of this aged rum, aged respectively three and five years. Our favorite is the Three-Barrel Parrot. In addition, Travellers produces several other lines of rums, including **Travellers Gold,** a light gold rum; a line of white and flavored rums including **Cristal Parrot Light Rum,** a premium white rum; a less expensive white, **Cristal White; Kuknat Rum**, a coconut-flavored rum; and Don Omario vintage rums, including **Don Omario Royal Edition,** a 15-year-old rum re-released on the occasion of Prince Harry's visit to Belize in 2012. **Bitters** (or *bittahs* in Kriol) is usually a homemade drink with herbs and barks, such as Billy Webb bark and contribo bark, soaked for a week or two in a high-proof rum. Often some anise is added to improve the taste. Travellers Liquors also sells a commercially made version of this drink. **Jackass Bitters,** made from the jackass bitter plant, is a folk remedy for upset stomach.

Travellers has an interesting small rum museum and tasting room in Belize City, **Travellers Heritage Center Museum,** (Mile 2½, Philip Goldson Highway, 501-223-2855, www.onebarrelrum.com, open Monday-Friday 8-5, free admission, small charge for tastings), well worth a visit.

Travellers and Cuello's also produce a number of other spirits, including vodka, gin and brandy. These are cheap but are truly awful. Avoid them. Of course, you'll pay a price. Any imported liquor or liqueur, whether from the U.S., Scotland, England, Mexico, France or elsewhere, will cost you two to three times as much as you'd normally pay. So, especially when ordering drinks in bars, stick to local rum drinks, such as rum and tonic, rum and Coke, rum punch or a daiquiri. Local rum drinks in bars generally cost US$2 to $4, whereas a margarita, martini or other drink using imported booze could be US$5 to $12 or more.

Wine: Imported wines are pricey in Belize, typically running about twice as much as you'd pay in a supermarket or wine shop in the U.S., due mostly to high import duties. In restaurants, even an inexpensive Chilean wine may be US$10 to $12 a glass. There are decent selections of imported wines at **Wine de Vine** (Coconut Drive, San Pedro, Ambergris Caye, 501-226-3430).

Belize grows no wine grapes, but local people make wine out of all types of tropical fruits. Among the wines you may want to try for the novelty of it are **Soursop Wine, Cashew Wine,** another sweet wine made from fermented fruits of the "crooked tree" and **Ginger Wine,** a strongly flavored ginger drink. Fandango is one brand of ginger wine. **Bel-Mer** is a local winery. A bottle of one of these local wines usually costs around US$6 in a grocery.

NIGHTLIFE

Many visitors to Belize, after full days of diving or snorkeling, are just too pooped to stay up late and party. At remote dive and fishing lodges, often the lights go out by 10 p.m.

On the islands and coast, Ambergris Caye has the most clubs and bars, and you can find good watering holes in Placencia, Hopkins and Caye Caulker, too.

CASINO GAMBLING

A law passed in 1999 permitted gambling in Belize, and several casinos opened in Belize; others are planned. Belize City has the **Ramada Princess Hotel and Casino,** with about 500 electronic machines plus live tables for poker, blackjack and other games. The Princess also has a branch in San Ignacio. Three casinos are in the Free Zone in northern Belize, including the large **Las Vegas Casino,** where a nice, new, 100+ room hotel associated with the casino opened in late 2015. The 54,000 square-foot casino has 600 video gaming machines and more than 30 poker, roulette, blackjack and other live tables. You get free drinks while gambling. San Pedro has a small gaming spot at **Captain Morgan's**, a resort and timeshare on North Ambergris. A casino has been proposed for Placencia in southern Belize, but when and whether it will open is anyone's guess.

HOLIDAYS

The following are legal public holidays in Belize:
New Year's Day - January 1
Baron Bliss Day - March 9 (date of celebration varies, usually being the Saturday preceding March 9)

Good Friday, Holy Saturday, Easter Sunday, Easter Monday (dates
vary)
Labour Day - May 1
Commonwealth Day - May 24
St. George's Caye Day - September 10
Independence Day - September 21
Columbus Day (also called Pan-American Day) - October 12
Garifuna Settlement Day - November 19
Christmas Day - December 25
Boxing Day - December 26

PRICE LEVELS

An old saying is that Belize is expensive for Central America but cheap
for the Caribbean. To some extent that's still true, and if you throw in the
high cost of imported goods, the 12.5% tax on most purchases,
accommodations that in-season can go for US$300 to $500 or more a night
for top end beach resorts and lodges and the 9% hotel tax on lodging plus,
at many resorts, a service charge of 10% or more, the inescapable
conclusion is that **for travelers Belize can be an expensive
destination.**

But note that we say "can be." **If you plan carefully, Belize can
also be a very affordable destination.** You can find attractive,
comfortable yet very reasonably priced mid-level lodging – say, from US$60
to $150 a night, double. Inexpensive guesthouses and hostels go for as little
as US$15 or $20 a night double. Unlike on pricey islands of the main
Caribbean, Belize has scores of affordable lodging choices and places to eat.
Restaurants that cater to Belizeans and budget-minded visitors are real
bargains by international standards. Even the top-end restaurants in Belize
are far less expensive than you'd pay in the U.S., Canada or Western
Europe. Yes, car and golf cart rentals are expensive, but bus travel is
downright cheap and in most areas taxis are reasonable. Some tours are
pricey, but in many cases you can do trips and tours on your own and save
a ton.

BANKS AND ATMS

Until 2015, Belize had five commercial banks, not including offshore
banks. Three were based in Belize, although with partial outside ownership
– Heritage Bank, Belize Bank and Atlantic Bank — and two, ScotiaBank
and First Caribbean International Bank (formerly Barclays), were
multinational banks with branches in Belize. In 2015, Heritage Bank bought
the assets and accounts of First Caribbean in Belize, and First Caribbean

closed its offices in Belize in early 2016. As of this writing, it is unclear how many First Caribbean Bank employees will move to Heritage Bank, or which if any First Caribbean offices will be rebranded as Heritage Bank.

Nearly all bank offices in Belize have modern ATM machines, and now most accept ATM cards issued outside Belize. Formerly Heritage Bank accepted ATM cards issued only in Belize, but it is expected that with the merger with First Caribbean most if not all of its ATMs also will accept foreign-issued ATM cards. Not infrequently, ATM machines may run out of cash on weekends or holidays, so don't wait until your wallet is empty to make an ATM run. **Belize ATMs issue cash in Belize dollars only.** There is usually a limit of BZ$500 (US$250) per day, but Atlantic Bank and ScotiaBank have higher limits. Your limit may also be affected by rules of your home bank.

Your bank back home may levy a foreign ATM fee of up to US$5 per ATM use, plus a foreign transaction fee of 1 to 3% of the money withdrawn, and the local bank in Belize may also hit you with a fee. These fees add up, so try to minimize the number of ATM withdrawals you make by withdrawing larger sums.

If for some reason you can't tap your funds with your ATM card, some banks in Belize will issue an advance on your Visa or MasterCard. The fee for this is usually less than US$10, depending on the bank, plus whatever fees and interest your bankcard charges. Getting a cash advance may take a little time and paperwork.

Here are the basic facts, including cities, towns and villages where each of the banks is located, number of ATMs and contact information for the main offices:

Atlantic Bank, founded in 1977, is 55% owned by Sociedad Nacional de Inversiones, S.A., a Honduran company, along with individual stockholders in Belize and Honduras. Atlantic Bank has 15 offices in Belize — including in Corozal, the Corozal Free Zone, Philip S. W. Goldson International Airport, Caye Caulker, San Pedro (two offices) and Placencia. Atlantic Bank has 16 ATMs that accept foreign-issued ATM cards on the Visa, MasterCard, Plus and Cirrus systems. Main office: Atlantic Building, Freetown Road at Cleghorn Street, Belize City, 501-223-4123, www.atlabank.com.

Belize Bank traces its history back to 1902 when it was founded as the Bank of British Honduras. It is owned by BCEB Holdings, shares of which trade on the London Stock Exchange in the United Kingdom. It has 12 offices around the country— including in Corozal Town, the Corozal Free Zone, San Pedro, Dangriga, Placencia and Punta Gorda. Belize Bank has 26 ATMs on its countrywide network around Belize. These ATMs accept foreign-issued ATM cards on the Visa, MasterCard, Plus and Cirrus systems. Main office: 60 Market Square, Belize City, 501-227-7132, www.belizebank.com.

Heritage Bank (formerly Alliance Bank) is the newest of the commercial banks in Belize. It has 10 offices – including ones in Caye Caulker, San Pedro, Independence (near Placencia) and Pomona (near Dangriga). In 2015, Heritage Bank bought First Caribbean International Bank's assets in Belize. First Caribbean closed its five offices in Belize in early 2016. As of this writing it's unclear as to how the banks will be integrated. Heritage Bank has more than 20 ATMs at its branch locations, plus ATMs at seven credit unions and at any remaining former First Caribbean International Bank offices. Main Office: 106 Princess Margaret Drive, Belize City, 501-223-6783, www.heritageeibt.com.

ScotiaBank, formerly Bank of Nova Scotia, is a large Canadian bank with operations in 50 countries. It has been operating in Belize since 1968. In Belize, it has 11 offices – including in Corozal Town, San Pedro, Placencia, Punta Gorda and Dangriga. ScotiaBank has 14 ATMs around the country accepting foreign-issued ATM cards. Main Belize office: 4A Albert Street, Belize City, 501-227-7027, www.scotiabank.com/bz.

Banks typically are open from 9 a.m. until 3 p.m. or later Monday to Thursday and until 4 or 5 p.m. on Friday. ATMs are 24/7 but as noted sometimes run out of cash, especially on weekends and holidays.

MONEY AND CREDIT CARDS

U.S. dollars (bills, not coins) are accepted everywhere in Belize, at a fixed rate of 2 Belize dollars to 1 U.S. dollar, although you often will receive change in Belizean money, or in a mix of Belizean and U.S. money. While there's no need to exchange U.S. dollars, sometimes you will get a better rate than 2 to 1 by exchanging with private moneychangers. At times when there's a shortage of U.S. dollars in Belize, you may be able to get up to 2.10 to 2.15 Belize dollars for each U.S. dollar.

Paper-money Belize denominations are the 100-, 50-, 20-, 10-, 5- and 2-dollar bills. Belize coins come in 1-dollar, 50, 25, 10, 5 and 1 Belizean cent units. The 25-cent piece is called a shilling.

Canadian dollars, euros and other foreign currencies are not widely accepted. These should be exchanged at banks or moneychangers. Traveler's checks in U.S. dollars are still accepted by most hotels and at some stores, restaurants and other businesses, but the use of traveler's checks is becoming less common due to the prevalence of ATM machines. You usually need to show your passport when paying with a traveler's check. Banks and some businesses only give about 1.96 Belize to 1 U.S. for traveler's checks.

As noted above, now nearly all **ATM machines in Belize accept foreign-issued ATM cards,** generally those on the Visa, MasterCard and PLUS ATM systems.

Visa and MasterCard credit cards are widely accepted, except at small shops. Debit cards, if they can be run as credit cards as most can, are also widely accepted. **American Express** is accepted by some hotels and larger businesses. **Discover** and European bank credit cards are rarely accepted. Sometimes there is a surcharge for credit card use, usually 3 to 5%. Surcharges are becoming less common, due to complaints by consumers and moves by credit card issuers. To avoid a surprise, ask about surcharges before using your card.

It's a good idea to alert your credit card issuer and/or your home bank that you are traveling to Belize, as otherwise foreign transactions on your debit and credit cards may be flagged and the transaction denied until you contact them, which can be a pain.

Increasingly, credit card companies are levying international currency conversion and foreign usage fees, from 1 to 3% of the transaction amount or even higher. Most products and services in Belize will be charged in Belize dollars, so the currency conversion charges apply. Even if the charges are listed in U.S. dollars, credit card companies usually charge an international exchange fee anytime a charge is made outside your home country. Some American Express, Capital One, Bank of America and other cards have no foreign transaction fees.

Savvy travelers bring a combination of cash in small U.S. currency denominations, an ATM card and credit cards, and, as old-fashioned as it may sound, perhaps a few traveler's checks, just in case your cards and cash are stolen or lost.

HOW TO STRETCH YOUR MONEY

Here are ways to stretch your travel dollars in Belize, while still having a great vacation:

Go in the off-season, when hotel prices are slashed by as much as 40% and some vehicle rentals and tours also are discounted.

Spend time in off-the-beaten path destinations, rather than the well-known and more expensive areas such as Ambergris Caye and Placencia. You can stay and eat in much of northern Belize, including the Corozal Town area, Cerros and Sarteneja, for probably one-half the cost of Ambergris Caye. Likewise, the Deep South of Belize, in and around Punta Gorda in Toledo District, is remarkably affordable for food and lodging, although less so for tours and trips.

Belize banknotes come in $2, $5, $10, $20, $50 and $100 denominations
Specimen illustration from the Central Bank of Belize

Look for mid-level accommodations rather than the tony resorts and lodges. You'll find lots of places that are charming and comfortable, yet priced under US$150 a night for two. We've included many in the sections on lodging, but to name just a few: Serenity B&B, Tony's Inn and Copa Banana in Corozal; Conch Shell Inn, Ak'Bol and Hotel del Rio on Ambergris Caye; Tree Tops Guesthouse, De Real Macaw, Caye Caulker Plaza Hotel, Maxhapan Cabañas, Barefoot Beach and Colinda Cabañas on Caye Caulker; Paradise Lodge and Reef's End Lodge on Tobacco Caye; Hopkins Inn B&B, Jungle Jeanie's, Tipple Tree Beya and Coconut Row Guest House in Hopkins; Maya Beach Hotel, Barnacle Bill's and Tradewinds on the Placencia peninsula; and Coral House Inn, Blue Belize and Hickatee Cottages in PG. If you really want to save money, there are plenty of basic but acceptable guesthouses and budget hotels in Belize for under US$50 a night.

Eat where Belizeans eat, and eat what they eat, such as stew chicken with rice and beans, and you'll find it difficult to pay more than US$10 a meal even with a couple of Belikins.

Drink local rums (often just US$2 or $3 a drink, and less than US$10 a bottle) instead of expensive imported booze.

Take local transport where possible – water taxis and buses.

Ask for discounts. Bargaining is not common in Belize, but when booking a hotel or tour, it never hurts to ask politely, "Is that your best available rate?" or "Is there a way I can save some money?"

Where possible, opt for do-it-yourself visits to attractions. Often you can go on your own and forego paying for a guide.

44

Plan to picnic for at least lunch, and also pick up inexpensive items for breakfast on your own. Local fruits in the markets or from roadside vendors are amazingly inexpensive compared with what you pay back home. We've seen star fruit for a few cents, pineapples for US$1 and bananas for 10 to 20 for US$1.

Side trips to Mexico may also save you money, given the current peso exchange rate.

WHAT TO PACK

Belize is a very casual country. You don't need evening clothes or even a coat and tie or other U.S.-style business dress. You'll live in tee shirts or collared casual shirts, shorts and slacks. A really dressy occasion for men might require a guayaberra or collared shirt and long pants; for women a simple skirt or dress. Leave all your fancy jewelry and Rolex watches at home. They will impress only thieves. Also leave your rain gear at home. It probably will rain, but most raincoats just make you sweat. At most, you could bring a light-weight plastic poncho that folds up into a small package.

Here are ideas for your packing list:

Lightweight cotton clothes or quick-drying cotton/synthetic blends.

Comfortable walking shoes. Consider light boots or walking shoes for hiking and sandals for the beach.

Extra swimsuits.

Unlocked cell phone.

Maps, guidebooks and paperback books (if you prefer paper to digital versions). If available at all in Belize, books and maps will cost more than back home and may be out of date.

Cap or hat for sun protection — be sure it's one that won't blow off in windy conditions on the water.

Sunglasses, the darker the better.

Small flashlight with extra batteries, baggies in various sizes, a roll of duct tape, a large garbage bag, pen and writing pad, and Swiss Army-style knife — with these you can go anywhere and do almost anything.

Replacement battery and memory stick (if needed) for your digital camera — you'll shoot many more photos in Belize than you think you will.

Single-use underwater camera, although some dive shops sell them.

Health kit consisting of your prescription medicines and a copy of your eyeglass prescription, plus aspirin, insect spray with 30% DEET, sunscreen (more than you think you'll need), baby oil or Avon Skin-So-Soft for sandflies, Pepto-Bismol or other tummy medicine, antibiotic lotion, bandages, sun-burn lotion, moist wipes, seasick pills and other over-the-counter medicines.

Optional:

Lightweight laptop or iPad or other tablet device, useful for getting on the internet at hotels and for storing books and other reading material. Some may prefer to just use their smartphone.

Lightweight battery-operated portable radio if coming during peak tropical storm and hurricane season (June-November).

Snorkel mask — you can rent snorkel and dive gear in Belize, but rental masks often don't fit well.

Fishing gear.

Cotton sweater or light jacket may be needed in the winter, especially on the water.

Frisbees, baseball-style caps with U.S. sports logos, tee shirts and boxes of crayons make good small gifts for kids. School supplies also make good gifts for children.

MAPS

Belize Traveller's Map from ITMB, at a scale 1:250,000, is still the best general map to Belize, but it was last updated as 6th edition in 2005. List price is US$10.95. This map is available from ITMB at www.itmb.com, from Amazon at www.amazon.com or at larger bookstores.

Other maps to consider:

Belize National Geographic Adventure Map, National Geographic Maps, 2009. Helpful, but it contains some errors.

Insight Fleximap Belize, American Map, 2003. It's sturdy and water-resistant but not fully up-to-date.

Laminated Belize Map, Borsch, 2012. German cartography company produced this handy, durable map. Scale 1:500,000. Would have been nice if the scale were a little larger. In English, Spanish, French and Italian.

Wall Map of Belize, Cubola Productions. This large 36 x 58 inch color map of Belize is suitable for hanging on your wall. Scale is 1:250,000.

Driver's Guide to Beautiful Belize, by Emory King, an American who was shipwrecked in Belize in the early 1950s and never left (or so the story goes) is a mile-by-mile guide to the main roads in Belize. The *Driver's Guide* also has maps of Belize City and major towns. It's really handy if you are traveling around the mainland. Rather than a folding map, it's 40-page booklet in 8½ x 11-inch format. Before Emory King's death in late 2007, it was updated annually, but as of this writing it is out of print. If you can find an old copy, the price is around US$15 in Belize and worth every penny.

Google Earth has satellite images of Belize. Some areas are in high resolution; others, not. **Google Maps** are available of Belize, but they often are out-of-date or contain errors, mainly in the location of hotels and restaurants. **Mapquest** also has Belize maps online. *See the GPS section below.*

GPS in Belize

Our experience with GPS in Belize has been mixed at best. We usually bring along our Garmin GPS for vehicles when in Belize. Garmin, a leading GPS provider, offers a Belize map at www.gpstravelmaps.com/gps-maps/central-america/belize.php as an add-on for US$29.95. It is helpful, but it does have limitations and some inaccuracies. You'll have the same issues with smartphone GPS maps.

Satellite Radio

Yes, satellite radio is available in Belize. Although Sirius and XM Radio have merged, and most of their programming is now shared, the two services use different satellites. Currently, Sirius can be picked up better than XM in most of Belize.

Population of Belize

Populated areas in Belize are officially designated as a city, town or village. Belize has no really large cities, and overall Belize is one of the least densely populated countries in the world, with about 55% of the population living in rural areas.

The country's urbanized areas, in order of population from largest to smallest, as of the 2015 estimates by the Statistical Institute of Belize (more or less the equivalent of the U.S. Census Bureau), are:

Urbanized Areas Population, 2015 Estimates

Belize City	60,963
San Ignacio/Santa Elena	20,582
Belmopan City	19,458
San Pedro Town	16,444
Orange Walk Town	13,687
Corozal Town	11,722
Dangriga Town	10,108
Benque Viejo Town	6,589
Punta Gorda Town	5,910
Country Total:	**368,310**

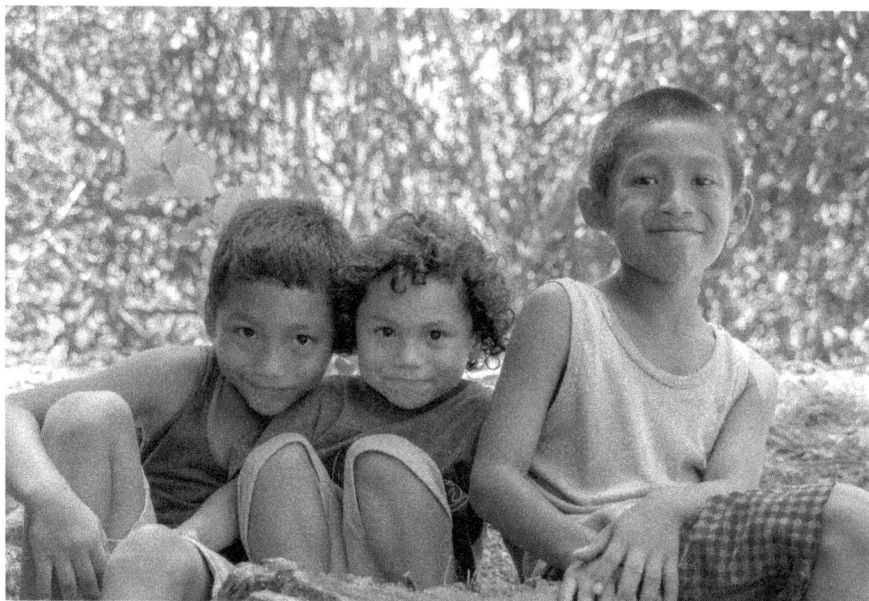

Three Belizean kids   Shutterstock

PEOPLE OF BELIZE

Belize is truly a multicultural society. **Mestizos** make up about 50% of the 368,000 population. These are persons of mixed European and Maya heritage, typically speaking Spanish as a first language and having social values more closely associated with Latin America than with the Caribbean. Mestizos are concentrated in northern and western Belize. There is often a distinction made between Mestizos who came to Belize from the Yucatán during the Caste Wars of the mid-19th century and more recent immigrants from Central America. Mestizos are the fastest growing segment of the population.

Creoles, once the dominant ethnic group in the country, now make up only about one-fifth of the population. These are people usually but not always of African heritage, typically speaking Bileez Kriol and English and often having a set of social values derived from England and the Caribbean. Creoles are concentrated in Belize City and Belize District, although there are predominantly Creole villages elsewhere, including the village of Placencia. "Royal Creoles" are the "aristocracy" of Belize, usually old families from Belize City, often better educated, more prosperous and with lighter skin color than average. Prime Minister Dean Barrow is considered a Royal Creole.

Maya constitute about 10% of the population. There are concentrations of Yucatec Maya in Corozal and Orange Walk districts,

48

Mopan Maya in Toledo and Cayo districts, and Kekchi Maya in about 30 villages in Toledo. These three Maya groups speak different languages. **Garifuna** (also known as **Garinagu** or sometimes Black Caribs) make up about 5% of the Belizean population. They are of mixed African and Carib Indian heritage. Most came to then British Honduras from Honduras in 1830s. Dangriga and Punta Gorda are towns with large Garifuna populations, as are the villages of Seine Bight, Hopkins and Barranco.

The "Other" group, making up about 14% of the population, includes about 19,000 people, or 6% of the population, who say they are of mixed ethnic heritage. About 11,000 **Mennonites,** mostly of European background, originally came to Belize from Canada and Mexico in the 1950s. Divided into conservative and progressive groups, they farm large acreages in Belize. Conservatives live mostly in Shipyard, Barton Creek and Little Belize, avoid the use of modern farm equipment and speaking German among themselves. Progressives live mostly in Blue Creek (Orange Walk District) and Progresso and Spanish Lookout in Cayo District. Mennonites and Amish, especially "Old Order" Mennonites and Amish, share many beliefs and practices. Mennonites and Amish come from a Protestant tradition known as Anabaptism, meaning to be baptized again, that dates to 16th century Europe.

Belize also has sizable communities of **East Indians,** who live mainly around Belize City and in Toledo and Corozal districts, **Chinese,** mostly from Taiwan, living all over the country, **"Lebanese"** (who may be from any part of the Middle East) and **gringos,** mostly expats from the U.S. and Canada concentrated in San Pedro, Placencia, Cayo and around Corozal Town.

LANGUAGES

English speakers should have no trouble traveling in Belize. The official language of Belize is English. Government documents are in English, English is the primary language used in schools and higher education, and most newspapers, television stations and other media are in English.

Bileez Kriol (that's the preferred spelling), a combination of mostly English vocabulary with elements of West African grammar, syntax and word endings, is used daily by many Belizeans of all backgrounds. Belizean Kriol is now accepted as its own language, and a dictionary of Kriol has been published. You will hear it spoken most in Belize City and in Creole villages around the country. Even though the vocabulary is based on English, it is unlikely that you will be able to understand more than a few words here and there, due to the way it is accented and the unique phraseology used.

Spanish is widely spoken as well, and in fact now is the first language of more Belizeans than is English. It tends to be the dominant language in areas bordering Mexico and Guatemala. Especially in small villages, you will run across quite a few Belizeans who speak only Spanish, so having a basic Spanish vocabulary is helpful. The Belize government has called on all Belizeans to learn both Spanish and English.

The Garifuna language and three Maya languages also are spoken in Belize. Some Mennonites speak a German dialect at home but generally also know English and perhaps Kriol and Spanish as well. As many as two-thirds of Belizeans are bi- or tri-lingual. *See the Appendix of this book for a sampling of common phrases in Kriol and Spanish.*

TAXES

Here are the main taxes you will pay as a visitor to Belize:

National Goods and Services Tax (GST) of 12.5% on nearly all products and services. The GST of 10% replaced a 9% sales tax in mid-2006 and later was increased from 10% to 12.5%. A few items are exempt: basic foodstuffs such as rice, flour, tortillas, eggs and beans; some medicines; school textbooks; and transportation on buses and airplanes. Like a value-added tax, the GST is supposed to be included in the final purchase price, rather than added on like a sales tax, but many businesses quote prices without the GST and just add it on at the cash register. Very small businesses, such as street vendors, don't have to register for the GST and don't charge the tax. You will pay 12.5% tax on most restaurant meals, tours and car rentals but not hotel stays. There are additional taxes on alcohol, cigarettes and a few other items. More than one-half the cost of gasoline is due to government tax.

Hotel tax: It's 9% on all hotel stays and short-term vacation rentals. There was an attempt to raise this to 12.5%, but this increase was at least temporarily beaten back by the hotel industry. If you eat and drink at your hotel, your restaurant bill will include 12.5% GST, not the 9% hotel tax, which is on lodging only.

Import duties apply to almost all goods imported to Belize. It is a major source of government income. On average, the import duty is around 20%, but it can range up to as much as 80 to 100% on some items such as cars and SUVs with V-8 engines. Some imported items, such as computers and books, do not incur an import duty but are subject to GST. You will not see the import duty broken out separately, but you will pay it in higher prices for many items not made, raised or grown in Belize.

SHOPPING

Frankly, few come to Belize to shop. Belize does not have the indigenous crafts traditions of Mexico, Guatemala and many other countries in Central and South America. You can find some Maya textiles and slate carvings, but in truth what is done in Belize pales in comparison with what's available in neighboring Guatemala. Beautiful native Belizean hardwoods show up in some carved items and in furniture. You'll find gift shops in San Pedro, Caye Caulker and Placencia as well as at some larger resort hotels. Check to see where the items were made; many craft items are imported from Guatemala or Mexico or even China. Art by Belizean artists is always a memorable purchase. (*See Souvenirs below and the Art and Crafts Galleries chapter for some ideas.*)

For more mundane purchases such as groceries, clothing and household items, Belize City offers by far the best choice, but again this is no mecca for shopaholics. The Free Zone near Corozal Town, with its cheap Asian-made junk, disappoints most visitors.

Business Hours: Most businesses open around 8 a.m. and close at 5 or 6 p.m. on weekdays. Some smaller shops close for lunch, usually from 1 to 2 p.m. Most stores are open on Saturday, or at least on Saturday morning. On Sundays, many stores and other businesses are closed, except in tourist areas like San Pedro.

BEST SOUVENIRS

If you want to bring back a souvenir of your trip to Belize, here are some ideas:

Original Belize art, art prints or photographs. The work of a number of artists born in Belize or resident in Belize is highly collectible. (*See Art and Crafts Galleries section.*)

Marie Sharp's hot sauces. It comes in a variety of degrees of hotness and with various base ingredients such as grapefruit and orange. The best selection is from the Marie Sharp's factory shop near Dangriga or the Marie Sharp's shop in Dangriga Town. Marie Sharp's is cheap, tasty and probably the country's most popular souvenir. Another Belizean company that makes hot sauces plus a large line of spices, condiments, sea salts and other products is **Caribbean Spice.** Many Belizeans also like **Hot Mama's**. Spices and flavorings grown in Belize, such as black pepper vanilla, also make tasty souvenirs.

Belizean rum from Travellers or Cuello's or Belikin beer. Duty-free shops at the international airport do not offer many bargains on Belizean rum or beer, but they are handy. The **Travellers Heritage Center** at Mile 2½ Philip Goldson Highway in Belize City is a good place to taste and buy a variety of rum products at moderate prices. There also is an outlet in San Pedro on Pescador Drive.

Handmade Belizean crafts such as Maya slate carvings, woven baskets, carved items from Belizean tropical hardwoods or small ceramic items. There are craft stores or co-ops in Belize City, Punta Gorda, Maya Center and elsewhere – *see Art and Crafts Galleries section.*

Gallon Jug Estates Coffee. Belizean coffee is virtually unknown outside Belize, even at the hippest "third wave" specialty coffee shops. Unfortunately, sometimes the Gallon Jug coffee sold in stores has been roasted and prepared long ago and is stale. Coffee shops in San Pedro, Placencia and elsewhere sell freshly roasted mostly Guatemalan coffee that is excellent. Gallon Jug Estates also produces sauces and condiments.

Belizean fruit wine made from cashew fruit, craboo (nance), soursop or other local fruits. Many groceries in Belize carry local fruit wines.

Handmade jewelry from shops in San Pedro, Caye Caulker or Placencia. Avoid jewelry made from coral or conch shells.

Belizean chocolate made by hand from Belize-grown organic cacao. Several small companies in Belize make their own chocolates, including Goss Chocolate in Placencia, Belize Chocolate Company in San Pedro and Ixcacao Maya Belizean Chocolate and Cotton Tree Chocolate in Toledo and Che'il Mayan Products at Maya Center.

Tee shirts with unique Belizean designs from local bars, restaurants and other businesses – we know you'll avoid the tacky ones sold in gift shops.

Belizean currency – if you can find lightly circulated bills you can have the colorful notes framed for display. However, if you change your mind, Belize dollars are almost impossible to exchange back home.

Belizean-made furniture such as a "clam chair" or small tables made from Belizean hardwoods like mahogany, rosewood or ziricote – shops in San Pedro including Graniel's and stores elsewhere can ship them home for you.

Garifuna drums make an interesting souvenir. They are available at some craft shops and from their makers in Dangriga, Hopkins, Punta Gorda and elsewhere.

While not made-in-Belize, **hand-woven Guatemalan textiles** such as blankets, tablecloths and *huipils* (colorful brocaded blouses worn by indigenous Maya women) are beautiful. The gift shops at Frances Ford Coppola's properties in Belize have high-quality items from Guatemala, albeit at higher prices than you pay from shops and craftspeople in Guatemala.

Do not bring back coral or conch shells. The coral reef is struggling to survive climate change and pollution, and the queen conch, while not yet on the endangered species list, is threatened and could become endangered. Do not even THINK of bringing back real Maya pottery or other artifacts, not even a tiny shard. That is illegal as well as irresponsible.

INTERNET

There are an estimated 91,000 regular internet users in Belize (2015 estimate), about one-fourth of the population. Internet access in Belize has been greatly improved over the past few years. **Belize Telemedia Ltd.** (www.belizetelemedia.net and www.digicell.bz) now offers DSL in most of the country, for both PC or Mac. It also offers wireless internet via line-of-sight towers. In 2016 BTL introduced fast 4G cell service. The LTE data network in theory supports download speeds of up to 100 megabits per second, according to BTL. BTL's competitor, **Smart** (www.smart-bz.com), also offers cellular internet. However, costs for both systems are higher than in the U.S. DSL and cellular data speeds, while increasing, still are slower than in some other countries in the region. If you have an unlocked smartphone and buy a SIM chip from BTL or Smart *(see Cell Phones below)*, you should be able to check email and such in most areas, though expect to pay more than you'd like.

Most hotels, from budget guesthouses to deluxe resorts, offer internet access to guests. It is usually free, but a few of the more upscale properties are still holding out for daily fees for internet. Even remote dive lodges offer guests internet access, but this usually is via satellite, which means slow connections and perhaps none at all during rainy weather. Many of these lodges limit guest access to email only, with no large uploads or lots of time checking websites. Cybercafés – that quaint word – are in all cities, towns and many villages where visitors are likely to go. Rates vary but are normally under US$5 or $6 an hour. BTL has hotspots around the country, but the cost is relatively stiff.

CELL PHONES

You can probably use your GSM or CDMA personal cell phone in Belize, but unless you have an unlocked phone and spring for a Belize SIM card or set-up you will pay high international roaming rates. Check with your provider to see current voice and data rates. Some providers now provide a daily international voice and data rate that can save you money.

Short-term visitors to Belize also can buy a SIM card for their unlocked cell phone, get a Belize telephone number, buy a prepaid phone card and use your phone for voice calls, short text messages and in some cases for internet data. There are two companies that offer cell services to visitors. One is **Belize Telemedia Ltd.** (www.telemedia.net) and its digital cell division, **DigiCell** (www.digicell.bz), mostly on the GSM system, and the other is **Smart** (www.smart-bz.com), using the CDMA system. DigiCell now offers 4G cellular in Belize.

Buy a SIM card from BTL for any unlocked dual band GSM cell phone for US$25 plus GST. This fee includes US$5 of usage time. You can buy additional phone cards in many shops and at BTL offices, or top off your account by dialing 135 or 10* and follow the automated instructions. Alternatively, you can rent a cell phone from Belize Telemedia Ltd. and its digital cell division, DigiCell, for US$5 a day (not including outgoing call usage). In both cases you get a temporary Belize telephone number.

With a pre-paid phone card, domestic outgoing calls are BZ47 to 50 cents a minute and test messages are BZ25 cents. International calls are around BZ65 cents a minute during the day and BZ50 cents a minute off-peak (9 p.m. to 6 a.m.). Incoming calls and texts are free. Note that domestic and international rates change frequently and may be different when you are in Belize than those shown here.

The BTL office at the Philip S. W. Goldson International Airport near Belize City sells SIM cards and rents phones. This BTL office is at the end of the rental car kiosk row at the far side of the parking lot across the street from the terminal building. You can also obtain SIM cards at BTL service centers in cities, towns and some villages in Belize or from authorized agents at stores.

Smart, also known as Speednet, is another digital cell service that began operating in 2005. It's on the CDMA system only, not GSM. Short-term visitors can also get their unlocked CDMA phone set up with Smart, including a Belize telephone number, for a fee of US$20. Smart has an office in Belize City (Mile 2½, Philip Goldson Highway, 501-678-1010) and also at a number of service centers around the country. Note that as elsewhere cellular plans in Belize change frequently.

MEDIA

With its high literacy rate and engaged population, for a small country Belize is media-rich. **Belize has a half dozen television stations, several radio stations and a number of weekly and monthly newspapers.** There is no daily newspaper in the country. Cable television companies operate in most populated areas, in some cases with pirated content.

Most of the **weekly newspapers** in Belize are based in Belize City, but a few other towns have weekly or monthly newspapers. The two best national newspapers in Belize are *Amandala* and *The Reporter*. These two weekly tabloids are independent and outspoken, though coverage runs to strident political and crime news. Since they are based in Belize City both have a Creole, port city orientation that does not fully reflect the views of all of Belize's diverse society. They have web editions: www.reporter.bz and www.amandala.com.bz.

The Guardian and the Belize Times are operated by the two leading political parties in Belize. The weekly Belize Times (www.belizetimes.bz) is the Peoples United Party paper, and The Guardian (www.guardian.bz) is the United Democratic Party's organ.

Ambergris Caye has weekly print and online newspapers of interest to visitors. The San Pedro Sun (www.sanpedrosun.net) is operated by expats from the U.S. It has both a print and an online edition. A Belizean-owned online weekly, Ambergris Today (www.ambergristoday.com), does a good job with news of island and of Belize nationally. There also are small newspapers in several outlying towns and villages: the monthly Placencia Breeze in Placencia, the quarterly Toledo Howler in Toledo and others. The Breeze and Howler have both print and on-line editions.

Two Belize City **TV stations**, Channel 5 and Channel 7, may also be picked up in a good part of the country and are carried on most cable systems. Channel 5 has an informative text version of its nightly news broadcast on-line at www.channel5belize.com. Channel 7 also has an on-line news summary at www.7newsbelize.com. Streaming video versions of the evening newscasts are now also available, though the quality can be spotty. Channel 3 in Orange Walk Town (www.ctv3belizenews.com), offers some news of Northern Belize and the nation. LOVE-FM radio also has a TV arm. While some of the equipment is primitive, it has some good locally produced programming. Plus TV and Open TV, both in Belmopan, cover capital and countrywide news.

KREM-FM 96.5 and LOVE-FM 95.1 (frequencies vary around the country) are the two most popular **radio stations** in Belize. KREM-FM has a morning talk and call-in show from 6 to 8:30 a.m., with host Evan Hyde Jr. During the day it broadcasts an eclectic mix of local music, rap, soul and other music, along with Belize news. LOVE-FM offers "easy listening" music during the day, with a morning call-in and talk show hosted by station owner Rene Villanueva from 6 to 8 a.m. This station has three full newscasts at 6:45 a.m., 12:30 p.m. and 6 p.m., Monday to Saturday, and news updates frequently. Both stations offer internet broadcasts. The website for KREM is www.krem.bz, for LOVE www.lovefm.com. Another station, this one with a UDP political slant, is WAVE-FM.

Belize First Magazine, an on-line **magazine** about Belize founded by Lan Sluder, author of this book, has hundreds of pages of articles and archives at www.belizefirst.com. Among its free offerings are ebooks on Belize and a news archive going back more than ten years.

Most of these media can be accessed through links from www.belizenews.com.

LGBT

It is worth quoting the U.S. Embassy in Belize statement about attitudes in Belize about gay and lesbian travelers in Belize:

"The tourist friendly San Pedro Town, Ambergris Caye, remains relatively open and welcoming to the LGBT community. **Outside of the tourist friendly cayes, LGBT persons, especially males, are reluctant to display affection in public (including holding hands) because incidents of verbal or physical assault have been reported.** There continues to be a significant hostile sentiment towards individuals who identify themselves as lesbian, gay, bisexual or transgendered. LGBT issues are frequently highlighted in the press and can spur passionate discussions at community forums or public protests, and there have been some instances of violence reported against LGBT individuals, and LGBT groups have reported that the police at times refused to accept reports of crime from LGBT persons."

The Embassy also notes: "The current criminal code states that 'carnal intercourse' with any person 'against the order of nature' shall receive a punishment of 10 years' imprisonment. This law is interpreted as including only sex between men, but the law is rarely enforced. Additionally, the Immigration Act prohibits 'homosexual' persons from entering the country, but immigration authorities have not enforced that law and the law is currently facing a challenge before the Caribbean Court of Justice."

We think the Embassy's statements are generally accurate. At the same time, we know a number of LGBT people who live in Belize and a number of LGBT expats who have moved to the country. They say that in general they have experienced few or no problems. In short, Belize remains far behind the more progressive parts of the U.S., Canada and Europe regarding public and governmental attitudes toward LGBT rights. Certainly there are social conservatives and some sexual bigots in Belize, as there everywhere, but on a one-to-one basis most Belizeans are accepting of individual preferences including sexual matters.

WOMEN TRAVELING ALONE

It is common to see women traveling alone in Belize, and **most report no special problems.** Of course, women – and for that matter, men – traveling by themselves need to practice the usual traveler's precautions. *Machismo* exists in Belize, but not to the degree that it is present in some Latin countries.

This is not to say that single travelers face no dangers. There have been some serious crimes, including murder, rape and assault, against women traveling alone. A few years ago, a female airline flight attendant was killed in San Pedro, and in early 2016 a 39-year-old Chicago woman staying alone at a small lodge in Cayo District near the Guatemala border was murdered in broad daylight while doing yoga. There is some evidence that single women travelers may be targeted by criminals.

One disadvantage to traveling alone in Belize is that there are not many true hostels or B&Bs where guests can mingle. There are only about a half dozen hostels countrywide, and a handful of B&Bs. Budget guesthouses and hotels are everywhere, and to some degree these function like hostels, but you may not get the same level of interaction with other travelers. Remote dive and fishing lodges, surprisingly, may be good places for singles, as guests get together at breakfast or in the evening in the bar to discuss the day's activities. Caye Caulker, Tobacco Caye and Placencia tend to get more younger people and more single travelers than other coastal, caye and atoll destinations.

TRAVELERS WITH DISABILITIES

The equivalent of the Americans with Disabilities Act (ADA) hasn't shown up in Belize yet. To be candid, **those with physical limitations face some challenges in Belize.** Getting in and out of rocking boats docked at piers with high step ups or step downs, flying in small Cessna airplanes with ceilings barely 5 feet high, walking up and down steep hillsides at old hotels with stairs and no elevator or slugging through slippery rainforest trails and sandy beaches require a lot of effort for the elderly or physically limited.

Having said that, we know people with severe physical limitations who have vacationed in Belize and who have had a great time. Almost always, Belizeans are quick to try to lend a hand or get you in and out of tight places. The author of this guide has rheumatoid arthritis and carries some extra avoirdupois and yet has been able go (almost) everywhere in Belize. True, on one ramble around Belize, the author did fall and fracture several spinal vertebrae and was only able to make it home and to a back specialist thanks to the help of his daughter, but the fall could have happened anywhere.

GREEN BELIZE

How green is Belize? That's a difficult question to answer. On the one hand, many average Belizeans are remarkably environmentally aware. They take great interest in sustainable activities, whether in tourism, agriculture or any other area of the economy. They are especially concerned about keeping the Belize Barrier Reef system alive and well. Many expats who have moved to Belize also seem to have authentic concerns about the environment. Some lodge owners and other tourism operators go out of their way to get green certifications.

Quite a few Belizeans go organic simply out of economic necessity. Chemicals and genetically modified seeds are expensive, and many Belizeans can't afford them, even if they wanted to buy them. Small farmers, such as the nearly 1,000 members of the Toledo Cacao Growers Association, produce their crops organically.

The government has preserved huge swaths of the country from development as national parks and forest reserves. In 2015, the UDP government passed laws preventing offshore oil exploration and development. Many individuals and Non-Governmental Organizations (NGOs) in Belize are involved in environmental and sustainable development projects. A 90-acre, 10MW solar array to generate solar energy is planned for Placencia.

At the same time, you can point to many examples where both Belizeans and foreigners in Belize have wrought destruction on the environment. In many coastal areas, mangroves have been cut down, potentially worsening erosion and damage to the coast during tropical storms and hurricanes. Resort owners, hoping to lure more beach lovers, rid the sea floor of seagrass, which is a nursery for marine life. Coastal areas not in front of hotels or home look like garbage dumps, albeit much of that washes in from Mexico or other parts of Central America and elsewhere. Logging, legal and illegal, is taking a toll on tropical hardwoods in Toledo and elsewhere. Fishing out of season for conch or lobster or taking endangered or threatened fish and sharks in nets is not uncommon. If caught, violators are fined, but many violators escape detection.

Although the government talks a good environmental game, many critics say some environmental impact studies are mere formalities, allowing developers to build in critical natural areas. The controversial Norwegian Cruise Line port on Harvest Caye is a case in point. Critics say it was approved without proper environment assessments and could cause major damage to reefs and marine life. At one time the government was considering approving a massive project for a causeway out to cayes off Belize City for a different cruise port. In Belize as elsewhere, money talks, and it is not uncommon for projects that are at best environmentally suspect to be approved by the government.

Much of the chicken, egg, corn, citrus and banana production in Belize still is done using chemicals. Some Mennonite large-scale farmers and ranchers in Spanish Lookout and elsewhere have yet to see the benefits of natural, organic methods. Thus, the environmental picture in Belize is mixed.

CHURCHES AND RELIGION

Although Belize was a British colony, the Catholic Church, not the Anglican Church, is dominant in Belize. About 40% of Belizeans are at least nominally Catholic. Nearly 9% of Belizeans belong to Pentecostal Protestant churches. Old Order and progressive Mennonites are a significant group in Belize. Anglicans represent only about 6% of the population. Other religious groups in Belize include Methodist, Baptist, Church of Christ, Presbyterian, Jehovah's Witness, Assembly of God and Seventh Day Adventist. Nearly anywhere you are in Belize, **you should be able to find some religious service to meet your spiritual needs.** Belize has one small Muslim mosque. There is no temple, but Jews meet in local homes in Belize City and elsewhere.

KIDS

Belize is a country of the young. The median age in Belize is only 22. Small children are everywhere in Belize. If you are traveling with young children, you should experience no special problems. Children are welcome at hotels and restaurants nearly everywhere – the few hotels that have age restrictions are noted in the lodging sections of this guide.

In general, **kids will love Belize.** They like climbing Maya ruins, hiking and exploring, beach and marine activities and the general outdoor adventure environment of Belize. The author often took his kids with him on travel writing trips to Belize, starting when our younger child was only about two years old.

However, there are a few things that are different about Belize, compared to the U.S. and Canada, as regards children accompanying parents: One is that "kids stay free" often doesn't apply in Belize. Except for very young children, under age 5 or 6, kids may be charged as extra persons for room and meal rates, albeit usually at a reduced rate of 50% or so. Another is that some tours, zip lines and some snorkeling trips have age or height restrictions. These are for the safety of the young.

For a parent, whether married, separated or divorced, traveling alone with his or her kids, it is a good idea to have a notarized statement from the other parent that permission has been granted for the child or children to accompany the traveler. You'll probably never need to show this letter, but it can be helpful should any official believe that you are in violation of custody rules or have kidnapped the child from the other parent.

PETS

In most cases, **dogs and cats can be brought into Belize without quarantine.** However, unless it is a service animal, in our opinion **traveling in Belize with pets is not a good idea.**

Bringing a pet into the country falls under live animal importation and is regulated by the **Belize Agricultural Health Authority** or **BAHA** (Forest Drive and Hummingbird Highway (P.O. Box 169), Belmopan City, Belize, 501-822-1378, www.baha.org.bz). Dogs and cats are allowed to enter the country provided that owners have a valid import permit, international veterinary certificate, valid rabies vaccination certificate and inspection by quarantine officer at the port of entry. Owners must get a certificate from a veterinarian at the owner's home country. The vet examination must take place within 14 days before arrival in Belize, and the certificate must state that the animal is in good health, is free from infectious diseases and has been vaccinated for rabies not less than one month and no more than one year prior to departure for Belize.

You should apply for an import permit for your cat or dog from BAHA. Permit application forms are available for download at the BAHA website. Send the permit application by email to bahasps@btl.net or fax to 501-824-3773. The date of arrival must be specified. There is a US$25 entry and inspection fee, payable in U.S. or Belize dollars at the port of entry. Approved permits are faxed to applicant at a cost of US$12.50 to be paid at the point of entry. If you don't follow this application process, you could be subject to a violation fine on top of the regular admission and inspection fees. In addition, any pet arriving without a valid permit or without a valid rabies vaccination may be confined at the owner's expense until the vaccination is valid.

The dog or cat must be inspected at the port of entry. Those coming from countries considered of risk (for example, pets from South American countries where there is the risk of screwworm) need to undergo veterinary inspection. There is an additional fee for this veterinary inspection.

One reason we advise against brings pets to Belize on your vacation is the expense and trouble of transporting the animal. Small dogs and cats can sometimes be carried in the cabin of scheduled commercial airlines for an extra fee. The kennel must fit under the seat. Reservations in advance are required, to assure that no more than a certain number, typically five to seven, animals are on a flight. A vet's certificate that the animal is in good health usually must be provided to the airline, with the certificate done typically within 10 days prior to the date of travel.

United and occasionally American are two of the airlines flying into Belize that ship pets and allow them as checked luggage, with some restrictions. In March 2016, Delta stopped accepting pets as checked luggage and even as cargo on international flights. American still carries pets but not on its small Airbus equipment, which is generally what is used on flights to Belize.

Pets are transported in the pressurized cargo hold. The kennel must be large enough for the animal to turn around in. Pets may not be accepted by the airline as checked luggage if the forecast temperature is too hot or too cold – typically above 85 or 90 degrees F. or below 45 degrees F. -- at any point on the air itinerary; in some cases, the airline may accept a letter from a vet stating that the animal can stand temperatures above or below these points.

Some airlines have restrictions on which breeds can be checked as luggage. American, for example, does not permit "pug nosed" dogs such as Boston terriers, bulldogs or boxers. The airline also prohibits Burmese, Persian, Himalayan and exotic shorthair cats in the cargo hold.

Charges vary. United charges $125 for an accompanying dog, cat, rabbit or bird and US$239 to US$709, depending on weight, for checked pets.

Contact the airline in advance to be sure you are following all its rules for pet travel; otherwise, you may be denied boarding.

Service animals generally are exempt from these rules and charges.

In Belize, both domestic airlines, Maya Island and Tropic Air, will carry your pet in its kennel. Tropic Air currently charges you for three seats for the pet, plus your own ticket. Maya Island Air currently charges only for one seat for your pet, plus your own ticket. You must notify the airlines in advance that you are transporting a pet. Water taxis usually allow pets, for a fee of around US$10 each way. These policies are subject to change.

Besides the hassle and cost of transporting pets, there are other reasons we advise against bring them to Belize. One is that there are a lot of stray dogs and cats in Belize, and your pet may pick up mange or other diseases from the strays. Some breeds don't quickly adapt to Belize's hot, humid climate. Your pet likely isn't familiar with wildlife in Belize, including poisonous snakes, scorpions, spiders and Africanized bees that could be dangerous. There are about 20 licensed vets in Belize, but most have large-animal farm practices only and do not care for domestic pets. While this is changing to some degree, Belizeans have a different attitude towards pets than do most Americans, Canadians and Europeans. For example, dogs in

Belize are usually kept as guard animals to prevent theft rather than as pets to be allowed in the home. Finally, quite a few hotels in Belize do not permit animals or will allow them only reluctantly.

DRUGS

Despite its reputation as a source of marijuana and, more recently, as a transshipment point for cocaine and other drugs from South America, **Belize has strict laws on the use of illegal drugs,** with prison terms and fines for offenders. Senior police officials have advocated decriminalizing the personal use of marijuana, or making medical and recreational use legal, but as of this writing Belize laws on the subject haven't changed. Police seem to find it easier to catch a small-time drug user than to solve serious crimes. Quite a few Belizeans smoke marijuana, some fairly openly, but it is still illegal.

Unfortunately, crack, heroin, meth and other hard drugs are a fact of life in Belize, as they are in many countries. Much of the crime in Belize City and in other parts of the country is related to drugs. Avoid buying drugs from street and bar touts, as they may turn you in to police for a small reward, and unless you are with friends who know the country well think twice before even smoking a joint.

HEALTH

Belize has relatively **high standards of health and hygiene,** and you're little more likely to become ill in Belize than in Florida. Not many visitors become ill from traveler's diseases or from drinking the water. While malaria, dengue fever and other tropical diseases are present in Belize, they rarely affect visitors in the more popular destinations of Belize. The **Zika virus** *(see below)* is a new and fast-growing threat, especially to pregnant women or those who may get pregnant.

Most travelers to Ambergris Caye or Placencia and other popular areas don't get any special shots or take other precautions before they come. No shots are required for entry into Belize, except for yellow fever if you are coming from an infected area such as parts of Africa. However, it's always a good idea to keep tetanus-diphtheria, hepatitis A and B and other vaccinations up to date.

About 85% of Belize has access to potable water. Thanks to the plentiful rain in Belize — from 50 to 200 inches or more per year — drinking water literally falls from the sky. In short, in most areas of Belize, including nearly all areas of interest to visitors, you can drink the water and not worry about getting sick.

Most hotels in Belize have water that's safe to use out of the tap. Ice for cold drinks in restaurants and bars is generally safe. However, many visitors to Belize prefer to drink bottled water, either for the taste or just to be extra safe. Most hotels provide bottled water, either free or at a modest charge, and it's available – Crystal is one popular brand bottled by Coca-Cola – in all groceries and many other stores.

The leading cause of death in Belize is not illness but **traffic accidents.** About one-fourth of all deaths in Belize are now due to traffic accidents, even though the vast majority of Belizeans don't own cars. Often the cause of accidents is alcohol-related. Such speed limits as there are in Belize, and most roads have no posted speed limit, don't mean much because Belize has very few traffic enforcement officers. The use of seat belts is required in Belize, but this rule, too, is rarely enforced. Finally, many Belizeans simply aren't good drivers. Driver's education programs are virtually unknown.

AIDS has become a serious problem in Belize, according to health officials. As many as 8,000 people in Belize are HIV-positive, a large number given Belize's small population.

In recent years, the number of reported cases of **malaria** in Belize has fallen to under 1,000 annually, mostly in remote bush areas and typically among recent immigrants from Guatemala or elsewhere in Central America. Another good thing is that more than 95% of the malaria cases in Belize are the *Plasmodium vivax* strain, which is less dangerous than *Plasmodium falciparum.* The *Plasmodium vivax* strain can be prevented with the use of a time-tested drug, chloroquine, taken once a week starting two weeks before arrival. Several other antimalarials also are effective. Most visitors to popular areas of Belize such as Ambergris Caye, Caye Caulker and Placencia don't take any anti-malarial drug. However, better be safe than sorry. Especially if you are going to be spending time in the bush, check with your family doctor or the **U.S. Centers for Disease Control** (404-332-4559, www.cdc.gov) for the latest information.

Dengue fever is transmitted by a mosquito active during the day, *Aedes aegypti.* It causes flu-like symptoms that are unpleasant but in most cases are not life threatening. Dengue has become epidemic at the end of the rainy season in many countries of the region. Dengue exists in Belize, especially during the rainy season but it is not very common. However, the number of reported cases has increased to around 600 annually. There is at present no widely available preventative medication for dengue fever; a vaccine is under development. The best prevention is to use mosquito repellents. Dengue symptoms can be treated with Tylenol or its generic equivalent. Avoid taking aspirin if you think you have dengue, as aspirin can exacerbate internal bleeding sometimes associated with dengue.

The **Zika virus** is believed present in Belize (although, as of this writing tests have not confirmed it), as it is in many countries in the Caribbean and in Central and South America, including in neighboring Mexico and Guatemala. Zika is now endemic in parts of the Americas, notably Brazil where as many as 1.5 million people there have had it. Projections are that it could affect at least 4 million in the Americas, including the United States and Canada. It is a viral disease transmitted mainly by the same vector as dengue, the *Aedes aegypti* mosquito. However, other ways of transmission, including sexual contact and blood transfusions, have been reported. The symptoms last four to seven days and are similar to dengue but usually much milder – rash, muscle and joint pain, headache and nausea. Complications from Zika in those who get the virus are believed to be relatively rare. However, it can be a **serious danger for pregnant women** as it can **cause malformations of the nervous system of fetuses, particularly microcephaly** (children born with unusually small heads and with brain damage.) Pregnant women should consult with their physician before traveling to countries where the virus is present. El Salvador has gone so far as to urge female citizens of that country to avoid becoming pregnant until at least 2018. Colombia has taken similar action. There is as yet no vaccine or treatment for Zika although vaccines are in development. In early 2016 the Belize Health Ministry released a national plan to clean up and reduce breeding areas for the *Aedes aegypti* mosquito. Overall, health authorities appear to believe that Zika in Belize will not become as severe a problem as it is in some other countries in Central and South America.

Leishmaniasis is a potentially serious skin infection caused by a parasite transmitted by sandflies in beach and some inland areas. Taking precautions against sandflies such as using an oily lotion on your feet and legs is recommended.

Both **cholera** and **typhoid fever** are occasionally present in Belize, but only a handful of cases have been reported in recent years. **Rabies** is also present in Belize. In 2016, Belize cattle ranchers were urged to have their cattle vaccinated against rabies, with the disease possibly transmitted by vampire bats.

The **biggest trip-spoiler in Belize is probably sunburn.** You're only 18 degrees of latitude north of the Equator, and the sub-tropical sun is much stronger than back home. Use a sunscreen when outdoors. Also, take precautions such as wearing a tee shirt when snorkeling.

HOSPITALS AND CLINICS

There are eight public hospitals in Belize. **Karl Heusner Memorial Hospital** City (Princess Margaret Drive, 501-223-1548, www.khmh.bz) in Belize City functions as the main public hospital in the country and as a national referral center. Also, there are three regional hospitals: the **Southern Regional Hospital** in Dangriga, the **Western Regional Hospital** in Belmopan City and the **Northern Regional Hospital** in Orange Walk Town. In addition, there are district public hospitals in San Ignacio, Punta Gorda and Corozal Town. Rockview Hospital in Belize City is a psychiatric center. Altogether, there are about 600 public hospital beds in Belize.

The public hospitals provide the basic medical specialties: internal medicine, surgery, pediatrics and OB-GYN. Karl Heusner Memorial also provides neuro, ENT, physiotherapy, orthopedic surgery and several other services, including trauma care and neurosurgery. The quality of these hospital services vary.

Public hospitals and clinics offer basic medical attention for at most a low fee, US$5 or less including meds such as antibiotics or painkillers. You should be prepared to wait several hours, unless it is serious emergency.

The regional hospitals in Belmopan, Orange Walk Town and Dangriga, plus Karl Heusner in Belize City, have walk-in service after working hours and on weekends, with physicians and specialists on duty. These hospitals also have pharmacies that offer free basic medications.

Several clinics are in San Pedro, but the island, the top area for tourism in Belize, still lacks a true hospital. For serious injuries or illness on the Northern Cayes or elsewhere off the coast you'll probably have to go to Belize City or to Chetumal or Mérida, Mexico. Some may need to return home for advanced care.

Besides these hospitals and larger clinics, Belize has a network of more than 60 public health clinics and rural health posts in towns and many villages around the country, providing primary medical and dental care. Some of these are staffed by Cuban doctors.

In addition to the public hospitals, Belize has a private hospital and a large private clinic in Belize City:

Belize Medical Associates (5791 St. Thomas St., Kings Park, Belize City; 501-223-0302; www.belizemedical.com). Established in 1989, Belize Medical Associates has a 25-bed hospital, along with two surgical suites, X-ray and ultrasound machines, a clinical lab, emergency services and pharmacy. It is affiliated with Baptist Health Systems of Miami.

Belize Healthcare Partners (Corner Chancellor and Blue Marlin Avenue, Belize City, 501-223-7870, www.belizehealthcare.com) is a health care facility with about 25 physicians on staff. Belize Healthcare Partners offers radiology, kidney dialysis and laboratory services for private patients.

A number of other **private physicians, dentists and medical clinics** also are in Belize City and a few are elsewhere in the country, including San Pedro.

Pharmacies: There are drug stores in Belize City, in all towns, and in some villages. Some common prescription drugs, usually generic ones manufactured in Asia or Canada, cost less in Belize than in the U.S., although pharmacies may not stock a wide selection of drugs. Some meds, notably those manufactured in the U.S., cost more in Belize than in the U.S. or Canada. In general, in Belize prescriptions usually are not needed for antibiotics, Viagra and some other drugs that require prescriptions in the U.S., even some painkillers containing codeine.

However, pharmacies owned by physicians or operated by hospitals, a common situation in Belize, may require or suggest a consultation with the doctor.

Among the larger independent drug stores in Belize are Central Drug Store, DRs Pharmacy, Goodcare, Safeway Drug Store, Family Health Pharmacy and First Choice Pharmacy, all in Belize City (there also are pharmacies catering to cruise ship passengers in the Tourist Village); Evergreen Pharmacy and Magana's Pharmacy in Corozal Town; St. Vincent's Drug Store in Dangriga; and NJV's Pharmacy in Punta Gorda. Also, Brodies supermarkets in Belize City have pharmacies. In addition, especially if you are in Northern Belize, crossing the border to Chetumal is an option. Chetumal has large *farmacias* that stock most medications at prices significantly lower than in the U.S., and usually lower than in Belize.

If you are taking prescription medications, when you come to Belize you should be sure you have the generic name of the drug, as local pharmacies may not have the same brand names as back home.

Cost of Care: Even if medical care isn't always up to snuff in Belize, at least it is cheap. **The majority of public health care is provided at little or no charge to Belizeans and sometimes to visitors.** Belizeans who can't afford to pay are treated in about the same way as those with more means. Only a tiny percentage of Belizeans have medical insurance. Private medical insurance coverage in Belize begins at US$150 to $300 a month, above what the average Belizean can pay.

Rarely in the public health system in Belize will anyone be turned away for lack of cash or insurance, as many may be in the U.S. Public hospitals and clinics may bill nominal amounts for tests and or they may ask for a donation. But even visitors are routinely treated for free or for a few dollars. A British friend was injured in a boating accident off

Dangriga. In great pain, he was taken to the hospital in Dangriga where he was he was diagnosed as having broken ribs. He was then transported by air to Belize City where he was hospitalized for several days. His total bill, including X-rays, hospital stay, transport and medications: zero.

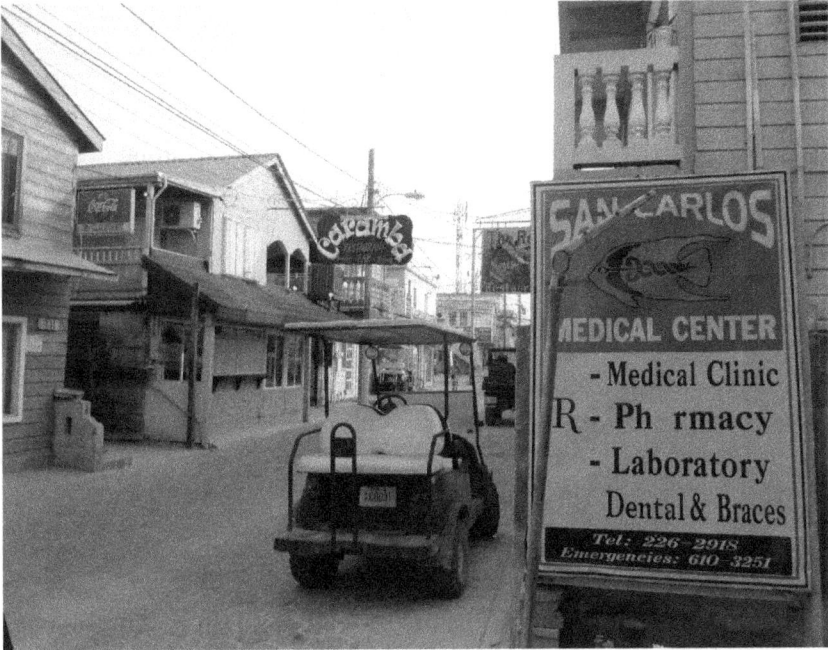

Medical clinic in San Pedro, Ambergris Caye

If you go to private physician or dentist, you will be charged. Rates vary, being higher in tourist areas such as San Pedro. However, overall you'll pay just a fraction of the cost you'd have to pay for an emergency room or doctor's visit in the U.S. Even in the private sector overall costs for health care in Belize are one-fourth to one-third that in the U.S. and may be even less. After a severe fall while on the cayes, the author recently got emergency care and prescription meds from a physician in San Pedro for a cost of less than US$100.

Some Belizeans physicians will make house or hotel calls. Check with your hotel for a list of recommended professionals.

POLITICS AND GOVERNMENT

Formerly a British colony, and known as British Honduras from 1862 to 1973, Belize became independent from Britain in 1981. It is now a member of the British Commonwealth, with a Westminster-style government system with a prime minister, an elected house of representatives and an appointed senate. **The current prime minister is Dean Barrow,** a Jamaica- and U.S.-educated lawyer whose main home is in Belize City. He heads the **United Democratic Party** (UDP), which swept national elections in 2008 and retained control of the government in March 2012 elections. The UDP won again in November 2015 general elections, and Dean Barrow was sworn in for his third, and likely final, term as prime minister. The opposition party is the **People's United Party** (PUP), currently headed by John Briceño of Orange Walk. Both parties are generally centrist in their economic and political policies. Third parties occasionally challenge the UDP and PUP, but in modern times none has received more than a token amount of votes.

The "George Washington of Belize" was George Cadle Price, an ascetic Creole who helped found the PUP and was Belize's first prime minister. George Price died in 2011.

Politics in Belize is a freewheeling affair and often intensely personal. Belize has strong ties with the United States and Britain, but it also has cultivated ties with Taiwan, Cuba, Venezuela, Jamaica, Japan, Mexico and other countries, often out of the need to seek foreign aid or development funding.

ECONOMY

The country of Belize **Gross Domestic Product** in 2014 (the latest year for which complete data is available) was US$1.7 billion, or around US$4,900 per capita. On a Purchasing Power Parity basis, the Belize GDP in 2014 was US$3 billion and the per-capita GDP on a PPPP basis was US$8,200. The PPP method involves the use of standardized international dollar price weights, which are applied to the quantities of final goods and services produced in a given economy. This method may be better for estimating true economic power when comparing countries.

By comparison, U.S. GDP in 2014 was US$17.4 trillion, and per-capita GDP in the U.S. in 2014 was US$54,600. Thus, per-capita GDP in Belize is less than 10% of that in the U.S. Belize's GDP growth averaged nearly 4% annually between 1999 and 2007 but fell to 0% in 2009 and stayed low through the international recession. However, in 2014, GDP grew by 3.4%, about 1 percentage point higher than the U.S. in the same year.

Average income figures in Belize mask a huge income disparity between rich and poor. About 40% of the Belize population is below the poverty line.

Although the estimated population of Belize is now nearing 370,000, the entire Belize national economy is about the size of the economy of a U.S. town of around 30,000 to 40,000 people.

Tourism and agriculture/marine products are the two major industries, each representing about one-fifth of GDP. In terms of foreign currency earnings, tourism is number one. Due to recent growth, tourism is now the largest segment of the economy in most years. Ambergris Caye, Cayo and Placencia are the major areas developed for tourism, with Hopkins and Caye Caulker also having significant tourism development.

Belize got about 341,000 international overnight visitors in 2015, a record, with more than 60% coming from the U.S. Nearly three-fourths of the overnight visitors arrived by air at Philip S. W. Goldson International Airport in Ladyville near Belize City, and most of the rest by land through Mexico or Guatemala.

These figures do not include nearly a million (958,000 in 2015) day visitors on cruise ships, which mostly call on Belize City, coming in on tenders as large ships can't dock at the Belize City port. In late 2016, despite construction delays, some cruise ships are expected to start calling on the US$100 million **Norwegian Cruise Line port** at Harvest Caye near Placencia village. How this will impact tourism and daily life in Southern Belize is as yet unclear.

The main **agricultural crops** are sugar cane, citrus, cacao, marine products, timber and bananas. Aquaculture, mainly shrimp and tilapia fish farming, has developed in Belize since the 1990s.

Agriculture has taken hits in Belize recently, with low prices for sugar, loss of jobs in the papaya sector due to competition from Guatemala, a significant decline in citrus production due to a disease called citrus greening and a drop in banana exports and shrimp farming.

Belize has a labor force of around 125,000. The official **unemployment rate** in 2014 was 12.9%, but in many rural areas of Belize it is much higher. In some parts of Belize, especially the far south, a significant number of Belizeans have never worked at a regular job, making a living of sorts through subsistence farming or doing odd day jobs. There is a shortage of skilled workers in some areas, notably Ambergris Caye.

Inflation in Belize has been low to moderate in recent years. It was 4.5% in 2007 but increased to over 6% in 2008, before dropping to just 0.5% in 2013 and 0.9% in 2014. **In 2015, there was a small deflation in Belize prices,** which dropped a negative 0.9%.

The government runs a **budget deficit** most years. The deficit was 3% of GDP in 2014. External debt was about US$1.25 billion in 2014. That is high given the small size of the Belizean economy, but relatively speaking it is better that the debt-to-GDP ratio of the U.S. In 2006, the government reached agreement with most international creditors to restructure its external debt, issuing new bonds at lower interest rates. Belize again renegotiated its external debt in 2013.

Concerns include a fairly large public debt relative to government income and GDP and a balance-of-trade deficit approach US$300 million a year.

Key Economic Numbers:
(Figures are the latest available, in most cases for 2014 and 2015):
GDP: US$1.7 billion
GDP Per Capita: US$4,900
GDP Growth: 3.4%
Inflation Rate: -0.9%
Unemployment Rate: 12.9%

BRIEF HISTORY OF BELIZE

The human history of Belize can be divided into **four broad periods: the ancient Maya period, the Spanish conquest, the British colonial period and modern Belize.**

The **ancient Maya,** whose ancestors likely came originally from Asia, settled in what is now Mexico 7,000 to 10,000 year ago. The Maya civilization was influenced by and grew out of the Olmec culture farther north. The Maya migrated to what is now Belize about 3,000 to 5,000 years ago, perhaps earlier. During the height of the Maya empire, called the Classic period, roughly 250 BCE to 900 CE (in this book we use BCE, Before the Common Era, instead of BC, and CE for Common Era instead of AD), the area that is now Belize had a civilization that included large-scale agriculture, sizeable cities of up to several hundred thousand people, formalized religion and a sophisticated knowledge of architecture, art, science and mathematics. As many as a million people lived in Belize during the late Classic period, compared to about one-third that number today. Caracol likely was the largest city-state in Belize, with a population perhaps three or four times larger than that of Belize City today.

Then, rather quickly, in a matter of at most a few hundred years, most of the great Maya cities were depopulated and the Maya civilization went into decline. There are many theories as to why this happened, among them that there was a change in weather patterns that disrupted agricultural, that epidemic diseases swept the region or that social changes – perhaps revolutions – transformed the society. It could have been a combination of reasons. Whatever the reasons, by around 1000 CE most of the major cities in Belize had been at least partially abandoned, though a few settlements, such as Lamanai in northern Belize, lasted for many more centuries.

The **Spanish Conquest** of Mexico and Central America began in the first quarter of the 16th century. Spanish troops and missionaries destroyed much of what was left of the Maya civilization, including burning nearly all of the Maya books or codices that they found. Soldiers killed many, and the European diseases they brought such as smallpox killed even more. Belize offered little to the Spanish in the way of gold or other riches, so Spain never paid much attention to it.

By the early 17th century, Belize drew the attention of a motley group of **British loggers and adventurers.** The original Brits in Belize sought logwood, a valuable hardwood used to make dyes. These Brits also did a little buccaneering on the side. One of the most fearsome was Edward Teach, called Blackbeard for his huge black beard. According to legend, Blackbeard used Ambergris Caye for his hideout, continuing to terrorize ships of all nations. He was finally killed off the coast of North Carolina in 1718.

By the beginning of the 18th century, several hundred British loggers, hangers-on and their slaves had settled around the mouth of the Belize River, near the bay of what is now Belize City. They were known as **Baymen.** British logging settlements grew over the course of the next 100 years or so. The loggers imported slaves from Jamaica to help cut logwood and mahogany.

There was continuing conflict between the British and the Spanish. Finally, in early September 1798, a Spanish fleet of 32 ships with about 2,000 men came to settle the score and wipe out the British once and for all. But it didn't work out that way. A ragtag band of Baymen assisted by a Royal Navy battleship on September 10, 1798, defeated the larger Spanish force in the **Battle of St. George's Caye.** That event helped end Spain's claims to Belize once and for all and is now celebrated as National Day.

Spain acknowledged British sovereignty in Belize in the Treaty of Amiens in 1802. Thus began the **British era** in Belize, which lasted until the mid-20th century. British Honduras, as it was then known, officially became a British colony in 1862, at the time of the U.S. Civil War. Following the Civil War, about 1,500 **Confederate supporters came to British Honduras.** They tried to establish the town of New Richmond, near what is present day Belmopan City. Others settled in Toledo District.

Much of the British period was marked by the traditional colonial approach of exploiting the natural resources of the colony. Though

slavery was abolished in Belize in 1838, almost three decades before it was abolished in the United States, English and Scottish companies employing hard-working Belizean blacks continued to log the native forests, exporting the timber back to Europe.

During this time, Belize began to become a melting pot of races and ethnic backgrounds. The old Baymen families, with names like Usher and Fairweather, married former slaves, creating a kind of provincial **Creole aristocracy** of "Royal Creoles" in Belize City. Some Mayas, fleeing the Caste Wars of mid-19th century Mexico, intermarried with the Spanish, and were then called Mestizos. Hundreds of Garifuna from Honduras, with African and Caribbean Indian heritage, settled in southern Belize.

As the 20th century dawned, British Honduras was a sleepy backwater of the British Empire. But underneath the sleepiness, things were stirring. Jamaican-born Marcus Garvey helped raise racial consciousness in Belize, as he did elsewhere in the Caribbean.

The worldwide Great Depression and a **terrible hurricane in 1931,** which killed some 2,000 people in and around Belize City, both had a great impact on Belize. The country was only tangentially involved in World War II, though many Belizeans served in British or other armed forces.

The end of World War II sparked anti-colonial feelings and marked the beginning of **modern Belize history.** The first major political movements favoring independence from Britain arose. Of these, the People's United Party (PUP) under George Price, an ascetic Creole educated at St. John's College in Belize City, was the most important. In 1954, a new constitution for the colony was introduced, for the first time giving all literate adults the **right to vote**. Until then only about 3 in 100 Belizeans were allowed to vote.

George Price negotiated the new constitution granting British Honduras full internal self-government, although it remained a British colony.

The country's **name officially was changed to Belize in 1973. On September 21, 1981, Belize became an independent nation,** with George Price as prime minister.

Small, unpopulated and undeveloped, modern Belize has struggled to create a viable economy and infrastructure. The country several times faced off with Guatemala, which had long maintained that Belize was simply a province of Guatemala. It was not until 1991 that Guatemala finally recognized Belize as a sovereign state, although even up until today populist flag-wavers in Guatemala occasionally threaten to invade *Belice* (as it is known in Spanish). Most recently, in 2015-16, there have been skirmishes in Southern Belize around the Sarstoon River.

In the 20th century, agriculture, especially citrus, bananas and sugar, replaced logging as the country's main industry. More recently, tourism has supplanted agriculture as the primary industry.

Democracy found fertile roots in Belize, and the little country has a dynamic two-party system. Occasionally, groups attempt to start a third party, but in recent times that's proved unsuccessful. The United Democratic Party (UDP), under the former schoolteacher Manuel Esquivel, first defeated the PUP in the 1984 national elections, and again in 1993, but the PUP under Said Musa regained power in 1998 and held it until 2008.

The current prime minister, Dean Barrow, heads the UDP, which won the general election in 2008 and again in 2012 and most recently in November 2015. Dean Barrow is the first black to hold the office of prime minister. After its third straight national election defeat, the PUP appears to be in some disarray, with efforts under way for new leadership and a new policy direction.

VISITING BELIZE ON A CRUISE SHIP

Cruise ships from the ports of Miami, Fort Lauderdale, Tampa, New Orleans and elsewhere make stops in Belize. Typically, these are ships doing a Western Caribbean itinerary.

Nearly a million cruise ship passengers visited Belize in 2015. Large cruise ships have called only on Belize City, docking offshore and tendering passengers on small boats into the city.

Tenders come into the **Tourism Village** docks in the Fort George areas near the main downtown area. The Tourism Village is well policed, and security is good. Cruise passengers with cruise ID have no difficulty entering, but locals and non-cruise international visitors are not warmly welcomed. Non-cruise tourists need to show and probably leave their passports to enter the Tourism Village.

In the Village are several bars and restaurants, gift shops, a Belizean chocolate shop, an internet café, five Diamond International stores, a pharmacy that sells some meds, including antibiotics, without a prescription. Viagra is advertised at US$4 a pill or US$90 for 30-day supply, no prescription needed. Outside the Tourism Village are a **flea market and local stands** selling snacks and local crafts. Activity varies depending on how many cruise ships are in port. Thursday is usually the busiest day.

The Celebrity Equinox *is one of the ships that visits Belize* Photo by Sheila M. Lambert

From the Tourism Village you can walk to most of the downtown attractions, including the Museum of Belize, Bliss Memorial and Lighthouse, the Swing Bridge and others. Several hotels, including the Radisson Fort George and The Great House, are nearby, as are a number of restaurants. During the day, the area is generally safe, although occasionally you may be approached by touts offering crafts or drugs.

The **most popular shore excursion** for cruise passengers is cave tubing at Caves Branch Archaeological Reserve (Nohoch Che'en) aka Jaguar Paw near Belmopan. Cave tubing tours from independent tour companies in Belize City start at around US$50, with add-ons for ziplines and other stops. Also very popular are snorkel trips to Hol Chan Marine Reserve or elsewhere off Belize City, the short trip to Altun Ha Maya site north of Belize City and the longer trip to the Lamanai Maya site on the New River Lagoon. Visits to the Belize Zoo, often paired with other tours, also are popular. It's usually more expensive to use the cruise ship's tour operators, but passengers who use them usually get preferential departures on tenders into Belize City.

With the expected opening of the controversial **US$100 million Norwegian Cruise Line cruise port on Harvest Caye near Placencia in late 2016** – it has been delayed several times due to environmental and other issues and could be further delayed – NCL ships will dock there for access to Placencia and Southern Belize instead of stopping in Belize City.

Among the cruise lines with itineraries that include stops in Belize are **AIDA** (www.aida.de), **Azamara Club Cruises** (888-532-5828, www.azamaracluBCEruises.com), **Carnival Cruises** (800-764-7419, www.princess.com), **Celebrity Cruises** (888-752-7762, www.celebritycruises.com), **Hapag-Lloyd Cruises** (www.hl-cruises.com), **Norwegian Cruise Line** (866-234-7350, www.ncl.com), **Oceana Cruises** (855-623-2642, www.oceanacruises.com), **Phoenix** (www.phoenixreisen.com), **Princess Cruises** (800-774-6237, www.princess.com), **Regent Seven Seas Cruises** (844-473-4368, www.rssc.com), **Royal Caribbean** (866-562-7625, www.royalcaribbean.com), **Thompson** (www.thomson.co.uk) and **Voyages of Discovery** (www.voyagesofdiscovery.co.uk).

VISITOR INFORMATION

Belize Tourism Board (64 Regent Street, Belize City, 501-227-2420 or 800-624-0686, www.travelbelize.org) is Belize's official governmental source of travel information. The BTB has a slick website, and it provides some useful information for visitors, such as contact information for all registered lodging properties in Belize.

Belize Tourism Industry Association (10 North Park Street, Belize City, 501-227-1144, www.btia.org), established in 1985 when Belize tourism was in its infancy, is a private-sector umbrella organization for the broad tourism industry, operating as a private-public partnership with representation on governmental agencies and departments. It has local information centers for visitors in Placencia, Punta Gorda and Orange Walk Town. BTIA also has chapters in most major visitor destinations in Belize. It puts on the BETEX industry show in Belize City, which brings around 40 travel agencies and other international tourism operators to Belize. In the past, BTIA has organized the publication of an annual magazine, *Destination Belize*, but the future of this magazine is unclear.

Belize Hotel Association (13 Cork Street, Belize City, 501-223-0669, www.belizehotels.org) is a private, non-profit organization that represents Belize hotels and allied tourism operators.

Besides these organizations, a number of individuals, companies and organizations have helpful websites. Among these are Marty Casado's **AmbergrisCaye.com** (www.ambergriscaye.com), which has an incredible amount of information on San Pedro and Ambergris Caye, along with some on Caye Caulker. It also has an active and helpful message board, mostly about the Northern Cayes. **Caye Caulker Vacation** (www.cayecaulkervacation.com) is the official site of the Caulker BTIA chapter.

Belize Forums (www.belizeforum.com) -- note the lack of the plural in the website URL – has what is arguably the most active and informative message board about Belize. It is operated by Tony Rath, a noted photographer and owner of the **Belize by Naturalight** website (www.belizenet.com) and is also associated with the Pelican Beach Resorts.

For information on Placencia, the Placencia BTIA chapter produces the newsy *Placencia Breeze* monthly tabloid newspaper and the **Placencia.com** website (www.placencia.com). The ***Toledo Howler*** is a quarterly newspaper on Punta Gorda and Toledo District put out by the PG BTIA – an online version is available at https://issuu.com/btia_toledo. *(See the Best Belize Websites appendix for more sites and blogs about Belize.)*

TRANSPORTATION

Philip S. W. Goldson International Airport near Belize City

GETTING TO BELIZE

The vast majority of the more than 340,000+ overnight visitors to Belize arrive by air at the **Philip S. W. Goldson International Airport** in Ladyville, about 9 miles north of Belize City.

Belize Prime Minister Dean Barrow announced in 2015 that following the completion of an 11-mile North Ambergris Caye road project, the Belize government will "redevelop, redesign and expand" the Basil Jones airstrip at the road's end into a new international airport. The airport will be called **Efrain Guerrero International Airport** in honor of a recently deceased Sanpedrano, PM Barrow said. Promises of an international airport on Ambergris Caye have been made before, so the new airport is not necessarily a done deal. A privately financed and developed international airport just north of the Placencia peninsula remains unfinished, and its future also is unclear.

ARRIVING BY AIR

At present, six major airlines fly to Belize: **American Airlines** (which recently merged with US Airways, www.aa.com), **Avianca** (formerly TACA, www.avianca.com), **Copa** (which in late 2015 began offering two weekly flights between Panama City, Panama, and Belize City, www.copaair.com), Delta **Airlines** (www.delta.com), **United Airlines** (which merged with Continental, www.united.com) and **Southwest** (which began service to Belize from Hobby in Houston in late 2015, www.southwest.com).

The gateways for nonstop flights from the U.S. include Atlanta, Charlotte, Dallas, Houston, Los Angeles, Miami and Newark. Avianca has service from San Salvador, and Copa has service from Panama City. In addition, Belize-based **Tropic Air** (www.tropicair.com) has service to the international airport from Cancún, Mérida, Flores, Guatemala City, Roatán, San Pedro Sula and Tegucigalpa. Not all international service is daily, and service may be reduced in the off-season. *(See Traveling Around Belize section below for details on Belize domestic air travel.)*

The international airlines use mostly Boeing 737, Airbus A320 or other smaller equipment to Belize, with the usual tight seating in coach and overpriced seating in first/business class, if there is any seating at all beyond coach. Tropic Air uses mostly 14-seat Cessna equipment.

Flights from Atlanta, Miami, Dallas, Charlotte and Houston take only two to three hours of airtime.

At present there is no scheduled non-stop or direct service from Canada or Europe. In-season, usually there are a few charter flights from Toronto.

One of the chief complaints from Belize travelers is the high cost of airfare. From the chief gateways you can expect to pay US$600 to $1,000 round-trip in coach. Airlines flying to Belize occasionally have internet specials with return prices as low as US$300, but you have to act fast as the windows for purchase and travel are narrow.

One idea is to fly into Cancún, Mérida or Cozumel, Mexico, on a cheap scheduled or charter flight and bus it from there. There is now daily first-class **ADO Express** bus service daily between Cancún and Belize City, and non-daily ADO Express service between Mérida and Belize City. In addition, there are many first-class and some executive-class ADO buses that run between Cancún and Chetumal, at the Belize border, and ADO buses from Playa del Carmen and Mérida to Chetumal. Also, there is a water taxi, usually daily, from Chetumal, Mexico, to San Pedro and Caye Caulker. *See below for more information and travel tips.*

Our advice: Sign up for internet fare notices on the airlines that fly to Belize. Keep checking the on-line reservation sites such as **Expedia** (www.expedia.com), **TripAdvisor** (www.tripadvisor.com) or **Travelocity** (www.travelocity.com). Also check meta-reservation sites – they compare fares from a variety of other sites – such as **Kayak** (www.kayak.com) or **Mobissimo** (www.mobissimo.com).

A travel agent specializing in Belize, such as **Barb's Belize** in Stuarts Draft, Va. (540-337-1103 or 888-321-2272, www.barbsbelize.com) may be able to find lower fares for you. The owner, **Barbara Kasak,** is very knowledgeable about Belize.

Another source of airfare deals and hotel and tour bookings in Belize is Katie Valk, a New Yorker and former music industry executive who has lived in Belize City, Cayo and Placencia for many years and is now based in Belize City. She knows just about everything about Belize and everyone in Belize. Email her at **Belize Trips** in Belize at info@belize-trips.com or visit www.belize-trips.com. Her U.S. telephone number is 561-210-7015. One big advantage to working with Katie is that she is usually on the ground in Belize, so she's there to help should anything go awry.

Arriving by Air -- What to Expect: The Belize International Airport (officially named as the **Philip S. W. Goldson International Airport**, after a long-time People's United Party politician, now passed to his reward) is about 9 miles north of the center of Belize City, off the Philip Goldson Highway (formerly Northern Highway) at Ladyville. The airport is small but fairly modern, having opened in 1990. It is believed to be the only "major" airport in the world with a mahogany ceiling in the original building. Another terminal area opened in late 1998 and since then the runway has been extended.

The airport has a 9,700-foot runway with three taxiways. Modern navigational aids are in place, including Doppler VHF Omni-Directional Radar (DVOR), Distance Measuring Equipment (DME), Digital Readout Directional Finder (DRDF), Non-Directional Beam (NDB), Instrument Landing System, Category 1 (ILS) and Secondary Surveillance Radio.

After your airplane taxis to the terminal building, you disembark the old-fashioned way, down a set of moveable stairs. You cross the tarmac and enter the immigration and customs area. Most days, you feel the humidity right away.

The immigration officer will look at your passport and usually ask the purpose of your visit and how long you are staying. You can be granted a visitor's entry permit of up to 30 days at no charge, but the 30-day period is not automatic. If you say you are staying 10 days, the officer on occasion may grant only that period or two weeks at most. If you think there's any chance you may want to stay a little longer than your current reservations, be generous about estimating the time you'll stay. The officer will then stamp your passport and enter the arrival and departure date.

From here, you move to a small baggage claim area, where there is a baggage carousel, restrooms and small duty-free shop selling liquor and a few other items. When entering Belize, you are permitted to bring in only one liter of alcohol, but you can buy an additional four liters of booze at the airport arrival duty-free shop, where you need to pay in U.S. dollars.

You then go through customs. Belize now has a Green/Red customs system. If you have nothing to declare, you can go through the Green line, though an officer may still ask to see inside your bags. On a typical flight, probably one-third of passengers have at least one bag inspected. Customs and immigrations officers generally are courteous and efficient, though like government officials in most countries they are not known for being overly friendly. Treat them with respect, and you'll be treated similarly. Do not even think of offering a bribe. That is not how things work in Belize, at least not at this level. The entire arrival, immigration and customs process usually takes from 15 minutes to half an hour.

After your bags pass customs, you can go into the main airport lobby or out to the taxi or rental car area. Porters are available to assist with bags, if necessary. A tip of US$1/BZ$2 per bag is standard, more if special services are provided. If you are continuing on a domestic flight and don't have reservations, move quickly to the **Maya Island Air** or **Tropic Air** check-in counter, as the domestic carriers use small airplanes, and they fill up quickly.

The rectangular main passenger lobby, which is usually bustling with people, has a **Belize Bank ATM** accepting all debit cards on the VISA, MasterCard, Plus, and Cirrus networks (however, Belize Bank's international airport office was relocated to Sky Plaza, Ladyville in 2013), a few tourist gift shops and airline ticket counters. The adjoining terminal 2 has an **Atlantic Bank** office (open 9:30 a.m.-3:30 Monday-Friday and 9:30-2:30 Saturday, closed Sunday) and an ATM. In the main terminal, upstairs to your left are bathrooms (clean) and a Global Spice restaurant and bar adjoining the "waving area" with views of the airstrip. There is another restaurant, Sun Garden, in terminal 2. A small bar, Jets Bar, is in the international and domestic departure area past security, along with four international duty free shops.

Taxis are available right outside the passenger lobby door. The taxis at the airport – cabs have green license plates – are regulated and you shouldn't be ripped off. The Airport Taxi Union (501-610-4450) operates the taxi service at the international airport. The fare is fixed at US$25 (BZ$50) to anywhere in Belize City — that's for the cab, not per person, although a small additional amount may be charged for extra luggage. In

Belize, you do not need to tip taxi drivers unless they perform extra service such as carrying luggage. There are no buses directly into Belize City from the airport. You can walk about 1½ miles to the Goldson Highway, or pay a taxi around US$6 to take you there. From the highway, you can flag down a bus going into Belize City (fare about US$1).

Belize Municipal Airport (TZA), located about 1 mile from the Belize City centre on the seafront, has Tropic Air and Maya Island Air domestic flights at somewhat lower rates than the international airport, but you'll need to transfer to that airport by US$25 taxi.

Overnight parking is available at the international airport for US$9 per day.

Rental car kiosks, including local offices of international franchised auto rental companies such as **Avis, Budget, Hertz** and **Thrifty**, along with locals **Crystal,** the largest rental firm in Belize, **Jabiru, AQ, Pancho's** and others, are on the far side of the airport parking area, a short distance. (*See the Rental Car section below for more information.*)

ARRIVING BY SEA

As noted in the Traveling Around Belize and individual destination sections below, there are **water taxis** carrying only pedestrians from Chetumal, Mexico, to San Pedro and Caye Caulker, from Puerto Barrios and Livingston, Guatemala, to Punta Gorda and from Puerto Cortés, Honduras, to Dangriga and Belize City. There are no ships that carry vehicles from the U.S., Mexico, Guatemala, Honduras or elsewhere in the region to Belize. There was briefly a ship from Tampa to a port near Cancún that carried vehicles, but it no longer operates. Attempts to restart a vehicular ferry service from the U.S. to Mexico or Central America have so far been fruitless.

Cruise ships from the ports of Miami, Fort Lauderdale, Tampa, New Orleans and elsewhere make stops in Belize. Nearly a million cruise ship passengers visited Belize in 2015. Until late 2016, the large cruise ships called only on Belize City, docking offshore and tendering passengers on small boats into the city. (*See section on Cruises in Know Before You Go.*)

Some cruise lines permit passengers to be dropped off at one of the ports of call, including Belize, rather than continue on with the cruise. This is rarely done, however, because it requires advance permission of the cruise line, which must arrange special immigration and customs procedures for the disembarking passengers.

Yacht owners arriving by sea in their own boats must check in with the Belize Port Authority (www.portauthority.bz) to arrange immigrations and customs procedures. Belize has two Port Authority offices in the country, one in Belize City and one in Big Creek near Placencia. Those arriving by boat at Belize City or Big Creek should report directly to the Port Authority office. In other areas, check with Immigrations and Customs offices. Immigrations and Customs offices are located in Belize City, San Pedro, Big Creek, Dangriga and Punta Gorda. The Port Authority communications center monitors on a 24/7 basis VHF radio channel 16 and HF radio channel 2182. The Maritime Emergency telephone line is 501-232-9440.

Incoming cruisers in their own boats should have updated and detailed charts and GPS equipment that clearly show the water depth and underwater formations. The Belize Barrier Reef and many patch reefs at the atolls and inside the Barrier Reef are extremely tricky for anyone not knowing local waters. Hitting the reef not only can cause serious damage to the boat and the reef but doing so also potentially exposes the boat owner to major criminal and civil penalties for damage to a UNESCO World Heritage Site. Yachters must have a valid passport, a visa if necessary (citizens of most countries don't need a visa), have cleared their last port and meet all the Belize entry requirements of those arriving by land or air.

Note that among the boating community Belize is not considered particularly yacht-friendly, with more red tape and higher costs than neighboring countries, especially Guatemala and Mexico. Many boaters gravitate to the Rio Dulce area of Guatemala's Caribbean Coast.

Also, there have been incidents of attacks on boaters in Belize, the most recent in January 2016, when four men boarded a yacht near Middle Long Caye, an island off Belize City, sexually assaulted one passenger and made off with thousands of dollars worth of equipment.

Arriving by Bus

From Flores, Guatemala, to Belize City, several bus companies including **Fuente del Norte** (www.grupofuentedelnorte,com) and **Linea Dorado** (www.lineadorada.info) provide bus service. The fares are around US$25 one-way. In Belize, the buses pick up and drop off at the Marine Terminal near the Swing Bridge in Belize City. The Guatemalan buses are not supposed to pick up or drop off passengers anywhere else in Belize, but drivers sometimes will do so. Fuente del Norte buses also run daily between Flores and San Pedro Sula, Honduras, and San Salvador, El Salvador. This and several other lines have frequent first-class service between Flores and Guatemala City. **Mundo Maya Travels** (Brown Sugar Market Place, North Front Street, Belize City, 501-223-1200, www.travelmundomaya.com) sells tickets to these and other bus companies, along with some water taxi and boat ferry tickets.

Marlin Espadas Ltd. (501-615-9009, www.marlinespadas.com) has begun a daily bus service between Flores, Guatemala, and Chetumal, Mexico. A bus departs from Flores daily at 7:30 a.m. and from Chetumal daily at 9:30 a.m. Stops can be made at Corozal Town, Orange Walk Town, Belize City, Belmopan, San Ignacio and Benque Viejo. The buses are air-conditioned and have wi-fi. The cost for the full trip is around US$40 one-way.

Mexican bus line **ADO** (www.ado.com.mx) has two **ADO Express** services to Belize City – a daily one from Cancún and one from Mérida that runs three or four days a week. The ADO Express buses have reserved reclining seats, videos, bathroom and air conditioning. ADO serves a number of other cities in southern Mexico with first-class and, on a few routes, even better executive class service. It is possible to board various bus company buses at U.S.-Mexico border cities and make connections to ADO, ending up in Chetumal or Belize City. **MexExperience** (www.mexexperience.com) is one of several websites that provides detailed information on traveling through Mexico by bus.

From Cancún to Belize City, the ADO Express bus departs from Cancún downtown terminal daily at 10:15 p.m., with stops at Playa del Carmen, Tulum, Corozal Town and Orange Walk Town. It arrives in Belize City about 6 or 6:30 a.m. The current fare (subject to increase) is 576 Mexican pesos one-way or about US$35 at current exchange rates. Trip time is about 8 hours.

Tica Bus (507-314-6385 in Panama City, www.ticabus.com) is a well-known bus company that provides express service between major cities, mostly capital cities, in Central America, from Panama City, Panama, through Costa Rica, El Salvador and Honduras to Guatemala City, Guatemala, and on to Chiapas, Mexico. In early 2016, a one-way ticket from Panama City to Chiapas was US$148 to $191, depending on the class. That doesn't include the cost of border crossings, which average US$5 to $7 for each border crossed. However, the Tica Bus route does not include Belize. Its closest destination to Belize is Guatemala City, which can be reached by express buses of Fuente del Norte and other companies from Flores, Guatemala. As noted above, there is daily service on Fuente del Norte and other companies between Flores and Belize City.

(For more information on getting to Belize by bus, see the Bus information in the Traveling Around Belize section below.)

ARRIVING BY CAR

A few intrepid travelers choose to drive to Belize, either through Mexico or if coming from other areas of Central America, through

Guatemala. Due to the drug cartel violence in Mexico, especially in border areas, and increasingly in Guatemala, many people who in previous years would have considered driving to Belize now are reluctant to do so. Some who do drive may try to convoy with other drivers or hire a Belizean who has made the trip frequently and knows the safest and best routes.

The drive from Brownsville, Texas, the nearest entry point in the U.S. to Belize, is about 1,250 to 1,500 miles, depending on the route you take. It usually takes three to four days to drive, although it can be done faster, staying in Mexico for only two nights. Total non-stop driving time is around 28 to 35 hours, depending on conditions, your driving speed and other factors.

The fastest route from Brownsville/Matamoros is via Tampico, Tuxpan, Veracruz, Villahermosa and Chetumal. From the border, take Mexico national route 101 to highway 180. Just north of Veracruz, take 150D (a toll road) to Villahermosa. (Alternatively you can stay on highway 180). At Villahermosa, take route 186 for 360 miles to the Belize border (the last 5 miles may be signed as route 307). The toll roads are expensive, around US$10 for each 100 miles, but you can make 70 mph on them, much faster than on the regular roads.

Driving in Mexico can be confusing, as road through towns and elsewhere are often poorly signed. In general, avoid going through the town centers *(Centro)*, as you can easily get lost and the hotels are more expensive. To enter Mexico (and later, Belize) by car, you need the original plus two copies of your passport, valid driver's license, vehicle registration card, original vehicle title, or if your vehicle is not paid for, a notarized letter of permission from the lien holder. Besides paying the Mexico tourist entry fee of about US$20, which allows entry for up to six months, you have to provide a credit card in lieu of posting a cash bond of up to US$400 to guarantee that you will bring the car back out of Mexico. Your credit card (MasterCard, Visa, American Express, Diners) must be in the name of the driver.

Upon arrival at the Belize-Mexico border, if you are not returning to the U.S., you must have the Mexican temporary entry permit canceled at Mexican customs. If entering Mexico by car as a tourist, as a resident of the U.S. or Canada you can bring in such personal items as luggage, binoculars, laptop computer, TV, camping equipment, up to three liters of alcohol and fishing equipment. Do NOT even think about bringing in a gun, as you will find yourself in serious trouble. If you are transporting goods of a value of US$1,000 or more and/or are going through Mexico to Belize to stay permanently, you are supposed to use the services of a customs broker at the U.S.-Mexico border and get trans-migratory status, which costs money in fees and, some say, in bribes to Mexican federal officers along the way. A broker at the U.S.-Mexico border will cost you about US$150 to $200. Unless you plan to stay in Belize, it is best just to enter Mexico as a tourist and not go the trans-mig route.

Except on toll roads, driving after dark in Mexico is not advised. You may be stopped frequently for inspections. You should exchange enough U.S. dollars to get you through Mexico, as U.S. dollars are not widely accepted, or are accepted at a low rate of exchange. The exchange rate for U.S. dollars in late 2015 was around 16.5 pesos to the dollar. Gasoline stations in Mexico sometimes do not accept credit cards.

Mexican auto insurance is required; liability costs from around US$75 for five days. It is now recommended that you get at least US$300,000 in third-party liability coverage. Collision insurance coverage can add to the cost, depending on the value of your vehicle. Insurance for a month or two, or even six months, is not much more than for a few days.

Here are typical quotes for 7 days and six months:

Extended coverage including US$300,000 third-party liability for nearly new vehicle valued at US$20,000: US$120 to $135

Six months: US$400 to $415

You MUST have Mexican auto insurance. Your U.S. or Canadian insurance is NOT valid in Mexico (or Belize.)

Sanborn's (800-222-0158; www.sanbornsinsurance.com) is a well-known source of information on travel in Mexico and for Mexican auto insurance, although their insurance tends to be more expensive than insurance from most other companies. Other companies include International Insurance Group (www.sb.iigins.com), which offers insurance through Grupo Nacional and ACE Seguros.

Do a Google search for other companies selling Mexican auto insurance, some of which can be purchased on-line in advance. One such is Mexican Auto Insurance (www.mexicanautoinsurance.com). Some U.S.-based insurance companies including GEICO and Progressive offer links to a Mexican insurance provider, with small discounts available for their U.S. or Canadian policyholders.

Sanborn maps, and in fact most maps to Mexico, may not be completely accurate. The *Guia Roji (Red Guide)* maps to Mexico are probably the best available, although ITMB maps also are good. A website with all types of helpful information on Mexico is www.mexconnect.com.

On arrival at the Mexico-Belize border, you again need your original title (no photocopies) for your vehicle, or, if you do not own it free and clear, a notarized statement from the lien holder that you have permission to take the car out of the U.S. You also have to buy Belize auto insurance, which is required by law in Belize. There are brokers at the border. Three months of insurance should cost about US$60 to $100, or one month or less about US$35. The cost may be higher depending on the coverage you get. Crossing the border you probably will have to have your car sprayed to kill hitchhiking bugs — the fee is around US$5.

Driving from other parts of Central America, you will enter Belize through Guatemala. Currently, the only legal entry point from Guatemala is at Melchor de Mencos, about 90 minutes by car from Flores/Santa Elena and around 10 hours from Guatemala City. Roads from Guatemala City to Flores and then to the Belize border are good, although there is the occasional risk of bandits.

Work is underway now on completing the paving of the San Antonio Road in Toledo from the Guatemala border near Jalacte village in Belize to the Southern Highway. When and if a border crossing station is completed near Jalacte, drivers can reach southern Belize via CA13 at Poptun, Guatemala, from Guatemala City. Auto liability insurance in Guatemala is not required, but it is recommended.

The Pan-American Highway, designated CA-1 in Central America, runs from the top of Alaska at Prudhoe Bay to the bottom of South America at Tierra del Fuego, Argentina. Although it is on the west side of Guatemala, from either border crossing you can wind your way to the Pan-American in Guatemala or Honduras. The only part of the PAH that can't be traveled by car is about 50 miles of the Darien Gap between Panama and Colombia.

Assuming that you are entering as a tourist, you should get free entry of your vehicles for 90 days, with no duty required. (However, we have heard of a number of exceptions to this statement.) Your car information is entered on your passport so you cannot sell it in Belize. You must leave the country with the vehicle.

TRAVELING AROUND BELIZE

Belize is a small country, with a mainland portion less than 70 miles wide and 200 miles long, plus cayes and atolls in the Caribbean. Despite its small size, travel from one point to another in Belize can take longer than you expect. As a rule of thumb, if you figure getting from Point A to Point B in the U.S. or Canada takes two hours, expect it to take four hours in Belize. It's a matter of road conditions and delays due to schedule delays and mechanical breakdowns, plus the usual "Belize time" factor. Note: **Belize Bus and Travel Guide** (www.belizebus.wordpress.com), run by an expat living in Belize, is an excellent source of information on bus and other travel options in Belize. It usually has the most reliable and most current information, although as things change so quickly in Belize, some information even on this site may be out of date.

TRAVEL BY AIR

Belize has two domestic carriers, **Tropic Air** (800-442-3435 from the U.S. and Canada, or 501-226-2012 in Belize, www.tropicair.com), which has service to 11 airports in Belize, plus seven destinations in Mexico, Guatemala and Honduras; and **Maya Island Air** (501-223-1140, www.mayaislandair.com), which serves nine airports only in Belize.

Tropic Air operates 11 Cessna Grand Caravans (208B), two Gippsland Airvans and one Cessna 172. These aircraft are configured for from three to 14 passengers. Maya Island operates eight Cessna Caravans, three Britten Norman Islanders, one Gippsland Airvan and one Cessna 182.

As of early 2016, Tropic has scheduled service at Belize City (both international and municipal airports), Belmopan City, Caye Caulker, Corozal Town, Dangriga, Orange Walk Town, Placencia, Punta Gorda, San Ignacio/Benque Viejo and San Pedro. Internationally, it services Cancún and Mérida in Mexico, Flores and Guatemala City in Guatemala and Roatán, San Pedro Sula and Tegucigalpa in Honduras. Some international flights are less than daily.

Maya Island Air has scheduled service at Belize City (both international and municipal airports), Caye Caulker, Corozal Town, Dangriga, Placencia, Punta Gorda, San Pedro and Savannah. Both airlines also offer charter flights and may offer non-scheduled stops at other airstrips in Belize such as Kanatik in Stann Creek or Caye Chapel near Caye Caulker.

Currently, Maya Island Air permits passengers to have one checked bag of up to 50 pounds, one carry-on and on small personal item (such as a computer or purse) as a carry-on, all at no charge. Additional checked items are charged excess baggage fees ranging from BZ41 cents to BZ$1.13 per pound. Tropic Air allows one small carry-on (such as a purse or computer bag) and two free checked bags on domestic flights. On Tropic's international flights, the first checked bag is free, and additional bags are US$35 each.

Domestic flights from the municipal airport, less than a mile from the center of Belize City, are cheaper than from the international airport in Ladyville. For example, a flight to San Pedro on Ambergris Caye costs approximately US$90 one-way from international and US$55 one-way from municipal. Savings to most other destinations are less significant. Of course, you have to pay a cab to transfer from one airport to the other – US$25 for up to four persons.

Usually there is little or no savings on roundtrip fares over two one-way fares, but there are exceptions so it's worth checking the airlines' websites. Except for occasional off-season specials, fares are about the same year-round, with no advance-purchase or other discounts. Sometimes you can get a 10% discount by paying cash rather than paying by credit card. It pays to ask.

The domestic airlines fly only during daylight hours, except at peak tourism periods when they have permission to continue flying into San Pedro until all waiting passengers are taken care of.

Which airline is better? In some ways, it's a toss-up. Tropic is larger, with 250 flights daily to 17 destinations in Belize and surrounding countries, but Maya Island has added new aircraft and several new terminals (at Belize municipal, Placencia and elsewhere). For most people, the decision comes down to which airline has the more convenient flight on a specific day and time. Fares on the two airlines are similar, although there are some small differences to specific locations.

Are advance air reservations necessary? Except at peak high-season travel periods, you can probably get on a convenient flight without advance reservations. Still, having a reservation gives you a little extra edge, and we recommend you book ahead if possible. It's essential you do so at holiday periods such as Easter and Christmas.

TRAVEL BY BUS

Travel by bus in Belize is inexpensive. You can travel the whole length of the country from the Mexican border in the north to Punta Gorda in the far south for about US$25 or go from Belize City to Cayo in the west for US$4 to $5. It's also a good way to meet local people and to get a real feel for the country.

In Belize City, local and the Mexican-based ADO buses use the main bus terminal on West Collet Canal. It is still known as **Novelo's,** the name of a former bus company. Buses to Guatemala stop at the Marine Terminal near the Swing Bridge in Belize City. Other places have a bus terminal or a central point where buses stop.

There now is limited bus service within Belize City. Around half a dozen lines offer service in the downtown area and in the north and west parts of the city. Fares are BZ$1 to $2.

Bus travel in Belize falls somewhere between the chicken bus experience in rural Guatemala and the deluxe coaches with comfortable reserved seats and videos in Mexico. Belize buses are usually recycled American school buses or old Greyhound diesel pushers. There are two types of buses in Belize — regular buses that pick up and let off passengers on demand, and express buses that are faster because they make stops only at a few places.

The country has a franchised bus system, with the government granting rights for certain companies to operate on specific routes. Belize City is the hub for bus service throughout Belize. Nearly all bus lines in Belize are small, with just a few buses and drivers. Only one or two bus lines have websites, and many operate out of the owner's home with just a cell phone.

Bus companies licensed to operate on the Philip Goldson Highway in the Northern Zone include BBOC, Cabrera's, Chell's, Morales, Tillett's, T-Line and Valencia. (Bus lines subject to change.) Northbound buses depart from Belize City about every half hour from around 5:30 a.m. to 7:30 p.m. Some of the northbound buses continue to Chetumal.

Companies authorized to operate on the George Price Highway in the Western Zone include BBOC, D&E, Guerra's, Shaw and Westline. Westbound buses depart Novelo's bus station roughly every half hour beginning at 5 a.m., with the last departure around 9:30 p.m.

Bus companies operating in the Southern Zone — most running between Belize City and Punta Gorda via Belmopan and Dangriga -- include **James Bus Line** (www.jamesbusline.com), the best bus company in the south), Cho, G-Line, Ritchie's and Usher. In addition, several lines are licensed to operate mainly in rural areas of the Southern Zone. These include A-Jay's, Chen, Martinez, Radiance Ritchie and Polanco. Keep in mind that many of these "bus lines" have just one or two buses. The small lines tend to come and go.

In some cases you can make advance reservations with the larger bus operations by calling the bus companies, although most people don't make reservations. If boarding at a terminal, you pay for your ticket at the window and get a reserved seat. If boarding elsewhere, you pay the driver's assistant.

Mexican bus line **ADO** has two express services to Belize City – a daily one from Cancún and one from Mérida (where Belizeans often go for medical care) that runs three or four days a week. The ADO buses are much nicer than Belize buses, with 44 reserved reclining seats, videos, bathroom and air conditioning. From Cancún, the ADO bus leaves from the Cancún bus station in downtown Cancún City. In Belize City, ADO uses the main Belize City bus terminal called Novelo's located on West Collet Canal near the City Centre.

From Cancún to Belize City, the ADO bus departs from Cancún terminal daily at 10:15 p.m., with stops at Playa del Carmen, Tulum, Corozal Town and Orange Walk Town. It arrives in Belize City about 6 or 6:30 a.m. The current fare (subject to increase) is 576 Mexican pesos one-way or about US$35 at current exchange rates. Trip time is about 8 hours.

TRAVEL BY RENTAL CAR OR GOLF CART
Vehicle Rental in Belize

Having a rental car is an excellent way to see the mainland part of Belize. Only golf cart and scooter rentals, not car rentals, are available on the cayes. Scooters are available for rent in a few areas, including Placencia and Ambergris Caye. *See the Ambergris Caye, Caye Caulker and Placencia sections for information on golf cart rentals.*

With a car, you can make your own schedule, going where and when you want. That's especially true of more remote areas of Belize that are not served by public transport.

Driving in Belize is generally not too difficult, as most roads are well-signed, traffic is light and, increasingly, main and even secondary roads are paved and in good condition. On the islands, only Ambergris Caye has some paved roads.

Due to high import duties on vehicles and the wear and tear vehicles get on Belize's roads, car and golf cart rentals are expensive. Fuel is also significantly more expensive than in the U.S. You may be able to offset some of that cost by visiting places on your own that you otherwise would have to visit on expensive tours or via expensive air trips. That's especially true if you are traveling in a family group or with another couple.

Car Rental Agencies

Belize has both franchise agents of international car rental companies such as Avis, Budget, Hertz, Alamo and National, and it also has local companies. In fact, the largest rental agency in Belize is an independent local, Crystal. Most rental agencies are based in Belize City, typically with **small rental offices across the main parking lot just outside the terminal exits at the Philip S. W. Goldson International Airport,** along with a location in Belize City. There are also a small number of car rental agencies in Corozal Town, Placencia and elsewhere.

At peak times, especially holiday periods such as Christmas/New Year's and Easter, it is vital to make **advance car rental reservations.** Most of the time you will find that cars are available, but we have occasionally visited Belize at the time of a large regional governmental meeting when virtually all vehicles were taken. Generally, even at times other than holidays, it's advisable to reserve a car in advance. If you don't mind taking a chance of not finding the car you want, you can wait until you get to the international airport where about 10 rental car kiosks are in a row on the far side of the main airport parking lot, just a couple of hundred feet from the terminals. You can compare vehicles and bargain for the best rate.

Belize City companies without a location at Philip S. W. Goldson International Airport offer pick up service at the international airport. For companies with locations at the international airport and also in Belize City, usually you can pick up at one location and drop off at the other. If you are dropping off at downtown area location, many car companies will have a driver take you to your destination in Belize, such as the municipal airport or water taxi terminal, at no charge (you should tip the driver a couple of dollars.) Some companies offer cell phone, GPS systems and child car seats for rent for an extra charge.

Most car rental agencies offer a variety of vehicles for rent, from sub-compact cars to small, mid-size and large SUVs, pickups and vans. Toyota, Kia, Jeep, Ford, Hyundai and Great Wall (from China) are among the car brands available.

Here are some of the car rental agencies in Belize City. Rental companies in other areas are listed in the destination sections. Over the years, we have had the best results with **Budget, Crystal** and **Hertz.**

Meta travel search sites such as **Kayak** (www.kayak.com) can help you compare rates and availabilities.

International Airport and Belize City

The following companies, listed alphabetically, offer rentals:

Alamo Car Rental (Philip S. W. Goldson International Airport and 1 Slaughterhouse Road, Belize City, 501-223-0641, www.alamo.com) is associated with National and shares its Belize City location with it.

AQ Auto Rental (Philip S. W. Goldson International Airport and Mile 5½ Philip Goldson Highway (Northern Highway), 501-222-5122, www.aqbelizecarrental.com) also has a location in Placencia.

Avis Rent a Car (Philip S. W. Goldson International Airport, 501-225-4400, www.avis.com.bz).

Budget Rent a Car of Belize (Philip S. W. Goldson International Airport and Mile 2½ Philip Goldson Highway, Belize City, 501-223-2435 or 501-225-2280, www.budget-belize.com) also has a location in Placencia.

Buy Belize/Belize Auto Rental (101B Freetown Road, Belize City, 501-223-2121, www.buy-belize.com).

Crystal Auto Rental (Philip S. W. Goldson International Airport and Philip Goldson Highway, Belize City, 501-223-1600 or 936-307-1325 in U.S., www.crystal-belize.com), founded by a former Texan, is the largest car rental company in Belize. It permits vehicles to be taken into Guatemala, but the advance paperwork requires 48 hours.

Explore Belize Auto Rental (Philip S. W. Goldson International Airport, 501-225-2709, www.explorebelizeautorental.com).

Hertz (Philip S. W. Goldson International Airport and 11A Cork Street, Belize City, 501-223-5395, www.carsbelize.com).

Jabiru Auto Rental (Philip S. W. Goldson International Airport, 5576 Princess Margaret Drive, Belize City, and Marine Terminal, Belize City, 501-224-4680, www.jabiruautorental.bz).

National Car Rental (Philip S. W. Goldson International Airport, 877-222-9058, www.nationalcar.com) is associated with Alamo and shares its Belize City office with that company.

Pancho's Auto Rental (Philip S. W. Goldson International Airport and 5747 Lizarraga Avenue, Belize City, 501-224-5554 or 501-225-2540, www.panchosrentalbelize.com).

Vista Auto Rentals (798 Vista Del Mar, Ladyville, 501-225-2292, www.vistarentalsbelize.com).

(For destinations other than Belize City, see Practicalities in those destinations chapters for information on vehicle rental including cars, golf carts, scooters and bicycles.)

Tips on Rental Cars in Belize

Here are questions to ask and things to check BEFORE driving off in your rental.

• **Take along a cell phone.** It's wise to have a cell phone if you are renting a car in Belize, not only to report any breakdown or accident but also on the small chance that you run into trouble of a more serious kind. As noted in the Cell Phone section (above) you can purchase a SIM card and Belize phone number for your unlocked mobile phone or rent one from Belize Telemedia Ltd. at the international airport. A few car rental companies rent cell phones or may provide them free with the rental.

• **Check the mileage on the vehicle you've been assigned.** Even "name brand" rental agencies often have high-mileage cars in their fleet, and local companies typically will provide a car with 50,000 to

100,000 miles on it, or more, (but usually in good mechanical condition.) If the mileage seems high, ask for another vehicle.

• **Check the tires.** High-quality radials or six-ply truck tires are best for Belize roads. At the very least, tires should have plenty of tread. Also, check the spare, and be sure you know how to locate and use the jack and related equipment.

• **Agree on pre-existing dents and scratches.** Most car rental agencies will point out existing dents and mark them on your rental agreement form. Walk around the car with the agent to be sure major problems, such as a cracked windshield, are noted on the form. You might consider taking a photo of the vehicle. But don't stress about this, as the rental companies are almost always fair about this and in most cases aren't trying to rip you off.

• **Ask what will happen if you have a breakdown somewhere in the boondocks.** Major companies, such as Crystal, will send a mechanic out to repair the problem. Others may not.

• **Don't be shy about asking for discounts off published rates.** During busy times, discounts are probably not available, but in the off-season or during slow periods you may be able to negotiate a little on rates.

• **Determine in advance whether you need to accept Collision Damage Waiver/Loss Damage Waiver coverage.** CDW/LDW, which is a waiver, not an insurance product, runs about US$14 to $20+ per day in Belize, and often the basic plan does not cover the first US$500 to $1,000 in damage, so you have to cough up for a windshield broken by a flying rock, for example. American Express and some other credit cards DO provide primary CDW coverage in Belize, but you probably need to pay for a premium credit card plan to get coverage for off-road travel and for larger SUVs and trucks. Call your card issuer to confirm. Note that liability insurance, required in Belize, is provided on rental cars, but liability insurance does not cover damage to your rental vehicle.

TRAVEL BY SHUTTLE

Another option for traveling around Belize is to use a private shuttle service. There are around a dozen of these shuttle services, some based in Belize City and others in Corozal and elsewhere. While the shuttles cost more than buses, they have small vans that are more comfortable and less crowded than buses. In some cases, shuttles will make stops on demand, and some drop and pick up as far away as Cancún. Among the shuttle services in Belize are **Belize VIP Transfer Service** (www.belizetransfers.com)

and **Moralez Travel Service** (www.gettransfers.com), both based in Corozal Town; **William's Belize Shuttle** (501-620-3055, www.williamshuttlebelize.com) and **Maya Heart World** (www.mayanheartworld.net) in Cayo; and **Discounted Belize Shuttles and Tours** (Philip S. W. Goldson International Airport, Ladyville, 501-620-1474, www.discountedbelizeshuttlesandtours.com) and **Belize Shuttles and Transfers** (Belize City, 501-610-2258, www.belizeshuttlesandtransfers.com) in Belize City.

TRAVEL BY WATER TAXIS

If you are going to San Pedro or Caye Caulker, you have the option of taking a water taxi. Note that since around 2012, the water taxi business in Belize has been in a state of flux, and the operators have changed several times. Check locally for current operators, schedules and prices.

As of this writing, there are two main water taxi companies, with boats that hold up to 50 to 100 passengers, connecting Belize City with San Pedro and Caye Caulker. From Belize City it's a 45-minute ride to Caulker and 75 minutes to San Pedro. Going between Caulker and San Pedro takes about 30 minutes. **Ocean Ferry** (501-223-0033, www.oceanferrybelize.com) boats leave from the Marine Terminal in Belize City at 10 North Front Street near the Swing Bridge. **San Pedro Belize Express** (501-223-2225, www.belizewatertaxi.com) boats leave from the Brown Sugar dock at 111 North Front Street near the Tourism Village.

Ocean Ferry, which currently has five departures daily from each location, charges US$24.50 round-trip between Belize City and San Pedro and US$14.50 between Belize City and Caye Caulker or between San Pedro and Caye Caulker. San Pedro Belize Express, which has around eight or nine departures from each location, charges US$35 round-trip between Belize City and San Pedro, and US$25 between Belize City and Caye Caulker or between San Pedro and Caye Caulker.

San Pedro Belize Express also has service every other day between the municipal pier in Chetumal, Mexico, and San Pedro and Caye Caulker, a trip of about 90 minutes to San Pedro, for US$50 one-way Chetumal-San Pedro and US$100 round-trip. To and from Caye Caulker the trip is nearer two hours and is US$55 one-way or US$110 round-trip. Yet another water taxi company, **San Pedro Water Taxi,** (501-226-2194, www.sanpedrowatertaxi.com) also has service between Chetumal and San Pedro and Caye Caulker. One-way fares are US$60 between San Pedro and Chetumal and US$65 between Caye Caulker and Chetumal. Round-trip fares are US$130 and US$120 respectively. The fares usually do not include US$5 port fees in Mexico or exit fee of US$18.75 leaving Belize.

You may also have to pay a 295 Mexican peso in Mexico, if you have not already paid it.

Thunderbolt has daily service between Corozal Town and San Pedro for US$25 one-way. The trip takes 90 minutes to two hours, and the boat will stop in Sarteneja on demand. In Corozal, the Thunderbolt leaves from the Reunion Pier in the center of town.

A local ferry company, **Coastal Xpress** (www.coastalxpress.com), provides scheduled boat transportation up and down Ambergris Caye, with rates from around US$5 to US$14 one-way.

There are four or five water taxis/pedestrian ferries daily between Punta Gorda and Puerto Barrios, Guatemala (US$25 one-way). **Requeña** (www.belizenet.com/requena) is probably the best operator. Also there's limited service to and from Livingston, Guatemala. *See the Punta Gorda and Toledo section for more information.*

A weekly boat, **D-Express,** operates between Placencia and Puerto Cortés, Honduras, for US$60 one-way. Also, the **Starla** boat (504-9545-9322 in Honduras) runs weekly between Belize City and Puerto Cortés for US$75, with a stop at Dangriga. Belize City to Dangriga costs US$50. The **Pride of Belize** boat also makes trips between Belize City and Puerto Cortés for US$75. Tickets are available from Mundo Maya Travels in Belize City (501-223-1200, www.travelmundomaya.com).

From Dangriga to Tobacco Caye, you can arrange a boat (around US$20 one-way) but service is not scheduled. Ask at the Riverside Café in Dangriga. *See the Dangriga/Hopkins and Offshore Cayes sections for more information.*

The charmingly named **Hokey Pokey** operates about eight round-trips a day between Independence (Mango Creek) across the Placencia Lagoon, and Placencia (MnM Hardware). Cost is US$5.

BELIZE IN DEPTH

This section provides information about key attractions of Belize, such as Maya and other archeological sites, national parks and reserves, wildlife, local art and crafts, outdoor sports and activities, festivals and events and key facts about Belize's tourism and hospitality industry.

Waves break over the Belize Barrier Reef off North Ambergris Caye – the barrier reef system and the atolls are part of a UNESCO World Heritage Site

MARINE RESERVES AND NATIONAL PARKS

Much of Belize's land is protected in national parks, monuments, sanctuaries, preserves and reserves. The exact amount is disputed, with figures ranging from around 20% to 45% of Belize's total land and sea area.

Several types of protected areas are included in this section, including:

• **National parks** are afforded the highest level of protection, but there are exceptions. National parks in Belize are managed under the National Park Systems Act of 1981, with the ministerial responsibility currently held by the Ministry of Forests, Fisheries & Sustainable Development. Management is usually in coordination with a local non-profit group or NGO.

• **National monuments,** which are similar to national parks but usually smaller, recognize a specific geographic site, such as the Blue Hole. They are sometimes referred to as natural monuments.

• **Wildlife sanctuaries and preserves** are established to protect certain types of wildlife. Some are managed by non-profit organizations or NGOs such as the Belize Audubon Society, and a few are on private land.

• **Marine reserves** are protected areas in the Caribbean and other waters off Belize. Fishing is prohibited in some parts of these reserves, and a user's fee is levied for visitors.

The following listing is alphabetical.

Bacalar Chico National Park and Marine Reserve, Ambergris Caye, Belize District: Established in the 1990s, Bacalar Chico encompasses 12,640 acres of land on North Ambergris Caye (mostly public lands, some privately owned) along with 15,530 acres of government-owned marine territory. Bacalar Chico covers a total of about 44 square miles of land and sea. The park has a number of habitats, including swamps, grasslands and tropical forests including a semi-deciduous forest and a rare littoral, or beach, forest. The park is home to all of Belize's wild cats, including jaguars and pumas, along with manatees and crocodiles. The park includes the largest nesting areas in Belize for green sea turtles and loggerhead turtles, and one of the largest nesting areas in the country for hawksbill turtles. Nine Maya sites are in the park. Bacalar Chico is most easily accessible by boat from San Pedro Town. There is a small visitor center at the park. Mexico Rocks, a popular snorkeling spot, is now marked as a recreational area and is transitioning into a protected marine reserve. Park fee US$10.

Bird Sanctuaries, Belize and Toledo Districts: There are seven areas, mostly cayes, totaling only 15 acres that are officially bird sanctuaries. These include Man of War Caye, Monkey Caye, Little Guana Caye and Bird Caye.

Blue Hole National Monument, Lighthouse Reef Atoll, off Belize District: Blue Hole Natural Monument and the Lighthouse Reef Atoll are located 55 miles east of Belize City. The Great Blue Hole of water, 1,000 feet across, is set in a ring of corals. It is approximately 450 feet deep, the world's largest oceanic blue hole. It is believed that Belize's Blue Hole became a kind of submerged cenote (a karst-eroded sinkhole resulting from the collapse of limestone bedrock) about 12,000 years ago. Divers in the Blue Hole can see stalactites, dripstone sheets and columns at the southern rim of the Blue Hole. Jacques Cousteau brought the Blue Hole to the attention of the world in 1971 through his television series. In 1996, the Blue Home National Monument, as part of the Belize Barrier Reef and atoll system, became a UNESCO World Heritage Site. Several PADI dive operators visit it out of San Pedro, Caye Caulker, Hopkins and Belize City, along with a couple of live aboard dive ships. Because of its depth, the Blue Hole is for experienced divers only. Over the years, several divers have died in accidents at the Blue Hole. Snorkelers also can accompany dive boats to the Blue Hole and snorkel its surface waters. In fact, the Blue Hole is best appreciated from the air, and Belize airplane and helicopter charters, including Maya Island Air and Astrum Helicopters and tour operators such as Tsunami Adventures in Caye Caulker do Blue Hole flights. Park fee US$30 plus US$10 for Half Moon Caye National Monument.

Burden Canal Nature Reserve, Belize District: This reserve encompasses more than 5,200 acres (eight square miles) of mangrove backswamps of the Belize River and Haulover Creek between Belize City and Gales Point. It is home to many birds, including kingfishers, herons, white ibis and egrets. The American crocodile is also present. Near Gales Point are nesting grounds for endangered turtles. The waterway continues south from near Belize City to the Sibun River to the Northern Lagoon near Gales Point. At the southern end of the Northern Lagoon a winding creek leads to Manatee Lagoon, a prime spot for seeing West Indian Manatees. At present there is no formal visitor center for Burden Canal Nature Reserve. Tour operators or guides in Belize City and Gales Point can guide you in the reserve.

Caye Caulker Marine Reserve, Caye Caulker, Belize District: Declared a marine reserve in 1998, this 61-square mile protected area includes the portion of the Belize Barrier Reef that runs parallel to the island along with the turtle grass lagoon adjacent to the Caye Caulker Forest Reserve.

Caye Caulker North Point Sanctuary, Caye Caulker, Belize District: This is a 100-acre reserve established in 1998 at the north end of Caye Caulker above the Split. It consists mostly of mangrove forest.

Corozal Bay Wildlife Sanctuary, Corozal District: Corozal Bay Wildlife Sanctuary (was established in 1998 to protect the West Indian manatee and the fisheries of Corozal Bay. This sanctuary covers approximately 178,000 acres (278 square miles) of Corozal Bay and the lagoon on the west side of Ambergris Caye. The sanctuary is managed by the Belize Forestry Department in coordination with the Sarteneja Alliance for Conservation and Development. This sanctuary connects with Sanctuario del Manati (Manatee Sanctuary) in Mexico and with the Belize Barrier Reef system through Bacalar Chico Marine Reserve and National Park, North Ambergris Caye. The Corozal Bay Wildlife Sanctuary can be accessed from Corozal Town, Chunox, Copper Bank and Sarteneja villages, Ambergris Caye and Caye Caulker. Sarteneja, with a population of more than 2,500, is considered the largest fishing village in Belize. Sarteneja fishermen harvest lobster, conch and several fish species including stone bass, snapper and barracuda from the sanctuary and surrounding areas.

Gales Point Wildlife Sanctuary, Belize District: This 14 square-mile sanctuary near Gales Point village covers two lagoons with sizeable West Indian manatee populations plus a coastal plain.

Glover's Reef Marine Reserve, Glover's Atoll, off Stann Creek District: Glover's Reef Marine Reserve was established as a national protected area in 1993. It covers 86,650 acres or 135 square miles of the marine area of Glover's Atoll, a main nursery and feeding area for finfish, lobster and conch. It is managed by the Fisheries Department of the Belize Ministry of Agriculture and Fisheries. In 1996 it was designated as one of the seven parts of the Belize Barrier Reef Reserve System, a UNESCO World Heritage Site. The Wildlife Conservation Society, a conservation group that dates back to 1895, has a research station in the reserve on Middle Caye. The Society has pioneered the use of drone airplanes to monitor the marine reserve. About 670 acres of the reserve is a wilderness area closed to visitors, and 3,800 acres are closed to fishing seasonally from December to February, with part of this section, a grouper spawning area, closed to fishing permanently. Visitors to the reserve pay a user's fee of US$30 weekly.

Gladden Spit and Silk Cayes Marine Reserve, off Stann Creek District: This protected marine reserve of about 26,000 acres (40 square miles) has long been known as a place where whale sharks congregate in the late spring during spawning of grouper and mutton snapper. The reserve has a number of pristine small cayes including North Silk, Middle Silk and South Silk south of Gladden entrance near Queen Caye. Since 2003, when the government established the reserve, it has been divided into a general use zone, a no-take zone around the Silk Cayes, a conch restoration zone and a whale shark and reef fish spawning aggregation conservation zone. Park fee is US$10.

Half Moon Caye Natural Monument, Lighthouse Reef Atoll, off Belize District: This was the first nature reserve to be officially established in Belize, in 1981. It was originally named as a bird sanctuary in British Honduras in 1924. Today, Half Moon Caye in Lighthouse Atoll is a breeding ground for a large colony of red-footed boobies, a nesting area for loggerhead, hawksbill and green turtles, all endangered, and home of the rare leaf-toed gecko and Allison's anole lizard. Off the caye is Half Moon Caye Wall, one of Belize's top dive sites. There's a lighthouse and campground on the caye, and visitors to the caye are charged a US$10 per day user fee. An additional park fee of US$30 is charge to visit the Blue Hole.

Hol Chan Marine Reserve, off Ambergris Caye, Belize District: Hol Chan ("Little Channel" in Maya, referring to a narrow channel through the Belize Barrier Reef) is a 4,450-acre (seven square mile) marine reserve about four miles south of Ambergris Caye, is Belize's most visited dive and snorkeling area. It is the oldest marine reserve in Belize, established in 1987. No fishing is allowed in part of the zone, and no commercial fishing is permitted in another zone, so the size and variety of fish species have increased in recent years. More than 160 species of fish have been recorded in the reserve, including large schools of jacks, groupers, snappers and barracuda, along with 40 types of coral, three species of sea turtles, nurse sharks, spotted eagle rays and stingrays, and three marine mammals, the West Indian manatee and two species of porpoises. The reserve can be visited by from San Pedro and Caye Caulker. It also gets visitors from cruise ships in port in Belize City. Visitors can enjoy the novelty of snorkeling with large numbers of nurse sharks and stingrays. While accidents are rare, at times, especially during windy periods, the wave energy through the narrow channel is strong, and several people have died from drowning or cardiovascular events. Mostly recently, in early 2016, an American tourist drowned while snorkeling in Hol Chan. A Hol Chan visitor center is in San Pedro Town. Two- to three-hour snorkel trips to the reserve from San Pedro cost around US$45 per person, not including equipment rental if needed, usually US$10 for mask, snorkel and fins, or the park fee of US$10. Rates from Caye Caulker are similar, although the snorkel trips usually last an hour or two longer and often include an additional snorkel stop.

Laughing Bird Caye National Park, off Placencia, Stann Creek District: Named after the colonies of laughing gulls that once lived on this 2-acre island (most have now moved on to a nearby caye, replaced by pelicans). Laughing Bird Caye, declared a national park in 1991, is 11 miles off Placencia, about half way to the Great Barrier Reef. The marine part of the park totals around 10,120 acres (16 square miles). There is excellent snorkeling around the caye, and good diving, although the fish and other sea life are perhaps better than the coral. Six-hour snorkeling trips to Laughing Bird from Placencia are around US$75 per person including gear, lunch and US$10 park fee.

Port Honduras Marine Reserve, off Toledo District: The 100,000-acre (156 square miles) marine reserve is in the Gulf of Honduras off Toledo District. It has nearly 140 small mangrove cayes and is home to a number of endangered or threatened species including the West Indian manatee, goliath grouper, hammerhead shark and hawksbill, green and loggerhead turtles. Seven jungle rivers flow into the marine reserve. Although fishing is permitted in most of the reserve, long lines, gill nets and beach traps are prohibited. The four Snakes Cayes, named for the boas that once lived on the islands, are located in the reserve. The southwest side of West Snake Caye has nice coral beach with white sand, good for swimming. Toledo Institute for Development and Environment (TIDE) co-manages it with the Government of Belize. Park fees US$5 per day.

Sapodilla Cayes Marine Reserve, off Toledo District: This 48-square mile marine reserve about 45 miles off Punta Gorda, established in 1996, is Belizean territory, but both Guatemala and Honduras have laid claim to parts of the area. Two of the cayes in the reserve, Hunting and Lime, have especially beautiful beaches. The reserve is administered by the Fisheries Department. Park fees are US$10 per day or US$25 per week.

Sarstoon-Temash National Park, Toledo District: This is the southernmost national park in Belize, located south of Punta Gorda on the Guatemala border. It consists of about 42,000 acres (66 square miles) of mangrove forest, wetlands and broadleaf jungle. Unfortunately, in late 2014, an oil company, US Capital Energy, began drilling for oil in the national park, after earlier being granted rights to do so by the Belize government over the opposition of local people. To date, no oil has been found.

Shipstern Conservation and Management Area, Corozal District: This 21,500-acre (34 square mile) protected area is in northeastern Corozal District near the Shipstern Lagoon system. It is owned and managed by Corozal Sustainable Future Initiative (CSFI), a Belize NGO financed in part by a group of European zoos that also co-manages Honey Camp Lagoon National Park and Freshwater Creek Reserve. Formerly called Shipstern Nature Reserve, the conservation area dates to 1990. It was formed from a parcel of land owned in the 1980s by a British butterfly enthusiast, Clive Farrell, who developed a butterfly farm near Sarteneja village that later failed. Today, a few butterflies are kept at the Shipstern visitor center for tourism purposes. The reserve is home to all five species of Belize's wild cats, both of Belize's peccary species, more than 300 species of birds (some from the Yucatán seen in Belize only at Shipstern), 300 species of butterflies of which about 30 are seen in Belize only at Shipstern and about 80 species of reptiles and amphibians. There is a visitor center about three miles from Sarteneja. Admission is US$5, which includes a short guided tour of the botanical trail and old butterfly facility. Sarteneja and Shipstern can be reached by bus from Orange Walk Town, by car from Corozal Town or Orange Walk Town and by boat from San Pedro or Corozal Town. Tropic Air in the past has offered a stop-on-demand service at Sarteneja airstrip on its San Pedro-Corozal Town route – check to see if this is still an option when you are in Belize.

Southwater Caye Marine Reserve, off Dangriga, Stann Creek District: Southwater Caye (also sometimes called South Water Caye) at 118,000 acres (184 square miles) is the largest marine reserve in Belize. This reserve, along with Gladden Spit Silk Cayes Marine Reserve, Laughing Bird Caye National Park and Sapodilla Cayes Marine Reserve, comprise the Southern Barrier Reef Complex, one of the areas with the highest biodiversity in the region. Among the cayes here are Southwater, which has one of the most beautiful beaches in Belize and three dive/fishing lodges, Carrie Bowe Caye, which has a Smithsonian Institution research station, Man-of-War Caye, a nesting site for the brown booby and the Pelican Cayes, with their deep, clear lagoons encircled by steep, lush coral ridges and coral reefs. This reserve is managed by the Belize Fisheries Department. Visitors to this marine reserve need a permit, which can be obtained from the Fisheries Department in Belize City or at the ranger station at Twin Cayes. Tour operators and lodges also can provide permits. Permits cost US$5 per day or US$15 for up to 10 days.

Spawning Aggregation Zones, Belize and Toledo Districts: These 11 marine spawning zones, mostly off Belize District, total 19,850 acres (31 square miles) of the Caribbean Sea.

Swallow Caye Reserve, Belize District: Located about 19 miles southwest of Caye Caulker and 28 miles south of Ambergris Caye, the 9,000-acre (14 square miles) Swallow Caye Reserve is dedicated to the West Indian manatee, many of which live in this reserve. You can do tours from Belize City, Caulker or San Pedro. Park fee is US$5.

ART & CRAFT GALLERIES

Although Belize does not have the great crafts tradition of indigenous cultures in neighboring Guatemala and Mexico, it offers paintings, art prints and photography by native Belizean artists or by artists living in Belize. It also has some authentic Maya textile, slate and ceramic crafts as well as sculptures carved from Belizean hardwoods.

In addition to the galleries list below, many individual artists and craftspeople in Belize sell their work at stands or from their homes. Here are some places to find quality art and crafts, listed alphabetically by place:

AMBERGRIS CAYE
Belizean Arts
Barrier Reef Drive at Fido's, San Pedro
501-226-3019
www.belizeanarts.com
Hours: Open daily "until late"
Reportedly this was the first art gallery in Belize, established more than 20 years ago by Londoner Lyndsey Hackston. Belizean Arts today has a large selection of art by Belizeans and Belize residents, with paintings by Walter Castillo, Pen Cayetano, Nelson Young, Leo Vasquez and others. The gallery also carries work by Cuban and other Caribbean artists.

Belizean Melody Art Gallery
Barrier Reef Drive near The Phoenix Resort
501-631-47481 Hours:
Various hours Monday-Saturday
This art gallery and paint studio has paintings, prints and jewelry. It's also a "paint-your-own" studio.

The Gallery of San Pedro
Pescador Drive (Middle Street), across from post office, San Pedro
501-226-4304
www.thegallerysp.com
Hours: 9-6 Monday-Saturday, 9-3 Sunday
The gallery says it has 1,800 paintings and 800 carvings from all over Belize, plus hammocks and other gift items.

Graniel's Dreamland
Pescador Drive, San Pedro
501-226-2632

www.danielsdreamlandbelize.com
Hours: Daily
Armando Graniel is a prominent homebuilder on Ambergris. His furniture workshop makes different kinds of tables, chairs, cabinets and other items from Belizean hardwoods. The shop ships to foreign countries.

Note: San Pedro also has about **30 craft artisan vendor stalls at the Louis Sylvester Sports Stadium parking lot.**

BELIZE CITY
Image Factory
91 North Front Street
www.imagefactorybelize.com
501-223-1149
Hours: 9-5 Monday-Friday
Established in 1995, the Image Factory became the center of Belize's art and cultural scene. It has shows featuring Belize's top artists and writers. There also is a good selection of books on Belize for sale.

Note: On days when there are cruise ships in port (passengers tender in), vendors including some **crafts vendors set up stalls near the Tourism Village, mainly along Fort Street.** You can haggle a bit for the best prices on crafts.

CAYE CAULKER
Caribbean Colors Art Gallery
Avenue Hicacao, Caye Caulker
501-226-0206 or 877-809-1659
www.caribbean-colors.com
Hours: 8-5 Monday-Saturday
Lee Vanderwalker's gallery, café and gift shop has wearable art by Vanderwalker, along with Christmas ornaments, jewelry and tiles.

Debbie Cooper's Art Gallery
4 Mangle Avenue near airstrip, Caye Caulker
501-226-0330
www.debbiecooper.artspan.com
Hours: Vary – call to ask
Co-owner Debbie Cooper, who spent years living in Hawaii, sells her own paintings and prints here, together with work by Walter Castillo, Nelson Young and other artists.

DANGRIGA
Besides art, Dangriga along with Hopkins and Punta Gorda offer Garifuna drumming schools, and authentic Garifuna drums may be available for sale.

Garinagu Crafts and Art Gallery
46 Oak Street at Tubroose Street
501-522-2596
Hours: 8:30-6 Monday-Friday
Owner Francis Swaso, a Garifuna art and culture expert, offers handmade Garifuna drums, dolls, wood carvings and masks.

Pen Cayetano Studio Gallery
3 Aranda Crescent at Gallery Street
501-628-6807
www.cayetano.de
Hours: 9-5 Monday-Friday, weekends by appointment
Admission US$2.50
Dangriga native Cayetano's well-known impressionist paintings depict Garifuna culture. Also sold here are CDs from Cayetano's band and needlework and other art by other members of the Cayetano family.

PLACENCIA PENINSULA
Art 'n Soul
South end of the Sidewalk, Placencia village
501-503-3088
Hours: 9-6 Monday-Saturday
Greta Leslie displays and sells her own work, together with that of Nelson Young, Lola Delgado, Omar Sierra and others.

Lola's Art
Seine Bight
501-6523-3342
Hours: 7-6 daily
Belize City native Lola Delgado displays and sells her own bold, strongly colored paintings of Garifuna women and Belizean seascapes, primitive in some ways but strangely appealing.

Treasure Box
Main Road, Placencia village
501-503-3145

This shop near the soccer field has interesting jewelry, some made from the lionfish that is devastating local fish species, along with paintings, prints and other items.

Painting of Garifuna women by Lola Delgado of Seine Bight

PUNTA GORDA
Fajina Craft Center
Front Street, Punta Gorda
501-600-9353
Daily except Sunday
This co-op has Maya crafts, chocolates and other items.

Maya Bags
www.mayabags.org
Airport Road near Tropic Air office at PG airstrip; main office in Manhattan, New York

Maya Bags contracts with nearly 100 Maya women in Toledo to make fabric and leather handbags, shoulder bags, clutches, weekend bags, home decor items and other crafts, then sells them on-line and in stores in the U.S. and elsewhere.

The great sport of relaxation awaits you!   Photo by James Bommarito

GREAT OUTDOORS: SPORTS & ACTIVITIES

Here is information about the outdoors sports and activities on the cayes, atoll and coast that you may want to enjoy in Belize. *See the various destination sections for more information.*

BEACHCOMBING

Although you can find some queen conch and other conch shells (technically not permitted to be exported) and other interesting shells in Belize, the beaches here are not especially good for seashell hunters. The Barrier Reef just offshore and the low tidal change mean that shells don't show up much on Belize beaches. However, garbage from other countries in the region and from cruise ships does pile up on Belize's beaches, and you might find the occasional piece of junque of interest, along with all the plastic soft drink bottles and trash.

BIRDING

With some 590 species of birds identified in Belize, about the same as the total number in the United States and Canada, Belize is a birding destination *par excellence.* Even small islands such as Caye Caulker have dozens of species of resident or migratory birds, many likely new to those from the U.S., Canada or Europe. Serious birders frequently spot 75 to 100 different species within a day or two of arrival in Belize and can chalk up several hundred on a stay of a week or 10 days. The *Birds of Belize* by H. Lee Jones is the Bible for most birders.

CAMPING

On the cayes, there's a small campground on Caye Caulker but currently none on Ambergris Caye. You can pitch a tent on Tobacco Caye – ask at the little lodges for permission and costs. Glover's Atoll Resort on Glover's atoll has camping in a beautiful but primitive setting. Also, you can camp at Half Moon Caye at Lighthouse Reef atoll.

CANOEING & KAYAKING

In Belize, you can canoe or kayak both on inland rivers and lagoons and in the Caribbean, the Gulf of Honduras and the Bay of Corozal. Sea kayaking isn't for amateurs, unless you go with an experienced sea kayak tour company such as Island Expeditions or Slick Rock Adventures. Companies in Placencia and elsewhere in Stann Creek *See tour operator listings in destination sections.*

DIVING

Belize is one of the top diving destinations in the Western Hemisphere. The Great Barrier Reef system, part of the Mesoamerican Reef, runs along the coast of Belize. The Barrier Reef and the atolls on the "Outer Reef" are part of a UNESCO World Heritage Site.

Dive experts divide Belize into three areas: the offshore atolls, the Belize Barrier Reef around Ambergris Caye and the Belize Barrier Reef and patch reefs off Southern Belize. The most pristine diving destinations are around the three Pacific-style atolls, Lighthouse, Turneffe and Glover's. The wall dives are rich with coral, crowded with schools of jacks, permit, spadefish and other tropical and semi-tropical fish. The topography around the atolls makes for spectacular tunnels and large spurs. Glover's Reef attracts whale sharks in the months in the spring when the snappers are spawning.

Probably the best-known dive attraction in Belize, although arguably not its best, is the Blue Hole, a 400-foot deep collapsed cave through Lighthouse Reef.

Despite some coral bleaching and other climate-induced degradation to the Belize Barrier Reef, plus damage by boats and careless divers, there is still good diving on and around most parts of the reef, even near busy Ambergris Caye.

The Belize Barrier Reef starts just north of Ambergris Caye, meeting the shore at Rocky Point on North Ambergris. Here you can dive or snorkel among coral skeletons or visit Bacalar Chico National Park. Just south of Rocky Point is one of the largest sea turtle nesting beaches in Belize. Immediately outside the Barrier Reef are a variety of dives, including wrecks, caverns and large spur and groove formations. Eagle Ray Canyon is a favorite due to the good chance of encountering spotted eagle rays. Hol Chan Marine Reserve between Ambergris Caye and Caye Caulker is Belize's most visited snorkeling and diving destination. It is known for its nurse sharks, stingrays and spotted eagle rays.

Farther south, Southwater Caye Marine Reserve, the Silk Cayes and Sapodilla Cayes have lightly visited dive sites.

From Southwater Caye Marine Reserve south, the Barrier Reef is nearly continuous, with many small cuts through the reef. The farther south you go, the farther the reef gets from the mainland. At Placencia, the reef is 20 miles from shore, making for diving with great visibility, big fish and little boat traffic.

Laughing Bird Caye National Park off Placencia sits atop a faroe, an atoll-shaped formation inside the barrier reef. Stands of staghorn coral lie on the windward side of the faroe, while dense stands of elkhorn coral form masses of tunicates.

Even farther south, off Toledo District is the Port Honduras Marine Reserve with its mangrove coast, scores of small cayes and extensive lagoons. These form one of the most important fish nurseries in the region. Snake Cayes, just northeast of Punta Gorda, have unusual marine life due to a combination of river run off and the clear waters of the Caribbean. Coral reefs surround many of the isolated islands, ideal for diving. The pristine reefs of the Sapodilla Cayes are about 40 miles off PG. The Sapodilla Cayes are at the extreme southern end of the Belize Barrier Reef. There are extensive reefs of lettuce corals. Deep channels separate the islands and lead to the gradual slope of the outer drop off, home to dolphins, turtles and sharks.

You can do dive trips from the Northern Cayes, mainly Ambergris Caye (the most visited dive destination in Belize) and Caye Caulker, as well as from Belize City, Dangriga, Hopkins, Placencia and Punta Gorda.

An even better option for the atolls and Sapodilla Cayes is to stay at one of the remote dive lodges, eliminating the need for long, rough boat rides from the mainland or Northern Cayes. U.S.-based live aboard dive boats, including Belize Aggressor and Wave Dancer, do week-long dive trips to Belize's atolls departing from Belize City.

FISHING

Belize has terrific catch-and-release sports fishing. Estuaries and river mouths are where the snook and tarpon are. The flats off Ambergris, Caye Caulker, Placencia, the atolls and elsewhere are where you'll find superb flyfishing for bonefish and permit. One of the world's great permit fisheries is off Stann Creek and Toledo districts in Southern Belize.

Bonefishing fishing is good year-round, as is permit fishing although summer isn't usually as good for permit as the rest of the year. Tarpon fishing is more seasonal, roughly from April to October, as tarpon are migratory. Snook and barracuda can be found year-round. Fishing is limited or prohibited in parts of some marine reserves.

The Belize Barrier Reef and patch coral reefs support grouper, snapper, jacks and barracuda while the deeper, blue waters off the drop off are home to marlin, sailfish, bonito and pompano.

The main fishing centers in Belize are Ambergris Caye, Caye Caulker, Sarteneja, Hopkins/Sittee River, Placencia and Punta Gorda, along with the fishing and dive lodges on Turneffe, Glover's and Lighthouse atolls.

Anglers have to buy a catch-and-release saltwater fishing license for US$10 a day or US$25 a week. Licenses are available from fishing guides or can be purchased online at www.coastalzonebelize.org. One-year licenses are available but generally are limited to Belizean citizens and have to be applied for in person at the Belize Coastal Zone Management Authority & Institute in Belize City.

GOLF

Belize is not much of a destination for golfers. There is a 9-hole "jungle course," Roaring River Golf Course near Belmopan. A residential development, Consejo Shores, near Corozal Town has a private 9-hole course for residents and guests. The 18-hole, 7,000-yard course on 265-acre Caye Chapel between Belize City and Ambergris Caye closed in 2012 when the long-time owner, a Kentucky coal baron, declared bankruptcy. In late 2014, the Government of Belize sold Caye Chapel to a Mexican company. Reportedly, former golf great Greg Norman will redesign the Caye Chapel Golf Course as part of the proposed redevelopment of the island. In the meantime, you can play the old course and even stay overnight in a casita or villa on the island, which at present is managed by Coldwell Banker real estate firm in San Pedro. Another course in the bush near Altun Ha north of Belize City was roughly laid out but now is reverting to jungle. Several real estate developments, including ones in Belize, Corozal and Stann Creek districts, have announced grandiose plans for golf courses, but to date these have not materialized. Don't be fooled by blue-sky promises.

SNORKELING

The number 1 outdoor activity in Belize, by far, is snorkeling. More than six in 10 visitors to Belize snorkel while in the country. Hol Chan Marine Reserve just off the southern end of Ambergris Caye, where you can snorkel with nurse sharks and stingrays, is the top snorkeling spot in Belize, but there's good to wonderful snorkeling elsewhere, including the Mexico Rocks area of North Ambergris, off Caye Caulker, around Laughing Bird Caye National Park off Placencia, in the lagoons of the atolls and elsewhere. Good snorkeling from shore is rare in Belize. It's only possible from the far northern end of Ambergris Caye where the Barrier Reef and patch reefs come close to shore and from islands that are on or very near the reef, such as Southwater Caye and Tobacco Caye and at some atolls. However, you can see marine life such as starfish and small tropical fish while snorkeling from shore off Ambergris Caye, Caye Caulker, Placencia and elsewhere.

SURFING

Belize has no surfing, unless you count high waves during tropical storms or hurricanes or rare waves through channels through the Belize Barrier Reef or at atolls. For surfing, go the Pacific Coast of Mexico and Central America. (Belize, of course, has no territory on the Pacific.)

SWIMMING

The Belize Barrier Reef ecosystem provides a wonderful nursery for sea life in the shore areas inside the reef, but for swimmers the seagrass off beaches can make sea swimming less than ideal. Some beach resorts remove seagrass from a small area for better swimming, and often there is good swimming off the end of docks or piers where there is little or no seagrass. Still, especially off the Northern Cayes and around the remote atolls and cayes, the Caribbean waters are gin-clear, warm (in the low to mid-80s F. most of the time and shallow, with little wave activity, perfect for a refreshing dip in the sea. Nearly all beach resorts above the budget level also have swimming pools, in some cases multiple pools.

TENNIS

Tennis enthusiasts traveling to Belize will want to choose their hotel carefully, because most resorts and hotels in Belize don't have tennis courts. Some which do include Placencia Hotel and Residences at the north end of the Placencia peninsula and Belizean Shores on North Ambergris.

WINDSURFING, KITEBOARDING AND PADDLE SPORTS

The coast and cayes of Belize offer near-perfect conditions for windsurfing and related sports, including kiteboarding and various paddleboard sports. Winds from the sea are consistently 10 to 20 miles an hour. The months of January to March usually offer the best conditions, with tradewinds of 15 mph and higher most days. Among the more recommended windsurfing and related board sports outfits in Belize, most of which offer lessons, are Contour Ocean Ventures in Caye Caulker, Kitexplorer in Caye Caulker and San Pedro, Windschief in Hopkins and Slickrock Adventures and Vela Windsports on Long Caye, Glover's Reef. There's also good windsurfing on the other atolls, and a number of dive/fishing lodges there offer windsurfing and other board sports equipment.

Take a boat to the beach – visitors relax on Caye Caulker

FESTIVALS AND EVENTS

Here are festivals and events held in Belize, in most cases annually. We've focused on the festival held on the cayes and in coastal areas. Some are major national festivals, some are designed to boost tourism during slow periods and some are more local, community-oriented events. In many cases specific dates vary from year to year. Also, the Belize Tourism Board's website (www.travelbelize.org) has info.

January
Krem New Year's Cycling Classic: Bicycle road race from Corozal Town to Belize City. Takes place New Year's Day, January 1.

February
Fiesta de Carnaval: Nationwide celebrations, parades and dance competitions at Mardi Gras time. The biggest celebrations are in Belize City and in San Pedro, Ambergris Caye, where celebrants throw paint at people, including visitors. Takes place during the week before Lent, exact dates vary from early February to early March.

Placencia Sidewalk Arts and Music Festival: 2016 marked the 13th annual Arts and Music Festival held on the Placencia's famous sidewalk. There are art displays, art for sale and music concerts. A number of well-known Belizean artists and galleries set up booths. Takes place on a Saturday and Sunday in mid-February, exact dates vary. For more information, visit the Placencia BTIA's site, www.placencia.com.

March
La Ruta Maya Belize River Challenge: This canoe race began in 1998 and has become a national event, with resorts and other companies sponsoring 30 or more canoe teams. It's a four-day race from west to east along the Macal and Belize rivers, from San Ignacio to Belize City. Held in early March, exact dates vary. For more information, see the La Ruta Maya's Facebook page.

Barron Bliss Day: Baron Bliss Day honors English Baron Henry Edward Ernest Victor Bliss (1869-1926), who donated his estate to Belize, although the Baron had never set foot in Belize. Baron Bliss Day is March 9, but it is usually celebrated the Saturday before that date, with a boat regatta in Belize City Harbour and other activities.

April
Easter Week: As in many other countries in Central and South America, Easter week is holiday time for Belizeans. Especially on Easter

weekend, from Good Friday through Easter Monday (both Friday and Monday are legal holidays), many Belizeans head to beach destinations including Placencia, Caye Caulker and Ambergris Caye. Many hotels are fully booked. Easter observances are held at Catholic churches, especially in San Pedro and Caye Caulker. A sailing regatta is held at Sarteneja on Easter Sunday. Exact dates vary.

May

Chocolate Festival of Belize: The annual Chocolate Festival, held in Punta Gorda and elsewhere in Toledo District, celebrates the cacao tree and its fruit. There are about 1,000 small cacao farmers in Toledo District, and some in Stann Creek and Cayo districts. A street fair on Front Street in PG has chocolate tastings, cooking contests, craft sales and activities for children. There also are trips to cacao farms in Toledo. Held Commonwealth Day weekend in late May, exact dates vary. More information at www.chocolatefestivalofbelize.com.

Naturally the Chocolate Festival of Belize is held in late May in Punta Gorda, Toledo District, "Chocolate Center of the Universe"

Mango Fest, Hopkins: This celebrates one of Belize's most popular and delicious fruits. Held on the beachfront in Hopkins village, the festival has music, food and crafts stalls and activities for children. Last weekend in May, dates vary.

June
Lobsters are in season June 15 to February 14, and Lobsterfests in San Pedro, Caye Caulker and Placencia celebrate the annual opening of lobster season. All the Fests have live music concerts, drink and food booths with lobster cooked and sold in various ways such as broiled, boiled, baked, fried, on pizza, along with craft shows, dances and other activities. Restaurants often tie in with their own lobster specials. All three Lobsterfests – San Pedro, Caye Caulker and Placencia – have Facebook pages.

San Pedro Lobsterfest: Lobsterfest activities in San Pedro extend over a period of about 10 days, with organizers and business getting the most they can out of the tasty lobsters. Held annually beginning June 15.

Placencia Lobsterfest: Lobsterfest in Placencia is held over a three-day weekend and rivals Caye Caulker's for the best Fest. In 2013 it won the Belize Tourism Board's award for Best Festival in Belize. It is a major fundraising event for the Placencia Village Council and the Placencia chapter of the Belize Tourism Industry Association (BTIA). Usually the third or fourth weekend in June, exact dates vary.

Día de San Pedro: This event, which goes on for more than a week, rather than just a day, honors the patron saint of the town, St. Peter. There's usually an all-day beach party at Boca del Rio park, dance and music concerts, a triathlon, a ceviche competition, a fishing rodeo, the blessing of the boats and various masses and other religious ceremonies. Held annually over a period of 10 days at the end of June.

July
Caye Caulker Lobsterfest: Caye Caulker was the birthplace of the Lobsterfest in Belize, with the first one held in 1994. It celebrates the opening of the lobster season and also the work of lobster fishermen from Caulker and from Sarteneja and elsewhere. Usually held on three days during the first weekend of July, exact dates vary.

August
Deer Dance Festival: This nine-day festival in the Mopan Maya village of San Antonio, Toledo District, features masked and costumed dance performances. There is marimba, drum and harp music. The festival starts with all-night vigils. The finale is a Holy Deer dance with hunters and a jaguar whose symbolism may date thousands of years. It also includes the

raising of a huge 60-foot sayuc tree pole, which is greased with lard and soap. Village boys and men try to climb it to claim a money prize. The festival weaves together Maya and Catholic ritual and Spanish history. Late August, dates vary.

International Costa Maya Festival: Billed as Belize's biggest festival, the International Costa Maya Festival in San Pedro, Ambergris Caye, features a beauty pageant with entries from Belize and most of the other Central American countries and Mexico. There also are music concerts and dances and other events. It's held over three days on the first weekend in August. For more information check the festival's Facebook page or visit www.internationalcostamayafestival.com.

September

The period between September 10, St. George's Caye Day, and September 21, Independence Day, is a time of celebrations and parties. Belizeans who have moved away from their home often come back to Belize during this period.

St. George's Caye Day: This special day commemorates the 1798 defeat of part of the Spanish navy by a ragtag band of Belizean Baymen and buccaneers, including former slaves, near St. George's Caye off Belize City. It is celebrated with patriotic speeches and parties (of course!) in Belize City and around the country. Sanpedranos crown a Miss San Pedro, and boats head to St. George's Caye for a regatta. Some Belizeans dress in the Belize flag's colors of blue, white and red. Celebrated annually on September 10.

Belize Independence Day: A British Crown colony from 1862, Belize formally was granted its independence from Britain on September 21, 1971. Belizeans celebrate with parades, parties and plenty of eating and drinking. Celebrated annually on September 21.

October

Pan-American Day: Formerly called Columbus Day, in Belize Pan American Day, or Día de la Raza, focuses on the migration of Mestizos and the Yucatec Maya from the Yucatán to the then British Honduras in the mid-19th century, but it also celebrates the history of other groups in Belize's diverse culture. It is most widely celebrated in Northern Belize, which has a large Mestizo population. Among other things there are the Corozal Bay Regatta and the Belikin Spectacular Blue Water Billfish Tournament in San Pedro. Observed as an official national holiday annually on October 12. (Some years it may be observed on a different date to give Belizeans a three- or four-day weekend.)

November
Garifuna Settlement Day: This official national holiday celebrates the arrival in Belize of the first Garinagu, who came in dugout canoes from Honduras. It is celebrated in all Garifuna communities in Belize, but the main celebration is in Dangriga, the town with the largest Garinagu population. In Dangriga and Punta Gorda a canoe is floated in early in the morning. Garifuna Settlement Day is November 19, but celebrations in Dangriga – parades, drumming, dancing and special Garifuna religious ceremonies – go on for several days around that date. For more information, see the website of the National Garifuna Council, www.ngcbelize.org.

December
Garifuna John Canoe Dance Festival: This Garifuna and Creole festival, also known as Habinahan Wanaragua Jankunu, revolves around masked male dancers and drummers, with women permitted only to sing. It probably evolved from male secret society rituals in West Africa and was brought to the New World by African slaves and by the Garinagu. The Garifuna people mostly were able to avoid enslavement and resisted British and other colonial domination. The dance is held in Dangriga Town, lately at the Ecumenical High School auditorium. It features competition among Jankunu dance groups from Southern Belize, especially Dangriga and Seine Bight. Celebrated on the last Sunday of the year following Christmas.

Christmas: As in many other places, Christmas in Belize is mostly a family affair. Belize does have some of its own traditions at Christmas, such as repainting and fixing up the house. Christmas and New Year's are peak times for tourism in Belize, and many hotels boost their rates by 20% or more. Many homes and businesses in Belize are decorated and lit with Christmas lights, and on some years there is a lighted boat parade in San Pedro. Only restaurants at hotels and those that predominantly serve tourists are open on Christmas Day. Regular businesses are closed, and buses and water taxis may run on a reduced schedule.

Boxing Day: With its British heritage, Belize celebrates Boxing Day as an official holiday the day after Christmas. Boxing Day is rooted in the British tradition of giving money and boxed leftovers to servants and other "lower classes" after Christmas. In Belize, it is a day for friends and extended family to get together. Celebrated on December 26.

WILD BELIZE

Hammerhead shark   Photo by Shane Gross/Shutterstock

For a small country, Belize has a large and diverse collection of mammals, reptiles and amphibians, birds and butterflies and moths, along with huge number of fish, corals and other marine life.

Numbers vary, but scientists and naturalists believe Belize has about 590 species of birds, 150 species of mammals, 160 species of reptiles and amphibians, nearly 600 species of fish, 65 species of living coral, 700 species of butterflies, perhaps 1,500 species of moths and more than 3,500 species of vascular plants and trees.

Here are just a few of the more important and more interesting of the fauna and flora of wild Belize.

MARINE LIFE

Spotted Eagle Ray (*Aetobatus narinari*) is among the most graceful swimmers in the Caribbean Sea off Belize. This ray, one of three rays found in Belize, is large, reaching 15 or 16 feet in length with wingspans of 10 feet. It has distinctive brown spots. A mature eagle ray can weigh 500 pounds, but **manta rays,** also found in Belize, are even larger, reaching 3,000 pounds. Although the spotted eagle ray has venomous spines on its long tail, it avoids human contact and poses little threat to divers, snorkelers or swimmers. It is listed as threatened.

West Indian Manatees (*Trichechus manatus*) are large aquatic mammals that typically grow to 9 to 12 feet long and weigh 800 to 1,500 pounds (females are usually larger than males). They prefer fairly shallow water in lagoons, rivers, estuaries and coastal areas. Manatees are seen in many areas of Belize, but your best chance of seeing one is at Swallow Caye Wildlife Sanctuary near Caye Caulker, the Northern Lagoon just south of Belize City, the Southern Lagoon near Gales Point and Placencia Lagoon west of the Placencia peninsula. It is estimated that there are about 1,000 manatees in Belize, the largest concentration in the region. Tour operators and guides in San Pedro, Caye Caulker, Belize City, Placencia and Gales Point offer manatee spotting tours. Also called sea cows, manatees are docile and spend up to half their days sleeping and much of the rest of their time eating. A manatee can consume 100 pounds of plant matter a day. Manatees are at risk from gill netting, mangrove habitat destruction and from collisions with boats and cuts from boat propellers. The West Indian manatee is listed as endangered by CITES.

Whale Shark (*Rhincodon typus*) is the largest fish in the world. The largest known whale shark was over 41 feet long and weighed 47,000 pounds. Even larger ones are thought to exist. Whale sharks are filter feeders, eating tiny plankton and eggs from fish and coral spawning. Despite their huge size, these sharks pose little or no danger to humans. They are gentle giants, sometimes allowing humans to touch or even ride them (something that is opposed by scientists). Whale sharks can live for 70 years or longer. These pelagic sharks congregate in large numbers in various places around the world, including off the Yucatán where 400 have been seen at one time, near the Bay Islands of Honduras, off Coiba Island, Panama and in Africa, Asia and the Middle East. In Belize, they gather at Gladden Spit in the Silk Cayes Marine Reserve off Placencia. The best months for seeing whale sharks in Belize are April and May, especially on the days around a full moon. However, most years they are present from mid-March to early July. In June and July the seas off Placencia tend to be rough, making it not a great time to go out in a relatively small boat. Tour operators and dive shops in Placencia, Hopkins and elsewhere schedule what shark trips for divers and snorkelers, who can swim with the big fish. Because of the unpredictability of when the sharks will be seen, visitors may have to spend a week or two in Belize to have a chance of seeing the sharks. Demand for a place on the whale shark trips is high.

Among the other species of sharks frequently seen by divers in Belize are the **hammerhead shark, black tip shark, bull shark, lemon shark, reef shark** and **tiger shark.** All of these sharks are potentially dangerous to humans, but few incidents involving divers, snorkelers or swimmers have ever been reported. The best-known shark attraction in Belize is Shark Ray Alley in Hol Chan Marine Reserve between Ambergris Caye and Caye Caulker. There you can swim, snorkel or dive with large numbers of **nurse sharks** along with **stingrays.** Nurse sharks are not usually dangerous, although if handled or provoked they have been known to bite. Stingrays do sting but rarely do so when swimming in the sea. You are more likely to receive a venomous sting when walking barefoot on the sea bottom where rays have burrowed into the sand. The best way to avoid this is with a shuffling walk through the water. Stingray stings are painful but rarely are fatal. Steve Irwin, the "Crocodile Hunter," did die in 2006 after being pierced in the chest by a stingray barb off Queensland, Australia.

REPTILES AND AMPHIBIANS

Crocodiles are usually called alligators by Belizeans, but Belize has no true alligators, just two species of crocodiles, the larger **American crocodile** (*Crocodylus acutus*), which can grow to 15 or 20 feet in length and weigh nearly a ton, and the smaller **Morelet's crocodile** (*Crocodylus moreletii*), which rarely reaches more than 8 or 9 feet in length with a weight of less than 75 pounds. The Morelet's lives in fresh water lagoons in Belize, while the American's habitat is coastal, preferring salt water, although it is also found in brackish lagoons, swamps and rivers. Both species feed on almost anything they can kill – birds, fish and mammals including deer, goats, cats and dogs. Occasionally, humans have been attacked by American crocodiles in Belize, and a few deaths have been reported. Until it was prohibited, a large American crocodile in a lagoon on the southern end of Ambergris Caye was regularly fed raw chicken for the entertainment of gawking tourists.

In September 2010, a crocodile sanctuary in Toledo District, the American Crocodile Education Sanctuary (ACES), founded by two expats, Cherie and Vince Rose, was burned to the ground by local residents, who reportedly believed that the expats were responsible for the disappearance of local children. The Roses were never charged with any wrongdoing. After the mob burning, ACES moved its facilities to Ambergris Caye and then a part of it to a 266-acre shrimp farm in Ladyville near Belize City. Now called **Caribbean Shrimp Farm & ACES Educational Crocodile Eco-Sanctuary** (501-623-7920 or 239-771-3252 in U.S., www.americancrocodilesanctuary.org) is home to rescued Morelet's and American crocodiles. The shrimp farm/croc sanctuary is open to the public. Indeed, the public is invited to net for shrimp and have their catch prepared at Captain Hook's Restaurant & Croc Bar. The Roses also offer "crocodile expeditions" in a 20-foot skiff from San Pedro for US$50 per person. Is there a movie in all this?

Fer-de-Lance *(Bothrops asper),* locally called **tommy goff,** is one of the most deadly of the approximately 20 poisonous snakes in Belize (only eight or nine of these are considered deadly to humans). This pit viper, with a brown and yellow pattern on its back and a broad, flattened head, doesn't avoid humans and will strike aggressively if disturbed. Many of the serious snakebites in Belize and the rest of Central America are from this viper. However, the good news is that hospitals in Belize usually have supplies of anti-venom serum. Although the bite is potentially fatal the victim usually has several hours to get treatment, and with the antivenom the death rate is near zero.

Green Iguanas *(Iguana iguana)* can be seen all over Belize, usually sunning on a tree limb. In Belize, the lizards are threatened because people hunt and eat these "chickens of the trees" and also take their eggs. A herbivore, the mature green iguana can be fairly large, with a body length as much as six feet including the tail and a weight of 20 pounds. When young, the lizard is indeed green but older iguanas are brown, brownish green or black. During mating season, mature males are orange and females are brown. The San Ignacio Resort Hotel is known for its **Green Iguana Conservation Project.** *(See What to See and Do in Cayo.)*

Jesus Christ Lizard, actually the **common basilisk** *(Basiliscus basiliscus)* gets its name because, using flaps of skin on its rear feet, it can run across water. An adult male can reach 30 inches or more in length, with three-fourths of its body being the tail.

Wish Willy *(Ctenosaura similis)* is a black spiny-tailed iguana, a cousin of the green iguana. This lizard, which when mature is 3 to 4 feet long but fairly light in weight, lives mostly in mainland coastal areas of Belize. It holds the record as the fastest lizard on earth, able to run 21.7 mph according to the *Guinness Book of World Records.*

BIRDS
Chachalaca, Crested Guan and Great Curassow are three members of the *Cracidae* family in Belize. They somewhat resemble turkeys. The **crested guan** *(Penelope purpurascens)* and **great curassow** *(Crax rubra),* rated as near-threatened or vulnerable, mostly live in trees, but the **common chachalaca** *(Ortalis vetula)* lives in scrubby brush. Although the crested guan and great curassow are larger and more impressive, the chachalaca is our favorite for its chuckling call, after which its name is derived. Some sexist biologists have described the call of the birds, which run in flocks of a dozen or so, to be like the sound of arguing women.

Parrots and Parakeets in Belize comprise 10 species including the beautiful **scarlet macaw** *(Ara macao)*, the endangered **yellow-headed Amazon parrot** *(Amazona oratrix)* and the green **Yucatan Amazon parrot** *(Amazona xantholora)*, found only in Belize, Honduras and Mexico.

Belize has 26 species of **hummingbirds,** about the same as the entire United States.

Jabiru Stork *(Jabiru mycteria)* is the tallest standing bird in the Americas and has the second-longest wingspan, after the Andean condor. Because of their size, with weights of up to 20 pounds, and coloration – their bodies are mostly white with a featherless black head and neck – you can recognize these storks in a lagoon or river even at a distance. They nest and are commonly seen at Crooked Tree Wildlife Sanctuary from around November to May. Belize has the largest nesting population of jabiru storks in Central America.

Keel-billed Toucan *(Ramphastos sulfuratus),* the national bird of Belize, is one of three toucan species found in the country. Toucans inhabit the high canopy of rainforests. They are social birds, usually traveling in small flocks. The Belize $100 banknote has a hologram of a toucan as a security feature, and the toucan along with Belize's national animal, Baird's tapir, are on the back of all denominations of Belize banknotes.

Red-footed Booby *(Sula sula)* lives on offshore cayes in Belize, most famously on Half Moon Caye National Monument at Lighthouse Reef Atoll, where an estimated 4,000 of these goony birds are in residence in ziricote trees most of the year. Boobies are clumsy during takeoffs and landings but graceful fliers that dive into the sea to catch small fish. They especially like flying fish. Plumage varies, although on Half Moon Caye it is mostly white, but the feet and legs are always a bright red.

MAMMALS

Agouti The Central American agouti *(Dasyprocta punctate) is* a rodent, generally brownish orange in Belize that weighs 6 to 10 pounds. It feeds mostly on fruit and seeds. Agouti, also called **paca** or **gibnut,** is on the menu in some restaurants in Belize. It has been nicknamed the Royal Rat because it was served to Queen Elizabeth II on her October 1985 visit to Belize. Its taste is sometimes compared to rabbit or pork.

Baird's Tapir *(Tapirus bairdii),* locally known as the mountain cow, is Belize's national animal. Tapirs, which are about 6 feet in length and weigh 300 to 500 pounds when mature, feed on fruit, grasses and aquatic vegetation. They are most likely to be seen in or near inland rivers. The best-known tapir in Belize was "April," who lived for more than 30 years at the Belize Zoo. Her birthday was celebrated on April 27, with April getting cakes made of horse chow, cucumbers, flowers and honey. She died October 31, 2013. The tapir, along with the keel-billed toucan, are on the back of all Belize banknotes.

Bats More than 50 species of bats are found in Belize, making bats by far the most common of all mammals in the country. Among the many general types of bats in Belize are mastiff bats, sac-winged bats, free-tailed bats, leaf-chinned bats, leaf-nosed bats, plain-nosed bats and one species of funnel-eared bat. Most bats in Belize feed on insects or fruit, but some, such as the **spectral bat** (*Vampyrum spectrum*), are carnivorous. The spectral bat, not a true vampire bat, hunts small mammals, birds, reptiles and amphibians. This is the largest carnivorous bat in the world, with a wingspan of up to 3 feet.

Are there true vampire bats in Belize? Yes, two of three known New World species of vampire bats**,** the **common vampire bat** (*Desmodus rotundus*) and the **hairy-legged vampire bat** *(Diphylla ecaudata)* are found in Belize. Vampire bats have razor-sharp front incisor teeth used for cutting the skin of birds or, in the case of the common vampire bat, mammals including humans. Vampire bats feed only when it is fully dark. They use infrared radiation to find blood hotspots on their prey. While most bats have lost the ability to get about on land, vampire bats can walk, jump and even run by using their forelimbs to produce a bounding gait.

Once the common vampire bat finds a host, such as a sleeping horse or human, it lands and approaches it on the ground. It locates a warm spot where blood is near the surface, bites it and laps up the blood. A typical vampire bite consumes about 1 fluid ounce of blood per feeding, up to about one-third of the bat's body weight. Sometimes the little sucker has to pee in order to be light enough to take off and fly back to its roost. The feeding, with the bat's saliva providing an anticoagulant effect, lasts about 20 minutes. Although rare, cases are known where vampire bats transmitted rabies to humans.

Black Howler Monkeys *(Alouatta pigra)*, called baboons by Belizean Creoles, were once near extinction in Belize, but restoration efforts such as the Bermudian Landing Baboon Sanctuary have greatly increased the numbers of howlers in Belize. Today, howler monkeys are making themselves heard all along the Belize River Valley and elsewhere in Belize. These primates can reach 3 feet in height. Entirely vegetarians, eating most leaves and fruit, they travel through the trees in troops of up to about 20. Only the adult male is black; females and juveniles are yellowish or whitish in color. The monkeys' extremely loud vocalizations, mostly in the early morning, can be heard for up to 3 miles. Howlers are not uncommonly, but illegally, taken from the wild as pets. Also present in Belize are **Yucatán spider monkeys** *(Ateles geoffroyi)*.

Coatimundi (*Nasua narica*). More properly the white-nosed coati, it is called **quash** by many Belizeans or *pizote* by Spanish speakers. Coatis are in the raccoon family, but unlike the common raccoons, which are mostly nocturnal, coatis are active by day. Very intelligent, they adapt quickly to humans, raiding garbage cans for food. In Belize, they sometimes are tamed and kept as pets. They are omnivores, eating fruit, vegetables, snakes, eggs and carrion. Large males can weigh more than 25 pounds.

Belize is home to hundreds of jaguars   Used under license from Adobe

Jaguar (*Panthera onca*), or *tigre* in Spanish, is the largest cat in the Americas and the third-largest cat in the world, after the lion and tiger. It is an apex predator throughout its range, from Arizona to northern Argentina, feeding entirely on meat. It will kill and eat tapirs, deer, peccaries, monkeys, fish (unusual for cats, it likes the water), birds, turtles and also dogs and farm animals. Rare attacks on humans have been reported but none in Belize in modern times. Large males can weigh over 300 pounds. Belize has both the more common spotted, tawny yellow variety as well as the black jaguar. The latter looks entirely black, but up close (as you can see for yourself at the Belize Zoo) spots are visible. Jaguars in Belize are primarily nocturnal, so it is rare to see them. A jaguar is on the front left of the Belize $20 banknote.

The **other wild cats of Belize** are the **cougar** *(Puma concolor)*, also commonly known as the **mountain lion, puma** or **panther,** the second-

125

largest New World cat after the jaguar, with males weighing up to 225 pounds, usually a tawny tan in color; **ocelot** *(Leopardus pardalis),* which looks like a domestic cat but is larger (20 to 40 pounds) and has a beautiful coat, varying from cream to reddish-brown in color, sometimes grayish, marked with black rosettes; the **jaguarondi** or **eyra cat** *(Puma yagouaround),* a small (rarely over 20 pounds) gray or chestnut in color; **margay cat** *(Leopardus wiedii),* a small (6 to 9 pound) brown or black spotted cat that is an exceptionally good tree climber. All are considered threatened to some degree. All five of Belize's wild cats range throughout the country, even on North Ambergris Caye, coming down from Mexico across a narrow channel. The jaguar and cougar in particular need a large territory, up to 150 to 200 square miles, so efforts by conservationists have been directed toward creating large and contiguous corridors in Belize for these animals.

Kinkajou *(Potos flavus)* is another member of the raccoon and coati family. Sometimes called a **nightwalker** in Belize, this 10-pound mammal spends its time mostly in the upper canopy of rainforest trees, eating fruits, flowers and insects and using its long, prehensile tail for balance. The kinkajou was one of the animals on the back of the Belize $20 banknote issued starting in 2003, but a commemorative edition of the banknote for the Central Bank of Belize's 30th anniversary in 2012 replaced the kinkajou with an illustration of the Central Bank Building in Belize City. *Sic transit gloria mundi.*

Peccaries are hog-like animals that run in herds, usually of 10 to 20 individuals, but the herds can be larger. Belize has two species, the **white-lipped peccary** *(Tayassu pecari)* and the **collared peccary** *(Tayassu tajacu).* Both species are fairly small by pig standards, weighing 40 to 90 pounds. You'll probably smell peccaries before you see them, as they have scent glands on their backs that secrete a pungent, musky oil.

OTHER CRITTERS
Here are a few other interesting creatures of Belize – insects, spiders and butterflies.

Africanized Bees Nearly all honeybees in Belize, as elsewhere in the region, have been Africanized, a result of interbreeding of local bees *(Apis mellifera)* with wild African bees *(April mellifera scutellata).* The so-called **"killer bees"** were accidentally released in Brazil in 1957 and have since migrated northward through South America to Central America and to the Southern United States. Both wild and domestic honeybees in Belize are Africanized. Their sting is no worse than the sting of a regular honeybees, but they are much more aggressive in defending their hives or nests than European and North American honeybees. They often chase animals or people that accidentally disturbed their nests and may sting them hundreds of times. Many cattle and other livestock have been stung to death in Belize, along with a few humans. Most recently, a 4-year-old Mennonite boy in Little Belize in Northern Belize died as a result of stings in 2013. Beekeepers in Belize have successfully adapted to keeping Africanized bees, using special protective gear. On the positive side, Africanized bees appear to be more resistant to mites and to Colony Collapse Disorder. Should you be attacked by killer bees, try to get into a vehicle or building, or go underwater.

Blue Morpho Butterfly *(Morpho peleides)* arguably is the most stunning and best known of Belize's 700 or so species of butterflies. The blue morpho has large (5- to 8-inch wingspan) bright blue wings, edged with black. The underside of the wings is a dull brown, to help camouflage the butterfly when it is at rest. You only see the flashing neon blue when the blue morpho is in flight. Blue morphos are widely dispersed in forested areas of Belize.

Botfly *(Dermatobia hominis)* is one of the more unpleasant bugs of Belize. The clever, hairy bug lays its eggs on a mosquito or tick. The mosquito or tick then bites you, or another mammal, incidentally depositing the botfly larva under the host's skin. The host can be a squirrel or other small mammal. Or you. The larva grows for several weeks under the host's skin until it is the size of a small grub worm, with spikes to keep the larva in the subdermal layer of the host. There's a tiny hole in your skin so that the larva can breathe. Yes, it's yucky but not serious unless infection results. A physician can remove the larva, or you can treat it yourself by cutting off the air to the larva. Use Vaseline, fingernail polish or a product called NewSkin to cover the hole, or tape a cotton ball soaked with camphorated oil or a piece of wet tobacco on the larva hole for about 8 hours. Those steps will kill the botfly larva, but you may have to remove the larva with a scalpel or sharp knife. Not many visitors to Belize get botfly larvae unless they spend a lot of time in the bush and are bitten by mosquitoes or ticks. If you are infected, you'll know it, because you will have a red, painful area on your skin (often in your hair) with a small air hole. Act quickly to kill the larva or see a dermatologist or other doctor.

Leaf-Cutter Ants *(Atta cephalotes)* Next to humans, leafcutter ants – known in Kriol as wi-wi or wee-wee ants – form the largest and most complex societies on Earth. The leaf cutter ants, of which there are nearly 50 species worldwide, have an advanced agricultural system that involves cultivating a certain type of fungus. The ants cut tree or vegetable leaves and carry them back to their underground nests to feed the fungi. As leaf cutters remove leaves from a tree, a line of ants may extend for distances of 200 yards or as workers carry their cargo back to their nest. Soldier ants with powerful jaws guard the workers. The jaws can inflict painful bites on humans. The underground nests are complex structures, with sophisticated farming, waste management and air-conditioning systems. The ants sometimes defoliate a tree but usually cause no long-term damage. A leaf cutter ant mound may cover hundreds of square yards and contain up to 8 million individual ants.

Mexican Red-Rump Tarantula *(Brachypelma vagans)* is the most common of the nine species of tarantulas found in scrubland and forests all over Belize. Although these hairy-eight-legged spiders, with a leg span of up to 5 or 6 inches, have a bad reputation from their appearance in horror movies, in fact they are gentle creatures that live in burrows. They attack and eat only insects and small lizards and rodents. The red-rump tarantula is listed as vulnerable in Belize. It is easiest to spot them using a flashlight at night.

Scorpions make their homes in Belize as they do in most other parts of the world, including England, continental Europe and the United States. The most common of four or five scorpions in Belize is the **slender brown scorpion** or **brown bark scorpion** *(Centruroides gracilis),* which can grow to 6 inches in length. This relative of the spider has a poisonous sting, but except in rare cases its sting is no worse than a wasp sting, causing serious problems only in those allergic to the venom. It usually lives under rocks or tree bark but can be found in the walls or dark spaces of homes. Of the 2,000 or so species of scorpions in the world, only 25 are known to be deadly to humans, and none of these is in Belize. If stung, wash the sting site with soap and water and take an aspirin or other painkiller. If you are one of those with an allergic reaction (such as fainting, extreme pain, cardiac symptoms) get to a doctor who will treat the allergic symptoms.

FLORA

Bukut *(Cassia grandis)* is a large deciduous native of Belize, growing to nearly 100 feet. Howler monkeys love to eat its leaves. In the early part of the dry season, it puts on a stunning display of salmon-colored flowers. Its seedpods, when broken open, smell like an old sock. Hence, its local name, **stinking toe** tree.

Cacao *(Theobroma cacao)* is the source of Maya and Belizean chocolate. Cacao trees grow especially well in Toledo District, where about 1,000 independent farmers depend on the crop.

Caribbean Pine *(Pinus Caribaea* var. *hondurensis)* is the only true tropical pine in Belize, reaching over 90 feet in height. The Caribbean or Honduran pine covers about 80% of the Mountain Pine Ridge, and it also is common in the palmetto-oak-pine forests at lower elevations. In the Pine Ridge, thousands of acres of these pines have been devastated by the

Southern Pine Bark Beetle, which bores into the tree and kills it. A government reforestation program has helped restore the pines in some areas of this forest reserve.

Cashew (*Anacardium occidentale*) is an evergreen tree that produces a fruit, cashew apple or *marañón* in Spanish, and the cashew nut. The fruit, actually an accessory or false fruit, is yellow or red in color and has a sweet, grape-like odor and taste. The cashew apple, which in Belize ripens in April and May, can be eaten raw, cooked, fermented into vinegar, or made in a wine or other alcoholic drink. High in Vitamin C and other vitamins, it also is used to make preserves and jams. The true fruit is a kidney-shaped drupe that grows at the end of the cashew apple. Within the true fruit is a single seed, what we know as the cashew nut. Before the nut can be consumed it has to be heated to get rid of the allergenic resin in the shell. The standard cashew tree can grow to almost 50 feet, but a dwarf version that grows only about 20 feet high is preferred in Belize. The tree tends to spread out horizontally and is often much wider than it is higher. The limbs are irregularly shaped and bent, giving it the named **crooked tree**.

Ceiba (*Ceiba pentranda*), also called **cotton tree** or **kapok tree,** is the national tree of Guatemala, but it also is native to Belize. The ceiba, which the ancient Maya cultivated in their plazas, is a huge tree, growing up to 230 feet high with a trunk 10 feet in diameter. The trees produce several hundred large pods containing seeds surrounded by a fluffy, cotton-like fiber sometimes used as filling for pillows and mattresses. Ceiba trees can live for hundreds of years.

Cohune Palm (*Attalea cohune*) is one of many species of palms in Belize. The cohune palm was of great importance to the Maya and is sometimes a marker for Maya ruins hidden under earth and jungle. It is a dominant plant in parts of Belize. The **warree cohune** also is found in Belize. The hard nuts of the cohune are a source of oil and a fuel for fires and the branches are used for thatch construction. Cohune palm hearts are a delicacy still eaten at Easter, and wine can be made from the heart of the palm. There are many other palms in Belize, including the **coconut palm** found along the coast (it has been subject to lethal yellowing and is being replaced in some areas with the Malayan palm), the stately **royal palm,** the distinctive fan-shaped **traveler's palm** (not a true palm, instead related to the banana) and the **xate palms,** three different small palms used for floral decorations that have been poached in the Mountain Pine Ridge and Chiquibul by *xateros* from Guatemala. The **bayleaf palm** (*Sabal mauritiiformis*) is the preferred material for making thatch roofs in Belize, because properly harvested and put together the palm makes a long-lasting, waterproof roof. It has been overharvested in Belize. Now the supply is limited, and the cost to do a bayleaf palm roof can run into many thousand U.S. dollars.

Copal *(Protium copal)* was a sacred tree to the Maya. It was mentioned in the *Popul Vuh*, the story of creation as told by the Maya priests. It can still be found growing around the ruins of Maya temples. The copal resin was burned as an incense in religious ceremonies and is still used today in Catholic churches in the region.

Craboo *(Byrsonima crassifolia)*, also known as nance, is native to Central America, South America and the Caribbean. Craboo trees have bunches of tiny orange and red flowers that bloom in May through June in Belize. They can grow to 30 feet and are found all over the country. The small fruits usually ripen in July and August. There are several different varieties of craboo -- some fruits are tiny and bitter and others are large and sweet. People enjoy the fruit mashed with milk or raw or in ice cream. They also are used to make nance liqueur and craboo wine.

Flamboyant *(Delonix regia)*, a native of Madagascar, is now widespread in the Caribbean and the Central American lowlands. It is a medium-size tree, growing to 50 feet, easily identified by its umbrella-like branches and from May to July by the brilliant blossoms, which vary in color from crimson to flaming orange. Parrots like the tree. When in bloom it is visited by leafcutter ants, carrying off the dropped blossoms. A flamboyant tree is in the middle of Elvi's restaurant in San Pedro.

Gumbolimbo *(Bursera simaruba)*, a medium-sized tree that is easily identified by its shaggy red bark that peels away leaving a smooth inner bark, like sunburned skin, earning it the nickname **tourist tree.** Its leaves have a turpentine smell. The gumbolimbo bark is boiled in water and applied as a soothing lotion to burning, itching skin from touching the sap of the **poisonwood** tree. The lotion is also good for sunburn. Gumbolimbo and poisonwood trees often grow near each other.

Mahogany *(Swietenia macrophylla)* is the national tree of Belize. It appears on the Belize flag, along with the Latin motto *Sub Umbra Floreo* ("Under the Shade I Flourish"). Although many of the large Honduran mahogany trees in the country's virgin forests were logged and shipped overseas from the 18th to mid-20th century, there are still impressive specimens in remote high bush. The trees, considered endangered in Belize, can grow to 150 feet with a diameter of 6 feet or more. The wood is still used in Belize for kitchen cabinets and trim and for furniture. Mahogany wasn't the first timber logged in the country. **Logwood** *(Haematoxylon campechianum)* was the first native tree harvested by loggers in the then British Honduras. It was exported to Europe beginning in the 17th century for use in dyeing textiles and paper.

Postage stamp featuring Belize's national tree   Photo used under Adobe license

Mammee *(Pouteria sapote)* is also called mammy apple and, in Spanish, *sapote*. The mammee is related to the sapodilla. This tree, which grows to over 90 feet, is widely cultivated in Belize mainly for its fruit. The fruit is ovoid in shape and has a light brown skin with a rough texture like sandpaper. It ripens in the dry season (February through May). Howler monkeys as well as humans find the fruit delicious.

Mango *(Mangifera indica)* originated in Asia but is now common all over Belize. Many homes have a couple of large mango trees, the fruit of which comes in many different varieties and is highly prized. In Belize, the mango fruits generally ripen from June to September, although certain varieties may ripen earlier or later. The mango is in the same family as poisonwood and cashew. The sap of the tree and the skin of unripe fruit can cause itching and redness around the eyes in some people. Hopkins village holds Mango Fest in late May.

Mangroves in the littoral forest protect the coast from erosion. Unfortunately, although protected by law in Belize many mangroves have been removed by real estate developers and homeowners so their properties have better water views. Belize has several species of including **red mangrove** *(Rhizophora mangle)*, **black mangrove** *(Avicennia germinans)* and **white mangrove** *(Laguncularia racemosa)*.

Orchids in Belize total more than 300 species, including the **national flower, the black orchid** *(Encyclia cochleata)*.

Papaya *(Carica papaya)* is another popular backyard fruit tree in Belize. It is also grown in large commercial plantations, especially in Corozal District, where the fast-growing tree can reach 30 feet. Many papaya trees bear fruit in the first year and in peak production have up to 150 large papaya fruits. The trees bear year-round. It is easy to recognize, with few branches except at the top and the fruit hanging from the trunk. The orange-yellow fruit, often eaten at breakfast with lime juice, is high in Vitamin C and supposedly is helpful with digestive issues, constipation and high blood pressure. Some commercial papaya plantations in Northern Belize have been shut down, with businesses moving to Guatemala, due to that country's lower labor costs. The latex in the tree contains papain, sometimes used in beer brewing to prevent cloudiness. In Belize, papaya leaves are used to tenderize meat.

Rosewood *(Dalbergia stevensonii)* is prized for its beautiful wood. It was used for interior trim in some Jaguar motorcars and in musical instruments. In Belize it grows in Toledo District, mainly around Monkey River. It is now illegal to cut a live rosewood tree in Belize, although there has been illegal logging of this endangered tree.

Santa Maria *(Calophyllum antillanum)* is a hardwood tree that is used for floors in homes in Belize and also for furniture and in boat building. It grows to nearly 100 feet.

Soursop *(Annona muricatga)* is another tree that Belizeans often have in their gardens. The oval or heart-shaped fruit is large, weighing 8 to 15 pounds, bright green with soft spikes. Each tree produces one to two dozen fruits annually. The soursop fruit is often used to make drinks and ice cream.

Ziricote *(Cordia dodecandra)* is a rare tropical hardwood that grows only in Belize and parts of Mexico and Guatemala. The heartwood of the ziricote is reddish-brown with black streaks. This contrasts with the blonde- or vanilla-colored sapwood, making striking furniture, musical instruments and wood carvings. The tree has vivid orange flowers that usually bloom in the hot, dry season during April and May.

Seasons for Selected Fruits in Belize

Banana	Year-Round
Breadfruit	October-November
Cashew	April-May
Craboo (Nance)	July-August
Dragon Fruit	August-December
Mammy Apple	February-June
Mango	June-September
Valencia Orange	August-February
Papaya	Year-Round
Pineapple	December-February & August-September
Sapodilla	May-September
Soursop	August-February
Star Fruit	June-February
Watermelon	Year-Round

TOURISM INDUSTRY IN BELIZE

Since our readers are mostly visitors to Belize we believe it is important to provide an overview of the tourism industry in Belize, especially in terms of where visitors to Belize go, how much they spend and what they enjoy.

A Belize visitor checks out the sea   Photo by Dann Hauer/Shutterstock

Here, in bullet form, are some of the key facts about the tourism industry in Belize. Information for this section comes from a variety of sources, but we owe the greatest debt to the Government of Belize, Belize Tourism Board and to the Inter-American Development Bank, which had a report on sustainable tourism prepared in 2015 by Manuel L. Knight of the tourism consulting firm of KnightConsult LLC, Washington, D.C. Numbers are rounded.

• In 2015, Belize had **341,000 overnight visitor arrivals.** Overnight arrivals were up 6.2% from 321,000 in 2014.

- Of all overnight arrivals, **77% came to Belize for leisure and vacations,** 18% came to visit family and friends and 5% were for business or governmental reasons.
- **Activities participated in by tourists to Belize,** ranked by order of popularity:

Snorkeling	**67%**	of tourists participate in activity
Jungle trekking	34%	
Caving and cave tubing	33%	
Island tour	25%	
Diving	24%	
Fishing	22%	
Canoeing/kayaking	22%	
Cultural event	15%	
Sailing	13%	
Birding	12%	
Gambling	2%	
Other	13%	

- **Types of attractions visited,** ranked by order of popularity:

Belize Barrier Reef	**53%**	of tourists go here
Marine Reserves	47%	
Islands	47%	
Archeological Sites	42%	
National Parks	40%	
Museums/Historical	19%	
Blue Hole	12%	
Other	4%	

- **Most-visited destinations** (2014), ranked by order of popularity:

Ambergris Caye	**45%**	of tourists visit this area
Caye Caulker	26%	
San Ignacio Area	22%	
Belize City/Belize District	16%	
Placencia	15%	
Hopkins/Dangriga	12%	
Offshore Islands	6%	
Belmopan	6%	
Corozal District	4%	

Orange Walk District   4%
Toledo District   3%

• **Fastest growing destinations** (2010-2014), ranked by percentage growth rates in visitation:

Hopkins/Dangriga   **23% increase** in visitation
Belmopan   18%
Placencia   16%
Ambergris Caye   8%
San Ignacio   8%
Toledo District   8%
Offshore Islands   7%
Caye Caulker   6%
Corozal District   4%
Orange Walk District   -1%
Belize City   -10%

• **Cruise tourism has seen huge increases** over the past decade and a half. **In 2015, cruise arrivals totaled 958,000,** up 10% from 871,000 in 2014 and up a whopping 1,800% from the year 2000, when the country had only 50,000 cruise ship visitors.

• Although cruise ship arrivals were nearly three times the number of overnight arrivals, **cruise tourism generated less than 15% of total direct tourism revenues.**

• **Three-fourths of overnight arrivals come in to Philip S. W. Goldson International Airport** near Belize City, while 11% come in from the northern border with Mexico and 10% from the western border with Guatemala. Nearly all cruise ship passengers arrive at Belize City, tendering in to the Fort Street Tourism Village from ships docked offshore. This may change in 2017, with the opening in late 2016 of Norwegian Cruise Lines' new cruise port on Harvest Caye off Placencia.

• **Tourism revenues in 2015 totaled US$250 million** (15% of total Gross Domestic Product) in direct expenditures and US$656 million in direct and indirect expenditures (39% of total GDP).

• Nationwide, the **tourism industry directly employs 18,850 people,** more than 14% of the total labor force. Nearly one-half of tourism employment is in Belize District, including Belize City, Ambergris Caye and Caye Caulker.

• Including both direct and indirect contribution, the **tourism industry in Belize provides 35% of the country's employment.**

• **Hotel occupancy in Belize in 2014 averaged 47%,** up strongly from the Great Recession of 2009-2011 when average occupancy rates sank into the mid- to high 30% range.

• **Hotel occupancy rate by destination and average room rate** (2015), ranked in order of occupancy rate:

Belize City & Rural Belize District: 59%, US$83

Hopkins/Dangriga & Rural Stann Creek: 53%, US$138

Ambergris Caye: 52%, US$229

Orange Walk District: 46%, US$68

Cayo District: 43%, US$110

Caye Caulker: 43%, US$69

Placencia: 37%, US$167

Offshore Islands: 35%, US$128

Corozal District: 33%, US$52

Toledo District: 30%, US$86

• Belize **overnight visitors stayed 6.7 days** on average. The typical **overnight visitor spends a total of US$1,085 while visiting Belize,** not including air or transportation to the country.

• **Belize's biggest competitor for ecotourism** in the region is **Costa Rica,** which got 2.5 million overnight visitors in 2014, nearly eight times as many as Belize.

• **Belize's biggest competitor for cultural tourism** and Maya sites is **Guatemala,** which had 1.5 million overnight arrivals in 2014.

• Belize's tourism industry is miniscule compared to that of **Mexico**, which got 29 million overnight tourists in 2014.

• **Overnight visitors to Belize come primarily from the United States** (63% in 2015), Europe including the U.K. (12%) and Canada (7%).

• Compared with Mexico and most other competing destinations, Belize's tourism industry is a cottage industry. **The typical Belize hotel has only 9 rooms.** Only four hotels in all of Belize have more than 100 rooms: Las Vegas Hotel & Casino, Corozal Free Zone (106 rooms plus 59 rooms in the adjoining Gardens Hotel) the Ramada Princess Hotel & Casino in Belize City (160 rooms), Radisson Fort George, Belize City (102 rooms) and The Placencia Hotel & Residences on the Placencia peninsula (about 100 condotel apartments, plus some other rental options).

• Number of **hotels and hotel rooms by destination** (as of 2015):

Ambergris Caye: 166 hotels with 1,833 rooms

Cayo District: 122 hotels with 1,144 rooms

Placencia: 136 hotels with 781 rooms

Caye Caulker: 107 hotels with 712 rooms

Belize City: 32 hotels with 684 rooms

Dangriga/Hopkins and rural Stann Creek: 80 hotels with 604 rooms

Offshore Islands: 43 hotels with 392 rooms

Corozal District: 33 hotels with 368 rooms

Toledo District: 40 hotels with 323 rooms

Orange Walk District: 23 hotels with 289 rooms

Rural Belize District: 25 hotels with 250 rooms

Total Lodging Places: 805

Total Rooms: 7,380

Tropical Paradise hotel in Caye Caulker village

TOP 10 EVERYTHING

We have selected our Top 10 beach resorts, budget (value) hotels, restaurants, bars, adventures and off-the-beaten-path places in Belize. These are *our* favorites. Your mileage, of course, may vary.

Blue Hole at Lighthouse Reef Atoll   Wollertz/Shutterstock

TOP 10 MARINE ATTRACTIONS

It's a bit difficult to select the Top 10 attractions in Belize, because they vary so widely. We've included a bit of explanation for each attraction. *For more information, see the various destination sections.*

1. **Belize Barrier Reef.** The Belize Barrier Reef system including hundreds of cayes, three atolls and seven marine reserves is a UNESCO World Heritage Site. It offers excellent diving and snorkeling and it is wonderful just to see it from places such as Ambergris Caye or Caye Caulker where the reef is only a few hundred yards from shore. A few cayes, including Southwater Caye, are on or very near the reef.

2. **Ambergris Caye.** Although more developed that some would like, and still growing, San Pedro and Ambergris Caye is still the most popular visitor destination in Belize, as well as the top pick for expats, for a lot of good reasons: It offers access to fine diving, snorkeling, fishing and other marine sports; it has Belize's best selection of resorts and restaurants, in all price ranges, although it trends to the high end; while it's a 90 minutes by

boat or 20 minutes by small plane from the mainland, you can use it as a base to see some of Belize's inland attractions.

South Water Caye Marine Reserve: Location

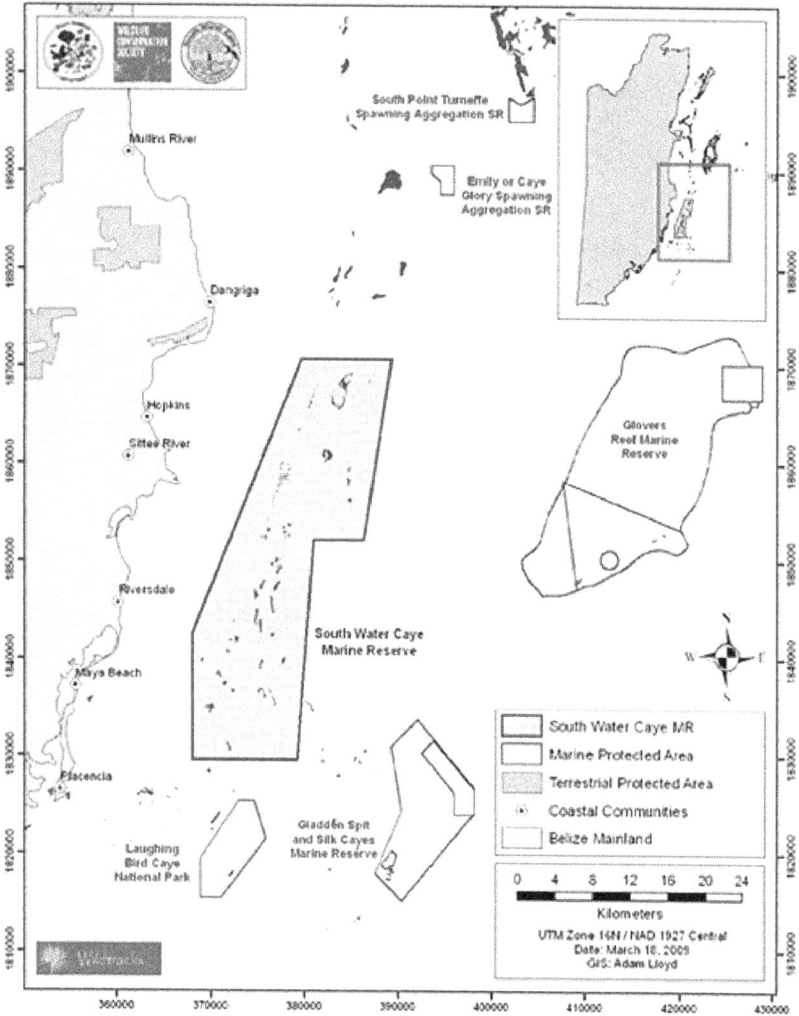

Map of Southwater Caye Marine Reserve area   Courtesy of SWCMR.org

3. **The Atolls.** Belize has three of the four Pacific-style atolls in the Western Hemisphere (the fourth is off Mexico). Getting to Lighthouse, Glover's or Turneffe atolls is a long and sometimes rough boat ride, but once there you're in a beautiful part of the Caribbean, with world-class diving, snorkeling and fishing. Especially on Glover's and Turneffe atolls

there are a number of good dive and fishing lodges, and Lighthouse Reef has the famous Blue Hole, along with Half Moon Caye National Monument.

4. **Caye Caulker.** Ambergris Caye's sister island is more like Belize used to be. Even if you don't stay there, at least take a day trip from San Pedro or Belize City.

5. **Placencia peninsula.** This is a highlight of Belize's Southern Coast, with 16 miles of tan sand beaches. While a lot is happening here now, and there are plenty of resorts, restaurants and watering holes, it's still a lower-key alternative to the bustle of San Pedro.

6. **Hol Chan Marine Reserve.** Hol Chan is Belize's most popular snorkeling spot, especially the Shark Ray Alley part where you can swim, snorkel and dive with beaucoup nurse sharks and stingrays. It's almost too popular, especially when several cruise ships are docked off Belize City. With cruise daytrippers and snorkelers from San Pedro and Caye Caulker, the snorkel boats line up like cars on the New Jersey turnpike. Well, almost.

7. **Southwater Caye Marine Reserve.** Located about 15 southeast of Dangriga and extending as far south as Placencia, this is the largest marine reserve in Belize, encompassing about 118,000 acres. Southwater Caye Marine Reserve (also referred to as South Water Caye Marine Reserve) along with Laughing Bird Caye National Park, Gladden Spit and Silk Caye Marine Reserve and the Sapodilla Cayes Marine Reserve make up the Southern Barrier Reef complex, one of the marine areas with the greatest biodiversity in Belize. Among the islands in the reserve are Southwater Caye with its beautiful beach and snorkeling from shore, Man-of-War Caye, a nesting site for brown boobies and Carrie Bow Caye, where the Smithsonian Institution has a research center.

8. **Hopkins village.** This friendly Garifuna village has one of the mainland's best stretches of beach and an increasing number of beach hotels and restaurants in all price ranges.

9. **Sapodilla Cayes Marine Reserve.** More than 40 miles off the coast of Toledo, the Sapodilla Cayes Marine Reserve is the southernmost marine reserve in Belize. Its pristine waters, cayes with fine beaches such as Hunting Caye and unique lettuce coral make for great diving and fishing. Both Guatemala and Honduras claim the Sapodilla Cayes as part of their national territory.

10. **Sarteneja village.** Located in an isolated area of northeastern Corozal District, Sarteneja is the largest fishing village in Belize, and it is also known for its old school boat builders. It is as yet undiscovered by most tourists, but those who visit are charmed by the quiet village.

Welcome to our resort!

TOP 10 BEACH RESORTS

Here are our picks for the Top 10 Beach Resorts in Belize. Most are more expensive, deluxe properties.

1. **Victoria House,** San Pedro, Ambergris Caye
2. **Phoenix Resort,** San Pedro, Ambergris Caye
3. **Grand Caribe Beach Resort & Condominiums,** North Ambergris Caye
4. **Hamanasi Adventure & Dive Resort,** Hopkins
5. **Pelican Reef Villas Resort,** San Pedro, Ambergris Caye
6. **Chabil Mar Villas,** Placencia
7. **Turneffe Island Resort,** Turneffe Atoll
8. **Cayo Espanto,** near Ambergris Caye
9. **Maya Beach Hotel & Bistro,** Maya Beach, Placencia peninsula
10. **Xanadu Island Resort,** San Pedro, Ambergris Caye

Honorable Mentions: Athens Gate, San Pedro; **Beaches and Dreams,** Hopkins; **Belizean Dreams,** Hopkins; **Coco Beach Resort,** North Ambergris Caye; **Iguana Reef Inn,** Caye Caulker; **Matachica,** North Ambergris Caye; **El Pescador,** North Ambergris Caye; **Seaside Cabañas,** Caye Caulker; **Las Terrazas,** North Ambergris Caye; **Turtle Inn,** Placencia; **Turneffe Flats,** Turneffe Atoll, **Villas at Banyan Bay,** San Pedro, Ambergris Caye

TOP 10 BUDGET/VALUE HOTELS

These are our picks for Top 10 Budget/Value beach hotels in coastal and island areas of Belize. Although they may not be the cheapest properties in their areas, they give real value and service for your money. All are on the water (those in Punta Gorda have water views but are not on a beach). *Read more about each of them in the Lodging sections of the various destinations.*

1. **Maya Beach Hotel,** Maya Beach, Placencia peninsula
2. **Coral House Inn,** Punta Gorda
3. **Tree Tops Guesthouse,** Caye Caulker
4. **Hopkins Inn,** Hopkins
5. **Sea Dreams Hotel,** Caye Caulker
6. **Coconut Row Guesthouse,** Hopkins
7. **Colinda Cabañas,** Caye Caulker
8. **Cerros Beach Resort**, near Copper Bank, Corozal District
9. **Serenity Sands Bed & Breakfast,** Consejo, near Corozal Town
10. **Blue Belize Guest House,** Punta Gorda

Honorable Mentions: Coconut Row Guesthouse, Hopkins; **D'Nest Inn,** Belize City; **Fernando's Seaside Guesthouse,** Sarteneja, Corozal District; **Maxapan Cabañas**, Caye Caulker; **OASI, Caye Caulker; Pedro's Hotel and Backpacker Inn,** San Pedro, Ambergris Caye; **Ruby's,** San Pedro, Ambergris Caye; **Seabreeze,** Corozal Town; **Tipple Tree Beya Inn,** Hopkins

TOP 10 RESTAURANTS

Here are the choices for the best places to eat on the coast and cayes in Belize. We've tried to include places serving authentic Belizean food as well as more upscale places. *Read more about each of them in the Dining sections of the various destinations.*

1. **Maya Beach Hotel Bistro,** Maya Beach, Placencia peninsula
2. **Tutti Frutti,** Placencia
3. **Casa Picasso,** San Pedro, Ambergris Caye
4. **Rojo Beach Bar,** North Ambergris Caye
5. **Chef Rob's,** Hopkins
6. **Blue Water Grill,** San Pedro, Ambergris Caye
7. **El Fogón,** San Pedro, Ambergris Caye
8. **Hidden Treasure Restaurant,** San Pedro, Ambergris Caye
9. **Riverside Tavern,** Belize City
10. **Barracuda Bar and Grill,** Hopkins

Honorable Mentions: Asha's Culture Kitchen, Punta Gorda; **The Baker,** San Pedro, Ambergris Caye; **Black Orchid,** Ambergris Caye; **Habaneros,** Caye Caulker; **Il Pellicano Cucina,** Caye Caulker **Palmilla,** Victoria House, San Pedro, Ambergris Caye; **Red Ginger,** The Phoenix Resort, San Pedro, Ambergris Caye; **Robin's Kitchen,** San Pedro, Ambergris Caye; **Secret Garden Restaurant,** Placencia; **The Truck Stop,** North Ambergris Caye; **Wild Mango's,** San Pedro, Ambergris Caye

The Lazy Lizard, Caye Caulker   Photo by James Willamor

TOP 10 WATERING HOLES

Bars and taverns come and go in Belize. Most of these have stood the test of time, even if they are not the local hottest spots. *For more information, see the various destination sections.*

1. **Lazy Lizard,** Caye Caulker
2. **Barefoot Bar,** Placencia
3. **Wayos Beach Bar,** San Pedro, Ambergris Caye
4. **Rojo Beach Bar,** North Ambergris Caye
5. **Crazy Canuck's Beach Bar,** San Pedro, Ambergris Caye
6. **Fido's,** San Pedro, Ambergris Caye
7. **Corozo Blue,** Corozal Town
8. **Driftwood Beach Bar & Pizza Shack, Hopkins**
9. **Truck Stop,** North Ambergris Caye
10. **Yoli's,** Placencia

Honorable Mentions: Feliz, San Pedro, Ambergris Caye; **Jaguar Bowling Alley,** Maya Beach, Placencia peninsula; **Katanga Beach Bar,** X'Tan Ha, North Ambergris Caye; **Palapa Bar & Grill,** (new location), San Pedro, Ambergris Caye; **Road Kill Bar,** San Pedro, Ambergris Caye; **Tipsy Tuna,** Placencia; **Waluco's,** Punta Gorda; **Y-Not Grill & Bar,** Tony's Inn, Corozal Town

TOP 10 SEA ADVENTURES

Some of these adventures will get your heart racing, and several are for the very fit and highly experienced only (unlike us.) Others can be enjoyed by most who are in reasonable shape.

1. **Go island hopping by sea kayak** in Belize's Caribbean
2. **Dive or snorkel the Blue Hole** at Lighthouse Reef Atoll
3. **Go for an angling grand slam** (permit, bonefish, snook and tarpon) off the coast, cayes and atolls
4. **Dive or snorkel with whale sharks** at Gladden Spit off Placencia
5. **Snorkel and swim with nurse sharks and stingrays** at Shark Ray Alley in Hol Chan Marine Reserve
6. **Charter a bareboat or captained sailboat** to explore the Caribbean inside the Belize Barrier Reef
7. **Try windsurfing or kiteboarding** on Caye Caulker
8. **Dive The Elbow** and its canyons and spur and groove formations at Turneffe Atoll
9. **Do a three-day sailing trip from Caye Caulker to Placencia,** with camping stops at two islands along the way
10. **Dive The Chimney** at Halfmoon Caye wall at Lighthouse Reef Atoll

TOP 10 OFF-THE-BEATEN-PATH SPOTS

Here are some of the places in Belize, with an emphasis on coastal, caye and atolls areas, that too frequently are overlooked by visitors:

1. **Sarteneja village** in northeast Corozal District
2. **Punta Negra village,** coastal Toledo District
3. **Punta Gorda,** Toledo District
4. **Bacalar Chico National Park and Marine Reserve,** North Ambergris Caye
5. **Half Moon Caye National Monument,** Lighthouse Reef Atoll
6. **Southwater Caye and Southwater Caye Marine Reserve,** off Dangriga
7. **Snake Cayes,** off Punta Gorda
8. **Cerros Maya site** in Corozal District
9. **Sapodilla Cayes,** off Punta Gorda
10. **Monkey River village,** Toledo District

A quiet street in the charming fishing village of Sarteneja

TOP 10 BEACHES IN BELIZE

While Belize is known for its snorkeling, diving, fishing and other activities on the water, its beaches don't win many "World's Best Beaches" awards. The Belize Barrier Reef along the coast reduces wave activity that, in other areas, over long periods, creates "dead zones" near shore and wide, sandy beaches. This plus the low tidal range in Belize means that in many areas there is seagrass off beaches. The grass is a wonderful nursery for sea life and is an integral part the barrier reef ecosystem, but for swimmers it can be, well, off-putting. Some resorts remove seagrass from a small area for better swimming, and often there is good swimming off the end of piers where there is little or no seagrass.

Still, many of the beaches are postcard-beautiful. We prefer the beaches, especially those on Ambergris, with a view of the reef just a short distance from shore. In general, beaches on Ambergris Caye, especially North Ambergris, have soft, nearly white sand, while those in the south of the country, on the Placencia peninsula and Hopkins, have tan or khaki-colored sand.

Keeping the above information in mind, here are our picks for the top beaches in Belize.

1. **North Ambergris Caye,** various beaches (mostly at resorts) from about 4 miles north of San Pedro
   2. **Southwater Caye,** south end
   3. **Maya Beach,** Placencia peninsula
   4. **Hunting Caye** in Sapodilla Cayes
   5. **Beach area just south of Hopkins village**
   6. **South Ambergris Caye** at and near Victoria House
   7. **Mar de Tumbo** beach south of San Pedro, Ambergris Caye
   8. **Ranguana Caye,** off Placencia
   9. **Southwest Caye** and other cayes at Glover's Atoll
   10. **Half Moon Caye,** Lighthouse Reef Atoll

DESTINATIONS

The sections that follow cover all the major destinations in Belize. We begin with the place where most visitors arrive and use as primary transit center, Belize City, even though it is not a beach destination.

Colonial architecture in the historic Fort George area of Belize City

BELIZE CITY AND ENVIRONS

If there were nothing to Belize but Belize City, the country would get very few visitors. Belize City has an image problem, and part of that image of high crime, gangs and not much worth the visitor's time is at least partially accurate. But there's no escaping Belize City, as it's where most visitors arrive. It's the commercial, media and transportation hub of Belize.

Give the city a chance, don't put your self in bad situations and you may just find there's a good deal to like about the city. Certainly, places near the city like the Belize Zoo, Altun Ha Maya site, the Baboon Sanctuary and Crooked Tree Wildlife Sanctuary are safe and well worth your time.

BELIZE CITY RATINGS

Ratings are on an A to F scale, with pluses and minuses, just like a school report card.

Popularity with Visitors	D
Popularity with Expats	D-
Cost Level	C
Safety	D
Lodging	B-

Dining	B
Nightlife	C-
Outdoor Activities	C-
Water Activities	C-
Cultural Activities	A-
Museums	B
Maya Sites	D+
Historical Sites	B
Tourism Infrastructure	B
Transportation	A
Medical Care	A-
Shopping	A-
Overall Visitor Rating	C-

BELIZE CITY OVERVIEW

ADVANTAGES OF BELIZE CITY: • Access to good restaurants and social and cultural activities • Business and transportation hub of the country • Availability of stores and shopping, some with lower prices • Good medical care

Belize City has a bad rep among visitors and even among Belizeans from other areas, who sometimes dread visiting the "big city" with its rude layabouts and drug touts. In truth, the city is hardly more than an oversized town, with ramshackle buildings set close to the street in the central areas but also with its share of stately old colonial houses in the Fort George section and 19th century landmarks such as St. John's Anglican Cathedral and the House of Culture, formerly Government House. And while crime is a considerable problem – hardly a weekend goes by without a murder or three – crime in Belize City is nothing like that you'd experience in the much bigger and meaner cities of the region such as Guatemala City and Tegucigalpa.

The city has an energy of its own. By day, Front, Queen and Albert streets swarm with shop clerks and shoppers. Restaurants are packed at lunchtime. On Regent Street you'll find lawyers and judges dressed in British-style robes. Day trippers from the cruise ships that now call on Belize City – nearly a million passengers make port here annually, much to the dismay of many resort and ecolodge owners who fear the impact of hordes of cruise tourists on environmentally sensitive ruins, caves and cayes – get on vans and boats for their shore excursions. (Some of the cruise tourists will be siphoned off to southern Belize, with the debut of the Norwegian Cruise Line cruise port on a caye off Placencia village sometime in late 2016.)

Everywhere you'll hear the sound of Kriol being spoken, as local residents greet friends and lovers amid a happy Caribbean-style gumbo of sounds and smells. At night, despite the street crime, Belize City lights up with parties, gallery openings and political and professional meetings, as Belize City remains in all but name the true political, as well as cultural, commercial and social, capital of the country.

Belize City Practicalities

As the largest urban area and commercial hub of the country, Belize City offers most of the amenities of a town of similar size in the U.S. or Canada, although don't expect to find international big box stores like Home Depot or Best Buy.

Airlines: Belize City is the air transportation hub of the country and offers more than 200 domestic flights a day by Maya Island Air and Tropic Air from the two Belize City area airports, Philip S. W. Goldson International Airport and Belize City Municipal to major destinations in Belize and in Guatemala, Honduras and Mexico. The international airport is served by major airlines including American, Avianca (formerly TACA), United, Delta, Copa and Southwest.

Buses: More than a dozen bus companies leave from the terminal in the Collet Canal area just west of the city center. This terminal is still called Novelo's, though the original Novelo's bus line, for which it was named, no longer operates. Local buses operate, under a franchise arrangement, in different neighborhoods of Belize City, with fares of US$1 or less.

Taxis: Most taxi trips within the city cost US$4 or less. The rate to and from the city and the international airport is fixed at US$25 (for the cab, not per person).

Car Rentals: Belize City has a largest number and variety of car rental agencies in Belize. Most have kiosks at the international airport along with offices in the city. *See contact information for Belize City car rental companies above.*

Banks: All of Belize's domestic banks -- Atlantic Bank, Belize Bank, Heritage Bank and ScotiaBank -- have offices and ATMs in Belize City. The larger banks have multiple offices, in several cases along with their international banking (offshore) subsidiaries. Branches in the "suburbs" have drive-up windows.

Embassies: Some diplomatic missions to Belize maintain their offices in Belize City rather than Belmopan. However, the U.S. Embassy moved to a new US$50 million compound in Belmopan in 2006.

Groceries: The two largest supermarkets in the Belize City area — indeed in all of Belize — are Save-U (San Cas Plaza by Belcan Bridge, 501-223-1291) and Brodies (Mile 2½, Philip Goldson Highway, 501-223-5587, www.brodiesbelize.com). Both are modern supermarkets with air-conditioning and free parking. Brodies was greatly expanded and redone in 2006-2007. They both have pharmacies and sell liquor, beer and wine. Brodies also has a fairly extensive dry goods section. There is another, older Brodies downtown. Premium Wine & Spirits (166 Newtown Barracks, 501-223-4984) has a good selection of imported wines.

Restaurants: Belize City has many good restaurants in all price ranges. Among the favorites are the Tender Bar & Grill, Riverside Tavern, Sahara Grill and Chon Saan Palace.

Other Stores: While there at present is no Walmart or Costco, Belize City does have a number of larger stores where you can buy everything from appliances to travel supplies. Among them: Mirab Department Store (501-223-2933, www.mirabsbelize.com, for appliances, home furnishings and other items); Courts (501-223-0775, www.shopcourts.com/belize, for electronics and other goods); Benny's Home Center (501-227-3347, www.bennys.bz, for hardware and construction supplies); and Hofius (501-227-7231, www.hofiusbelize.com), a hardware store with a good reputation for appliances and kitchen equipment.

Medical: Belize City is the medical center of Belize, with the largest hospital (Karl Heusner Memorial Hospital, Princess Margaret Dr., 501-223-1548, www.khmh.bz) and by far the largest number of physicians, dentists and other healthcare professionals. Belize Medical Associates (5791 St. Thomas St., Kings Park, tel. 501- 223-0302) is a 25-bed private hospital.

Among the several dozen physician practices in the city are Family Medical Center (3 Newtown Barracks, 501-223-2647, email b.e.bulwer@btl.net) and Caribbean Shores Medical Center (5756 Princess Margaret Drive, 501-224-4821, email fdsmith@btl.net). Among recommended dentists are Dr. Osbert O. Usher Dental Clinic (16 Magazine Road, 501-227-3415) and Heusner's Professional Dentistry (42 Albert Street, 501-272-2583).

Infrastructure: Belize City has the most advanced electrical, water, sewerage and internet/telecommunications systems in the country. Larger villages in rural Belize District also are generally well served, but more remote areas are exceptions.

For More Information: The Belize Tourism Board (www.travelbelize.com) is headquartered in Belize City and covers it fairly well. Cruise Critic (www.cruisecritic.com) has information on Belize City for daytrippers. The passenger reviews are the most helpful.

GETTING TO BELIZE CITY

Coming into Belize you most likely will land in Belize City. Many Belize travelers will tell you the best way to see Belize City is through your rear view window. However, with an open mind to its peculiarities, and with a little caution (the city's drug, gang and crime problems rarely affect visitors, and the areas usually frequented by visitors are watched by tourist police), you may decide Belize City has a raffish, atmospheric charm. You might even see the ghost of Aldous Huxley or Graham Greene at a hotel bar.

Belize City is the hub of transportation in Belize. *See the Transportation section above for information on flights and other types of transport to and from Belize City.*

WHAT TO SEE AND DO IN BELIZE CITY

Belize City, if nothing else, has character. It's full of interesting faces, ramshackle shops and charming old colonial houses. The city rewards travelers with a surprising number of interesting sights and memorable places, among them the colonial-era buildings in the **Fort George** and **Southern Foreshore** sections. For the most part, the colonial buildings are wood with zinc roofs.

Belize City is divided into the North Side and South Side, with the Swing Bridge effectively diving the two sides. The Fort George section on the North Side bordering the Belize City Harbor is Belize City's most photogenic area.

There are at least a half dozen buildings and sights especially worth seeing, including the Fort George Lighthouse, the Museum of Belize and the Swing Bridge, the Supreme Court Building, St. John's Anglican Cathedral and the House of Culture. These are described briefly below, roughly from north to south. The Fort George Lighthouse and Bliss Memorial and the Museum of Belize are on the North Side of the city. The Supreme Court, House of Culture, St. John's Cathedral and Yarborough Cemetery are on the South Side.

All of these places are safe enough to visit during the day, but should be avoided after dark unless you are with people who know the area. At the very least, take a taxi to them.

Fort George Lighthouse and Bliss Memorial. Fort George Point, Fort George area, North Side. Admission free. The Fort George Lighthouse, on the tip of Fort George Point near the Radisson Fort George Hotel, was designed and funded by Belize's great benefactor, Baron Henry Edward Ernest Victor Bliss. The Edwardian nobleman never actually set foot on the Belizean mainland, but he sailed his yacht in the 1920s to the coast of British Honduras. For unknown reasons, in his will he bequeathed most of his fortune to the people of Belize. The date of his death in 1926, March 9, or on a closed weekend day, is celebrated as a national holiday. Bliss is buried here, in a small mausoleum perched on the seawall.

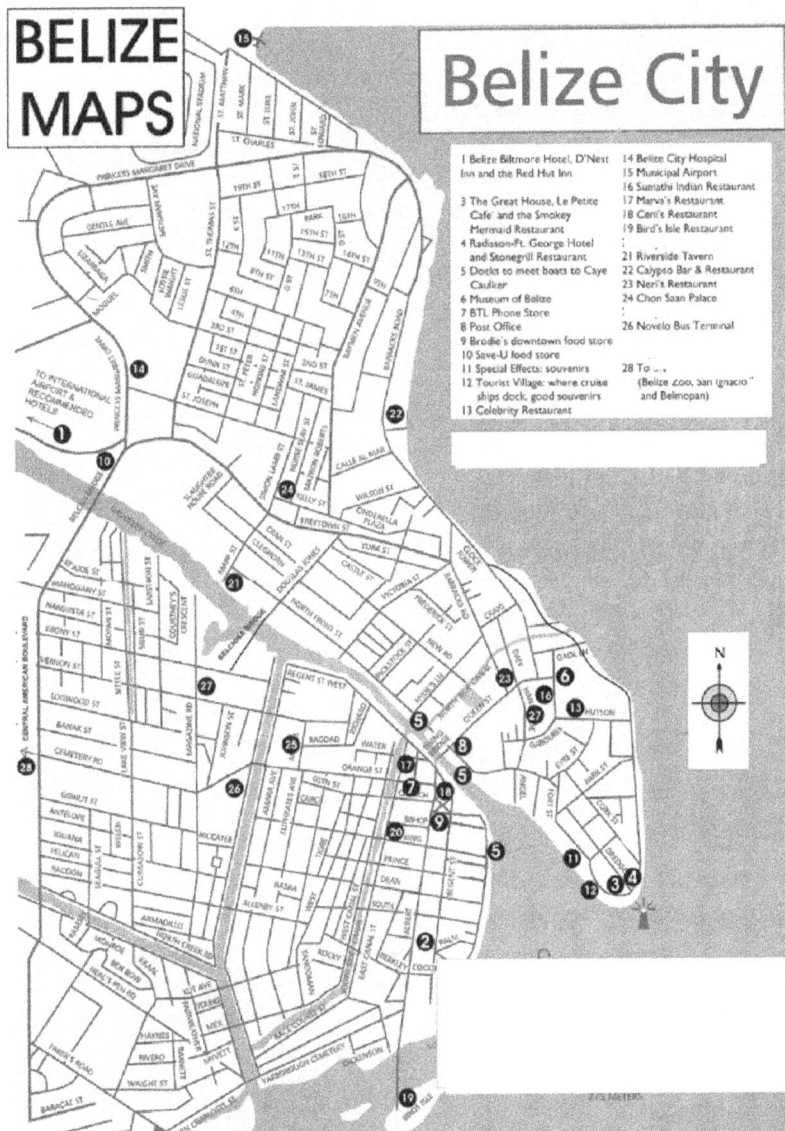

BELIZE MAPS

Belize City

1 Belize Biltmore Hotel, D'Nest Inn and the Red Hut Inn
3 The Great House, Le Petite Cafe' and the Smokey Mermaid Restaurant
4 Radisson-Ft. George Hotel and Stonegrill Restaurant
5 Docks to meet boats to Caye Caulker
6 Museum of Belize
7 BTL Phone Store
8 Post Office
9 Brodie's downtown food store
10 Save-U food store
11 Special Effects: souvenirs
12 Tourist Village: where cruise ships dock, good souvenirs
13 Celebrity Restaurant

14 Belize City Hospital
15 Municipal Airport
16 Sumathi Indian Restaurant
17 Marva's Restaurant
18 Cerri's Restaurant
19 Bird's Isle Restaurant

21 Riverside Tavern
22 Calypso Bar & Restaurant
23 Neri's Restaurant
24 Chon Saan Palace

26 Novelo Bus Terminal

28 To ...
(Belize Zoo, San Ignacio and Belmopan)

Map of Belize City Univ. of Texas Map Library, Adaptations by Slick Rock Adventures

Museum of Belize. 8 Gabourel Lane, North Side, 501-223-4524, www.museumofbelize.org, open 9-4:30 Tuesday-Friday, 9-4 Saturday, admission US$5. This fascinating museum was the main Belize City jail from the 1850s to 1993. Displays on Belize history and culture include ancient Mayan artifacts, colorful Belize postage stamps, colonial-era bottles and an actual jail cell. Exhibitions change regularly.

Swing Bridge. The bridge spanning Haulover Creek actually swings, when needed to allow a boat through or by special request of visiting dignitaries. Four men hand-winch the bridge a quarter-revolution so waiting boats can continue upstream. The large creek over which it swings was so named because before the bridge livestock were "hauled over" the stream, an inlet of the Belize River. The bridge, made in Liverpool, England, opened in 1923. It was upgraded in 1999. It's the only one of its kind left in Central America and one of the few in the world.

Near the Swing Bridge is the **Image Factory** (91 Front Street, 501-223-4093, www.imagefactorybelize.com, open 9-5 Monday-Friday, 9-noon Saturday), an art gallery and foundation. It is the focus of Belize's contemporary art and cultural scene. The Image Factory also has a nice selection of books on Belize for sale.

Belize Supreme Court. Regent Street, South Side. The 1926 Belize Supreme Court building was modeled after its wooden predecessor, which burned in 1918. The current building, of reinforced concrete painted white, has filigreed iron stair and balcony rails, similar to what you might see in New Orleans (the construction company was from Louisiana) and above the balcony a four-sided clock. (The clock faces usually tell different times.) Belize's Supreme Court for Belize and Cayo districts meets here four times a year. There are two other Supreme Court buildings, one in Corozal Town and one in Dangriga. You can't enter the building, but you can admire it from the outside.

House of Culture. Regent Street, South Side, 501-227-3050, www.nichbelize.org, open 8:30-5 Monday-Thursday, 8:30-4:30 Friday, admission US$5. Formerly Government House, the city's finest example of colonial architecture is said to have a design inspired by Sir Christopher Wren. Built in 1814, it was once the residence of the governor-general, the queen's representative in British Honduras. After Hurricane Hattie in 1961 the house became a place for tony social functions and a guesthouse for visiting VIPs. Queen Elizabeth stayed here. Now it's open to the public. View art, silver, glassware, and furniture collections.

St. John's Cathedral. 8 Albert Street at Regent Street, South Side, 8-7 daily, admission free. This cathedral, built starting in 1812, is the oldest Anglican church in Central America and the only one outside England where kings were crowned. Four kings of the Mosquito Coast (a British protectorate in Honduras and Nicaragua) were crowned here. The cathedral, built of brick brought to British Honduras as ballast on English ships, is thought to be the oldest building in Belize, other than Mayan structures. Its foundation stone was laid in 1812. The roof is constructed of local sapodilla wood, with mahogany beams.

Yarborough Cemetery, Between Yarborough Road and Cemetery Lane, South Side, daily during daylight hours, admission free. Located about a block from St. John's Cathedral and the House of Culture, Yarborough was the first public colonial-era cemetery in British Honduras. It was established in 1787. The ground was consecrated by the Bishop of Jamaica in 1826. Until 1877, it was the only public cemetery in Belize. It was designated an archeological reserve by the Belize Institute of Archeology in 2009.

Suburbs

Outside the downtown area to the west of the city, **Old Belize** (Mile 5, George Price Highway, 501-222-4129, www.oldbelize.com) has a cultural and historical museum (open 10-8:30 daily, admission US$2.50), a manmade beach area, overpriced restaurant/bar, waterslide and a marina. We wouldn't make a special trip just for Old Belize.

To the north of the city centre, **Travellers Liquors Heritage Center** (Mile 2½, Philip Goldson Highway, open Monday-Friday 8-5, 501-233-2855, www.onebarrelrum.com) is a small museum dedicated to the history of Travellers brand rum, and rum in general, in Belize. You can enjoy free samples (extra tastes are US$1 for two rums) and watch rum being made in the back. This is also a good place to buy rum to take home. Bring cash, as credit cards aren't accepted.

Tours from Belize City

Belize City is home to a more than 50 tour operators. Most are focused on the cruise ship market, which brings in nearly a million cruise passengers annually. *(See the Cruise Ship section of the Know Before You Go chapter.)* The most popular tours from Belize City are the cave tubing trips to Caves Branch/Jaguar Paw, the Altun Ha Maya trip, the Belize Zoo (often paired with cave tubing and/or ziplining or another tour) and the snorkeling trips to Hol Chan Marine Reserve near Ambergris Caye or to area off Belize City such as Goff's Caye.

The number 1 tour, cave tubing, involves an hour's drive to Nohoch Che'en Caves Branch Archeological Site, also called Jaguar Paw after a jungle lodge that used to be here. The drive is not particular scenic, as it goes through Belize City and savannah areas on the west of the city. You hike for about 20 to 30 minutes to the entrance of Caves Branch River, hop on large yellow inner tubes and float through a series of caves. You'll see some Maya artifacts along with cave structures. There is a zipline and some vendor stalls at the cave tubing site visitor area and parking lot. The total tour takes about 5½ hours, although it can be combined with ziplining or a stop at the Belize Zoo, adding two hours or more to the total trip. Note: Cave tubing cannot be done after heavy rains in the rainy season (roughly June-November) because the river levels are too high to safely float through the caves.

Many of the tour operators have kiosks or simply hang out at the Fort Street Tourism Village where the tenders come in. They just have a cell phone and a website or Facebook page. The Government of Belize licenses all guides. Of course, some tour operators have better management practices than others, but the biggest factor in your satisfaction with the tour is likely to be the individual guide you happen to get, which is difficult to control.

Here are some of the more recommended tour operators working out of Belize City. Where a street address is not shown, tour operators are at one of the terminals of the Tourism Village.

Butts Up Cave Tubing (501-605-1575, www. www.cave-tubing.com)

Cave Tubing Paradise (501-601-0060, www.cavetubingparadise.com)

Charlie's Cave Cubing (501-607-2128, www.charliescavetubing.com)

Experience Belize (501-629-2115, www.experiencebelizetours.com)

Explore Belize Caves (501-605-6823, www.explorebelizecaves.com)

Exotic Belize Day Trips (501-610-4109, www.exoticbelizedaytrips.com)

King David (501-667-2741, www.altournativebelizeservices.com)

Reggie's Tours (501-601-7221, www.regtourbz.com)

Sea Sports Belize (83 North Front Street, 501-223-5506, www.seasportsbelize.com)

Vital Nature and Mayan Tours (501-601-8975, www.cavetubing.bz)

V.I.V. Tours (501-604-1105, www.vivtours.com)

Typical Tour Costs and Time Required

These are typical prices for the various tours, per person. The amount of time may vary depending on road and weather conditions and other factors. Most of these tours are for the cruise passenger market. Rates vary slightly among different tour operators, but prices are similar due to competition. Prices shown may not include 12.5% tax and definitely do not include gratuities. Cruise ship shore excursion prices typically are significantly higher, but shore excursion guests get priority on tenders into Belize City and are guaranteed the ship won't leave without them.

Altun Ha Maya site US$45-$55 3½ to 4 hours

Belize Zoo US$45-$60, 3 to 3½ hours

Lamanai Maya site US$75-$85, 5 to 6 hours

Cave tubing US$45 to $70, 5 hours

Cave tubing and zipline US$65 to $90, 5 to 8 hours

Shark Ray Alley US$150-$175 (includes air transportation to San Pedro) 5 to 6 hours; if going by water taxi the cost will be less but the time longer

Xunantunich US$70 to $90, 6 to 7 hours

BELIZE CITY LODGING
Belize City Lodging
Rates shown are plus 9% hotel tax and in some cases a service charge, usually 10%. Hotels are listed alphabetically.

City Center Area

Best Caribbean Pickwick Hotel. 160 Newtown Barracks, 501-223-2950; www.bestcaribbean.bz. Opened in 2014, this hotel is on the fourth floor of a commercial building (you take an elevator up to the hotel). It is named after a prominent private club, the Pickwick Club, formerly in this area. The small hotel has 24 air-conditioned rooms. Of these, the 13 deluxe rooms have 45-inch flat screen TVs, king beds and sea views. The hotel is across from the Ramada Belize City Princess Hotel and Casino (we don't recommend you stay there) and the locally popular BTL Park, where you can sometimes rent paddleboats or jet skis. Guests have free use of a swimming pool and can play tennis on two courts, for a fee. Rates are US$128 to US$138 double, plus 9% hotel tax.

The Great House. 13 Cork Street, 501-223-3400; www.greathousebelize.com. The Great House offers spacious air-conditioned rooms with polished pine floors in a modernized and expanded colonial house, originally built in 1927. It is in the historic Fort George area, located a short stroll from the harbour and directly across the street from the Radisson Fort George. All 12 rooms, half on the second and half on the third floor (there's no elevator), have a balcony, private bath, mini-fridge, safe, TV and phone. There is also a fairly good, if somewhat pricey, restaurant in the courtyard, the Smoky Mermaid. Doubles are US$173 May-October and US$183 November-April, plus tax.

Radisson Fort George Hotel and Marina. 2 Marine Parade, 501-223-3333 or toll-free from U.S./Canada, 800-333-3333; www.radisson.com/belize-city-hotel-bz/belize. This is the flagship of the city's international-style hotels, and the most expensive, though you may be able to get reductions from the rack rates. It was the first major hotel built in the country, opened in 1953 as the Fort George Hotel with 36 rooms. Today, all rooms have cable TV, fridge and minibar, and those in the Club Wing, reached by a glass elevator, have sea views. Most of the rooms, including those in the Villa Wing (once a Holiday Inn) across the street, have been remodeled. There are good restaurants, a bar, and the grounds are an oasis of calm on the edge of the sea. The hotel has two pools and a private dock. The marina can take large boats of up to 250 feet in length with a 10-foot draft. Management is solid, and the staff is friendly and helpful. In-season rates start at around US$250 double, a little less the rest of year.

If you're looking for a **budget hotel,** keep in mind that most are in less desirable downtown areas, with high crime rates. If you can live with that, for centrally located budget lodging under US$50 a night double, our picks are **Belcove** (9 Regent Street West, 501-227-3050, www.belcove.com), which offers a central location near the Swing Bridge with views of Haulover Creek, a short walk to the water taxi terminals and a friendly if somewhat funky atmosphere -- rooms with air-conditioning are around US$40 to $50; **Bella Sombra Guest House** (36 Hydes Lane, 501-223-0223, www.lasbrisasdelmar.net), a four-room guesthouse in a somewhat dodgy area but with clean rooms and affordable prices; and **Smokin' Balam** (59 N. Front Street, 501-651-0839), near the water taxis and other attractions in the city centre, a family-run hostel-type place with four small rooms for around US$30 double.

Between Airport and City Center

Best Western Biltmore Plaza. Mile 3½, Philip Goldson Highway, 501-223-2302, U.S./Canada 800-528-1234; www.belizebiltmore.com. If you must have a U.S.-style motel, this 75-room is your option between the international airport and downtown. It does have a pool and an okay bar, but the restaurant isn't as good as it used to be. (Consider going to the **Sahara Grill** across the highway instead). Rates in-season start around US$140 double, plus tax, but it pays to get a nicer "premier" room at around US$160 and up. Parking, while limited, is in a guarded and fenced lot.

D'Nest Inn. 475 Cedar Street, 501-223-5416; www.dnestinn.com. D'Nest Inn is a B&B run by Gaby and Oty Ake. Gaby is a retired Belize banker, and Oty is originally from Chetumal. The Caribbean-style house is on a canal 50 feet from the Belize River. It's in an area called Belama Phase 2, a generally safe, middle-class section between the international airport and downtown. Oty's gardens around the house are filled with hibiscus, roses and other blossoming plants. The four guest rooms – all on the second floor up a flight of stairs – are comfortable rather than deluxe, furnished with antiques such as a hand-carved, four-poster bed, but they also have modcons like free wi-fi, air-conditioning and cable TV. Some could use a little upgrading. With a private entrance and your own key, you come and go as you like. Rates are US$82-92 double and include a delicious breakfast. Recommended, mainly due to the gracious hospitality of the owners.

Global Village Hotel. Mile 8½, Philip Goldson Highway, 501-225-2555; www.globalvillagehotel.com. If you have an early morning flight out or you're overnighting en route somewhere else, the Global Village Hotel (actually it's more of a motel than a hotel) is a decent choice near the international airport. The 40 rooms are clean and modern, at around US$55 double, including a basic continental breakfast and airport shuttle. This Chinese-owned place is located just south of the turnoff to the international airport.

Villa Boscardi. 6043 Manatee Drive, Buttonwood Bay, 501-223-1691; www.villaboscardi.com. This quiet and tasteful bed and breakfast is in an upscale part of Belize City north of the city centre. It's usually rated the best B&B in the city. It's near the current prime minister's home. European-owned, Villa Boscardi has eight clean, attractive rooms, all with air conditioning, private bath, fan, desk, hair-drier, cable TV, wi-fi and phone. Rates are around US$100-$115 double, plus tax.

For another choice in lodging outside the city, see **Black Orchid Resort** *in Burrell Boom, below.*

BELIZE CITY DINING

If you're shopping for groceries while in the city centre, **Brodies** is worth a look. It's on Albert Street, just past the park, and its selection of food is good if expensive, reflecting the fact that much is imported. Milk and dairy products, produced locally by Mennonite farmers, are delicious and good quality. Two modern supermarkets, **Save-U** and a branch of **Brodies**, are on the way to the international airport. This Brodies outpost has been remodeled and expanded, with dry goods as well as groceries, and is the largest and most modem supermarket in the country.

Naturally enough, local fruit is cheap and plentiful, though highly seasonal — Belizean citrus fruits are among the best in the world. Fruits and vegetables are available at the Queen Square market near the Novelo's bus station. It has been renovated.

In addition to the better dining choices listed below, greasy fried chicken is available as takeaway from small stands and stalls all over the city — a Belizean favorite still known as "dollah chicken" whatever the price. The big hotels have their own restaurants, quite expensive but with varied menus and usually good service.

Most restaurants in Belize City are closed for lunch on Sunday, and many are closed all day. Some are also closed for lunch on Saturday.

The pricing system for restaurants in all areas is as follow:

Inexpensive: Under US$7

Moderate: US$8-$19

Expensive: US$20-$39

Very Expensive: Over US$40

Prices don't include tax, tips (Belizeans usually leave 10% or less; we suggest 15%, more for great service) or alcoholic drinks. If not otherwise stated, the price range is for one person for dinner. Restaurants are listed alphabetically.

Bird's Isle. 90 Albert Street, South Side, 501-207-2179. This is an institution in Belize City. Its location on the water is nice, and service is good, but of late reports on the food have been mixed. If going after dark by all means take a taxi. Moderate to Expensive.

Celebrity. Volta Building, Marine Parade, 501-223-7272. Celebrity is perhaps Belize City's swankiest restaurant, although everything is relative. It has an extensive international-style menu of appetizers, salads, seafood, steaks, pasta and sandwiches, most well prepared with fresh ingredients. Business people frequent it for lunch and some of the city's elite come at dinner. There's a dining room and separate full bar. Expensive to Very Expensive. Open daily for lunch and dinner.

Chon Saan Palace. 1 Kelly Street, 501-223-3008. This was considered the best Chinese restaurant in Belize City for 30+ years, although the **Friendship** restaurant on the Goldson Highway now is preferred by some. Chon Saan serves fresh seafood and is Hong Kong style. Good fried chicken, too. Moderate.

Neries and Neries II. Corner of Queen and Daly Streets, 501-223-4028, and at Douglas Jones Street, 501-224-5199. Popular local joints, serving Creole favorites including cow foot soup, barracuda, stew chicken and gibnut. Inexpensive to Moderate. Open for breakfast, lunch and dinner. Take a taxi after dark.

Riverside Tavern. 2 Mapp Street at North Front Street, 501-223-5640. Opened in 2006, this Bowen family-owned restaurant has become very popular. It's still our favorite spot to eat in the city. Riverside Tavern has the biggest and best burgers in Belize City and arguably in all of Belize, with a variety of other well-prepared dishes, including steaks from Angus cross-bred cattle at Gallon Jug Estates. You can dine outside overlooking Haulover Creek or inside in cold air-conditioning, with views of the large bar and its TV sets. Parking is safe, in a fenced, guarded lot right in front of the restaurant. Recommended. Moderate to Expensive.

Sahara Grill. Vista Plaza, Mile 3½, Philip Goldson Highway, 501-203-3031. Reasonably priced Lebanese/Middle Eastern food. Try the chicken kabobs, falafel or hummus. Popular lunch spot, but also open for dinner. Closed Sunday. Inexpensive to Moderate.

Tender Bar & Grill. 8 Fort Street, Pier 1, 501-605-1620. Although it focuses on the cruise ship crowd – it's located where the cruise ship tenders drop off passengers, hence the name – other visitors and some locals praise it for its breezy waterside location, cheap drinks (the "soup of the day" sometimes is a two-buck daiquiri), good seafood and Belizean dishes such as stew chicken. Music is loud. Moderate. The **Wet Lizard** is another option at the Tourism Village where the tenders from the cruise ships come in. It's a fun bar, but the food isn't as good as at Tender Bar & Grill.

Where to Party in Belize City

Unless you know the city well, and go out with local friends, it's best to do your drinking and partying at the bars of the city's main hotels, such as the **Radisson Fort George** and **Ramada Princess Hotel & Casino**, or in the more upscale restaurants, such as the **Riverside Tavern, Celebrity** and the **Hour Bar & Grill** (1 Princess Margaret Drive, 501-223-3737), which has great drinks and okay food. Don't venture out alone after dark in Belize City. If you need to go somewhere at night, take a taxi or park somewhere with a guarded lot, such as Riverside Tavern.

AROUND BELIZE CITY
BABOON SANCTUARY

The **Community Baboon Sanctuary** (Burrell Boom village, 501-245-2009, open 8-5 daily, admission US$7) is a community organization of around 200 members in seven villages. They banded together in 1985 to protect black howler monkeys, called baboons by local people. The effort was successful, and there are now about 3,000 monkeys in the sanctuary. Spend a few minutes in the small visitor center and then take a guided tour to see and hear monkeys.

Black Orchid Resort *(see below)* is nearby, and the **Belize River Lodge** (501-225-20002, www.belizeriverlodge.com), the oldest fishing lodge in Belize, isn't too far away.

Black Orchid Resort. 2 Dawson Lane, Burrell Boom Village, 501-225-9158 or 866-437-1301 in U.S./Canada; www.blackorchidresort.com. This is a relaxing alternative to the crime and bustle of Belize City, and it's about the same distance from the international airport as the city centre. The Belizean-owned resort is on the Belize River. You can launch a canoe, kayak or powerboat from the hotel's dock, or just laze about the riverside swimming pool and thatch palapa. The air-conditioned gardenview rooms start at US$150 double in-season, US$125 off-season, plus 9% tax and 10% service are large, with custom-made mahogany furnishings. Riverview rooms are more expensive, US$225 in-season and US$195 off, plus tax and service. New luxury suites top out at over US$300 with tax and service. The on-site restaurant serves good Belizean food.

BELIZE ZOO

Belize Zoo (Mile 29, George Price Highway, 501-822-8000; www.belizezoo.org, open daily 8:30-4:30, admission for non-Belizeans US$15 adults, $5 children) bills itself as "the best little zoo in the world," and we won't argue with that. Established in 1983 by Sharon Matola, who remains its director, the zoo has become the pride of Belize, every year hosting and educating thousands of Belizean schoolchildren as well as their parents and many, many visitors. It is entirely devoted to the natural creatures of Belize. You can see many of the most interesting of Belize's 150 species of mammals, its roughly 590 species of birds and its 140 species of reptiles and amphibians. Highlights include jaguars plus the four other wild cats of Belize, tapirs, howler monkeys, Morelet's and American crocodiles, fer de lance snakes, toucans and jabiru storks. Animals are in their natural habitats, not in small cages. Seeing the entire zoo takes a couple of hours. Safe parking is available at a lot at the zoo. Night tours also are available. Access to the zoo from either Belize City or Belmopan or San Ignacio areas is easy by car, tour or bus (almost any local bus running between Belize City and Cayo will drop off and pick up passengers right in front of the zoo for a fare of around US$2.) Tip: Try to avoid visiting the zoo on days when large cruise ships are in Belize City, or get to the zoo early in the morning before cruise daytrippers arrive. Several websites provide cruise ship schedules including www.cruiseportschedules.com and http://ports.cruisett.com.

Lodging Near Zoo

Belize Zoo Jungle Lodge. P.O. Box 178, Belmopan, 501-822-8000; www.belizezoo.org. Also called the **Tropical Education Center,** the

Belize Zoo Jungle Lodge is on 84 acres across the highway from the Belize Zoo, but not immediately adjoining it. It has a large dormitory that sleeps up to 30, plus forest cabins and a cottage by a pond. Accommodations have electricity, potable water and baths, but not air-conditioning. Rates, which *include* tax plus breakfast and dinner, are US$35 per person in the dorm and US$76 to $87 for two persons in the cabins and cottage. One-way transfers from the international airport are US$70 for two persons and US$5 each per additional person.

Savanna Guest House. Mile 28, George Price Highway, 501-822-8005; www.belizesavannaguesthouse.com. This is a great choice for lodging near the Belize Zoo, about a mile away. Emmy Award-winning nature photographers and filmmakers Richard and Carol Foster, who have done great work on Belize for National Geographic TV, the BBC and others, run it. There are three rooms that go for US$60 each double, plus tax. Book ahead, as it is frequently full. Recommended.

MONKEY BAY WILDLIFE SANCTUARY

Monkey Bay Wildlife Sanctuary, Main Campus, Mile 31½, George Price Highway, (P.O. Box 270, Belmopan), 501-822-8032 or 770-877-2648 in the U.S.; www.belizestudyabroad.net is a private, not-for-profit education, conservation and training center. The main campus is a 1,060-acre reserve near the Belize Zoo. Monkey Bay solicits students for study abroad programs and also offers internships and seeks volunteers. Visitors can stay (and pay) for lodging in a campground (US$10.95 per person), 50-bed dorm (US$21.80 per person) or private rooms in cabins (US$32.70 to $109 single or double) and can also get meals at the sanctuary. Buffet meals also are available for a fee. In early 2016, an Atlanta ninth grade student died, apparently of drowning, while on a study abroad field trip at Monkey Bay Wildlife Sanctuary.

CROOKED TREE

Crooked Tree Wildlife Sanctuary, the name a reference to the bent and crooked cashew tree, is famous for the number and variety of birds that flock here, especially in the dry season (February to early June). The sanctuary and village are a little over 30 miles north of Belize City. You may see the jabiru stork, the tallest flying bird in the Americas. It stands nearly as tall as a human, with a wingspan of up to 12 feet. Even if you're not a birder, you'll appreciate the beauty of the Crooked Tree lagoon. Coming from the Philip Goldson Highway across the causeway toward Crooked Tree village, an old and predominantly Creole settlement, you'll see cattle cooling themselves in the lagoon, with their egret pals. Check in at the visitor center at the end of the causeway. You'll get a map and can walk or drive around the village, nearby bush trails and the lagoon front. Or ask about a local guide. Canoes are available for rent, too. Camping is available. Sanctuary admission: US$4.

Lodging at Crooked Tree

Crooked Tree Lodge. Crooked Tree Wildlife Sanctuary, 501-626-3820; www.crookedtreelodge.com. Formerly Paradise Lodge, this lodge on more than 11 acres was rebuilt and redone by a Belizean-English couple. It's now the best place to stay in Crooked Tree. There are six nice cabañas (starting at around US$60-$75 plus tax) on the shores of Crooked Tree Lagoon. A main lodge building houses a restaurant and bar. Camping (US$10) also available.

Birds Eye View Lodge. Crooked Tree Wildlife Sanctuary, 501-203-2040, fax 222-4869; www.birdseyeviewlodge.com. Birds Eye View Lodge is a modern two-story concrete hotel, just a few steps from the lagoon, covered with climbing vines and flowers. The hotel's 20 renovated rooms are modest but clean – rooms on the second floor generally are larger and you have access to the patio with great views of the lagoon. The Belizean management and staff are friendly. The hotel's dining room serves tasty Creole fare. Doubles are around US$80 to $120 in high season, plus hotel tax and 10% service. Continental breakfast is US$6, lunch is US$12, dinner US$15. The hotel can arrange birding, local tours, canoe rentals and such.

ALTUN HA

Altun Ha (off Old Northern Highway about 35 miles north of Belize City via the Philip Goldson Highway, Old Northern Highway and Altun Ha access road, daily 9-5, admission US$5) is currently the most-visited Maya site in Belize, mainly because of day trippers from cruise ships and from Ambergris Caye who go on day tours that include a quick visit to this Preclassic site settled some 2,000 years ago. There's a visitor center, gift shop and craft sales area.

If you decide you want to stay overnight near Altun Ha, or just have a nice lunch, the main choice is **Maruba Resort Jungle Spa** (Mile 40.5, Old Northern Highway, Maskall village, 501-713-799-2031 or 800-617-8227, www.maruba-spa.com). Overnight rates start at around US$200 and go up to several times that amount. We don't recommend that you buy the viper rum, in a bottle with a snake in it. Even snakes don't deserve to be pickled in rum.

GALES POINT AREA

The Northern and Southern lagoons near Gales Point, about 55 miles south of Belize City by road, are excellent places to spot West Indian manatees. There is a "manatee hole" fed by warm under-water springs, about 200 yards northeast off the peninsula point, where manatees are commonly seen. Some of the manatees have been tagged with radio transmitters, which permit researchers to track their movements. Tours from Belize City will take you on manatee watching trips, or you can arrange with someone in the Creole village of Gales Point to take you out. The village has a manatee guides association. When out manatee spotting, please be respectful of your fellow mammals. Responsible guides (and visitors) don't get too close to these huge, gentle creatures, nor do they try to swim with them or touch them. Gales Point is off the regular tourist track in Belize. There is no longer bus service to Gales Point from Dangriga or elsewhere, so you'll need a car or take a taxi from Dangriga. Very basic accommodations are available in local homes in Gales Point village. Near Gales Point are several miles of beach — not so good for swimming, but hawksbill turtles nest here.

Manatee Lodge. Gales Point (P.O. Box 1242, Belize City), 501-532-2400; www.manateelodge.com. If you like the British Honduras colonial atmosphere, with a truly lovely setting on a lagoon, this might be your cup of tea. There are eight rooms with polished hardwood floors, private baths, 24-hour electricity and jalousie windows in an old white frame building beside the Southern Lagoon. Doubles start at about US$90 plus 9% tax and 10% service. Package plans including transportation from Belize City, meals and tours are available, starting at around US$600 per person for three nights. Canoes are complimentary. Among other tours, the hotel offers a half-day boat tour, which includes manatee watching and a visit to Ben Loman cave.

NORTHERN BELIZE

For purposes of this travel guide, we consider Northern Belize Orange Walk and Corozal Districts. These areas, like the Far South of Belize, Toledo District, are relatively less visited. Yet, with proper planning they can offer the Belize traveler a lot to see and do, with generally much lower costs for food and lodging than the more popular destinations in Belize such as Ambergris Caye and Placencia.

COROZAL DISTRICT

COROZAL RATINGS

Ratings are on an A to F scale, with pluses and minuses, just like a school report card. In the case of Corozal, its proximity to Chetumal, Mexico, is taken into account in the ratings.

Popularity with Visitors	C
Popularity with Expats	B
Cost Level	B+
Safety	B
Scenic Beauty	C
Lodging	C+
Dining	C
Nightlife	B- (Free Zone)
Outdoor Activities	C
Water Activities	C+
Cultural Activities	C+
Museums	C
Maya Sites	C-
Historical Sites	C+
Tourism Infrastructure	B
Transportation	B-
Medical Care	A- (Chetumal)
Shopping	A- (Chetumal)
Overall Visitor Rating	**B-**

COROZAL OVERVIEW

ADVANTAGES OF COROZAL AREA: • Low cost of lodging and dining • Proximity to Chetumal, Mexico, for medical care and shopping •

Pleasant location on Corozal Bay • Casino gambling in Corozal Free Zone • Few sandflies in most areas and fewer noxious bugs than in some other areas of Belize • Pleasant sub-tropical climate with lower rainfall than Southern Belize • Generally safe, friendly area, though property theft is an issue • Easy access by several modes of transport to Ambergris Caye and other areas of Belize and to the Yucatán

Few Belize casual visitors to Belize, except medical missionaries and tourists passing through from Mexico, pay much attention to Corozal District and its main population center, Corozal Town. Yet this part of Northern Belize is **one of the friendliest and least expensive areas of the entire country.**

For visitors, it's a place to slow down, relax and enjoy at least a few days of easy living by the beautiful turquoise waters of Corozal Bay, aka the Bay of Chetumal. True, there's not a whole lot to see here, not many tourist sites, no real beaches though nice swimming is yours in the bay and lagoons, and few memorable hotels or restaurants. But the climate is appealing, with less rain than almost anywhere else in Belize, and the sunny dispositions of residents are infectious.

Corozal District is 718 square miles in area, with a district population of 46,000, according to the Statistical Institute of Belize estimates for mid-2015. The largest town by far is Corozal, with 11,700 residents. Spanish is spoken more widely than English here, although you can get by in English at least in Corozal Town. The town is laid out on a small grid, with the most appealing part along the bayfront, with its colorful houses and parks.

Nearby on and near the Philip Goldson Highway are "suburbs" — the small villages of Ranchito, Xaibe, Calcutta, San Antonio and others.

The **Corozal Free Zone,** just south of the Santa Elena border crossing from Mexico, is starting to make a name for itself as a place for businesses to set up free from many of the restrictions and high import duties of the rest of Belize. The Free Zone employs some 2,000 Belizeans. Mexicans and some Belizeans and visitors come here for relatively cheap gas.

There are **three casinos at the border,** on the Belize side, including a large 54,000 square foot casino, Las Vegas, which also sports a new 106-room upscale hotel. Another casino, The Grand Belize Casino, formerly was the Princess. These casinos, like the Free Zone, mostly depend on business from Mexico.

Unfortunately, to visit the casinos and Free Zone from Belize, tourists have to pay the **Belize land exit tax of US$18.75.**

The district can be divided into two main sections. The west part is still sugarcane country, once anchored by Libertad, the now-closed sugarcane processing plant and farther north by Corozal Town on Corozal Bay. The main road artery of this hemisphere is the Goldson Highway, a good two-lane paved road. From the southern edge of Corozal District near San Pablo village, it is about 28 miles to the Mexican border at Santa Elena. The border is about 9 miles from Corozal Town. The Consejo area about 7 miles north of Corozal Town on an all-weather unpaved road, on Corozal Bay, has attracted a number of expats at Consejo Shores, Mayan Sands and other residential developments.

The eastern hemisphere consists of the **Cerros/Copper Bank area** and the **Shipstern/Sarteneja peninsula.** This peninsula has far more trees than people. It is an area mostly of swamp and savannah, with the bulk of the peninsula's small population living in villages along the beautiful Progresso Lagoon and Chetumal Bay. Little Belize, a Mennonite area, is another population center, with around 2,000 residents. For visitors, a main reason to come here is the **Shipstern Nature Preserve,** a 22,000-acre reserve originally started and funded by a Swiss organization. The **fishing village of Sarteneja** (pop. 2,500) is charming as well.

A mostly unpaved road runs from Orange Walk Town to Sarteneja village, a distance of about 40 miles.

You also can get to the peninsula from Corozal Town via a free, hand-pulled vehicular ferry across the New River and another hand-pulled ferry over the mouth of Laguna Seca. Several residential developments, including Cerros Sands and the aggressively marketed Orchid Bay, are on the bay, and Progresso Heights, which sold many lots but has few homes, is on the Progresso Lagoon. **Orchid Bay,** despite its rather isolated location has a sizeable number of completed homes, condos and even a restaurant/bar and a bed and breakfast inn.

Corozal is one of the safer places in Belize. Even so, burglary and property theft are fairly common. One survey of expats in Corozal Town some years ago found that about 80% had been victims of theft, burglary and even home invasions over a period of four years.

One of Belize's two main land border crossing points is north of Corozal Town at Santa Elena (the other is at Benque Viejo del Carmen in Cayo, and a third is planned for Toledo District.) The Rio Honda marks the boundary between Belize and Mexico. Once across the border, some knowledge of Spanish is helpful. Chetumal has large supermarkets (San Francisco is one) and a modern mall with department stores, a multiplex cinema and food court. There are McDonalds and Burger King fast-food restaurants in Chetumal, along with a Sam's Club,

Walmart and other big box stores. Again, to cross into Mexico visitors to Belize must pay the US$18.75 Belize land exit fee.

Sarteneja village mural displayed at Candelie's in Sarteneja

Corozal Practicalities

Banks: Scotia Bank, Belize Bank, Heritage Bank and Atlantic Bank have branches and ATMs in Corozal Town.

Groceries: Corozal Town has more than a dozen small groceries and tiendas and a market with fruits and vegetables. (No, despite the name, the author does not own Lan's grocery in Corozal Town.) Large supermarkets are in Chetumal.

Restaurants: Among the best of the small bunch of restaurants in Corozal Town are Patty's Bistro, June's Kitchen, RD's, Jam Rock, Corozo Blue and the bayside restaurant at Tony's Inn. Near Consejo village is Smuggler's Den and in the village Buccaneer Palapa restaurant.

Other Stores: Corozal has a selection of small home furnishings, construction supplies and hardware stores, many run by Chinese immigrants. Chetumal across the border has larger stores of all kinds. There also are nearly 300 stores in the Free Zone, most of them selling cheap clothing and other items from Asia.

Vehicle Rentals: Corozal Car Rental (Mile 85, Philip Goldson Highway, Corozal Town, 501-422-3339, www.corozalcarrental.com) and Belize VIP Service, the same folks who have shuttle and transfer services, (Caribbean Village, South End, Corozal Town, 501-422-2725, www.belizevipautorental.com) offer car rentals in Corozal.

Medical: Corozal Town has a district hospital and several doctors and clinics, including Five Rivers, Maranatha, Bethesda and Ebenezer medical clinics. Nearby Chetumal offers low-cost and high-quality dental and medical care.

Infrastructure: Corozal Town and surrounding villages are on the power grid and generally have municipal water supplies with potable water, along with sewerage. They also have DSL and cellular internet. If in doubt, ask locally. Sarteneja and other areas have less modern infrastructures. Remote areas depend on water from cisterns or wells, power from solar or wind and sewerage from septic systems, along with satellite internet. Some developments, such as Orchid Bay, have built their own sophisticated infrastructure. In 2010 the AARP ranked Corozal a top retirement destination.

For More Information: The community website for Corozal is www.corozal.com, run by expats Jan and Judy Wilson, who have lived in Corozal since 1994.

GETTING TO COROZAL

From Mexico: ADO (in Mexico 52-5-133-2424, www.ado.com.mx) and other Mexican bus lines serve Chetumal, capital of the Mexican state of

Quintana Roo and, with a metro population of more than 300,000, far larger than any city in Belize. Buses run frequently from various towns and cities in the Yucatán, including Playa del Carmen and Mérida. Fares for first class buses — with reserved seats, videos, and bathrooms — are around 312 pesos or US$20 at current exchange rates from Playa del Carmen to Chetumal. It's a little over four hours from Playa del Carmen and six from Mérida. At the Chetumal bus station, you change to a Belize bus to Corozal Town (fare US$1.50), or take a taxi to the border and then a taxi or bus into Corozal, or use a transfer service. Belize buses leave Chetumal for Corozal Town and points south beginning well before daybreak. At the border, which sports a new Belize customs and immigration office, marked by a bridge over the Rio Hondo, you get off the bus to go through customs and immigration and then reboard for the 15-minute ride into Corozal Town. A taxi into Corozal Town from the border is around US$10.

Another option for some is the **ADO Express** between Cancún and Belize City and also between Mérida and Belize City. The daily Belize-City-Cancún bus is a comfortable, air-conditioned bus with reserved seats and videos. It costs 576 pesos one-way (about US$35 at current exchange rates.) Schedules change, but as of this writing the ADO Express departs from the Cancún bus terminal at 10:15 p.m. with stops at Playa del Carmen, Corozal Town and Orange Walk Town. It arrives in Belize City about 6:30 a.m. From Belize City, the current schedule is departure from the Belize City Novelo's station at 7:30 p.m., with stops at Orange Walk (9 p.m.), Corozal (10 p.m.), and then on to Tulum, Playa del Carmen and Cancún. The ADO Express to Mérida, also known as the hospital run, due to the number of Belizeans who get medical care in Mérida, currently isn't daily but three or four days a week.

Transfer services in Corozal and elsewhere in Belize will also pick you up in Cancún or elsewhere in Mexico and bring you to Corozal. One of the good transfer services is **Belize VIP Transfer Service,** formerly Menzies Tours (www.belizetransfers.com, 501-422-2725). You'll pay around US$400 for up to four persons from Cancun to Corozal, US$350 from Playa del Carmen, US$300 from Tulum, and US$45 from Bacalar or US$35 from Chetumal. Other shuttle services also operate.

It's also possible to **rent a car** in Cancún, Playa del Carmen, Chetumal or elsewhere and drive it into Belize (only a few Mexican agencies permit this). You will have to stop at the Belize border and purchase Belize auto insurance.

From points south in Belize: Corozal Town is about 83 miles by road from the international airport in Ladyville and 9 miles from the Mexican border. Figure about two hours by car on the Philip Goldson

Highway (formerly Northern Highway) from Belize City. Belize Bus Owners Cooperative (BBOC), Cabrera's, Chell's, Joshua's, Morales, Tillett's, T-Line and Valencia are among bus lines on this route, with frequent service in both directions, starting early in the morning and continuing to the early evening. Fares are about US$6 between Belize City and Corozal Town. Buses on this route use the main bus terminal in Belize City, Novelo's on West Collet Canal; in Corozal Town the bus station is on the main road toward the north end and just a few minutes walk to the main part of town. By regular (local) bus the trip takes about three to four hours. Most buses on this route are retired school buses or other older equipment, and currently there are no express buses.

From San Pedro, Ambergris Caye:

Maya Island Air (www.mayaislandair.com) and **Tropic Air** (www.tropicair.com) each fly four or five times daily between Corozal's tiny airstrip and San Pedro, Ambergris Caye (around 25 minutes and roughly US$72 one-way). The airstrip is about 2 miles south of Corozal Town, a US$5 cab ride.

A **water taxi** with enclosed seating area, ***Thunderbolt,*** (501-620-4475, www.ambergriscaye.com/thunderbolt) connects San Pedro and Corozal Town. Daily – though at times service may be less than daily -- it leaves Corozal from the municipal (Reunion) pier at 7 a.m. and San Pedro at 3 p.m. for the 1½- to 2-hour trip. Fare is US$25 one-way, US$45 round-trip. On demand the boat stops at Sarteneja.

WHAT TO SEE AND DO IN COROZAL

Ho hum, Corozal Town has few must-see attractions. It's more of a place just to visit, wander around the main plaza or waterfront, have a soft drink or beer and enjoy the Latin-Caribbean ambiance. Outside of Corozal Town, if you have the time and hemorrhoid meds for it, you really must drive up the Sarteneja peninsula to experience Belize off-the-beaten track. Also, go for a swim in Four Mile Lagoon or a take a boat or fishing trip in the beautiful Bay of Chetumal.

Corozal House of Culture. 1st Avenue, 501-422-0071, www.nichbelize.org. You'll recognize this place, in a landmark building over 100 years old, by its clock tower and new red roof. In the waterfront park, between 2nd Street South and the bay, the museum has, among other interesting artifacts, hand-blown rum bottles, a traditional Maya thatch hut and displays from the lighthouse that once stood on this site. It also presents rotating art and history displays. After renovation, it reopened in early 2012 and is now operated by the National Institute of Culture and History (NICH). Admission US$5.

Gabriel Hoare Market. This market, which replaced the old one by the bay, is in a two-story concrete building on 6th Avenue near the center of town. The first level has numerous fruit and vegetable stalls, with good seasonal selections of local items such as papaya, mangos, watermelon, citrus, bananas, onions, potatoes, peppers, ginger and beans. Upstairs are several inexpensive restaurants for a quick breakfast or lunch, along with some shops selling clothing and other items.

Corozal Town Hall. 1st Street South. Stop by on weekdays for a look at the mural by Manuel Villamar Reyes depicting local history. Nearby are the ruins of Fort Barley, built by the English to thwart attacks by Maya.

Maya Sites
Cerros

Cerros Maya (sometimes referred to in the singular as Cerro) was an important jade and obsidian-trading center during the Late Preclassic Period, with its heyday being from 400 BCE to 100 CE. The site apparently suffered an economic decline and was mostly abandoned in the Early Pre-Classic period after 250 CE, although there were residents there until around 1300 CE.

This site is on 53 acres on a hill beside the Corozal Bay. Cerros was first studied by the amateur archeologist Thomas Gann in the early 1900s. It was surveyed and excavated by David Freidel of Southern Methodist University in the 1970s. More recently a group of archeologists including Debra Walker, Kathryn Reese-Taylor and Beverly Mitchum Chiarulli brought to light several new structures including a ball court and a major monument. Three main structures have been excavated, along with plazas and ball courts. One structure rises about 65 feet. The site is of special interest because of its location overlooking the bay. Its waterfront location is reminiscent of better-known Tulum in the Yucatán.

A pedestrian and auto ferry across the New River reduces travel time from Corozal Town by car to Cerros. Drive to Copper Bank village and turn left, following signs. A faster way is by boat from Corozal Town. Expect to pay around US$20 and up per person for someone with a skiff to take you and your party to Cerros. Admission: Daily 8-5, US$5.

Santa Rita

The Santa Rita archeological site is thought to be a small remnant of the Maya city of Chetumal, or Chactemal, an important Maya center since it controlled trade routes along the coast and into what is now Mexico and Guatemala. This center was occupied by the Maya from at least 2000 BCE to the 16th century CE.

Thomas Gann worked here around the turn of the 20th century. Diane and Arlen Chase did systematic excavations from 1979 to 1985.

Only a small area has been excavated, and it is thought that much of the ancient city of Chetumal is now covered by the town of Corozal.

Santa Rita is located on a small hill at the northwest edge of Corozal Town, near the Coca-Cola plant. Follow the Santa Rita Road toward the Mexican border. About ½ mile from Corozal, bear to the right at the statue. Then, in a few hundred yards, take the first road to the left and then go about 2/10ths of a mile to the site.

Currently Santa Rita is closed, though you can walk around it. There are plans to develop the site for visitors and even weddings. Admission free.

COROZAL LODGING

Lodging options in Corozal Town, even when you include the Corozal Free Zone area, are somewhat limited. The good news is that prices for accommodations are low. Properties below are listed roughly by average cost.

George Hardie's Las Vegas Hotel & Casino. Mile 91.5 George Price Highway, Corozal Free Zone. 501-423-7000; www.lvbelize.com. Located in the Corozal Free Zone area at the Belize-Mexico border, this is the newest and best hotel in the casino area. The main hotel is 106 rooms with a large pool, bar and fitness room. It opened in late 2015. Also at the casino is a smaller, older hotel, Las Vegas Gardens. Rates at the hotels are around US$115-$150 double, plus tax. The hotels are associated with the 54,000 square foot Las Vegas Casino, the largest in the region.

Almond Tree Hotel Resort. 425 Bayshore Drive, South End, 501-628-9224; www.almondtreeresort.com. This small inn is a fine upscale choice at reasonable rates. Set directly on the bay at the South End of town, Almond Tree has a nice fresh water swimming pool. There are eight rooms/suites. Rates range from US$98 and $119 double, plus tax. There is air conditioning in rooms, cable TV, laundry services, bikes and wi-fi access throughout most of the premises.

Tony's Inn. South End, Corozal Town, 501-422-2055; www.tonysinn.com. A longtime favorite of travelers to Corozal, Tony's, just off the Philip Goldson Highway as you enter Corozal Town from the south, has 24 motel-like rooms with tile floors, cable TV and A/C. Many rooms recently have been renovated and upgraded, and rates for these have gone up. The breezy bayside palapa restaurant, Y Not Grill, is one of the most pleasant places to eat in Corozal. Rates: Upgraded rooms, US$120 double January-April, US$100 rest of the year; standard rooms US$80 in-season, US$70 off-season. All rates plus tax.

Serenity Sands Bed & Breakfast. Mile 3, Consejo Road (P.O. Box 88, Corozal Town), 501-669-2394; www.serenitysands.com. Serenity Sands B&B is serenely hidden away off the Consejo Road north of Corozal Town. On the second floor of a large modern concrete home, there are four tastefully decorated rooms with private balconies, Belizean art and locally made hardwood furniture. Although not directly on the water, Serenity has a private beach on the bay a few hundred feet away. Rates are an excellent value for the high quality you enjoy, from US$90 to $95 in high season, US$80 to $85 off-season, plus tax. Full breakfasts, mostly organic, are included. Best visited with a rental car. Recommended.

Copa Banana Guesthouse. 409 Bay Shore Drive, South End, (P.O. Box 26, Corozal Town), 501-422-0284; www.copabanana.bz. Whether you're just passing through or in town shopping for property around Corozal, you couldn't do much better than this guesthouse. There are five rooms/suites in two guesthouses. All have air-conditioning and wi-fi. There's a pool. The rates are affordable; you can cook meals in a common kitchen, complete with dishware, stove, coffeemaker, microwave and fridge. Rates: US$60 to $70 double, plus tax, with reduced rates for stays of at least 10 days. Complimentary bikes for rides into town from the South End.

Las Palmas. 123 5th Ave., Corozal Town; 501-422-0196; www.laspalmashotelbelize.com. This was formerly the budget-level Nestor's Hotel. It has was renovated and rebuilt, moving the whole property somewhat upmarket. The 27 rooms, with A/C, microwave, small fridge and wi-fi, go for about US$60 to $80 a night, double, plus tax.

Hok'ol K'in Guest House. 89 4th Avenue, 501-422-3328; www.corozal.net. Hok'ol K'in ("Coming of the Rising Sun" in Yucatec Maya) was one of the first places we stayed at in Corozal Town, back when it was run by a former Peace Corps volunteer. Today, it's under the ownership and management of local Belizeans, and it's still a good option in the low-moderate category. The 10 guestrooms have verandas that catch the breeze from bay, just across the street. One is handicap-accessible. You're centrally located here and can walk to most things in town. The guesthouse serves a good, inexpensive breakfast. Rooms with fans are a good buy at US$52 double and those with A/C are US$60.

Sea Breeze Hotel. 19 First Avenue, Corozal Town, 501-422-3051; www.theseabreezehotel.com. The Sea Breeze is a good budget choice in Corozal. In 2015, the owner moved the inn to a new location about 150 feet from where it had been since 2008. There are now only three rooms that share two baths. The two economy rooms are US$25, and the "premium" room is US$30 (US$40 with A/C), all plus 9% tax. Sea Breeze has a boat that will take you across the bay to the Cerros ruins.

COROZAL DINING
Dining in Corozal Town

Price ranges shown are for typical meals for one (usually dinner), not including tip, tax or alcoholic drinks. Price ranges:

Inexpensive: Under US$7
Moderate: US$8-$19
Expensive: US$20-$39
Very Expensive: Over US$40
Restaurants here are listed alphabetically.

Corozo Blue. South End, Corozal Town, 501-422-0090. In a beautifully redone stone building on the bay, this is a good spot for drinks and wood-fired pizza. Moderate.

Jam Rock. 1st Avenue, Corozal Town. Jam Rock is a laid-back open air spot on the bayfront for ceviche, chips and salsa and drinks. It's more of a bar than a restaurant. Some expats hang out here, and there's a monthly expat meet-and-greet held here. Open for lunch and dinner. Inexpensive to Moderate.

June's Kitchen. Third Street South, Corozal Town, 501-422-2559. Miss June's Kitchen is the total favorite of many locals for its flavorful Belizean food. Breakfast is great, and there are specials for lunch every day, such as ribs, conch soup or a boil-up. Open for breakfast and lunch daily. Inexpensive to Moderate.

Patty's Bistro. 2nd Street North, Corozal Town, 501-402-0174. You can eat your fill of fried chicken, pork chops, stew chicken, conch soup and other local dishes for very modest prices. It moved to its present location in 2009. Inexpensive to Moderate.

RD's Diner. 7 4th Avenue, Corozal Town, 501-422-3796. An alternative to Patty's Bistro, RD's is a family-style place serving a good variety of dishes including fish, shrimp, pizza, ribs and stew chicken at low to moderate prices. Try the cheesecake for dessert. Open daily except Sunday for breakfast, lunch and dinner. Inexpensive to Moderate.

Smuggler's Den. Old Smuggler's Den Road, off Consejo Road, Consejo, 501-629-9460. This restaurant/bar has been around for more than a decade, catering especially to expats in the Consejo area. There's pizza, steak, shrimp, burgers and more, in a nice atmosphere with a view of Chetumal across the bay. Open Friday and Saturday for dinner, Sunday for brunch/lunch and dinner. Moderate to Expensive.

Venky's Kabob Corner. 5th Avenue, Corozal Town, 501-402-0536. For takeout curries and other Indian food at modest prices, Venky's across from the Immigration Department office, is the place. Open daily. Inexpensive to Moderate.

Y Not Grill. Tony's Inn on the South End, Corozal Town. Y Not is Tony spelled backwards, get it? It has some of the best fajitas in Belize, and good conch fritters, too, in a pleasant, breezy bayside setting. A little more expensive than most other eateries in Corozal. Open daily. Moderate to Expensive.

Other favorites in Corozal include **Scottie's Crocodile Cove.** **Wood House Bistro** serves Chinese food. **Jo-Mel-In** is okay for breakfast. Also, check out the **Buccaneer Palapa** in the Consejo area.

Rural Corozal District
COPPER BANK/CERROS AREA
Getting Here from Corozal Town: You can drive from Corozal Town, crossing the New River on the hand-pulled ferry. To get to the ferry from Corozal, take the Goldson Highway south toward Orange Walk Town and watch for ferry sign just south of Corozal Town's South End. Turn left and follow this unpaved road for 2½ miles to the ferry landing. At a T-intersection, turn left for Copper Bank. The trip to Copper Bank takes about a half hour, but longer after heavy rains, as the dirt road can become very bad. As you enter Copper Bank, watch for signs directing you to Cerros Maya.

You can also hire a boat in Corozal to take you across the bay. Rates vary but can be as low as US$20 per person one-way.

Cerros Lodging
Cerros Beach Resort. Near Cerros Maya site on north side of Cerros peninsula -- entering Copper Bank village watch for signs to Cerros Beach Resort, 501-623-9763 or 518-872-3052 in U.S.; www.cerrosbeachresort.com. This is a laid-back, off-the-grid option for good food and simple lodging on Corozal Bay, near the Cerros ruins. For overnight stays, four small solar-powered cabañas go for US$60 year-round. Cerros Beach Resorts offers complimentary kayaks, bikes, snorkeling gear, fishing poles and wi-fi. There's cable TV in the lounge.

ORCHID BAY
Orchid Bay Lodging
Crimson Orchid Inn. 59 Pescadores Park, Orchid Bay, Chunox, 501-669-5076; www.thecrimsonorchidinn.com. Opened in late 2012, the

Crimson Orchid Inn is located in the heart of the Orchid Bay development. Those checking out Orchid Bay for a home or lot stay here while visiting the property, but it's also open to the public. Stephen and Laurene Honeybill, who were in the theater and entertainment in Britain, are the innkeepers. The B&B-style inn has nine rooms, with rack rates of US$100 to $200 in-season and US$80 to $150 off-season, plus 9% tax. Casitas at Orchid Bay also are offered for overnight guests, at US$95 to $175 plus tax, depending on the unit and the time of year. Crimson Orchid Inn guests can eat at the restaurant at Orchid Bay, Tradewinds *(see below)*.

Dining at Orchid Bay
Tradewinds Restaurant. Orchid Bay, 501-650-1925. Although most of the diners here are part of the "captive audience" of residents, visitors and would-be buyers at Orchid Bay, the food is pretty good, and the beer is cold. The menu is a combination of bar food, seafood and Belizean dishes. The clientele seems friendly and happy to be here. Moderate to Expensive.

SARTENEJA
This small Mestizo and Creole community enjoys waterside setting that makes it one of the most relaxed and appealing in all of Belize. It's one of the few places where you can see the sunset over the water. Lobster fishing and pineapple farming are the town's two main industries, although tourism is creeping in. Sarteneja is also known for building wooden boats. Most residents speak Spanish as a first language, but many also speak English. Real estate investors are beginning to discover Sarteneja.

How to Get There: Driving to Sarteneja from Corozal Town takes about 1½ hours via the New River ferry and a second ferry across the mouth of Laguna Seca. The road is unpaved and can be very muddy after heavy rains. On the way here you'll pass several developments, including Orchid Bay. You also can drive to Sarteneja from Orange Walk Town, a trip of about 40 miles and 1½ hours. There are several buses a day, except Sunday, from Belize City via Orange Walk Town.

The daily water taxi, Thunderbolt, between Corozal Town and San Pedro, will drop you at Sarteneja on request.

Sarteneja Lodging
Backpackers Paradise. Bandera Road, Sarteneja, 501-403-205; www.bluegreenbelize.org. This is basically a hostel. Rates are US$11 double for a small cabaña with shared outside bathrooms or US$3.25 per person for camping. A "honeymoon cabaña" with private bath is US$19 double. The cabañas are barely large enough for a double bed, lacking

chairs, closet and frills. Free wi-fi. **Nathalie's Restaurant** on-site serves inexpensive dishes including French crepes, at low prices. There's also a common kitchen for those who want to do their own cooking.

Fernando's Seaside Guesthouse. 62 North Front Street, Sarteneja, 501-423-2085. This is one of Sarteneja's first lodging spots, and it still enjoys a great location, on Front Street across the street from the water. Rooms are clean and have A/C and TV, but only the two at the front have views of the water. The owners live on the first floor. Rates around US$50 double, plus tax.

Oasis Guest House. Verde Street, Sarteneja, 501-601-3401. This centrally located guesthouse in Sarteneja, about a block back from the water, has two pleasant rooms for around US$50 double.

Sarteneja Homestay Program. (501-634-8032, email sartenejahomestay@gmail.com) can provide accommodations in local homes for around US$25 per person, including meals.

Our long-time favorite, **Candelie's Seaside Cabañas** (North Front Street, Sarteneja, on the seafront at the west end of the village, 501-423-2005), as of this writing doesn't seem to be open, but perhaps it will reopen. Candelie's has two charming cottages by the sea -- Wood Stork and Brown Pelican. When open, they rented for around US$60 double.

Dining in Sarteneja

Liz's Fast Food. 501-665-5998. Liz's is a snack shack two blocks back from the water, in the center of town near the old Catholic church. It's super cheap, with three small tacos or empanadas for US$1 – very tasty! Usually open for breakfast, lunch and dinner daily. Inexpensive.

Pablito's. No phone. Open for lunch and dinner daily. Also known as Estrella del Mar, serves cheap local food, notably fresh seafood, at a few tables under a thatch palapa. Open for lunch and dinner daily. Inexpensive.

Ritchie's Place. Front Street, 501-668-1531. Ritchie's has been around for a good while, serving fried seafood and other dishes. Owner Ritchie Cruz will also arrange fishing trips. Inexpensive to Moderate.

CAYES AND ATOLLS

Seafront in San Pedro   Photo by James Bommarito/Shutterstock

AMBERGRIS CAYE

The two main Northern Cayes are Ambergris Caye and Caye Caulker. The first area we'll look at is the most popular destination in Belize for visitors: Ambergris Caye.

There are good reasons for the island's popularity, both with tourists and expats: Ambergris Caye has a pleasant, laid-back attitude. Folks are friendly. There's a wide selection of hotels and restaurants and quite a few little shops. And of course, there's the Caribbean – big and blue and beautiful, with the barrier reef only a few hundred yards off the shore. This isn't a large island, although it's by far the biggest in Belize. It's only 25 miles long and 4 miles wide at its widest point, about one-half the size of Barbados. Much of the island is low mangrove swamp, and there are a dozen lagoons.

With the paving of 11 miles of the former golf path on North Ambergris, now underway as of this writing, and the prospect of a possible international airport also on North Ambergris, you can expect to see continued growth of tourism and foreign investment on the island.

AMBERGRIS CAYE RATINGS

Ratings are on an A to F scale, just like your old high school report card. A is the top grade; F is failing. Grades are relative compared to other areas in Belize.

Popularity with Visitors	A
Popularity with Expats	A-
Cost Level	C-
Safety	B-
Scenic Beauty	B+
Lodging	A
Dining	A
Nightlife	B+
Outdoor Activities	B-
Water Activities	B+
Cultural Activities	D+
Museums	D+
Maya Sites	C-
Historical Sites	C-
Tourism Infrastructure	B+
Transportation	B
Medical Care	C+
Shopping	B
Overall Visitor Rating	**A**

AMBERGRIS CAYE OVERVIEW

ADVANTAGES OF AMBERGRIS CAYE: • Busy resort island atmosphere with the country's best selection of restaurants and resorts • Offers some of Belize's better beaches • Provides excellent water sports opportunities – diving, snorkeling, boating, fishing, windsurfing, kitesurfing, paddleboarding and more • No need for a car, although many visitors rent a golf cart, which costs nearly as much as a car • Reasonably safe though burglaries and thefts are common, and with growth in visitation and population violent crime has increased

A Tour of the Island

The experienced Caribbean traveler may recognize San Pedro Town immediately: In some ways, it's the Caribbean of 25 years ago, before the boom in international travel, a throwback to the days before cruise ships turned too many Caribbean islands into concrete mini-malls hustling duty-free booze and supposedly discounted jewelry.

While Belize City is a cruise ship port, only a relatively small number of cruise daytrippers make it out to Ambergris Caye, and most of those head to Hol Chan Marine Reserve for the snorkeling.

Yet, first impressions may hide the huge changes that have taken place in Ambergris Caye, especially in the past 10 or 15 years. Old wood houses and shops are painted in bright tropical colors, fading in the sun, but newer homes, resorts and commercial buildings are of reinforced concrete, optimistically girded for the next big hurricane. Once the island limited to construction "no higher than a palm tree." Now, there are five-story buildings on the island, and large steel, concrete and glass bank and office buildings. Fortunately, the caye doesn't yet have true high rises.

While many people still get around by foot and bicycle, and the back streets are still sand, there are more and more paved streets. Many are busy with golf carts. Keep a close eye, as the electric ones sneak up behind you silently. Also on the island are an ever-increasing number of pickups and cars. In fact, there are so many taxis and private cars that there are occasional traffic jams downtown, and at times you take your life in your hands crossing the street.

To the north of town, over the new bridge over the channel, the large expanse of North Ambergris is being opened up to additional development due to the paving of a what until recently was a dirt and sand golf cart path.

The name of Front Street (dozens of Caribbean islands have main streets named Front, Middle and Back) was changed years ago to the more romantic-sounding Barrier Reef Drive. It is paved and one-way, with carts and vehicles allowed to go north only for most of its distance, to Caribena Street. On weekends, the entire street is closed to all but pedestrians. Middle Street, or Pescador Drive, one-way south from the intersection with Caribena Street, also is paved and heavily trafficked.

Many hotels, restaurants and larger businesses are on Barrier Reef Drive. Just beyond the primary school and the bite-sized San Pedro Library, you'll see Ruby's and part of the old San Pedro: the San Pedro Holiday Hotel, a pioneer in the hotel industry on the island. Then, near "Central Park" Big Daddy's and Jaguar's clubs are across the street from each other. The Catholic church, cool and welcoming, stands guard. Farther up on the right there's Fido's (pronounced FEE-does), a popular waterfront bar and restaurant, and the Mayan Princess. On the left is the big, modern Belize Bank building. As Barrier Reef Drive peters out, dead ahead is the ultra-deluxe The Phoenix resort and Red Ginger restaurant.

To the east, beyond the line of buildings, only a few feet away, accessible through many alleys, is the Caribbean. There's a narrow strip of beach and in most places a seawall between the buildings and the sea, used as a pedestrian walkway. A number of piers or docks jut out into the sea.

The patch of white you see a few hundred yards out is surf breaking over the barrier reef. Even if you're a strong swimmer, don't try swimming out to the reef from the shore, especially not in or near town. There is a lot of boat traffic inside the reef, and over the years several swimmers have been killed or injured by boats.

Pescador Drive, the other main north-south venue, is also busy. It's home to several restaurants, including Elvi's Kitchen, which got its start out of the owner's window, Cocina Caramba, The Reef and others. Farther north on Middle Street, San Pedro becomes slightly more residential, and more local. You'll see the San Pedro Supermarket, Ritchie's and Island Supermarket (there's another one south), Belize Electric and Belize Telemedia Ltd. facilities, a high school, a children's playground and then the Boca del Rio or "the river mouth" or "the channel." Cross the Sir Barry Bowen Bridge (before his death in an air crash in San Pedro, he loaned the town the money to build the bridge), and you're on North Ambergris, with its newly paved road.

Ambergris Caye Practicalities

Banks: Retail banks on the island include all four of Belize's banks: Belize Bank, Heritage Bank, Atlantic Bank and ScotiaBank. All have one or more ATMs on the island. Caye Bank, on Coconut Drive south of town, is an international (offshore) bank and cannot do retail banking in Belize.

Groceries: There are a number of small groceries on the island. Among the largest are San Pedro Supermarket at the north end of town, Richie's (across the street from San Pedro Supermarket) and Island Supermarket with locations north and also south of town. Other small groceries are located around the island, including the popular Marinas south of town. Super Buy on Back Street is where many locals shop. Another Super Buy is south near Marinas. Mata Grande, a small grocery, served North Ambergris residents for a number of years. A grocery near Grand Caribe, Beach Basket, is a new option north. Most of these and other groceries each have approximately the inventory of a large convenience store in the U.S., plus items such as frozen meats. An excellent bakery and breakfast spot or for fresh sandwiches is The Baker, south of town near Super Buy South, and a long-time local bakery is Casa Pan Dulce (formerly La Popular).

Fruits and vegetables can be purchased from street vendors or at small specialty shops in town. Costs for most food items, especially imported items, are higher than in the U.S., sometimes twice as high. Belikin beer can be ordered by the case from the Belikin distributor just south of town, near the Island Supermarket. However, even by the case you'll pay over a U.S. dollar a bottle, including deposit, but that's still a savings over supermarket prices. At last check a case of Belikin or Lighthouse at the Bowen & Bowen distribution center (501-226-4441) south of town was around US$31 including refundable bottle deposit; stout is a little more. Bowen also delivers for an extra charge. Liquor is sold in grocery stores – imported brands cost about twice U.S. prices, but several local rums are under US$10 a fifth.

There are wine shops on the island, including Wine DeVine on Coconut Drive near the airstrip. You'll generally pay twice U.S. prices for most wines, due to high import duties and taxes.

Other Stores: Ambergris Caye has hardware stores and other shops that provide the basics, but for some items you'll need to visit Belize City. There are gift shops galore on Front and Middle streets and also a few along Coconut Drive south of town.

Vehicle Rentals: You cannot rent a car on Ambergris Caye, but a number of companies offer golf carts for rent, including:

ATM Golf Cart Rental (Coconut Drive, San Pedro, 501-226-4803, www.atmgolfcartrental.com).

Boaz Golf Cart Rental (Coconut Drive, San Pedro, 501-226-4466, www.boazgolfcartrentals.com).

Carts Belize (P.O. Box 109, San Pedro, 501-226-4090, www.cartsbelize.com) has two locations, one near the airstrip and another next to Xanadu.

Cholo's Golf Car Rentals (Jewfish Street, behind Police and Fire Station, San Pedro, 501-226-2406, www.choloscartrentals.com) has a fleet of 100 4- and 6-passenger gas carts.

Island Adventures Golf Cart Rentals (Coconut Drive, San Pedro, 501-226-4343, www.islandgolfcarts.com).

Ocean Breeze Cart Rental (Seagrape Drive, San Pedro, 501-206-2575, www.oceanbreezecartrental.com).

Your hotel can also arrange a rental, either directly or with one of the above companies. Gas carts are preferable to electric carts, and most companies have only gas carts now. Many companies will drop off a cart at your hotel, but there may be an extra drop-off charge on North Ambergris. Rental companies can also have a cart waiting for you at the San Pedro airstrip. Typically you'll pay around US$60 to $65 for a one-day 4-passenger rental and US$275 to $325 for a weekly rental. Charges for a 6-passenger cart start around US$75 a day or $326 a week. Rates are usually plus 12.5% GST and sometimes plus insurance. To compare prices, you need know what is and is not included in the rate. Off-season, some companies offer specials or discounts. You must return the cart with a full tank of gas. A driver's license and a credit card are required for rentals.

DC Island Scooter (Barrier Reef Drive, 501-652-0307) rents nice two-person scooters for US$50 a day or US$235 a week, plus 12.5% tax. Many resorts provide complimentary bikes. Among those that rent bicycles (US$20 a day) is **Joe's Bike Rentals.**

Medical: There are medical clinics on the island and several physicians, nurses and other medical professionals. However, there is still no full-fledged hospital. The San Pedro Polyclinic II (501-226-2536), which is the closest thing to a hospital, was established in great part due to the long-time efforts of the San Pedro Lions Club. In 2005, the year the new clinic opened, the San Pedro club was named the international Lions Club of the Year, selected from more than 46,000 clubs in 193 countries.

Some of the other medical services on the island:

Lions Clubs Health Clinic 501-226-4052, emergencies 600-9071

Los Pinos Clinic 501-602-6383 and 226-2686

San Pedro Chiropractic Clinic 501-600-7119

Hyperbaric Chamber 501-226-2851 (or Antonia Guerrero, 600-5475 or Eleazar Portillo, 610-4560); this is the only hyperbaric chamber in Belize

Ambergris Hopes Clinic 226-2660, emergencies: 606-2316

Dr. Lerida Rodriguez 501-226-2197 or cell 620-1974

Dr. Teresa Damera 501-226-2686 or cell 602-6383

Dr. Giovanni Solorzano, San Carlos Medical Center, 501-226-2918 or cell 614-9251

Dr. Daniel Gonzalez 501-226-2660 or cell 606-2316

Dr. Miguel Allison 501-226-4052

Wings of Hope Medical emergency air ambulance, 501-223-3292

Infrastructure: San Pedro Town has a modern water and sewerage system. The power grid now extends far up North Ambergris, but most residents there have to depend on cisterns and wells for water and on septic systems for sewerage. Cable TV and DSL and cellular internet are available on much of the island, except the far north.

For More Information: Marty Casado's Ambergris Caye site (www.ambergriscaye.com) is the best source by far for information on the island.

GETTING TO AMBERGRIS CAYE

Getting to San Pedro is easy as caye lime pie, but it does require at least one stop along the way. There is no international air service direct to San Pedro's little airstrip, although the current Belize government supports building a new international airport on North Ambergris.

From Belize City: You can either fly or take a water taxi to San Pedro (or to Caye Caulker). It's a 20-minute flight to San Pedro; the boat trip takes about 75 minutes. The two Belize airlines, Maya Island Air and Tropic Air *(see below for more information)*, each have about one flight per hour every day to San Pedro, starting at around 7:30 a.m. and ending around 5:30 p.m. In peak visitor season, additional flights may be added to accommodate demand.

Flights originate from both the Philip S. W. Goldson International Airport in Ladyville about 9 miles north of Belize City, where your international flight arrives, and Municipal Airport, a small airstrip in Belize City. In some cases the same Maya Island and Tropic flight picks up and drops off passengers at both airports, making the short hop between the two in a few minutes.

Should you fly to San Pedro from International or Municipal? The answer depends on whether you'd rather save time or money. It's easier just to fly into international and walk over to the domestic check-in desk and catch your connecting puddle jumper.

But you'll save a little money, especially if traveling in a party of several people, by flying from Municipal. Adult and child one-way fares on both Maya Island and Tropic are approximately US$85 to $90 from international; from municipal, adult one-way is around US$50 to $55. So you're saving roughly US$35 to $40 per person. Round-trip fares usually are just slightly less than twice one way. Only rarely are there bargain fares or discounts for advance booking. Sometimes, mainly in the summer, the Belize airlines will offer discounts if you pay cash, rather than use a credit card.

Transferring between the airports requires a 20-minute taxi ride. A taxi from international to municipal is US$25 for up to three or four passengers. A tip isn't necessary unless the driver carries a lot of your luggage, in which case add a couple of bucks. Taxis – they have green license tags – are plentiful and await passengers just outside the main lobby on the international airport. You can do the math for your family or group.

Do you need to make reservations for Maya Island or Tropic flights in advance? Off-season, it's not really necessary, though having a reservation won't hurt. In-season, a reservation might save a wait. Most hotels on Ambergris Caye will arrange for your air travel to the island at the time you make your hotel reservations, and there's usually no extra cost to you (the hotel gets a small commission). You also can book direct with the airlines by telephone or over the internet. Here's contact information:

Maya Island Air: 501-226-3838; schedules, fares and reservations at www.mayaislandair.com. Maya Island Air is headquartered at the

Municipal Airport in Belize City, with its main base being Philip S. W. Goldson International Airport.

Tropic Air: 800-422-3435 or 501-226-2012; schedules, fares and reservations at www.tropicair.com. Tropic Air was founded in and is based in San Pedro.

Astrum Helicopters (Mile 3½, George Price Highway, near Belize City, 501-222-5100, www.astrumhelicopters.com) offers VIP transfers of guests to selected hotels on Ambergris Caye and elsewhere. Four resorts on Ambergris Caye have helicopter landing pads. Astrum also offers helicopter charters, tours, and aerial photography trips, plus medevac service. Helicopters aren't cheap. You'll pay US$1,000 to $2,000 for most trips, in five-place turbine-powered Bell 206B equipment.

If you are going to San Pedro or Caye Caulker, you also have the option of taking a **water taxi.** There are now two main water taxi companies (subject to change!) connecting Belize City with San Pedro and also Caye Caulker. From Belize City it's 75 minutes to San Pedro.

Ocean Ferry (501-223-0033, www.oceanferrybelize.com) boats leave from the Marine Terminal in Belize City at 10 North Front Street near the Swing Bridge. **San Pedro Belize Express** (501-223-2225, www.belizewatertaxi.com) boats leave from the Brown Sugar dock at 111 North Front Street near the Tourism Village.

Ocean Ferry, which currently has five departures daily from Belize City to San Pedro, charges US$14.50 one-way and US$24.50 round-trip between Belize City and San Pedro. San Pedro Belize Express, which has around eight or nine departures to San Pedro from Belize City, charges US$20 one-way and US$35 round-trip between Belize City and San Pedro.

Coming from Mexico or Northern Belize:

An option that became available recently is to fly from Cancún to Belize City (the international airport) on **Tropic Air.** From there you can fly or water taxi to San Pedro. Currently there are two flights daily from Cancún International Airport, one in the early afternoon and one in the late afternoon. The regular one-way fare is a rather pricey US$292. Tropic also flies from Mérida to Belize City.

A cheaper option from Cancún to Belize City is to take the ADO *bus (see below).*

Another option from Chetumal is to take a pedestrian ferry. **San Pedro Belize Express** (501-223-2225, www.belizewatertaxi.com) has service between the municipal pier in Chetumal and San Pedro a trip of about 90 minutes to San Pedro, for US$50 one-way Chetumal-San Pedro and US$100 round-trip.

Another water taxi company, **San Pedro Water Taxi,** (501-226-2194, www.sanpedrowatertaxi.com) also has service between Chetumal and San Pedro. One-way fares are US$60 between San Pedro and Chetumal and US$120 round-trip. The two companies each operate every other day, so that customers get daily service.

Water taxi fares usually do not include US$5 port fees in Mexico or the US$3.75 conservation fee of when leaving Belize by sea. You may also have to pay an approximately US$20 fee leaving Mexico, if you have not already paid it on arrival (if you flew into Cancún, it probably was included in your air ticket.)

Note that the water taxi business in Belize is changing. Check locally on providers, schedules and prices.

Many travelers, however, will come from Mexico or from northern Belize. To get to San Pedro, you have several options:

1) Take the **ADO Express** overnight bus from Cancún to Belize City, then fly or water taxi to the island. In late 2011, ADO began two express services to Belize City – a daily one from Cancún and one from Mérida (where Belizeans often go for medical care) that now runs three or four days a week. The ADO buses are much nicer than Belize buses, with 44 reserved reclining seats, videos, bathroom and air conditioning. From Cancún, the ADO bus leaves from the Cancún bus station in downtown Cancún City. In Belize City, ADO uses the main Belize City bus terminal (still known as Novelo's) located on West Collet Canal.

From Cancún to Belize City, the ADO bus departs from Cancún terminal daily at 10:15 p.m., with stops at Playa del Carmen, Tulum, Corozal Town and Orange Walk Town. It arrives in Belize City about 6 or 6:30 a.m. The current fare (subject to increase) is 576 Mexican pesos one-way or about US$35 at current exchange rates. Trip time is about 8 hours.

2) Transfer services in Corozal and elsewhere in Belize will also pick you up in Cancún or elsewhere in Mexico and bring you to Corozal or to Belize City. Belize **VIP Transfer Service** (www.belizetransfers.com) is one of several. You'll pay US$400 for up to four persons from Cancún to Corozal, US$350 from Playa del Carmen, US$300 from Tulum, US$45 from Bacalar and US$35 from Chetumal.

3) There is a water taxi from Corozal directly to San Pedro. There's one boat a day, the ***Thunderbolt.*** It departs Corozal from the pier near Reunion Park at 7 a.m. and returns from San Pedro at 3 p.m., stopping at Sarteneja on demand. Fare is US$25 one-way. Check departure times locally, as they may change, and service may be reduced at times in the off-season.

4) If you are coming from Corozal you can fly nonstop to San Pedro, a trip that takes about 25 minutes. **Tropic Air** has five flights a day from

Corozal to San Pedro, for around US$72 one-way. **Maya Island Air** has several flights a day, for about the same price.

WHAT TO SEE AND DO ON AMBERGRIS CAYE

You come to Ambergris Caye to relax, enjoy good food and drink and take part in beach and water activities, especially snorkeling and diving.

Snorkeling and Diving

Hol Chan Marine Reserve (www.holchanbelize.org), which includes Shark Ray Alley, is the most popular snorkeling site in Belize. On nice days, especially when cruise ships are in port in Belize City, small dive and snorkel boats are lined up at Hol Chan and especially at Shark Ray Alley, where you can swim with nurse sharks and sting rays. The reserve, which covers about 3 square miles, is located 4 miles off the southern tip of the island, accessible only by boat. Hol Chan, Maya for "Little Channel," is on the west side of a narrow cut or channel, only about 80 feet wide, in the barrier reef. *CAUTION:* Due to the wave and current activity through the narrow channel, snorkelers and divers must be cautious. Several snorkelers have died in accidents here. Most recently, in February 2016, a 55-year-old American drowned while snorkeling at Hol Chan. Weak swimmers and small children probably should not get in the water here, especially on windy days with choppy seas and heavy currents. In San Pedro Town is the Hol Chan visitor and information center on Caribeña Street, open daily 9 to 5. The marine reserve fee is US$10 per person, usually collected by the dive and snorkel tour operators that take visitors out to the reserve. Fishing is not permitted within the reserve. It is also not permitted to touch or hold sharks, rays or other sea life here, although guides routinely do it. Snorkel trips of about 2½ hours to Hol Chan typically cost around US$40 to $65, depending on the operator and whether or not marine reserve fees, taxes and snorkel gear are included. Two-tank local dives to Hol Chan and elsewhere on the reef near San Pedro generally are US$75-$95 plus any rental fees. When booking dive or snorkel trips, ask if the reserve fee, GST and equipment rental are included. (*See below for some of the many dive and snorkel operators on the island.*)

Bacalar Chico Marine Reserve (501-226-2833) is at the opposite end of Ambergris Caye from Hol Chan. It comprises about 23 square miles of sea and land area, from the Mexican border at the north tip of Ambergris Caye, where Maya traders cut a narrow channel between what is now Belize and Mexico, to the Robles Point area of the island. It includes areas of both the Caribbean Sea and Corozal Bay. At Rocky Point in the reserve the reef comes close to the shore, the only point on the island where it does.

191

There is a loggerhead and green sea turtle nesting site between Robles and Rocky Point. Offshore is a seasonal spawning area for Nassau and yellowfin groupers and a breeding area for the endangered queen conch. The national catch limit for the 2016 conch season was set at 800,000 pounds.

Manatee and bottlenose dolphins visit Bacalar. A popular snorkeling area, Mexico Rocks, is now within the marine reserve. On land are a surprisingly large number of animals, including on occasion all five of Belize's five wild cats, plus crocodiles and hundreds of species of birds. On the small cayes on the back side of Ambergris are the "bird isles" where you can see breeding colonies of roseate spoonbills, white ibises, tricolor heron, egrets, cormorants, frigatebirds and others. There are at least nine known Maya sites in the reserve, including a small one near the visitor center. **Bacalar Chico Expeditions** (www.bacalarchico.org) is an organization established by Green Reef Environmental Institute of Ambergris Caye. Bacalar Chico Expeditions trains guides to operate tours of the reserve, runs diving, fly fishing, kayaking and canoeing and other trips to Bacalar Chico. It also operates education programs and offers stays at cabins near the reserve. There is a US$10 per person marine reserve fee.

Belize Barrier Reef runs all along the east side of Ambergris Caye. It comes almost to the shore at Robles Point but is about a half mile from the beaches along most of the island. You can watch the waves break on the reef. The reef, part of the Meso-American Barrier Reef system, is a UNESCO World Heritage Site.

Mexico Rocks is a popular snorkeling site off North Ambergris, a little over 4 miles north of San Pedro. Water depth is only about 10 to 12 feet. With a patch reef system known for its live formations of staghorn, elk horn, brain and other coral, along with tropical fish, Mexico Rocks is transitioning into a protected marine reserve area.

Ambergris Caye Dive Shops and Tour Operators

Nearly every hotel on Ambergris Caye has a dive shop or a relationship with one. Most are pretty good, although your experience may vary depending on the particular dive master and crew you happen to draw. Prices are a little higher than you'd probably like, especially compared with Honduras and Mexico. Add-ons typically including 12.5% tax, equipment rental and marine reserve fees. Here are a few of the recommended dive shops (not a complete list), listed alphabetically:

Ambergris Divers Belize (Beachside, pier off Front Street and Black Coral Street, San Pedro, 501- 226-2634, www.ambergrisdivers.com)

Amigos del Mar (Beachfront, San Pedro, 501-226-2706, www.amigosdivebelize.com)

Belize Pro Dive Center (San Pedro, 501- 226-2092, www.belizeprodivecenter.com)

Ecologic Divers (Beachfront, just south of The Phoenix, San Pedro, 501-226-4118, www.ecologicdivers.com)

Hugh Parkey's Dive Connection (Beachfront, SunBreeze Hotel, San Pedro, 501-220-4024, www.hpbelizeadventures.com)

Island Divers Belize (Beachfront, Sea Grape Drive, San Pedro, 501-226-4800, www.islanddiversbelize.com)

Patojo's Scuba Center (Beachfront, Ocean Tides Resort, 501-226-2283, www.ambergriscaye.com/patojos)

Ramon's Village Dive Shop (Ramon's Village pier, San Pedro, 501-226-2071, www.ramons.com)

Scuba School & Family Dive Center (1788 Sea Grape Drive beside San Pedro Hardware, 501-226-2886, www.scubaschoolbelize.com)

White Sands Dive Shop (Las Terrazas Resort, North Ambergris, 501-226-2405, www.whitesandsdiveshop.com)

Other island **tour companies** offer day sails usually combined with snorkeling and a beach barbecue. Many also offer day trips to the mainland to visit Lamanai or Altun Ha Maya sites, the Belize Zoo, cave tubing at Caves Branch and other activities and sites; several do fishing trips. Many of the hotels and resorts on the island have relationships with both tour companies and dive/snorkel shops, so it's convenient to book through your hotel. However, most island dive/snorkel shops and tour operators can be booked direct and will pick you up at your resort. Here are some of the more recommended operators, listed alphabetically:

Belize Parasail (501-671-3866, www.belizeparasail.net) does parasailing, plus day trips to mainland sites, fishing and other tours

Catamaran Day Tours (501-621-7245, www.catamaranbelize.com) offers day and overnight sail trips, snorkel trips with open bar from US$85 to $100 per person plus marine reserve fees, mainland tours, Blue Hole trips and fishing trips

GoFish Belize (501-226-3121, www.gofishbelize.com) arranges flats and reef fishing trips, with full-day trips for one or two persons about US$425

Grumpy & Happy Snorkeling Tours (501-226-3420, www.grumpyandhappy.com)

Inland and Sea Adventures (501-610-1114, www.inlandandsea.com)

Lady Leslie Catamaran (501-226-2279, www.ladylesliebelize.com), day sails, scuba trips and beach barbecues, with a 38-foot Athena cat

Lil' Alphonse Snorkeling (501-226-3136, www.ambergriscaye.com/alfonso), long-established snorkeling operation

SEAduced by Belize (501-226-2254, www.seducedbybelize.com), run by a long-time San Pedro tour guide, does cave tubing and other mainland trips, plus snorkel trips and day charter sailing trips

Searious Adventures (501-226-4202, www.seariousadventures.com) has been in San Pedro for more than 15 years, running Lamanai, Xunantunich and Altun Ha Maya trips, cave tubing, along with snorkeling and sailing trips

Tanisha Tours (501-226-2314, www.tanishatours.com) is an established tour operator with a full complement of tours – manatee watching, cave tubing, ziplining and other sea and land tours

Tuff E Nuff Tours (501-226-2944, www.tuffenuffbz.com)

Typical Rates for Dive, Snorkel and Tours

Tour operators in busy San Pedro are pretty competitive, with rates tending to be about the same for the comparable tours or trips. Hotels may charge a little more than if you book direct. Shop around and compare prices and equipment. Look at the boats and be comfortable with the safety systems. Be sure to compare oranges to oranges – some operators include tax, use of equipment, admission fees and complimentary rum punch, while others do not. Rates below are per-person and with few exceptions include lunch if an all-day trip, transportation, guide, any needed equipment rental, GST and admission or park fees (tips not included):

2½-hour snorkel trips to Hol Chan: US$45 to $75

2-3 hour snorkel trips to Mexico Rocks: US$55 to $80

2-tank dive trips to Hol Chan: US$95 to $120

Full-day Blue Hole dive trip: US$275 to $400

Full-day Turneffe Atoll dive trips: US$225 to $325

Full-day snorkeling trips: US$90 to $130

Full-day catamaran sail, snorkeling and beach barbecue: US$100-$140

Full-day reef fishing with boat & guide for 1 or 2 persons: US$375-$450

Full-day flats fishing with boat & guide for 1 or 2 persons: US$400-$450

Cave tubing Caves Branch: US$125 to US$215

Day trip to Lamanai: US$175 to US$250

Altun Ha tour: US$75 to $200

For sailors, **TTM Yacht Charters** (Coconut Drive, San Pedro, 501-226-3026, www.sailtimm.com) has an operation on Ambergris Caye. It currently has only three catamarans for charter from San Pedro, ranging from 38 to 46 feet. Bareboat charter rates (no captain) range from US$4,500 a week in the low season (mostly summer) to US$9,000 a week for the largest boat from February to early April and at Christmas. The rates do not including provisions, extras like diving or fishing equipment rental or a fishing license (saltwater fishing licenses cost US$25 a week). A captain, mandatory for sailing outside the Belize Barrier Reef, is US$150 a day, plus food and tip. A cook is US$100 a day, plus food and tip.

Other Attractions

There are not many cultural or historical attractions on the island, but there are a few:

San Pedro House of Culture (Angel Coral Street, 501-226-4531, 8-5 daily, free admission) is the newest National Institute of Culture (NICH) House of Culture in Belize. It's small, but it's a start. There are a few artifacts from Marco Gonzalez Maya site (see below) along with some exhibits relating to life in San Pedro.

Marco Gonzalez Maya Archeological Site (501-662-2725, www.marcogonzalezmayasite.com) is the most significant of about 19 known Maya sites on Ambergris Caye. At the height of the Maya settlement of Ambergris Caye, an estimated 20,000 Maya lived on the island, about the present-day population of the island. There's evidence that during the Maya period the island was larger than it is now, since the sea level here has risen as much as 2 feet over the past two millennia, capturing much of the land area. Many Maya were engaged in trading with other Maya cities to the north and south. Marco Gonzalez dates back to around 100 BCE with occupation until at least 1500 CE.

The site is located at the far south end of the island, about a half-hour golf cart ride from San Pedro Town. Marco Gonzalez has been partially excavated, but much of it was looted. Since 2011, the site has been under the supervision of the National Institute of Culture. There's a visitor center, and tours are available for US$10, not including transportation to the site, which costs around US$8 if you don't provide your own transportation.

AMBERGRIS CAYE LODGING

WHERE TO STAY: TOWN? NORTH? SOUTH?

Probably the biggest decision you'll make about Ambergris Caye is where to stay. We're not talking about a specific hotel but about the general area. The area you choose will determine to a great degree the experience you have on the island. You have four basic options:

MEXICO

BELIZE CITY

BELMOPAN

BELIZE

GUATEMALA

AMBERGRIS CAYE

6-11 miles north

To
El Secreto
Tranquility Bay
X'tan Ha

Costa Blue
Portofino
La Perla del Caribe

Playa Blanca Isuana Vista
Mata Chica/Mambo
Azul Belize / Rojo Lounge
Mata Grande Grocery
Casa Turquesa
Ambergris Divers Resort

North End

About 4+ Miles from Town

Journey's End
Rendezvous
Las Terrazas
Blue Dolphin
Belizean Shores
Seascape Villas
Caliente North Essene Way
Capt. Morgan's Retreat

El Pescador
Cocotal Inn
White Sands Cove
Grand Caribe Ak'bol

About 2.5 Miles from Town

Agape House
The Cloisters
Ma 'Lo Ha

San Pedro River

Bridge
BOCA DEL RIO

Tanisha Tours

SAN PEDRO LAGOON

Freedom Tours

Heart of Town
(See hotel at San Pedro map)

Sunset Grill

Brahma Blue
1 mile

Hyperbaric Chamber
Sports Arena
Maya Island Air

Cayo Espanto
2.5 miles

Sun Breeze Hotel/ Blue Water Grill
Air Strip   Diamante Suites
Tropic Air   Belizean Reef Suites
Runway Bar & Grill   The Palms
Ramon's Village

Airstrip South

Changes in Latitude B&B
Coconut's Hotel & Casino
Isla Bonita Yacht Club
Exotic Caye Beach Resort
Corona del Mar/Woody's
Wine Devine
George's Kitchen Coral Bay Villas
Caye Coffee Caribbean Villas
Sausage Factory   Saltsports
Iguana   Xanadu Resort
Gardens
Antojitos   Marthas   Rico's
Santaelito Villas at Banyan Bay

Casa Picasso

About 1.5 Miles from Town

Belize Hutz   Grand Colony
Banana Beach & El Divino
Happy Grumpy Mata Rocks
Royal Palm Condos

Medical Univ of the Americas

Victoria House
Royal Caribbean Resort

Lions Club Park

Caribe Island Resort

Sunset Beach

South End
About 3 Miles from Town

Water Taxi

Barrier Reef

Hol Chan
Marine Reserve
Shark-Ray Alley

Caye Caulker & Caye Chapel

N

NOT TO SCALE

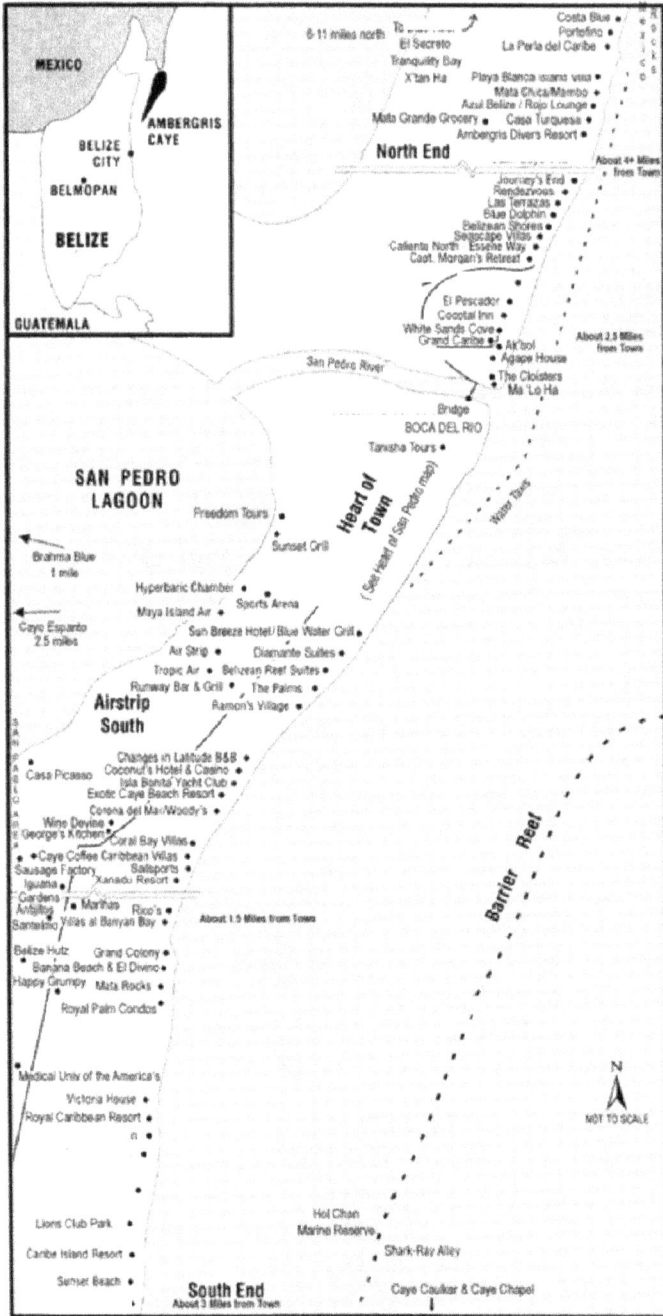

*Ambergris Caye map: Not all restaurants and resorts shown
due to space limitations*

1) In the town of San Pedro

2) Just to the south of San Pedro near the airstrip, within walking distance of town

3) On the south end, beyond easy walking distance to town

4) On North Ambergris, above the channel.

There is no one "best" place to stay. Each of these four areas has advantages and disadvantages. Which area you choose depends on what you want from your vacation. If you're looking for less bustle and the feeling of being away from it all, consider the south end 2 to 3½ miles south of town, or North Ambergris, especially the far north. If you prefer easy access to restaurants, nightlife, shops and other activities, you'll likely be happier in San Pedro town or just to the south. There's little advantage to any one area in terms of beaches, except in one way: The beaches in town tend to be more crowded with boats than those outside of town and in general are less desirable for swimming.

IN TOWN: Hotels in the town of San Pedro, with a few notable exceptions, are older spots, among them the original tourist hotels on the island. They are, again with a few exceptions, less expensive digs. If you're looking to save a buck or two, this may be the place for you. You also will be right in the heart of things, no more than a few blocks from some of the best restaurants, bars, shops and dive operations on the island. Party animals will want to stay here or just the south of town. Accommodations here include Ruby's, Holiday Hotel, Spindrift, Lily's, Martha's, Sanpedrano, Mayan Princess, Hotel del Rio and Ocean Tides. More expensive options in town include The Phoenix, which is ultra-deluxe, SeaBreeze Suites and Paradise Villas.

AIRSTRIP SOUTH: If you want a larger variety of moderate and upscale lodging but still want to be within walking distance the attractions of San Pedro Town (in the case of the ones about 1 mile south of town, consider it a hike along the beach), think about staying at the south edge of town and the area just to the south of town. The San Pedro airstrip is here, near town, but you should have few or no problems with airport noise, since the planes are small one- and two-engine prop jobs. This is a good compromise between the activity of town and the remoteness of the north end and far south end. Among the hotels here are SunBreeze, The Palms, Belizean Reef Suites, Ramon's Village, Exotic Caye, Coral Bay Villas, Changes in Latitudes, Caribbean Villas and Xanadu.

SOUTH END: Although most of this area is beyond a quick walk to town, this is a major growth area for tourism on the island. Some of the nicer upmarket hotels are located here, and more are on the way. An increasing number of restaurants and amenities also are located here. At the

197

far end, you're 2 to nearly 4 miles from San Pedro, so for visits to town you'll need to rent a golf cart (US$60 to $75 for 24 hours), ride a bike (some hotels offer them free to guests), take a taxi (about US$10 to $15 to town, for the taxi, not per person) or take a hotel shuttle, if available. Among the choices here are Villas at Banyan Bay, Grand Colony, Banana Beach, Mata Rocks, Royal Palm, Royal Caribbean, Victoria House, Athens Gate, Pelican Reef Villas and Hol Chan Resort Villas.

NORTH AMBERGRIS: By all accounts, the area north of "the River" or "the Cut" – a narrow channel of water separating the south and north ends of the island – is where much of Ambergris Caye's growth will occur over the next decade or two. Houses, resorts and restaurants have been going up here at an increasing pace.

At present, though, access is limited by how you get here: One is by boat, usually a water taxi, either scheduled or on-demand. The other is via a golf cart or taxi over the Bowen Bridge, which opened in 2006. In 2014-2015, part of the former golf cart path up North Ambergris was paved. Currently paving is under way to the Portofino area and eventually will go about 11 miles north of the bridge past La Beliza Resort (formerly Blue Reef). Crossing the bridge costs US$2.50 each way for a golf cart, US$1 for a pedestrian. Work trucks and taxis pay more. Weekly and longer passes are available. The Coastal Xpress water taxi costs US$5 to $20 per person one-way, depending on destination. Weekly and monthly passes are available, starting at US$75. When going north, bring plenty of bug spray for mozzies when you're away from the water. The same is true when going to areas at the far south end of the island.

You also may want to stock up on snacks, groceries (if you're doing a lot of cooking in your condo) and rum. Isolated resorts on North Ambergris may have set, and limited, restaurant and bar hours. You never know when the munchies will strike!

Accommodations on the north end include Cocotel Inn, White Cove Resort, Ak'Bol Yoga Retreat & Eco Resort, Grand Caribe, El Pescador, Capricorn, Captain Morgan's, Coco Beach, Belizean Shores, Seascape Villas, Las Terrazas, Azul, Matachica, Portofino, Tan Ha, La Beliza, Sapphire Beach Resort, El Secreto and Tranquility Bay.

Not on Ambergris but close by, off the backside of the island, is the ultra-expensive all-inclusive, Cayo Espanto.

Here are approximate distances, in driving miles, of hotels and resorts from Central Park, more or less in the center of San Pedro Town. Your mileage may vary.

SOUTH END
Hol Chan Reef Resort   3.5 miles south

Pelican Reef	2.8 miles south
Athens Gate	2.6 miles south
Miramar Villas	2.5 miles south
Sunset Beach Resort	2.5 miles south
Royal Caribbean Resort	1.9 miles south
Victoria House	1.8 miles south
Mata Rocks	1.4 miles south
Banana Beach Resort	1.4 miles south
Grand Colony	1.3 miles south
The Villas at Banyan Bay	1.2 miles south

AIRSTRIP AREA AND SOUTH

Xanadu	1 mile south
Caribbean Villas	1 mile south
Coral Bay Villas	1 mile south
Coconuts Caribbean	.9 miles south
Corona del Mar	.9 miles south
Exotic Caye Beach Resort	.8 miles south
Changes in Latitudes	.6 miles south
Pedro's Hotel	.6 miles south
Ramon's Village	.4 miles south
The Palms	.4 miles south
Belizean Reef Suites	.3 miles south
Sunbreeze Hotel	.3 miles south

IN TOWN

Ruby's	.2 miles south
Holiday Hotel	.2 miles south
Coral Beach Hotel	.2 miles south
Spendrift Hotel	.1 miles south
Martha's Hotel	.1 miles south
Hostel La Vista	.0 miles
Mayan Princess	.0 miles
Hotel Sanpedrano	.0 miles
Conch Shell	.1 miles north
SeaBreeze Suites	.1 miles north
The Phoenix	.3 miles north
Paradise Villas	.3 miles north
Blue Tang Inn	.4 miles north
Caye Casa	.5 miles north
Ocean Tides	.5 miles north

| Hotel del Rio | .7 miles north |

NORTH AMBERGRIS

Ak'Bol	2.0 miles north
Grand Caribe	2.5 miles north
Cocotal Inn	2.5 miles north
El Pescador	2.9 miles north
Capricorn	3.0 miles north
Capt. Morgan's Retreat	3.1 miles north
Coco Beach	3.1 miles north
Seascape Villas	3.2 miles north
Belizean Shores	3.3 miles north
Las Terrazas	3.8 miles north
Azul Resort/Rojo Bar	5.1 miles north
Matachica	5.2 miles north
Portofino Resort	6.0 miles north
Xtan Ha	7.1 miles north
La Beliza	8.1 miles north
Sapphire Beach Resort	10.0 miles north
El Secreto	11.0 miles north
Tranquility Bay	12.0 miles north

How to Get the Best Hotel Rates

Ambergris Caye hotel rates are not cheap, running US$150-$400+ double in high season, averaging US$229 year-round, although rooms are available for under US$30, and also for US$600 or more a night. Rates in San Pedro, however, are about the same as in resort areas of Mexico and Costa Rica and generally are far less than on Caribbean islands such as St. Maarten/St. Martin, Anguilla or St. Thomas.

There are several things you can do to enjoy lower prices. The most obvious is simply to go off-season, when most hotels drop rates 20 to 40%. Exact dates vary from hotel to hotel, but the low season generally starts just after Easter and runs until around Thanksgiving to mid-December.

The island has more than 160 hotels, resorts, inns and condotels with a total of more than 1,800 rooms. Annual occupancy rates on the island average in the low 50% range (10 to 15 percentage points lower than the average in the United States), and there are normally rooms available even in high season, although some popular spots may be full in-season. Easter and Christmas/New Year's periods are usually almost fully booked.

With most hotels having excess capacity in the off-season months, discounts of several types are available. In the off-season, many hotels have "walk-in" rates. These rates, typically 15 to 20% off the already discounted summer rates, can be real values.

Some hotels on Ambergris Caye also post special discounted rates for September to mid-November period, the slowest time of the year for tourism. Often you can get an extra day or two free – for example, stay four nights and get the fifth free.

Hotels usually also offer sizable discounts for stays of a week or longer, or have a value package such as "stay seven nights/pay for five." Frequently, hotels offer discounts for internet or other direct bookings, saving them travel agent or wholesaler commissions. These direct booking discounts usually range from 10 to 20% and may be higher.

We've noted recently that more and more properties are posting supposed rack rates on their websites and then showing "Special" or "X% Off" rates. These may or may not be true discounts.

When booking, always ask, "Is that your best rate?" or "Do you have a lower rate?" or "That's a little more than I was hoping to pay – is there a way I can get a better rate?" Keep probing to find out if you're getting the best price. Most hotels require a deposit to hold reservations, usually nonrefundable or only partially refundable.

Nearly all hotels on the island accept Visa and MasterCard. Some accept American Express. Only a few accept Discover. If credit cards are not accepted, this is noted in the hotel reviews. A few hotels still surcharge credit cards by 5% or so, but this practice happily is rare now.

A further note about seagrass and seaweed: In the last year or two (2015 and 2016), there has been an unusually abundant crop of seagrass or Sargasso seaweed on beaches in Belize, especially on Ambergris Caye. The hotels do what they can to keep their beaches cleared, but often it gets ahead of them, piles up and raises an unpleasant odor. Keep telling yourself that this is part of the natural ecosystem of the sea and the barrier reef.

Types of Lodging

You have several different types of lodging from which to choose on Ambergris Caye:

Condotels: These are condominiums run like a hotel. Units are individually owned and rented to visitors by on-site management that typical takes 40 to 60% of the gross. They have most of the same amenities as a regular hotel, except in some cases not a full-service restaurant. Most condotels on Ambergris Caye are not the large sprawling condo complexes found in Florida or Hawaii. They are small, only two or three stories high, with from one to three dozen units. Typically they have a mix of one- and two-bedroom units; some have three-bedroom suites. The advantage of a condotel is that you get a lot more space, including a kitchen, for a price not much more than for a regular hotel. The drawback is that most condotels do not offer the range of services of a hotel, such as room service. Condotels range in price from under US$100 to over US$600 a night. Among the condotels on Ambergris Caye are Villas at Banyan Bay, Belizean Shores, Coral Bay Villas, Mayan Princess, Grand Colony, Grand Caribe, Coco Beach, La Terrazas, Pelican Reef Villas, Athens Gate, Hol Chan Resort Villas and Xanadu.

Beachside cabañas and cottages: These come in two flavors – thatch and not. Thatch cabañas have thatch roofs, usually over concrete or wood walls. Among resorts with thatch cabañas (in some cases, only some units are thatch) includes Portofino, Captain Morgan's, Ramon's Village, Exotic Caye, Matachica, Xanadu and Victoria House. Note that a fire destroyed much of Ramon's Village in 2013, but it was quickly rebuilt. Another fire destroyed three buildings at Exotic Caye in 2015. As of this writing the Exotic Caye structures have not been rebuilt; it is likely the entire complex eventually will be replaced with a more upscale resort. Other properties have more traditional wood-frame or concrete cottages or cabins. Beachside cabañas are available from around US$75 to more than US$600 a night.

Hotels: Many of the hotels, even larger ones, on the island are personality inns. Most are small, with fewer than 40 rooms, and all are low rise. Hotels come in all price ranges, from US$15 to over US$400 a night. Nearly all the hotels, except for a few budget places, are on the water.

Privately owned houses for vacation rental: Scores of private homes and villas are available on Ambergris Caye for weekly rental. Rates start at around US$1,500 a week and go up to US$8,000 or more. Check Airbnb (www.airbnb.com), Vacation Rentals by Owner (www.vrbo.com) and TripAdvisor (www.tripadvisor.com) for listings and availabilities. Also, a local company, Caye Management (www.cayemanagement.com) has some listings.

Longer-term rentals: Monthly rentals of houses and apartments are available, starting at around US$400 for a small apartment, though most rentals are US$500 to $2,000 and up. The best way to find a rental is to ask around in person.

Camping: There are currently no campgrounds on Ambergris Caye, and camping, unless on your own land or on other private land with permission, is prohibited. Caye Caulker has a small private campground, and primitive camping is available on some outlying cayes, including Half Moon Caye.

Park/Playground •

Hotel Del Rio •
Caye Casa •
Seven Seas Hotel •
Casa Caracol •
The Tides •

Casa Pan Dulce Bakery •

Emerald Reef Suites •

• High School

Blue Tang Inn •
Paradise Villas •
The Phoenix •
Premium Wine •
Ecologic Divers •
Sunbreeze Suites •

• Barber Shop

Laguna Drive

Sandpiper St.

• San Pedro Market

Los Cocos •
Richie's •
Castillo's Hardware •
Fire & Police Station •

Belize Bank •
Pelican Property •

Caribena St.

Conch Shell Hotel •

Amigos del Mar Dive Shop •

San Carlos Pharmacy •
Reef Restaurant •

• Cocina Caramba
• D & E Frozen Custard
Footprints •
Javi Gift Store •
Lions Club •

• San Pedrano
• Tomas Hotel
• The Greenhouse
• Coconet
• Salty Dog

Cholo's Bar •
Lily's •
Mayan Princess •

• Coastal Xpress

Pelican Street

• Hardware
Island Plaza •

Hollywood Realty •
Ambergris Delight •

• Just For You Boutique

Fido's Courtyard / Belizean Arts •

Social Security •
Milo's Enterprises •
Papo's Art Gallery •
Warpoint •
St Francis Xavier Credit Union

Gift Shop •
• The Reef Radio
• C's Cellphones

Catholic Church •

Barrier Reef Drive (Front Street)

Ambergris Street

Heritage Bank •

Blue Moon •
Big Daddy's Disco •

Elvi's Kitchen •

• Island Vibes Boutique
• Martha's Hotel
Taxi Stand •
Jaguar Temple •

Grocery •

4 Sisters Plaza •

La Antorcha •
• Sea Turtle Gift Shop

Central Park •

Pescador Drive (Middle Street)

• Rum & Cigar House

Boledo Place •
Martha's Ice Factory •

Post Office •
Southwind Properties •
Alijua Building •

• Wood Carvers

Buccaneer Street

Casa Pan Dulce • Bakery

Estelle's •

Gecko Graphics •
• Lino's Meats
Amigo Travel •
Danny Boy Tours •
Rubimoon •

Marino's Bar •
Mash Enterprises •
Krystal Shipping •

Pier Lounge •
Spindrift Hotel •
Vero's Cafe •

Sunrise Realty •
• Graniel's Dreamworks
Jam-Bel Jerk •
Coral Beach Hotel
Black Coral Street

El Patio Tortillas •

Pupusa Food Stands •

Rock's •

Town Hall •

← Graniels

Loca Luna •

Nellie's
Laundromat

Holiday Hotel/Celi's •

Toucan Gift Shop •
San Pedro Sun •
Love Belize •
• Moondancer

Alliance Bank •

A & R •
Ecologic Divers •

• SeaDuced

Tarpon Street

Ruby's Hotel •
Searious Adventures •

Tackle Box Bar •

Ambergris Divers •

• Wild Mango's
• Belize Chocolate

Primary School •

Library •
Wood Carvers • • AquaDives

Esmaralda Lane

Caribbean Sea

N
NOT TO SCALE

San Pedro Town map: Not all restaurants and resorts shown

SAN PEDRO TOWN
(Listed from north to south. From Hotel Del Rio, Ocean Tides and Caye Casa, it is about a 10-minute walk along the beach to the main part of town.)

Hotel Del Rio. Boca Del Rio Drive, 501-226-2286; www.hoteldelriobelize.com. At this small seafront operation, you have the choice of several types of rooms and cabañas, some with thatched roofs. This is not a fancy resort, but it has personality some other places lack. In-season doubles are US$60 to $150, off-season US$50 to $130, plus 9% tax. Weekly rates are US$600 except at Christmas. Worth considering if you're watching your pennies and want a bit of thatch ambiance.

Ocean Tides Beach Resort. 57 Boca Del Rio Drive, 501-631-6863; www.tidesbeachresort.com. Formerly The Tides and started by well-known Sanpedrano divemaster Patojo Paz, this little resort has been upscaled and slightly expanded. It still focuses somewhat on divers, and you'll often see wet suits and dive gear hanging over the balcony. The three-story hotel has rooms and suites with pleasant furnishings. No restaurant, but several good ones are nearby, and there's a small beach bar and a pool. Rates range from around US$100 to US$275, plus tax, depending on the time of year and unit. Dive packages also available.

Caye Casa. Beachfront, San Pedro, 501-226-2880 or 888-480-4535 in U.S./Canada; www.cayecasa.com. Caye Casa, developed by the multi-talented Julie Babcock, is on the beachfront at the north end of town. Although there's some seagrass off the beach, swimming is good from the pier. The resort has three types of accommodations – rooms, casitas and deluxe one- and two-bedroom villas. Though modern, it has tropical colonial touches, such as thatch-roof porches. Rates in-season range from US$125 for a room to US$410 for a two-bedroom villa, off-season from US$110 to $350. Rates are plus a total of 15% tax and service charge.

Paradise Villas. Pescador Drive, San Pedro. Paradise Villas is an older but still attractive low-rise condo colony at the north end of town. The units, individually owned, are managed and rented by several different companies, plus several owners of one or two units. This can make it difficult to compare rates and accommodations. Choose from one-, two- and three-bedroom condos. Though units vary in furnishings and amenities, they are basically similar. There's an attractive seaside pool area, and a small artificial reef at the end of the pier (built by the condo owners) to attract fish for snorkeling. Rates vary slightly among the different agents, but most are in the range of US$125 to $275 in-season and US$100 to $235 off-season, plus tax. Rates are higher at Christmas. Among the companies offering rentals here are Paradise Villas in Belize (www.paradisevillasinbelize.com), Nellie Gomez (www.nelliesproperty.com) and Tradewinds Paradise Villas (www.tradewindsparadisevillas.com), which manages eight Paradise Villas units. You may also find units offered through Vacation Rentals By Owner (www.vrbo.com).

Blue Tang Inn. Sand Piper Street, 866-881-1020 in the U.S./Canada, 501-226-2326; www.bluetanginn.com. Blue Tang Inn, at the north end of town, is sometimes billed as a B&B, although we think inn describes it better. The 14 studio-type suites with kitchenettes in this three-story beachfront building are in good conditions, and there's a "cozy" swimming pool. There's also one small apartment. Rates US$129 to $229 off-season, US$155 to $255 in-season, plus 9% hotel tax. (For those who aren't divers, a Blue Tang is a colorful tropical fish seen around the barrier reef.)

The Phoenix. Barrier Reef Drive, San Pedro; 501-226-2083; www.thephoenixbelize.com. This beachfront condo resort is one of the best and most luxurious lodging spots on the island, if not in all of Belize. The winner of several "Best of" awards, The Phoenix is on the site of what used to be a retreat for Catholic nuns and later the location of the Paradise Hotel, one of classic old resorts on the island. The 30 condo units are absolutely gorgeous. The two-bedroom, two-bath units are around 1600 square feet, with deluxe kitchens, custom cabinets, closets and trim of Belizean hardwoods, broadband internet and all the upscale amenities. There also are one-bedroom and three-bedroom units. If you can, get a ground floor unit right on the beach. There are two swimming pools, and an upscale restaurant, Red Ginger. Rates are US$425 to US$675 in-season and US$350 to US$575 in low season, plus tax. No service charge is added. Highly recommended.

Conch Shell Inn. 11 Foreshore Street, San Pedro; 501-226-2062; www.ambergriscaye.com/conchshell/. This heart-of-town, beachfront two-story hotel is an option for money-conscious travelers who just want a clean, simple place to stay. There are fans but no air-conditioning in the 10 rooms. Second-floor rooms are probably a little cooler, as they catch the breeze off the sea, and quieter, too. Recently renovated. Rates US$74 to $94 double mid-November to mid-April, US$64 to $84 off-season, plus tax. Free wi-fi and mini-fridges.

Sanpedrano. Barrier Reef Drive, San Pedro; tel. 501-226-2054. Budget, six-room spot near but not on the water, located over a convenience store. Clean rooms starting at around US$35 with fan, US$45 with air-con, plus tax. Free wi-fi.

Mayan Princess. Barrier Reef Drive, San Pedro; 501-226-2778 or 800-250-6972 in U.S./Canada; www.mayanprincesshotel.com. This three-story, seafront condotel, painted a distinctive coral pink, has 23 large one-bedroom suites (king or queen beds) with air conditioning, kitchenettes, phones and cable TV. Rates are a good value at US$120 double off-season, US$155 in-season, plus 9% hotel tax and 10% service. Get 10% off if you book at least 90 days in advance. Dive packages available. Amigos del Mar dive shop is nearby. No pool, but each suite has a balcony with wonderful views of the sea, although swimming here, in the middle of town, isn't the best on the island. The atmosphere is comfortable and homey.

Hostel La Vista. Barrier Reef Drive, San Pedro, 501-627-0831; www.hostellavista.com. Right in the middle of things, across from Central Park and the sea, and next door to Jaguar nightclub, this purple hostel with green trim has space from around US$20 per person, plus tax. There's an eight-bed dorm, a six-bed dorm, some private rooms and a kitchen, plus space outside to lounge in a hammock. Free wi-fi and air conditioning. Before it opened as a hostel in late 2014, it was the old Sands Hotel, which was one of the early hotels on the island, dating from the 1970s.

Spindrift. Barrier Reef Drive, San Pedro, 501-226-2174; www.amberbriscaye.com/spindrift. This three-story concrete hotel won't win any awards for design, but it is on the water in the center of town, with reasonable rates. It has 20 rooms with A/C, four with fans and three one-bedroom apartments with kitchenettes. Caliente restaurant is on the first floor. Rates year-round around US$53 to $150 including tax and service.

Holiday Hotel. Barrier Reef Drive, San Pedro, 713-893-3825 in the U.S./Canada; www.sanpedroholiday.com. This was one of the first hotels on the island, opening with five rooms June 15, 1965. Built by Celi McCorkle, an island native and near-legend in the hospitality industry, the three-story Holiday Hotel has been well maintained and remains a pleasant spot convenient to most everything in town. All rooms have A/C and some have refrigerators. Island Divers Belize dive shop is located on the hotel's pier. Celi's Deli across the street and the Caprice Bar in the hotel are handy. Room rates: Off-season doubles are US$97 to $135, US$134-$212 in-season. Rates plus 9% tax and 6% service charge.

Ruby's. Barrier Reef Drive, San Pedro; 501-226-2063; www.rubyshotelbelize.com. This 23-room hotel at the south end of town is the favorite of many budget-oriented visitors. Rooms in the old wooden building section of the hotel, which opened in 1987, are basic but clean, some with shared baths; those on the street side can be a little noisy. Newer rooms, also basic, have private baths and most have air-conditioning. Some have sea views. Rates off-season range from around US$20 to $38 with fans, US$50 with air-conditioning; in-season, rates are US$22 to $42 for rooms with fans, US$65 with air. Get inexpensive breakfasts and light meals in the first-floor restaurant, Ruby's Deli, which opens early to catch the fishing crowd. The hotel is often full. Free wi-fi.

SOUTH EDGE OF TOWN/AIRSTRIP SOUTH:
(Listed from north to south, with those nearest town listed first.)

SunBreeze Beach Hotel. Coconut Drive (P.O. Box 14) San Pedro, 800-688-0191 or 501-226-2191; www.sunbreeze.net. The SunBreeze has a good location, just steps from the San Pedro airstrip (but you won't be bothered by airport noise) and within walking distance of most of what there is to do in town. SunBreeze has been upgraded and considerably improved. A number of the rooms have been refurbished. There's a freshwater pool, above ground but nice. The pool is just steps from the Blue Water Grill restaurant. Many other restaurants are within a few blocks. SunBreeze has 43 large rooms, configured in a two-story motel-style U-shape. Five of them are billed as "premier" with amenities such as Jacuzzi tubs. All have strong air conditioners, telephones, cable TV and tile floors. SunBreeze is directly on the water, with a dock and an independent dive shop, but there's a seawall and no real swimming beach. A good beach (all beaches in Belize are public) is at Ramon's nearby. The SunBreeze has some handicap-accessible rooms, uncommon in Belize. Rates for doubles, in-season, US$188 to $248; off-season, US$156-$215, plus 9% tax and 6% service. Discounts may occasionally be offered. The same Belize City-based company, Roe Group, also operates San Pedro's **SunBreeze Suites** (www.sunbreezesuites.com) north in town, with small suites from US$173 off-season and US$199 in-season, plus tax and 6% service. Roe also operates the Belize Biltmore Plaza in Belize City and Hidden Valley Inn in the Mountain Pine Ridge.

The Palms. Coconut Drive (P.O. Box 88), San Pedro, 501-226-3322; www.belizepalms.com. This three-story condotel on the water has a lot going for it: attractive and well-decorated condominium apartments plus a small casita near the pool, which is small and on the back side but surrounded by tropical greenery, a sandy beach and a convenient location at the south edge of town. Rates off-season: casita, US$170; one-bedroom condo, US$219; two-bedroom US$244 to $271; three-bedroom, US$349; in-season: casita, US$204; one-bedroom, US$259, two-bedroom, US$289 to $319; three-bedroom, $399. Rates are for up to four persons, except in the casita, which is for double occupancy, but do not include 9% hotel tax and 10% service charge. Three-night minimum stay required.

Ramon's Village. Coconut Drive, San Pedro, 800-624-4215 in the U.S./Canada or 501-226-2071; www.ramons.com. Anyone who has heard of San Pedro has probably heard of Ramon's Village, the creation of Ambergris native and pioneering hotel operator Ramon Nuñez. Now American-owned, over the years it grew from a small, moderately priced collection of thatched cabañas on the beach into a much larger group of multiunit buildings and individual cabañas, with more than 70 rooms, suites and cottages. In August 2013, much of Ramon's was destroyed in a fire, but it was rebuilt and quickly reopened for the Christmas 2013 season. Ramon's retains its sand-and-thatch ambiance, and the resort has one of the better beaches on the island. Certainly, the beach is the best in or near town, part of the hotel's 500-foot water frontage. A small artificial reef near the 420-foot pier brings fish to snorkelers. The pool is gorgeous. Ramon's has room service, free wi-fi, a popular bar and a so-so restaurant called Pineapple. It has a dive operation, which it says is the oldest in Belize, with two big dive boats and four skiffs. Lodging is divided into several categories, depending on location and size. All are air-conditioned. Across the street, not on the water, is a sister property, the Belizean Princess, with small cottages at lower rates. Ramon's location, just south of the airport, and a five-minute stroll from town is a draw, although street traffic in this area is active, to say the least. Ramon's does a first-rate job of marketing, especially to travel agents, and it enjoys one of the higher occupancy rates on the island. Rates vary depending on location and date. In-season, cabañas are US$180 to $295 double, and suites are US$345 to $510. Off-season rates are a few dollars less. Rates at the cottage colony annex across the street are US$155 double in-season, US$150 off. All rates are plus 9% tax and 10% service.

Corona Del Mar. Coconut Drive, San Pedro, 501-226-2055; www.coronadelmarhotel.com. This is a low-profile lodging spot, but regulars know it offers pleasant rooms, recently renovated apartments on the water, a penthouse suite and a cottage, at fairly moderate rates (although they have increased some with the renovations and additions). It now has a pool. Point of history: Corona del Mar was the first hotel on the island with an elevator. Off-season rates US$90 to $180 (US$250 for the penthouse, cottage US$180); in-season US$130 to $250 (penthouse US$350, cottage US$225), all plus tax and 6% service. As elsewhere on the island, rates are higher during the peak Christmas season. Friendly, homey place and one of the better values on the island.

Pedro's Hotel. Seagrape Drive, San Pedro, 501-226-3825 or 800-213-8347 from U.S./Canada; www.pedroshotel.com. This budget hotel south of town isn't on the beach, but it does offer affordable, even cheap (for San Pedro), accommodations. The 32 standard rooms start at US$50 off-season, and the 12 "deluxe" rooms start at US$70. Rates plus 9% hotel tax. All hotel rooms have A/C, free wi-fi and cable TV, and you have a choice of one king or two twin beds. On the grounds is a sports bar with pool table and projection TV. If you're looking for something cheaper, check out **Pedro's Inn Backpackers Hostel** (www.backpackersbelize.com) with 14 hostel-style rooms, each with two beds. Rates are US$12.50 per person, plus tax. The hotel has two small swimming pools, and guests have access to the nice beach at **Caribbean Villas,** a short hike away. The owner of Pedro's Hotel, the hostel and also Caribbean Villas, garrulous Englishman Peter Lawrence, claims Pedro's has the best pizza in Belize.

Changes in Latitudes B&B. 36 Coconut Drive, San Pedro, 501-226-2986; www.changesinlatitudesbelize.com. This small gay-friendly inn has six small but pleasant and very clean rooms on the first level, plus a suite upstairs sleeping up to six. The included breakfast is served from 7 to 11 a.m. Changes in Latitudes isn't directly on the water, but it's close, perhaps 150 feet away. The owners have redecorated all the rooms (all have private bath, A/C and fan.) Rates start at US$85 double off-season, US$125 in-season, plus hotel tax (no service charge). There's a minimum stay of three nights at most times, and five nights during peak holiday period from mid-December to mid-January.

Coral Bay Villas. Coconut Drive (P.O. Box 1), San Pedro, 501-226-3003 or 214-396-3218 in U.S.; www.coralbaybelize.com. This small condo resort has six one-bedroom beachfront suites in a white two-story concrete building with red tile roof. There's a new pool. Rates are US$135 double, off-season, US$175 in-season, plus tax. No service charge. Complimentary bikes and kayak.

Xanadu Island Resort. Coconut Drive, San Pedro, 501-226-2814 or 866-351-4752 in U.S./Canada; www.xanaduislandresort.com. Xanadu, located about 1 mile south of San Pedro, bills itself as the "world's first monolithic dome resort," a description that might sound good to an engineer but doesn't exactly get our poetic juices flowing. Happily, the resort's five monolithic domes look much nicer than they sound. The building process is costly, but the result is a masonry dome with foam insulation that, according to the resort, can withstand winds of up to 300 mph. The domes are covered with thatch palapa roofs, giving them a tropical look. Inside, the 20 condo suites (studio lofts, one-, two-, and three-bedroom) are attractively furnished in earth tone colors, with central air-conditioning, fans, phones, free wi-fi and cable TV. You get the use of bikes and kayaks gratis. Jet skis, small sailboats, windsurfers and kite boards, plus golf carts, can be rented on-site. There's a nice stretch of seaside sand (though with a seawall), a 350-foot pier and an attractive freshwater swimming pool, with lush landscaping. The resort has no restaurant, but there's a snack bar, and for self-catering a small grocery is just outside the resort. Several restaurants also are nearby. Xanadu consistently is rated on TripAdvisor and other social media sites as one of the top resorts on Ambergris Caye. Rates range from US$220 (studio) to $650 (three-bedroom beachfront) in-season and US$180 to $545 May to mid-December, plus hotel tax and service. Rates higher at Christmas and Easter periods.

Caribbean Villas. Coconut Drive, San Pedro, 501-226-2715 or 800-213-8347 in U.S.; www.caribbeanvillashotel.com. The folks who originally built and ran this place for many years, Wil and Susan Lala, sold out in 2004, and new management added a beach bar and swimming pool. Later, the owner of Pedro's Hotel, Peter Lawrence, took over Caribbean Villas. The resort has a variety of accommodations, pleasant but not deluxe, in the two-level whitewashed buildings with tile roofs, from small studios to two-bedroom suites. You'll enjoy the nice beach area and pier, with a little artificial reef for snorkeling. The open-air bar near the water serves booze and pretty good food. Rooms are air-conditioned, with phones and TVs. There's free wi-fi, but it may not reach inside all rooms. Rates are a good value, considering San Pedro prices, at US$135 to $245 year-round, higher at holidays. Three-night minimum, with seven-night minimum at holiday periods. All rates plus tax (no service charge). There's also an all-inclusive option, with all meals, local beers, rum and other drinks, for US$99 per person per day. (With all the great restaurants on the island, we wouldn't go for this option). In 2015, Caribbean Villas hosted the first gay pride week on Ambergris Caye.

SOUTH END:
(This area begins about a mile south of town. Properties are listed from north to south, with those nearest town listed first.)
Villas at Banyan Bay. Sea Grape Drive (P.O. Box 266), San Pedro, 866-352-1163 or 501-226-3739; www.banyanbay.com. At this 42-unit condotel, you have all the pleasures of home ... if your home happens to be just steps from the Caribbean. Many of the guests here appear to be families, taking advantage of the big two- and three-bedroom units. The kids love the large, three-tiered pool, and dad and mom go for the fully equipped kitchen and the whirlpool off the master bedroom. The beach here, Mar de Tumbo, less than a mile and a half south of town, is one of the best on the island, although as most beaches in Belize, it does have some seagrass. There's a dive shop, Belize Pro Dive, on the pier. The food at Rico's Restaurant on-site doesn't always knock us out, but service is good, and it has a beautiful setting on the water for drinks or dinner; breakfast is handy and well done. Overall, we're impressed by the high degree of maintenance. The apartments look almost as good now as when they were built years ago. The woodwork and cabinets are mahogany. The cathedral ceilings in the main living area sport a stunning array of tropical hardwoods. Some units here were sold as timeshares, before the resort was taken over by its lender during the Great Recession. Rack rates: US$275-$475 for a two-bedroom condo in-season, depending on location and number of people, and US$250 to $350 in the summer. For a three-bedroom beachfront unit,

for up to six people, you'll pay US$675 in-season, US$550 off. Discounts may be available.

Grand Colony Villas. Sea Grape Drive, San Pedro, 501-226-4270 or 866-620-9521 from U.S./Canada; www.grandcolonyvillas.com. Built in 2005, the Grand Colony Villas are among the most upscale – and expensive – condotel units on the island. The 15 large two- and three-bedroom villas have 10-foot ceilings, marble and hardwood floors, mahogany doors and cabinets and deluxe furnishings. There is also a three-bedroom presidential suite. Rates: US$599 to $899 in-season and US$499 to $799 off-season, higher during holidays, plus 9% tax, for up to four persons in the two-bedroom units and up to six in the three-bedrooms. The rates include wi-fi, use of bikes, paddleboards and kayaks. The beach here is one of the best on the island.

Banana Beach. Coconut Drive, San Pedro; 501-226-3890, 877-288-1011 in U.S. and Canada; www.bananabeach.com. This older South End resort has affordable rooms and one- to four-bedroom suites with kitchens, two swimming pools and a setting just steps from the sea and Mar de Tumbo beach (however, there's a low seawall directly in front of the hotel, and the usual seagrass). The 35 original one-bedroom units are in a single three-story building, designed in a style similar to Mexican hotels, around a courtyard with pool. These units and indeed much of the resort are overdue for a facelift. A three-story addition, which went up in 2002, has a variety of "expandable" suites, regular rooms and also some one-bedroom efficiencies. There is an air-conditioned restaurant, El Divino, featuring steaks and martinis and excellent ceviche. The hotel's tour office, Monkey Business, can set you up with tours, cart rentals and diving. Off-season, they start at US$95 double for a room or US$120 for a courtyard suite, US$145 for a seafront one-bedroom suite and top out at US$430 for a four-bedroom seafront suite. In high season, rates range for US$110 to $495. All rates are plus 9% tax and 6% service and include continental breakfast.

Mata Rocks. 45 Coconut Drive, San Pedro; 888-628-2757 or 501-226-2336; www.matarocks.com. Mata Rocks is a small, long-established beachfront hotel with 17 rooms and junior suites, comfortable rather than deluxe, just south of Banana Beach hotel. With its white stucco and wood exterior, Mata Rocks has a relaxed, laid-back atmosphere. The little thatch Squirrel's Nest beach bar often hops, however, and if you want to pop into town, about 1½ miles away, bikes are complimentary. All units have A/C and little fridges, and the junior suites have kitchenettes. There's a small pool. In-season, doubles are US$155 to $180 for rooms and US$205 to $220 for junior suites. Summer rates range from US$120 to $180, with some discounts offered. Rates are plus tax and include continental breakfast.

Victoria House. Coconut Drive (P.O. Box 22), San Pedro, 800-247-5159 or 713-344-2340; www.victoria-house.com. If what you want is an upscale but not stuffy resort vacation, Victoria House is just about perfect. About 2 miles south of town, Victoria House is a quiet hideaway on 19 acres, with a variety of accommodations ranging from comfy motel-like rooms in two buildings at the back of the resort to rooms and suites in the main lodge to thatch casitas to deluxe villas and gorgeous condos. There has been lots of remodeling and upgrading in recent years, including adding a second fabulous main pool, along with a group of condo villas at the south edge of the resort. These condo villas are our pick for some of the most beautiful beach accommodations in Belize. The hotel's restaurant, Palmilla, remains an asset. A full meal plan is US$75 per person per day, but many guests prefer not to be locked into a meal plan and dine around the island. Admiral Nelson's, the freestanding bar cabaña on the beach, is ideal for sipping rum drinks or Belikins. Head to the lovely sandy beach area for relaxing, or swim off the pier. The hotel also has a gift shop and a dive operation. A spa is opening in 2016. With its long-time management team, service is top-notch everywhere at this resort. Victoria House is a popular place to get married, and the hotel has honeymoon packages. Rack rates for rooms in-season, December-May, US$199 to $335, suites US$375 to $545; villas, condos and houses, US$650 to $1975, all plus 9% tax and 10% service. Prices are a little lower off-season and higher during holiday periods. Highly recommended.

Royal Caribbean Resort. Coconut Drive, San Pedro, 501-226-4220; www.royalcaribbeanbelize.com. The little yellow cabins lined up in rows at Royal Caribbean, which opened in 2005, remind some people of army barracks. However, the cabins are fairly spacious, with tile floors, wicker furniture, and kitchenettes, and all have cable TV and air conditioning. There's a pool, beach bar that serves some food and 300 feet of beach. Prices are US$140 to $175 double off-season and US$150 to $185 in-season. All rates plus tax.

Athen's Gate. South Coconut Drive, San Pedro, 501-226-4151, 713-609-9457 in U.S.; www.athensgatebelize.com. Athens Gate, which features some Greek design flourishes, has 12 two- and three-bedroom luxury condo units in four-story buildings (and there is no elevator!) There's an infinity swimming pool with waterfall, and the condo has 100 feet of beachfront. Rates for two bedroom units are US$375 to $450, and for three-bedroom US$500 to $575, but currently in-season rates are discounted 30% and off-season 40% off. Rates are plus tax, but service charge is not added. "Tipping is up to you." Neither Athens Gate nor Pelican Reef Villas nearby has an on-site restaurant, but there are several places to eat nearby.

Pelican Reef Villas Resort. South Coconut Drive, San Pedro, 501-226-4352, 281-394-3739 in U.S.; www.pelicanreefvillas.com. While listening to the pool's tinkling waterfall, it is easy to believe you've stumbled upon a hidden tropical treasure, when really the faux cave is a swim-up bar and Pelican Reef is 3 miles south of San Pedro's bustle. This condotel is one of the most popular on the island, despite relative spendy rates. Service here is top-notch, and the resort has won a number of "best of" awards. Large alabaster buildings with butter-yellow trim house the 24 two-bedroom (US$289 to $549 in-season, plus 9% tax and 6% service) and three-bedroom (US$449 to $699 in-season for up to six people, plus 15% tax and service) suites. Rates are lower off-season (May-mid-December). The resort sometimes offers discounts, with rates for two-bedroom units as low as US$175 plus tax and service, off-season. Tastefully decorated, with fully equipped kitchens, mahogany cabinets, granite countertops and plush sleigh-beds, the villa suites are gorgeous, and the oceanfront views are stunning. The same owners developed Athens Gate nearby. Recommended.

Hol Chan Reef Resort & Villas. South Coconut Drive, 3½ miles south of San Pedro, 501-661-7712 or 866-955-4433 in U.S./Canada; www.holchanreefresortvillas.com. This new condotel, about 3½ miles south of town, currently is the resort that is at the far south end of major hotel development on the island. It is located just south of Pelican Reef Villas. The road south is paved to around Victoria House but currently is packed sand after that. A taxi from here to town will run you US$10 to $15 or so, or you can rent a golf cart and drive it in about 15 minutes, or take a water taxi to town. However, several restaurants and a convenience store are within walking distance (the resort has a bar but not a full-service restaurant). Hol Chan has beautifully furnished and decorated 1,200 square feet two-bedroom and 1,800 to 2,400 square feet three-bedroom apartments. The two-bedroom units, sleeping four, are US$325 in-season, US$250 off-season; three-bedroom units, sleeping six to eight, are US$399 to $499 in-season and US$325 to $399 off-season. Rates plus tax and service. Condo villas have fully equipped kitchens including granite countertops, mahogany cabinets and stainless steel appliances. The complex has elevators, and guests get the use of a pre-paid cell phone. There's a large pool and a nice beach, although the water here is shallow. Not all units have sea views. In 2016, construction was still under way on new units.

NORTH AMBERGRIS ABOVE BRIDGE

These hotels are all north of the river channel and the bridge. With the paving of much of the former cart path to the north, it's much easier to go by golf cart or by taxi to resorts on North Ambergris. Within the immediate future, the golf cart path is supposed to be paved to about 7 miles north of the bridge and eventually some 11 miles north of the middle of town. Many people, however, still take a boat or the scheduled water taxi Coastal Xpress.

(Hotels are listed south to north, with those nearest town listed first.)

Grand Caribe Suites and Residences. Tres Cocos, North Ambergris, 501-226-4726 or 800-488-5903; www.grandcaribebelize.com. Tim Jeffers' latest project on the island is a winner! Set in an arc on a 5-acre beachfront site about 2 miles north of town, Grand Caribe's 72 luxury condos, in eight four-story, red-tiled-roof clusters, plus a large villa, all face the sea and a fine stretch of sandy beach. Grand Caribe debuted in 2008, with additional units finished over the next several years. It has since won several awards as one of the top resorts in Belize. The one, two-, three- and four-bedroom suites, for two to eight people (US$449 to $1,049 in-season, US$379-$1,049 off-season, plus 9% hotel tax and 10% service/resort fee). If you stay at least four days, or a week or longer, there are significant rate drops. The suites have Brazilian floor tiles, kitchens with granite countertops and mahogany cabinets and high-quality furnishings. Some units have elevator access. There's also a five-bedroom beachfront villa, for up to 10 people. The regular rate for that villa is US$20,000 a week plus 19% fees and taxes. Whew! Resort amenities include a restaurant, Rain, with indoor and rooftop dining, room service, concierge service, a new grocery, Beach Basket, free wi-fi, five swimming pools, pool bar and a fitness room. The resort's windsports shop rents aquatic sports equipment to guests and the public. An unusual feature of Grande Caribe is the long, curving pier with berths for a number of boats. Highly recommended.

White Sands Cove Resort. North Ambergris (P.O. Box 192, San Pedro), 602-733-1322 or 501-226-3528; www.whitesandscove.com. This little colony, about 2 miles from town, was closed to visitors for a time but has reopened. Those who want to be within a short bike or taxi ride to town, but a bit away from the hustle and bustle, seem to like it. The 14 units go for from US$116 to $395 a night, depending on time of year and size and location of unit. There's a pool.

Ak'bol Yoga Retreat & Eco-Resort. North Ambergris, 501-226-2073; www.akbol.com. This hip little resort has seven simple thatch cabañas (US$145-$165 in-season, US$10-$120, plus 9% tax and 6% service), some with sea views, around a natural stone swimming pool. You'll love the outdoor showers in the cabañas. On the lagoon side is a three-story building with 30 single rooms with shared baths for those attending yoga retreats. Rates for these rooms start at US$50 double, year-round, plus 15% tax and service. Daily group yoga lessons, open to the public, are US$15 per session. Private lessons are US$75. Ak'bol regularly holds yoga retreats with visiting masters. Soul Kitchen, the restaurant, serves local foods such as salbutes, panades, and pupusas at modest prices, and it also offers pizzas and vegetarian dishes.

Cocotal Inn & Cabanas. North Ambergris, about 2½ miles north of the center of town, 501-226-2097; www.cocotalbelize.com. Looking for small, comfy, affordable spot on the beach? Cocotal could be it. There are only six units - four cottages and two suites in the main house. Our favorite is the casita, with vaulted hardwood ceiling and a four-poster queen bed. It's closest to the beach and also overlooks the pool. All have fully equipped kitchens, so you can cook your own meals, or hop on one of the complimentary bikes and ride to a nearby restaurant. If you're thirsty, there's a beer and soft drink honor bar. Kayaks also available at no charge. The helpful owners are on-site. Rates are US$150 to $260 in-season, US$115 to $200 off. All rates plus 9% tax.

El Pescador. North Ambergris (P.O. Box 17, San Pedro), 501-226-2398 or 804-661-2259; www.elpescador.com. Since 1974, El Pescador has been the island's leading fishing lodge. Today, it's bigger and more upmarket than it used to be, with three pools, upscale villas and other resort amenities, but it's still devoted to anglers and angling. After fishing for tarpon, bonefish, permit and jacks, you can enjoy a fine meal, served family style in the dining room, or enjoy a drink and a cigar on the verandah. The lodge has 14 comfortable units, recently redone, in a rambling two-story colonial-style building with lots of mahogany. Adjoining the lodge are newer three-bedroom villas, and these are deluxe, with prices to match. Most can be divided and reserved as either one- or two-bedroom units. Nightly rates for rooms are US$275 in-season and US$185 off-season; villas are US$400 to $850 per night depending on the number of bedrooms in-season, US$280 to $595 off. Rates plus 9%, with a three-night minimum, and meals are extra. El Pescador offers all-inclusive fishing packages, which include guide, boat, transfer from Belize City, local drinks, all meals and taxes, but there also are dive and resort packages. Fishing packages start at US$1,895 per person for three nights with two days of fishing (two persons per room and two per boat) and range up to over US$5,915 per person for a week (one person in a room and one per boat.)

Seascape Villas. North Ambergris, 501-226-2119 or 888-753-5164; www.seascapebelize.com. This collection of villas on four beachfront acres 3½ miles north of town, built by noted island developers Bob and Diane Campbell, opened in 2006. Villas have sunken living rooms, slate floors, outdoor garden with hot tub and unobstructed views of the sea. Four rental villas are privately owned but available for rent when the owners aren't in residence. In-season, expect to pay around US$550 to $975 per day for up to six people, and US$459 to $559 off-season, plus tax.

Coco Beach Resort. North Ambergris (P.O. Box 1, San Pedro), 844-360-1553 or 501-226-4297; www.cocobeachresort.com. This is the newer, more upscale sister resort to Belizean Shores *(see below)*. It's about 3½ miles north of town. Coco Beach has deluxe one- and two-bedroom suites, plus penthouse suites and casitas. On-site is the Cocoblanca Restaurant. In-season rates are around US$280 to $850, plus tax, off-season rates lower. Discounts from rack rates are frequently offered.

Belizean Shores. North Ambergris (P.O. Box 1, San Pedro), 844-360-1553 or 501-226-2355; www.belizeanshores.com. Belizean Shores is an older but still popular condotel, developed by the same company that did the newer Coco Beach Resort nearby. It offers good rates and a lot of space in the units. The pool is a beaut, with a swim-up bar, and huge. The beach is small but fairly nice. There's a 350-foot pier, a tennis court (a rarity in Belize), basketball court and a dive shop. The resort has a restaurant. Rates US$275 to $325 in-season, lower off-season, plus tax. Discounts frequently offered.

Las Terrazas Resort & Residences. North Ambergris, 4 miles north of town; 800-447-1553 in U.S./Canada, 713-780-1233 or 501-226-4249; www.lasterrazasbelize.com. Las Terrazas, which opened in late 2007, is a luxury 37-unit, three-level condominium resort with one-, two- and three-bedroom suites. Rates are US$300 to $600+ in-season, plus tax and service, depending on the unit and number of people; lower rates off-season. The condos have 9-foot ceilings, travertine tile floors, fully equipped kitchens with Brazilian granite countertops, and all the amenities including cable TV and wi-fi. A two-level pier sweeps out into the sea. O Restaurant is at the resort, but other restaurants are not far away. White Sands Dive Shop in on-site.

Azul Resort. North Ambergris, 501-226-4012; www.azulbelize.com. Azul has only two beach villas, but, man, they are nice. The two-level villas have 20-foot ceilings with beams of mylady wood. Custom kitchens feature Viking appliances, and the cabinets and most of the furniture are made of zericote wood. Each villa has a 50-inch plasma flat-screen TV and Bose theater system. On the rooftop, you can relax in your own hot tub. The two beach houses share a beautiful pool, 400 feet of beach, and about 11 acres of prime property. Rates start at US$550 a day double, plus tax. Rojo Beach Bar is next door for drinks in a romantic beachside setting and some of the best food on the island. Some more changes at Rojo may be coming, but Matachica and its bar and restaurant are literally steps away.

Matachica Resort & Spa. North Ambergris, 501-220-5010; www.matachica.com. When it opened in 1997 about 5 miles north of San

Pedro, Matachica raised the bar on what constituted deluxe lodging on Ambergris Caye. Matachica's original owners designed this resort to the hilt. Each of the cabañas had a fruit theme -- mango, watermelon, banana and so on -- a theme that began with the exterior color and was carried through down to the tiles in the baths. It all might have been a little much for some, but others said the colors reminded them of Gauguin. New owners (who also bought the former Five Sisters lodge in the Mountain Pine Ridge) made some much-needed renovations, added a pool and new cabañas. The resort now has 30 one-bedroom and one two-bedroom cabañas. The beach here is postcard lovely though swimming isn't that great. We recommend the beachfront units, if available. They get a breeze and sometimes the A/C in the back units can't keep up due to the high thatch roofs. If a spa is your thing, Matachica has the Jade Spa & Gym. Mambo, the hotel's expensive restaurant, offers an eclectic menu, albeit emphasizing seafood. It's definitely a romantic spot for dinner. Doubles US$275 to US$625 in-season and US$225 to $495 off-season, plus tax and service. Package rates also available. No children under 14.

Portofino. North Ambergris (P.O. Box 36, San Pedro), 501-220-5096 or 800-813-7880; www.portofinobelize.com. One of Portofino's drawing cards is that it has thatch cabañas, fairly rare on the island. The resort, which opened in 2001 on the site of an old resort, the Green Parrot, has lushly landscaped grounds, a restaurant, dive shop, thatch units including beach cabañas, tree house suites, beachfront suites, honeymoon suite with whirlpool and a four-bedroom villa. Rooms have A/C, wi-fi, mini-fridge and cable TV. There's a circular swimming pool. Complimentary kayaks and free boat transfers to town, about 6 miles away. Rates: US$310 to $450 double in high season, US$280 to $380 in low, plus taxes and 10% service charge.

X'Tan Ha. North Ambergris, 844-360-1553 or 501-226-2846; www.xtanha.com. Formerly the Belize Legacy condotel, which closed during the Great Recession, X'Tan Ha (pronounced ISH-tan-HA) has been reborn as a small resort a little over 7 miles north of town. Just offshore is Mexico Rocks, one of the most popular snorkeling spots around Ambergris. X'Tan Ha has one-bedroom units with kitchens. Kayaks, paddleboards and a water trampoline are comped. There's a restaurant, Temple Run Tavern. The burger – one of the best on the island -- and fries meal is around US$15 while fish dishes are US$25 at dinner. A good beach bar, Katanga, is on the water. Two pools. Rack rates start at around US$275 in-season plus tax but often are discounted.

La Beliza Resort. North Ambergris Caye, 786-472-9664; www.vivabelize.com/la-beliza/. About 8 miles north of San Pedro Town, this was originally called Blue Reef, which opened in 2005 with construction continuing in 2006-2007. La Beliza is now part of a group of about a half dozen properties under one umbrella in Belize, including Jaguar Reef and Almond Beach in Hopkins and Sleeping Giant Rainforest Lodge and part of Ian Anderson's Caves Branch on the Hummingbird Highway, among others. La Beliza has 18 one- and two-bedroom condo units. The apartments are attractive, with granite tile floors and 10-foot ceilings, and all have sea views. The swimming pool also overlooks the water. La Beliza has no restaurant, but staff will cook meals for you and deliver to your condo. There's little within easy walking distance, so for company you'll have to try biking or carting south or depend on the hotel's boat or the Coastal Xpress water taxi, a 25-minute ride each way. This is one of the last stops north for the water taxi, which does make stops at resorts on the way to town. Coastal Xpress has weekly passes. "Soon come" the golf cart path up North Ambergris will be paved all the way to this resort. Year-round rack rates at La Belize are US$340 to $499, plus 9% hotel tax and service, but significant discounts are frequently offered, often bringing the real rate down by US$100 to $200 or more per night.

Sapphire Beach Resort. North Ambergris Caye, 501-671-2552 or 866-290-6342 in U.S./Canada' www.sapphirebeachbelize.com. Located about 10 miles north of San Pedro, Sapphire Beach Resort is another of the fairly remote resorts that have opened at the far north on Ambergris Caye. It is accessible by Coastal Xpress water taxi (tip: if you want to go into town regularly, it may pay to buy a weekly pass, around US$135 per person), but it's a 30-minute boat ride each way, sometimes longer. This development was built as condos and casitas for sale (there was controversy early on) and as of this writing more units are being constructed. One-bedroom units start at around US$150,000 and other flats go up to around US$400,000. Rental rates range from around US$200 to $450 in-season and US$375 off-season, depending on number of bedrooms and location. Higher rates at Christmas. Rates are plus 9% hotel tax and 5% service charge. There's a minimum stay of three nights in the off-season, five nights in-season and seven nights at Christmas. The development has a nice white sand beach and a swimming pools. It's about a 15-minute paddle out to the reef.

El Secreto. North Ambergris Caye, 501-236-5111 or 800-479-5037 in U.S.; www.elsecretobelize.com. Located about 11 miles north of San Pedro, El Secreto, like the other resorts in this area, is relatively isolated. The 11 thatched cabañas are expensive, and it is time-consuming to get to other resorts or restaurants or into town. For the money El Secreto charges and the ratings its gets, you may want also to look at other options. However, some people report they have enjoyed their stays here. The resort is beautifully designed, and it does some steep discounting, even in-season, to attract guests. With discounts, in-season you may be able to get a villa for around US$400 a night including taxes and service, subject to minimum-stay requirements.

Tranquility Bay. North Ambergris, in Bacalar Chico Marine Reserve, 501-236-5880; www.tranquilitybayresort.com. You're really, really away from things at Tranquility Bay, about 10 miles and a 35-minute boat ride from San Pedro Town. It's too far to go to town by the cart path, and the Coastal Xpress water taxi doesn't schedule stops this far north, so you have to depend on the resort's little boats. The good news is a new management team is making some improvements and upgrades, the restaurant is pretty good and that this far north you are closer to the barrier reef than at other resorts on the island. The reef is about 250 yards offshore, within swimming or kayaking distance if you're comfortable in the sea. You're also close to nature, as Tranquility is the only resort in the Bacalar Chico reserve. The one-bedroom cabañas are US$290 double in-season, $210 off, Also available are two-bedroom units (US$340 to $370 in-season, $268 to $307 off.) A budget room is US$170 in winter, US$135 May to mid-December. Rates are plus 9% tax and 10% service and include breakfast. All lodging is air-conditioned and has kitchenettes, but there are no TVs.

AMBERGRIS CAYE DINING

Ambergris Caye has Belize's widest selection of restaurants, ranging from inexpensive local spots and pizza joints to a couple that will have you reaching for your Platinum Amex. The emphasis is on seafood, of course, but many restaurants also serve chicken and pork, and even steak. Lobster is usually the most expensive item on the menu (in-season mid-June to mid-February), at around US$20 to $35. Pasta and Mexican-style dishes also are popular. After all that pricey seafood, an honest plate of Belizean beans and rice will taste real good.

Vegetarians can get by okay in San Pedro, even if you don't eat seafood. Rice and beans are ubiquitous (but often these are seasoned with lard or meat). Many Mexican places do up vegetarian burritos, and of course pizza is available at many spots. Fruit plates, with mangos, pineapple, watermelon and other local fruits, are a part of breakfast at a lot of places. Many restaurants will do vegetarian versions of their specialties – just ask.

Dress on the island is very casual. Even at the spiffiest places, tee shirt and shorts are okay, although some guests at the top restaurants will wear casual resort clothes – a light summer dress or a golf shirt with khakis. Socks optional.

Reservations are usually not necessary, except where noted. During the season, at popular dining spots you may have to wait a few minutes, or longer. Grab a Belikin and relax while you wait.

Keep in mind that small restaurants on a resort island can change overnight, with the loss of a cook or a setback in the personal life of the owner. Always ask locally if the restaurant you're thinking about is still good.

Restaurants are listed alphabetically.

Price ranges shown are for typical meals for one (usually dinner), not including tip, tax or alcoholic drinks. Price ranges:

Inexpensive: Under US$7
Moderate: US$8-$19
Expensive: US$20-$39
Very Expensive: Over US$40

IN TOWN OR NEARBY

Belize Chocolate Company. Barrier Reef Drive, 501-226-3015. Located next to Wild Mango's at the south end of town, Belize Chocolate Company makes it own chocolates from Belizean cacao. There are Kakow chocolate bars to go and chocolate cheesecake and chocolate coffee to eat in. Currently open from 3 to around 9:30 p.m. Closed Monday and Tuesday. Inexpensive to Moderate.

Blue Water Grill. At SunBreeze Hotel, Coconut Drive, 501-226-3347. Blue Water Grill aims high, and usually hits the spot. Try the mixed seafood grill or the local snapper dusted in cumin. The crispy Coconut Shrimp is always a winner. Many dishes are Asian-influenced. Tuesdays and Thursdays sushi is offered. Blue Water is often jammed, so in-season you may be in for a wait. Open for lunch and dinner daily. Expensive/Very Expensive.

Cocina Caramba. Pescador Drive, 501-603-1652. Owner Rene Reyes made a big success out of Caramba by simply serving good food in large portions at moderate prices. This spot is usually packed. Just about all of the seafood and Mexican dishes are tasty and well-prepared. Open for lunch and dinner. Closed Wednesday. Moderate.

Caliente. Spindrift Hotel, Barrier Reef Drive. This restaurant gets attention for its spicy versions of traditional favorites such as conch ceviche, its big variety of seafood and Mexican dishes and for its delicious soups. Locally popular for lunch, and open for dinner, too. Moderate/Expensive.

Caroline's Cookin'. Coconut Drive, beside airport, 501-226-3188. Great spot for breakfast, but jerk dishes, conch fritters, burritos and pork chops are good for lunch or dinner. Open for breakfast, lunch and dinner. Moderate.

Coconut Café, Coconut Drive, 501-226-4311. Casual spot on the beach at Exotic Caye with breakfast menu of pancakes, burritos, banana bread and eggs served all day. Also pizza and wraps. Open for breakfast and lunch. Most items under US$12. Closed Wednesday. Moderate.

DandE's Frozen Custard. Pescador Drive next to Cocina Caramba, 501-608-9100. Dan and Eileen (DandE, get it?) Jamison, who used to run the local weekly paper, the *San Pedro Sun*, now operate this custard and sorbet shop. For something with an island flavor, try the mango sorbet or the soursop frozen custard. Now open evenings only. Closed Tuesday. Inexpensive. Cash only.

El Fogón. 2 Trigger Fish Street, 501-206-2121. A fogón is an open-hearth grill that harkens back to the old Belize. El Fogón cooks Creole and Mestizo favorites that Belizeans love, and you will, too. It's family-run and a good value, especially at lunch. Dinner, focusing on seafood, is more expensive. Open for lunch and dinner daily except Sunday. Moderate.

Elvi's Kitchen. Pescador Drive, 501-226-2404. Yes, it's a little touristy, and, yes, it's a little more expensive than some, but Elvi's still does a fine job with fish and just about everything. Doña Elvia Staines began her restaurant as a take-out burger stand in 1974. It has grown in fame and fortune year after year, until today it is one of the best-known restaurants in Belize. There are still beefburgers on the lunch menu along with shrimp and fish burger versions. At dinner, you choose from large selection of seafood, chicken and other dishes, and almost all of it is good, with prices mostly under US$20 for entrees. The sand floor and the frangipani tree (now dead) around which the main dining room is built add atmosphere. Open for lunch and dinner. Closed Sunday. Moderate/Expensive.

Estel's-by-the-Sea. Barrier Reef Drive, 501-226- 2019. Charlie and Estella Worthington run this little seaside restaurant near Central Park. With its sand floor this place can legitimately boast of real island atmosphere. It's a favorite spot for breakfast, with all the usual egg-and-bacon basics including fried potatoes, but you'll also enjoy the burritos and *huevos rancheros*. The menu is on a board inside. Estel's may have the best Bloody Marys on the island. There's a good barbecue on Sunday. Opens early. Moderate. Cash only.

Fido's. Barrier Reef Drive, 501-226-3714. (Pronounced FEE-doh's.) Extremely popular, centrally located spot for a beer and a bite. Sit under the big palapa by the sea and enjoy burgers, fish and chips or lobster burrito. Live music many nights. Moderate.

Neri's Taco Place. Chicken Street. New to San Pedro, Neri's is popular for its cheap and delicious local food. You order at a window and if there's space eat at a picnic table outside. A little hard to find, it's one street back of El Fogón just north of the airport. Open for breakfast and dinner (breakfast only on Sundays.) Inexpensive.

Palapa Bar & Grill. San Pedro. If you were going to invent the platonic Caribbean bar on the beach, the original Palapa Bar & Grill in the Tres Cocos area of North Ambergris, which went strong for 20 years, might have been it, a thatch-roof two-level not on the sandy beach but at the end of a pier jutting out into the sea. Due to a change of ownership of the land and the loss of the lease, the original Palapa Bar moved in late 2015 to a location in San Pedro, at the end of the former Wet Willy's pier at the north end of town. The food is still mostly just bar stuff, burgers and BBQ wings and fish platters, but the beer is cold and the drinks are not very expensive. As of this writing, the old Palapa Bar is still open on North Ambergris, but changed somewhat in appearance. Confused yet? Stay tuned. Moderate to Very Expensive (depending on how much you drink.)

Red Ginger. Barrier Reef Drive, at The Phoenix, 501-226-4623. With its stylishly minimalist décor, this restaurant could be in L.A., but it's actually at The Phoenix resort at the north end of San Pedro. No sea views here. You gaze at deep red and rich cream walls, with brown earth-toned accents, and tropical wild ginger plants in glass vases. The specialty is seafood. The service is a notch above most other places in San Pedro. Expensive/Very Expensive.

The Reef. Pescador Drive, 501-226-3212. This old local favorite serves tasty Belizean fare such as stew chicken with rice and beans in large portions at small prices. Open for lunch and dinner. At lunch, there's a daily special for a few dollahs. Inexpensive to Moderate.

Ruby's. Barrier Reef Drive, 501-226-2063. If you can't sleep or are heading out for a day of fishing, get up early and grab a casual breakfast at Ruby's. For a few bucks, you can enjoy coffee, burritos and the best coconut tarts on the island. Later in the day, there are sandwiches and daily specials. It starts serving before 5 a.m., and stays open until late afternoon. Closed Sunday. Inexpensive.

Wild Mango's. Barrier Reef Drive, 501-226-2859. Award-winning chef Amy Knox brought her "New Wave Latin" cooking to this little spot at the south edge of town, on the water. Ms. Knox quickly made Wild Mango's one of the top restaurants on the island. One of the specialties is a ceviche sampler. Knox also delivers some great Mexican dishes and, of course, seafood. The snapper is particularly good. Open for lunch and dinner. Closed Sunday. Moderate/Expensive.

Other good places to eat, for not a lot of money, in town include **Melt Cafe, Lick's Beachside Café, Latitudes Café. My Secret Deli** on Caribena Street is known for its local food. A couple of Salvadoran *pupuserias* in the center of town, **Pupuseria Salvadoreno** and **Waraguma,** are very popular. *Pupusas* at these places are served only in the evening.

Controversial clock town in San Pedro's Barrier Reef Drive
Leonard Zhukovsky/Shutterstock

Street vendors in San Pedro offer food that is cheap, good and safe to eat. You can get a whole plate full of delicious food for a few bucks. Don't worry – it won't upset your tummy. Also don't miss the Lions Club barbecue on Friday night. The barbecue is great and the flan is out of this world. The money also goes to a good cause – improved health care on the island. Inexpensive/Moderate.

SOUTH OF TOWN

Antojitos San Telmo. Coconut Drive, 501-226-4575. It's just a joint, but a good joint, with snacks like tacos and burritos for almost nothing. Good service, too. Open for breakfast and lunch (closes at 3 p.m.) Inexpensive. **Robin's Kitchen** a bit farther south is another good local place.

The Baker. Sea Grape Drive, 501-629-8030. Now located near Xanadu Resort and next door to Marina grocery, The Baker is the island's best spot for delicious baked bread, croissants, pastries and sandwiches. Open from 7:30 to 5:30 Monday-Friday and 7:30 to 2 on Saturday. Inexpensive to Moderate.

Black Orchid Restaurant. South Coconut Drive, 501-206-2441. Located about 2½ miles south of town, beyond the croc pond and just before Athens Gate condotel, Black Orchid gets five stars for hard work and trying to please guests. Relaxed atmosphere, open to the fresh air, with good fish, lobster, lasagna and other dishes. Open for lunch and dinner. Closed Sunday and Monday. Expensive/Very Expensive.

Casa Picasso. Sting Ray Street, 501-226-4443. Closed for several years, Casa Picasso reopened under new ownership and almost instantly became a big new hit. Many consider it the best restaurant on the island. Billed as tapas dining with global flavors, besides small plates it features wonderful local seafood, pork and other entrees, with paired wines. There are interesting takes on most everything. Closed Sunday and Monday. Reservations suggested. Expensive/Very Expensive. One of the few independent restaurants on the island that takes American Express.

Hidden Treasure. Escalante area, 501-226-4111. It is hidden away indeed on a back street in a residential neighborhood south of town. At dinner you dine by candlelight, in the sultry tropical air under a pitched roof set off by bamboo, mahogany and cabbage bark wood. Although the restaurant is under new management, one of the longtime signature dishes, Mojarra a la Lamanai, remains on the menu – it's a snapper fillet topped with bell peppers, onions, tomatoes and capers in a coconut sauce and cooked in a banana leaf. Almond-crusted grouper also is popular. Open for dinner only. Closed on Tuesday off-season. Expensive/Very Expensive.

Palmilla at Victoria House. Coconut Drive at Victoria House, 501-226-2067. The main restaurant at Victoria House, Palmilla, once dependent on unexciting buffets, has had a marked change for the better under its current chef and kitchen team. For dinner, dine by romantic candlelight. Breakfast by the pool with views of the sea isn't to be missed. Expensive to Very Expensive.

NORTH AMBERGRIS
Aji Tapa Bar and Restaurant. Beachfront, Buena Vista area, North Ambergris (about 2½ miles north of town), 501-226-4047. Relax in a shady, romantic seaside patio, with views of the beach and barrier reef in the distance, and snack on shrimp in garlic and other small plates. For a treat, try the seafood paella. Aji is under new management, so things may change. Closed Tuesday. Expensive.

Mambo. North Ambergris at Matachica Resort & Spa, 501-220-5010. If you'd visited the island a few years ago, you'd never have thought Ambergris Caye would get this kind of place. The restaurant space is open, appealing and upscale. Everything is designed to the hilt – even the menus show hours of quality design time. On those menus is a selection of sophisticated Italian dishes and seafood, along with daily specials. But you need to bring plenty of money or plastic. Open for breakfast, lunch and dinner. Very Expensive.

Rain. 2 miles north of the bridge at Grand Caribe, 501-226-4000. This restaurant at the Grand Caribe resort has both indoor seating and rooftop dining with tremendous views of the reef. The setting is great, and the food, by the former chef at Aji, is very good, but the prices are at or near the top end of Ambergris Caye restaurants. For example, in-season, grilled lobster is US$35, Lobster Thermidor is US$38. Grilled fish dishes are US$22 to $28. A Cobb salad is US$16, and ceviche is US$14. Open daily for breakfast, lunch and dinner. Expensive to Very Expensive.

Rojo Beach Bar. North Ambergris, 501-266-4012. About 5 miles north of the bridge, Rojo enjoys a totally romantic beachside setting next to Azul Resort's two beachside villas. It's evolved into more of a bar, with the dining scaled back some, but you'll still find delicious lobster pizza, ceviche, conch fritters and such. And there's a pool to splash in. Closed Monday. Expensive to Very Expensive.

The Truck Stop. 1 mile north of the bridge, North Ambergris Caye, 501-226-3663. Built from containers, The Truck Stop is a newish choice on North Ambergris. It's been getting raves from local and visitors for its inexpensive Cuban and Asian sandwiches, noodle dishes, Mexican items and ice cream. Think of it as a kind of permanent food truck with a full bar.

There's live music on some days, and The Truck Stop now has an 18-foot screen for "movie nights." Open Wednesday-Sunday for lunch and dinner. Inexpensive to Moderate.

Where to Party on Ambergris Caye

For visitors, San Pedro is the nightlife capital of Belize. Still, it's not exactly a world-class party town. Nightlife usually consists of drinks and dinner at a local restaurant, with perhaps a later visit to one of the clubs or hotel beach bars. Quite a few expats on the island have made a second career out of drinking.

Keep in mind that bars come and go on a resort island like this. **Big Daddy's** near Central Park has been the hottest spot on the island, although it's going through some changes. Across the street, **Jaguar** hops, too, especially on weekends. **Fido's** is always busy, with lots of people dropping in for a drink or to hear some music. **Palapa Bar** (the new location on a pier at the north end of town), **Wahoo Lounge** (home of the "chicken drop"), **Wayos Beach Bar, Road Kill** and **Crazy Canuck's** are popular bars where you can get a cold beer or something stronger. **Pedro's**, also south of town, is a local expat hangout south, with hot pizza and disgusting shots of Jaegermeister.

On North Ambergris, **The Truck Stop** is a popular bar about 1 mile north of the bridge. It has live music at times and movie nights on an 18-foot outdoor screen. **Rojo Beach Bar** has one of the most romantic settings in Belize, and the food is good, too. **Kama Bar** has a nice setting for drinks and snacks.

Several hotels have popular beach bars, including **Caprice** at the Holiday Hotel, Ramon's **Purple Parrot,** and Mata Rocks' **Squirrel's Nest**. You can stroll along the beach south of town and slake your thirst at a half dozen beach bars.

Cholo's Sports Bar and a couple of other small local bars have pool tables. **Wine de Vine** has wine by the glass in the afternoon as well as bottles for sale (at higher prices than in the U.S., due to import duties.)

A small casino is open at **Captain Morgan's Resort** on North Ambergris. For more action, you can try the **Ramada Princess Hotel & Casino** in Belize City. There also are casinos in the Corozal Free Zone (a 25-minute flight and a taxi ride away), of which **Las Vegas Casino,** with 54,000 square feet of gaming space, is the largest. It also has a new hotel.

CAYE CAULKER

Laid-back Caye Caulker   Photo Angela N Perryman/ Shutterstock

CAYE CAULKER RATINGS

Ratings are on an A to F scale, just like your old high school report card. A is the top grade; F is failing. Grades are relative compared to other areas in Belize.

Popularity with Visitors	B
Popularity with Expats	C
Cost Level	B+
Safety	B-
Scenic Beauty	B-
Lodging	C+
Dining	B-
Nightlife	C-
Outdoor Activities	C
Water Activities	B+
Cultural Activities	D
Museums	F
Maya Sites	F
Historical Sites	D
Tourism Infrastructure	C

Transportation	C+
Medical Care	C-
Shopping	C
Overall Visitor Rating	**B**

CAYE CAULKER OVERVIEW

ADVANTAGES OF CAYE CAULKER: • Small, laid-back island atmosphere • Excellent opportunities for water activities – boating, fishing, diving, snorkeling, windsurfing • Less expensive than San Pedro • No need for a car or even a golf cart • Caulker is a little like Isla des Mujeres or Holbox in Mexico

Caye Caulker is Ambergris Caye's "little sister" island – smaller, less developed and a cheaper date. Caulker, whose name derives from the Spanish word for coco plum, *hicaco*, has the kind of laidback, sandy-street, tropical-color, low-key Caribbean charm that travelers pay thousands to experience, but here they can have it for peanuts. Well, almost. Less than 10 miles and about 30 minutes by boat from San Pedro or 45 minutes from Belize City, Caye Caulker is definitely worth a visit, and perhaps you'll like it well enough to stay.

Here are some of the key comparisons between Caye Caulker and Ambergris Caye:

Caye Caulker is physically much smaller, under 5 miles long and half a mile wide at its widest point, roughly one-tenth the size of Ambergris Caye. Hurricane Hattie in 1961 divided the island in two parts. North of "the Split" it is mostly uninhabited mangrove, and much of this area is protected as a nature reserve. As on many islands, there are basically just three streets running down the island, Front, Middle and Back streets being the main ones, though there are few street signs and locals usually give directions just by saying "go down to yellow house and turn right." Most of the 300 or so listings in the Caye Caulker section of the Belize telephone directory don't even include a street name or address, just the person's name and phone number. Nearly all of 1,500 people on the island live in the village south of the Split.

Unlike Ambergris Caye, where most of the main streets are now paved, Caye Caulker has streets of hard-packed sand and far, far, far fewer cars than San Pedro. Almost everybody gets around on foot or bike.

As on Ambergris, a majority of local residents are Mestizos who originally came to the island from Mexico, and who until recently made their living by fishing, but the island also has Creoles, some of whom

228

consider themselves Rastafarians, gringos and others. Some of the hawkers along Front Street overdo it and make themselves a little obnoxious.

While it is quickly going upmarket, Caye Caulker remains to some extent a budget island. In the 1960s and 1970s, the island was on the "backpacker trail," a cheap place for longhaired visitors to relax and smoke a little weed or sip a beer. Today, a very expensive hotel on Caulker goes for around US$250 a night, and most of the hotels charge under US$100 double, with some as low as US$15. Many of the older buildings on the island are wooden clapboard, often painted in tropical colors, but more recently constructed houses and hotels are of reinforced concrete. Only a few hotels on the island have swimming pools.

Caye Caulker has much the same mix of tourist-oriented businesses as San Pedro, but in most cases there are fewer of everything. The island has perhaps 25 simple restaurants, if you include those that operate out of somebody's back window or BBQ grill, some casual bars, a handful of dive shops and tour guides, several pint-sized groceries, a few gift shops, a bank and several cybercafés.

Beaches? Caulker has much less beachfront than Ambergris Caye, and what beaches it has don't compare with the better stretches of beach on Ambergris Caye, Hopkins or Placencia. Beach reclamation projects did widen and improve the beach along the east side of the village (though storms have taken away and then given back sand). Swimming in the shallow water close to shore is mainly from piers and at "the Split," which is very popular for sunning and swimming. There's a good bar with cold beer close by.

In the past, the pipe water on Caulker was not as good as on Ambergris Caye. On Caulker, it often had a sulfur smell and came from shallow wells, some which were close to septic systems. A reverse osmosis water plant is now operating on the island, but not all homes and businesses are on it.

Caye Caulker, like most other coastal areas and cayes, also has sandflies. Especially on calm days, at certain times of year, they can be a nuisance.

Ambergris Caye still has many more restaurants than Caye Caulker. However, in the past several years a flood of new restaurants has opened on Caulker, and you now have a much broader selection of types and quality of restaurants.

Caye Caulker Practicalities
Banks: Caye Caulker has only one bank, Atlantic Bank. It has an ATM that accepts international debit cards.

Groceries: Chan's Mini-Mart on Middle Street near the Caye Caulker Plaza Hotel is the most-frequented grocery, although there are other places to buy beer, booze, snacks and other basics on Front Street and elsewhere. Near Chan's are some fruit and vegetable vendors.

Other Stores: Caye Caulker doesn't have much shopping, beyond some gift shops on Front Street, a couple of art galleries and a few other shops. Most residents go to Belize City for their big shopping trips.

Rental Vehicles: Most people walk or bike around the island, but golf carts are available for rent from a couple of vendors, as are bicycles. Ask at your hotel.

Medical: Caye Caulker doesn't have a hospital, but there is a small medical clinic (Front Street at the south end, 501-226-0190), staffed as of this writing by a Belizean nurse and a Cuban doctor. It is open daily, usually until 7 p.m. and has a supply of commonly needed medications. For a real emergency, fly or take a water taxi to Belize City. Your hotel will assist in getting you to Belize City the fastest way.

Infrastructure: Caye Caulker now has a reverse osmosis municipal water system in the village. Sewerage is still an issue. DSL and cellular internet are available. North of the Split, residents must rely on their own resources for power, water and sewerage.

For More Information: The BTIA website for Caulker Caye Caulker Vacation (www.cayecaulkervacation.com). Another site is Go Caye Caulker (www.gocayecaulker.com).

GETTING TO CAYE CAULKER

You can fly to Caulker's little airstrip on **Tropic Air** (www.tropicair.com) or **Maya Island Air** (www.mayaregional.com) from Belize City. Flights from either International or Municipal to San Pedro will stop, on demand, at Caye Caulker. Fares about the same as to San Pedro – in spring 2016 around US$85 to $90 from the international airport and US$50 to $55 from municipal. Flights from San Pedro to Belize City also drop passengers at Caulker's airstrip, again for the same fare as to Belize City itself.

Most visitors to Caulker, however, come by boat. Two water taxi companies, with fast boats that hold up to 100 passengers, connect Belize City with Caye Caulker via a 45-minute ride.

Ocean Ferry (501-223-0033, www.oceanferrybelize.com) boats leave from the Marine Terminal in Belize City at 10 North Front Street near the Swing Bridge. **San Pedro Belize Express** (501-223-2225, www.belizewatertaxi.com) boats leave from the Brown Sugar dock at 111 North Front Street near the Tourism Village. Ocean Ferry has five departures daily from to Caulker. It charges US$14.50 one-way between Belize City and Caye Caulker. San Pedro Belize Express, which has around eight or nine departures to Caulker, charges US$15 one-way between Belize City and Caye Caulker.

The water taxi business in Belize is in flux; schedules, rates and companies are subject to change.

The water taxis boats mostly come in at two piers on the front side of the island. If you come ashore at the main public pier, the pink and green Trends Beachfront hotel is on your right, and the mustard-colored Seaside Cabañas is on your left.

Walk a few sandy feet and you'll come to Front Street. Go right, or north, and in 15 minutes or so you'll pass several good hotels, some restaurants, shops and tour operators, plus a few touts, and end up at "the Split," the main place to swim on the island. Go left or south and you'll find some of the island's better beachfront properties. Many of the island's restaurants, shops and hotels are on Front Street or on the beachfront. Go straight west, and you're in the heart of the village.

In general, hotels to the south are quieter than those north toward the Split. However, if you're staying a good ways south, it's a bit more of a walk to most restaurants and bars. For those who really want to get away from things, try the North Island, the area north of the Split. However, this part of the island is accessible only by boat, and except for some off-the-grid homes, there's little development.

If you come by air, the little airstrip is at the south end of the island. You can walk the 20 or 25 minutes or so back to the heart of the village, or you can get a golf cart taxi.

WHAT TO SEE AND DO ON CAYE CAULKER

Caye Caulker isn't so much about seeing and doing as being. On this l little island kick back, relax and just enjoy life.

From Caulker, you can visit most of the same attractions as from Ambergris Caye. Rates from Caulker are usually a little less than from San Pedro.

See the Ambergris Caye section above for information on **Hol Chan Marine Reserve** and other dive and snorkel sites. The **Caye Caulker Marine Reserve** is Caulker's own mini-Hol Chan snorkeling area, just 10 minutes from Caulker.

In addition, you may also want to visit **Swallow Caye Wildlife Sanctuary** (www.swallowcayemanatees.org), 9,000 acres of protected sea and mangrove habitat for manatees and other wildlife. Swallow Caye trips are around US$85.

Caye Caulker Dive/Snorkeling Shops and Tour Operators
There is no shortage of tour operators and snorkel and dive shops to take you out. There are at least three dive shops on the island and perhaps a dozen snorkel and tour operators, most of which have locations on or near the beachfront along Front Street.
Frenchie's Diving Services (beachfront pier, toward the Split, 501-226-0234, www.frenchiesdivingbelize.com) is the island's oldest dive shop under continuous ownership. It has four dive boats, the largest of which is a 38-footer.
Belize Diving Services (Chapoose Street, near soccer field, 501-226-0143, www.belizedivingservices.com) is a well-respected dive operation, founded in 1978, and owned since 2009 by Chip and Dani Petersen. It has a 46-foot dive boat.
Among the established snorkel and land tour operators are the following shops:
Anda de Wata Tours (Luciano Reyes Street, 501-666-7374, www.snorkeladw.com)
Anwar Tours (501-226-0327, www.anwartours.com)
Caveman Snorkeling Tours (Front Street, 501-605-0345, www.cavemansnorkelingtours.com)
Spearfishing Shack, Crocodile Street at Bella's Backpackers hostel, 501-666-4654)
Tsunami Adventures (501-226-0462, www.tsunamiadventures.com)
Local snorkeling trips around Caye Caulker are about US$35 per person, while five-hour snorkel trips to Hol Chan and other stops are US$65 to $75. Land tours for cave tubing or to visit Altun Ha Maya site are around US$85 per person. Some rates may not include tax, marine reserve fees or equipment rental.
With any of the Caulker dive shops, you'll pay around US$95 to $145 including marine reserve fee for a two-tank dive trip to the Caye Caulker Marine Reserve or to Hol Chan, and up to about US$285 for three-tank dive trips to Lighthouse Reef Atoll and the Blue Hole, including US$40 reserve fee. Day trips to Turneffe Atoll are less than to Lighthouse Reef.

Sailing, Windsurfing and Fishing
Caye Caulker also is home to a growing scene of other water and windsports, including paddleboarding, windsurfing and of course fishing.
Steve Wright's **Blackhawk Sailing Tours** (501-607-0323, www.blackhawksailingtours.com) has day snorkeling tours, sunset tours and overnight and longer sail trips on a 32-foot sailboat to English Caye, Tobacco Caye and Placencia.

Raggamuffin Tours (501-226-0348, www.raffamuffintours.com) has overnight sailing trips a 56-foot ketch, plus a three-day sailing trip to Placencia, with a stopover for camping on Tobacco Caye. The Placencia trip goes for US$350 per person including meals. It also does day sails and snorkel trips.

Kitexplorer (501-635-4967, www.kitexplorer.com) offers beginner to advanced kiteboarding, windsurfing and paddle surfing.

Anglers Abroad (Sea Dreams Hotel, 501-226-0602, www.anglersabroad.com) does half-day fishing trips for around US$220 and full day for around US$350, including guide, boat and lunch.

CAYE CAULKER LODGING

This is not a complete list of island hotels, but these are among our favorites in all price ranges. They are arranged by location, either north or south of Main Street and the main "front pier" where some water taxi boats arrive, and then (roughly) by price range, from most to least expensive.

North of the Main Front Pier:

CayeReef Condos. Front Street, Caye Caulker, 501-226-0381; www.cayereef.com. CayeReef Condos are relatively new upscale accommodations. The six condo apartments are on Front Street not far from the Split, with a small swimming pool at the front, hidden behind a wall. You can book either a two-bedroom entire unit or just one of the bedrooms. All units are fully air-conditioned, with tile floors, custom kitchens, private verandas with sea views (second and third floors), free wi-fi and cable TV. The units have Belizean art on the walls and flat-screen TVs. There are great views of the reef from the fourth floor roof top patio, where there is a rooftop whirlpool. Rates vary by the floor level – the higher the floor the higher the rate. In-season two bedroom units are US$210 to $247, and one-bedroom units are US$173 to $210. Off-season, the two-bedrooms are US$159 to $206, and the one-bedrooms are US$124 to $165. All rates plus tax and are higher at Christmas-New Year's.

Iguana Reef Inn. Middle Street next to soccer field (P.O. Box 31, Caye Caulker), 501-226-0213; www.iguanareefinn.com. This is the Ritz-Carlton of Caye Caulker. Sort of. The suites have air-conditioning, Belizean-made furniture, queen beds and local artwork. A swimming pool was added in 2006, and there's a nice bar with some 20 brands of rum. Considering the size and amenities of the 11 suites, the rates, US$159 to $259 in-season, and US$139 to $189 off-season, plus tax, are reasonable, and they include continental breakfast and complimentary kayaks and bikes. A penthouse suite on the third level with two bedrooms and two baths is pricey in-season at US$469, and a cabaña is US$289 (US$389 and $209 off-season, respectively). If there's a downside, it is that the hotel is on the backside of the island and not on the Caribbean, though the plus of that is from some suites and the back of the grounds you have a view of sunsets over the lagoon. The hotel's website is a good source of information about the island.

Sea Dreams Hotel. Front Street near the Split, Caye Caulker, 501-226-0602; www.seadreamsbelize.com. This is a great spot for anglers or just those who want to enjoy a relaxing stay at a well-run place. The "lobby" is sand with a large tree in the middle of it. Sea Dreams, located off Front Street on the west side, near the Split, has a variety of accommodations, including five courtyard rooms, three two-bedroom apartments, a penthouse and a cabaña, a bungalow and a house. All have A/C, cable TV and wi-fi; larger units have full kitchens. Sea Dreams has a rooftop terrace with panoramic views, plus a pier/dock on the lagoon side. Rates from around US$115 to $225, plus tax, including full breakfast. Owner Haywood Curry is known as an excellent fly fisherman and guide. Co-owner Heidi Curry helped found Caulker's first high school.

Caye Caulker Condos. Front Street (P.O. Box 52, Caye Caulker), 501-226-0072; www.cayecaulkercondos.com. Want a suite with a full kitchen to prepare some of your own meals? Try these condo apartments not far from the Split. Each of the eight cozy units, on the west side of Front Street, has a private verandah facing the water, less than 100 feet away; those on the second floor have the better views. All the units have A/C, tile floors, satellite TV and wi-fi. Bikes are free. There's now a swimming pool, too. Rates US$99 to $139 double in-season, US$79-$99 off-season, plus 9% hotel tax.

Caye Caulker Plaza Hotel. Avenida Langosta and Calle del Sol 501-226-0780; www.cayecaulkerplazahotel.com. This modern 30-room, concrete hotel has a central location in the middle of the village. It's about a 5-minute walk to either the sea or the lagoon. While not on the water, it does offer sea and lagoon views from the fourth-level rooftop deck. Rooms are clean, with mini-fridge, cable TV and really cold air-conditioning! In-season, rates are US$90 to $110, off-season US$75 to $95, plus tax.

De Real Macaw. Front Street, Caye Caulker, 501-226-0459; www.derealmacaw.biz. This friendly American-owned lodging, on the west side of Front Street but still close enough to catch the breezes, has a variety of accommodations -- rooms, a beach house, cabañas and a two-bedroom condo. More-expensive units have A/C. There's a porch with hammocks. Rates are US$25 to $130 for most of the year and US$20 to $110 September to mid-November, plus tax. Some units have minimum stay requirements.

Yuma's House. Beachfront just north of public pier, Caye Caulker, 501-206-0019; www.yumashousebelize.com. For US$17.50 per person, you can grab a bunk bed at this hostel on the beach. Formerly it was the very laidback Tina's; now it is less laid back. Its policies include no children under 15, zero drugs, no unregistered guests on the property, quiet time after 11 p.m. and other rules that are strictly enforced. A few private rooms with shared baths are about US$42.50, plus tax. Rates a little lower mid-May to mid-December. Though the hostel dorms are basic, you're right on the water, and the price and location mean this place is usually packed with young people. Reservations are a good idea – see the Yuma's website for a schedule for the earliest times reservations are accepted for a given date.

Sandy Lane Guesthouse and Cabañas. Corner Chapoose and Langosta Streets, Caye Caulker, 501-226-0117. This longtime budget favorite has nine rooms, some with private baths and some with shared baths, and four basic cabañas. Rates are a bargain at around US$13 to $17 for rooms and US$30 for the cabañas. There is a common kitchen outdoors.

South of the Main Front Pier:

Seaside Cabanas. Main Street, beachfront (P.O. Box 39, Caye Caulker), 501-226-0498; www.seasidecabanas.com. Rebuilt after a 2003 fire, this seafront hotel, with 17 rooms plus a seafront suite, is a high-profile spot near the village's main front pier. You're just a short walk from many of the island's restaurants, bars and shops. Painted a mustard color, with a combination of tropical thatch and concrete constructions, the Seaside buildings are in a U-shape around a pool. Una Mas is the bar. Several of the rooms have private rooftop terraces for sunning or watching the sea in privacy. The hotel has in-room phones and free wi-fi. Rates around USS129 to $199 in-season and US$115 to $189 off-season, plus 9% tax.

Colinda Cabañas. Beachfront, Caye Caulker, 501-226-0383; www.colindacabanas.com. Colinda Cabañas (the owners are named Colin and Linda) enjoys a great reputation and many repeat guests. Located away from the main part of the village toward the south end of the island, it has three beachfront suites, two second-row suites, five cabañas and a two-bedroom house on the breezy sea side of the island with a fine view of the reef. You can lounge on hammocks or swim (although swimming here isn't that great) from the 175-foot private pier with thatch palapa. Year-round rates range from US$69 to $159, plus tax. Weekly or longer bookings and returning guests enjoy a US$10-a-night discount. Complimentary bikes, kayaks and snorkeling gear. Wi-fi is free, but the signal isn't strong in some rooms.

Barefoot Beach Belize. Beachfront, south of the public pier, Caye Caulker, 501-226-0205; www.barefootbeachbelize.com. Formerly the Seaview Guest House, the current owners have turned this little seafront place into one of the more popular spots on Caulker. There are a total of 17 rooms, including seven budget rooms in "The Huts." Rates in-season range from US$55 to $129, and US$40 to $99 off-season, plus tax. Don't confuse this place with the similarly named Barefoot Caribe.

OASI. Front Street, Caye Caulker, 501-226-0384; www.oasi-holidaysbelize.com. Located about 5 minutes south of the main public pier, in a quieter area, OASI has four lovely rental apartments with air conditioning, wi-fi, cable TV, fully furnished kitchens and verandahs with hammocks. It is set in tropical grounds, with a fountain, barbecue grill and small bar for guests, Il Baretta, which serves real Italian espresso, wine and drinks. Complimentary bikes. Rates are a good value at US$95 to $105 double in-season, US$85 to $95 in low season. All rates plus 9% tax. Get the top floor apartment if you can. Recommended.

Tree Tops. Beachfront, (P.O. Box 29, Caye Caulker), 501-226-0240; www.treetopsbelize.com. Set back a little from the water, Tree Tops is run by Austrian-born Doris Creasy. All rooms have air-conditioning available, cable TV and a fridge. The four regular rooms are US$70 to $90 double year-round. Two third-floor suites (US$120 year-round), Sunset and Sunrise, have king-size beds and private balconies with views of the sea. Rates plus 9% tax. A small courtyard is a great place to read or just lounge in a hammock. Belize needs more places like this one – the guest rooms are clean as a pin, the entire place is meticulously maintained and the owner is helpful. Highly recommended.

Pancho's Villas. Pasero Street (P.O. Box 80, Caye Caulker), 501-226-0304; www.panchosvillasbelize.com. Owned by the same people who run Pancho's Auto Rentals in Belize City, Pancho's Villas has six rooms and three one-bedroom suites in a yellow three-story concrete building. All units have air-conditioning and ceiling fans, cable TV, wi-fi, fridge and microwave. The seafront is a short walk away. Rates US$70 to $95 in-season, US$60 to $85 off-season, plus tax. Weekly and monthly rates available.

Maxhapan Cabañas. 55 Avenue Pueblo Nuevo, Caye Caulker, 501-226-0118. This little spot is in the center of the village and not on the water, but it's very popular because it's neat and clean and a good value. Set in a small, sandy and shady garden, there are only a total of three rooms in a two-story cabaña and in a one-level building. They have tile floors and a veranda with hammocks. Complimentary bikes and snorkel gear. Rates start around US$65 plus tax.

Caye Caulker Vacation Rentals

For a vacation rental house on Caulker, expect to pay around US$350 to $1,000 a week, or US$75 to $200 a night. Rentals incur the 9% hotel tax.

Caye Caulker Accommodations. (P.O. Box 88, Caye Caulker), 501-226-0382; www.cayecaulkeraccommodations.com. This company manages more than two dozen houses and other rental units (some listings shared with other firms) on the island. Several have pools.

Caye Caulker Rentals. Front Street, Caye Caulker, 501-226-0029; www.cayecaulkerrentals.com. This rental agency also has some two dozen houses for rent, some from as low as US$50 a night, and others, including beachfront houses, from under US$500 a week.

Casitas Carinosa. (P.O. Box 48, Caye Caulker), 501-226-0547; www.cayecaulkercasita.com. Amanda Badger offers three nice rental options, all with pools – Amanda's Place, with two studio apartments, the three-bedroom Casita Carinosa and the one-bedroom Casa Amancer. Weekly rates range from US$575 to $1,295, plus 9% tax.

CAYE CAULKER DINING

Caye Caulker has at least 30 restaurants, mostly small spots with a few tables and sand or wood floors, where you can get a tasty meal for a few dollars. Several are more upmarket. Some don't accept credit cards.

With the increasing popularity of Caye Caulker, there has been a boom in the restaurant business on the island over the past two or three years. More than a dozen new eateries have opened. Locals also operate "pop up" restaurants – just a grill where they prepare fresh fish or chicken for you at modest prices.

Note that some restaurants close during the slow September-October period or at the whim of the owner. Opening times and days may vary seasonally.

Price ranges shown are for typical meals for one (usually dinner), not including tip, tax or alcoholic drinks. Price ranges:

Inexpensive: Under US$7
Moderate: US$8-$19
Expensive: US$20-$39
Very Expensive: Over US$40
Restaurants here are listed alphabetically.

Alladins. Beachfront, near the Split, Caye Caulker, 501-660-1550. Alladins serves tasty, authentic Middle Eastern dishes such as kebabs, falafel, hummus and baba ghanoush at modest prices. Inexpensive to Moderate.

Amor y Café. Front Street, Caye Caulker. Formerly Cyndi's, Amor y Café is another good place for breakfast, along with love and coffee. Open for breakfast daily. Inexpensive to Moderate.

Au French Corner. Front Street at Avenida Hicaco, Caye Caulker, 501-624-7374. Who would have thought you could get authentic French savory and sweet crepes on Caye Caulker? The new Au French Corner, with a chef from Paris – really – pulls it off. There are banana crepes, curry crepes, spinach crepes, strawberry nutella crepes, breakfast crepes, dessert crepes and others. Open for breakfast Wednesday to Saturday and dinner Tuesday to Saturday. Moderate.

Caribbean Colors Art Café. Front Street, Caye Caulker, 501-668-7205, Come for the art by Lee Vanderwalker. Stay for the coffee, omelets, salads and sushi. Open for breakfast, lunch and dinner. Closed Tuesday. Moderate.

Glenda's. Back Street, Caye Caulker, 501-226-0148. Come to Glenda's for a cinnamon roll, johnnycake and fresh-squeezed orange juice for breakfast, and come back at lunch for rice and beans. Open for breakfast and lunch Monday to Saturday. No credit cards. Inexpensive.

Habaneros Restaurant. Middle Street, Caye Caulker, 501-626-4911. Caye Caulker's most upscale dining and some think the best. Try the Lobster Newburg (in lobster season) or voodoo cakes. Everything tastes better with frozen mojitos. Dinner daily. Live music many evenings. Expensive. Reservations suggested in-season.

Il Pellicano Cucina Italian Restaurant. 49 Pasero Street, Caye Caulker, 501-226-0660. Authentic Italian food prepared by Italians. This has quickly become one of the most recommended restaurants on Caye Caulker. Open for dinner. Closed Tuesday. Expensive.

Pasta Per Caso. Avenida Hicaco, Caye Caulker, 501-634-5641. It's always seemed odd to us that visitors to a tropical island would choose Italian food for dinner, but in the case of Pasta Per Caso, we can understand it. The chef here, from Milan, does fresh pasta with light and tasty sauces, usually just two dishes each evening for you to choose between. Desserts are good, and try the Compari orange and rum punch. Open for dinner. Closed Tuesday and Wednesday. Expensive.

Roses Grill & Bar. Calle del Sol, Caye Caulker, 501-206-0407. This "open door" restaurant under a large thatch palapa is one of the best-known spots on the island, and the tables are often packed. However, some think Roses is a victim of its own popularity and that it's not as good as it once was. The specialty is seafood, and it's all fresh. Dinner daily, open for breakfast and lunch during high season. Moderate to Expensive.

Syd's. Middle Street, Caye Caulker, south of public pier, 501-600-9481. Locals often recommend Syd's, one of the old-time places on the island. It serves Belizean and Mexican faves like beans and rice, stew chicken, garnaches, tostadas along with lobster and conch, when in season, at prices lower than you'll pay at many other eateries. Breakfast, lunch and dinner daily. Moderate.

Wish Willy Bar & Grill. Located on a side street off Front Street near the Split, across from Frenchie's. At Wish Willy you eat in the back yard of the owner, Maurice. He tells you what's on the menu today. It may be fresh fish, lamb or chicken. In most cases, the prices are low, and the rum drinks cost less here than almost anywhere else on the island. You may share a table with other guests, and the service is sometimes slow, but keep in mind the money you're saving. Moderate.

Frenchie's Dive Shop on Caye Caulker

OFFSHORE CAYES & ATOLLS

Belize has some 1,000 islands in the Caribbean. The vast majority are small spits of sand and mangroves. Many are either privately owned (by old Belize families or by wealthy foreigners) or are government property. Around 15 to 20 have a fish or dive lodge or other resort. In most cases, you'll pay a pretty penny to visit and stay at these remote lodges, but there are a few exceptions.

Thatch Caye off Dangriga

OFFSHORE CAYES & ATOLLS RATINGS

Ratings are on an A to F scale, just like your old high school report card. A is the top grade; F is failing. Grades are relative compared to other areas in Belize.

Popularity with Visitors	B-
Popularity with Expats	D
Cost Level	C-
Safety	B+
Scenic Beauty	A
Lodging	B
Dining	B-

Nightlife	D
Outdoor Activities	C+
Water Activities	A
Cultural Activities	F
Museums	F
Maya Sites	F
Historical Sites	D+
Tourism Infrastructure	C-
Transportation	C-
Medical Care	D
Shopping	D
Overall Visitor Rating	**B-**

OFFSHORE CAYES & ATOLLS OVERVIEW

ISLAND ADVANTAGES: • Beautiful tropical islands in the Caribbean • Easy access to recreational activities on the water • You can really get away from it all

Belize's two main northern cayes, Ambergris and Caulker, are the largest and by far the most popular of Belize's islands, both for visitors and expats. However, Belize has about 1,000 other islands in the Caribbean. Most are small, remote and unpopulated. They are wonderful if typically somewhat expensive to visit. Building and living on the islands also is expensive.

GETTING TO OFFSHORE CAYES & ATOLLS

In almost all cases, you'll have to use the boat transfers offered by the individual resorts. Water taxis from Belize City or the Northern Cayes don't go to the remote islands. In many cases, the boat runs offered by the lodges operate only on certain days. While it's usually possible to charter private boats to the offshore cayes and atolls, they are very expensive. There are a few exceptions: Boats from Dangriga make regular daily trips to Tobacco Caye – check with the captains at the Riverside Café in downtown Dangriga for times and rates. You'll normally pay under US$25 per person one-way. Blackbird Caye Resort has a small airstrip, so it's possible to fly there. The resort will arrange your charter flight.

WHAT TO SEE AND DO ON REMOTE CAYES & ATOLLS

Why do you go to Belize's remote islands? A) To get away from it all, beachcomb and relax B) To dive and snorkel some of the most pristine waters and reefs in the Western Hemisphere C) To fish for game fish such as tarpon, permit and bonefish and also for snapper, jack, barracuda and other eating fish D) All of the above.

Of course, the correct answer is D) All of the above.

Belize's offshore islands and atolls are among the most beautiful places in the Caribbean. On the Belize Barrier Reef and around the atolls the diving and snorkeling is extraordinary. At some atoll lodges and at islands directly on the reef, such as Southwater Caye and Tobacco Caye, you can snorkel from shore, unlike in most of the rest of Belize. The fishing, whether it's trolling or fly fishing, is superb, too. And, of course, you don't have to do anything more than laze in a hammock, sip something cold and gaze at the sea.

If there's a downside, it's that most of the offshore cayes and atolls are a good ways out – it can take two hours by boat to get from the mainland to the atoll lodges – and due to the costs of transportation and running these remote lodges, you'll pay a pretty penny to enjoy them. However, there are exceptions, such as Tobacco Caye, which is affordable even for most budget travelers.

Note on fishing licenses: If you plan to fish in Belize, whether around the cayes or even from a pier on the mainland, in most cases you now need a saltwater fishing license. For visitors, licenses are US$10 per day or US$25 per week. Your fishing guide or hotel can assist in getting you a license, or failing that, contact Belize Coastal Zone Management (www.coastalzonebelize.org, 501-223-0719, and buy a license on-line.

OFFSHORE CAYES & ATOLLS LODGING AND DINING
NEAR AMBERGRIS CAYE

Caye Chapel. This 265-acre island was purchased by a Kentucky coal baron and developed primarily as a corporate retreat, with a group of upscale villas and casita rooms, an 18-hole, 7,000-yard golf course, a clubhouse with restaurant and swimming pool and an airstrip. The coal baron ran into financial difficulties, and in 2012 the lender took back the property. In late 2014, the Government of Belize sold Caye Chapel to a Mexican company that is involved in resort development in Cancún and elsewhere. Reportedly, former pro golfer Greg Norman will redesign the Caye Chapel Golf Course as part of the proposed redevelopment of the island. In the meantime, you can play the old course and even stay overnight in a casita or luxury villa on the island. Transport to Caye Chapel is via water taxi or air. For information, contact **Coldwell Banker** on Ambergris Caye (11 Coconut Drive, San Pedro, 501-226, 4599, www.buyrealestatebelize.com).

Cayo Espanto. 888-666-4282 in U.S. and Canada, or 910-323-8355; www.aprivateisland.com. Ready, willing and able to pay nearly US$20,000 a couple for a week's pampering, not including airfare to Belize? Then Cayo Espanto, a tiny private island on the backside of Ambergris, about 3 miles west of San Pedro, may be for you. At Cayo Espanto, the resort staff lines up, as on the old TV show "Fantasy Island" to greet you on arrival. Cayo Espanto's American owner quickly figured out that, in Belize's economy, it's not that expensive to hire a bunch of workers to keep the staff-to-guest ratio at two to one. So if you like attentive service, you definitely will get it at Cayo Espanto, including your own "houseman" who cares for your every need day or night. Start with breakfast in bed and end the evening with pisco sours (all meals and most drinks are included in the price) on your private dock, before bundling off to your king-size bed with its luxurious Yves de Lorme sheets. Currently there are seven villas, four one-bedroom, two two-bedroom and one over-the-water bungalow. The villas are quite large, and all but one has small private "plunge" pools. We especially like the units with open-air design, with walls that fold out let the Caribbean in, such as Casa Estrella. Meals are created by Cayo Espanto's crew of award-winning chefs and brought to your villa. You can dine at your own table by the sea, which will be set up for you down to the candlelight. The resort offers a full range of tours, dive and snorkel trips, fishing and all the rest, but most guests seem to spend most of their time at their villas (and for the US$75 more per hour they're paying to stay here, who wouldn't?) You can also get spa services in your villa. The rates are like the money-is-no-object rates on villa rentals on St. Barths: US$1,595 to $2,295 double in winter, and US$1,495 to $2,195 off-season – that's per night, not per week -- including meals and most drinks. However, 9% tax and 15% service/resort fee are additional. There's a minimum stay of five nights (some exceptions to this may be made). Rates are higher during the Christmas season. Occasional promotional rates may be offered. Is it worth it? Cayo Espanto stays pretty busy, so obviously there are people who figure it is.

Besides Cayo Espanto, another resort may be developed on the backside of Ambergris Caye. Film star Leo DiCaprio in 2005 purchased with Cayo Espanto owner Jeff Gram the 104-acre **Blackadore Caye** about 15 minutes by boat from San Pedro. The Academy Award-winning movie actor says he and a partner, Paul Scialla, a New York City-based developer, have plans to build a five-star resort there, tentatively named **Blackadore Caye, a Restorative Island,** with opening planned for

2018. Originally the resort was to be a Four Seasons hotel, but that deal fell through. The guest villas are to be built on a large platform stretching in an arc over the sea, with artificial reefs underneath. Environmental impact studies and architectural planning are under way. At public meetings, some local people have raised objections to the super-luxury development.

NEAR BELIZE CITY

Historical St. George's Caye is only about 8 miles or 20 minutes by boat from Belize City. It was the site of perhaps the most famous event in Belize history, when, as the story goes, in September 1798 a ragtag group of Baymen defeated a larger Spanish fleet from Mexico. St. George's Caye Day on September 10 celebrates the culminating Belizean victory. Today, St. George's Caye is home to one dive resort and to a number of weekend and holiday homes of Belize City's economic and social elite. Ask about the small aquarium on the island.

St. George's Caye Resort. St. George's Caye, 800-813-8498; www.belizeislandparadise.com. This long-established resort, now under new management, has 12 cabañas, including some that are set over the water, and a main lodge building with seven rooms. It's the exact opposite of a large resort. You get personal attention here, and sometimes you may be the only guests at the hotel. Cabaña rates are US$119 to $159 per person. Simple rooms are US$99 per person (double occupancy) All units have air-conditioning. Full meal plans are an additional US$60 per person per day. There are also dive and other packages, starting at US$826 to $1,066 per person for four nights. Rates are plus 9% tax. Rates include transfers from the international airport (minimum four-night stay), unlimited use of kayaks, Hobie Cats, windsurfers and snorkeling equipment and wireless internet in the main lodge. There is a salt-water pool. A bar serves beer and drinks.

Royal Palm Island Resort. Little Frenchman Caye, 501-223-4999 or 888-969-7829; www.royalpalmisland.com. This resort on 7-acre Little Frenchman Caye is about 9 miles off Belize City and within about a mile of the barrier reef. Accommodations are in air-conditioned two-bedroom beachfront cottages. All-inclusive rates include full breakfast, lunch with beverage of choice, three-course dinner with beverage of choice, mini-bar in room and return transfers from the international airport. Day trips to the island from Belize City are around US$100 including lunch. All-inclusive rates are from US$342 to $430 per person per day, depending on the time of year. Rates include taxes and service.

Hugh Parkey's Belize Adventure Lodge. Spanish Lookout Caye, 501-223-4526; www.belizeadventurelodge.com. Named after a well-known dive and hotel operator who with his wife for many years ran the famous Fort Street Guesthouse in Belize City. He died in 2002, while diving

244

in Mexico. Now it has 12 cabañas on 186-acre Spanish Caye about 25 minutes from Belize City. The cabañas are built over water. Five day/four-night dive packages, including transfers, lodging in an over-the-water cabaña, meals and four dives are around US$950 per person, double occupancy. Prices include taxes but not dive equipment or entries to marine parks.

OFF DANGRIGA
RAGGED CAYES

Royal Belize. Ragged Caye Range, 800-348-0546; www.royalbelize.com. Want to rent a private island for yourself and your closest friends? There are four deluxe, air-conditioned cottages on the island 25 minutes by boat from Dangriga. For around US$5,600 a night (US$4,400 September to mid-November) on an all-inclusive basis, including transfers from Belize City, meals, drinks and many water activities, you can enjoy the entire island for your party of up to 10 people. For weddings and other groups, the island comes with manager, concierge and cook. Off-island tours are not included in the all-inclusive rates. Minimum four-day stay, and taxes are additional. Rates for couples may also be available at times.

SOUTHWATER CAYE MARINE RESERVE

About 10 miles off Dangriga, **Tobacco Caye** is a tiny 5-acre coral island. Some people think Tobacco Caye is a funky island paradise; others think it's a bit junky. The accommodations on Tobacco Caye are all quite basic, simple wood cabins without air-conditioning. There's no scheduled water taxi service, but you can hook a boat at Dangriga to take you out – around US$17.50 to $20 one-way. **Captain Buck** (501-669-0869) is reliable, as are **Campa** (501-666-8699) and **Captain Doggie** (501-627-7443). Check at the **Riverside Café,** where the boat captains hang out.

Paradise Caye Cabins. 501-532-2101 or 800-667-1630 in U.S./Canada; www.tobaccocaye.com. Paradise has six simple but clean over-the-water cabins at the north end of the island. Rates around US$25 per person for room-only, US$50 per person including meals. All plus 9% tax. If you're buying meals separately, they're US$7.50 for breakfast or lunch, US$10 for dinner. Paradise Cabins is part of the Belize Adventure Group, which also runs Island Expeditions, Island Adventures and Bocawina Rainforest Resort.

Tobacco Caye Lodge. 501-532-2033; www.tclodgebelize.com. Rooms in six duplex wood cabañas, with all meals, are around US$55 per person in-season and US$48 per person off-season, plus 9% tax. Other choices on the island include **Reef's End Lodge** (www.reefendslodge.com, which has the island's only dive shop, and **Jo-Jo's by the Reef** (www.jojosbythereef.com.)

Southwater Caye's beautiful water and beach   Licensed from Adobe

Southwater Caye, about 15 acres in size, is one of the most beautiful small islands off Belize. The south end of the caye, where Pelican Beach's cottages are located, has a nice little beach and snorkeling right off the shore.

Pelican Beach Resort, Southwater Caye. (P.O. Box 2, Dangriga), 501-522-2044; www.pelicanbeachbelize.com. This is a wonderful place, comfortable rather than deluxe. The resort has three charming duplex cottages, two stand-alone casitas plus five rooms in the main building on 3½ acres at the south end, the best part of this beautiful island. In-season, nightly rates are US$350 double in a Pelican Pouch room to US$475 double in a freestanding casita, including three meals. Off-season, rates are only slightly less -- US$315 to $430. Rates do include taxes and service. Boat transfers from Dangriga are around US$70 person extra. Packages are also available, which include lodging, meals and transfers. A three-night package is US$850 to $885 per person, including taxes and service, a few dollars less off-season.

Other choices on the island are the expensive **Blue Marlin Lodge** (501-520-2243, www.bluemarlinlodge.com), with good dive and fishing options, and the less expensive **International Zoological Expeditions Cottages** (501-520-5030, www.ize2belize.com), which caters to educational groups in a dorm, but which also has private cabins and a dive shop.

Note: Visitors to Southwater Caye Marine Reserve (including those staying on Tobacco Caye and Southwater Caye) pay US$5 a day per person marine reserve fee, or US$15 for up to a week's stay.

COCOPLUM RANGE

These islands are about 8 to 9 miles off Dangriga. Unlike Southwater Caye and Tobacco Caye, they are not directly on the reef, so the shore snorkeling is fair at best.

Thatch Caye. (P.O. Box 133, Dangriga), 501-532-2414 or 800-435-3145 in U.S./Canada; www.thatchcayebelize.com. There are five overwater bungalows, one three-bedroom over-the-water villa and four seaside cottages on this "hand built" island. (The developers spent years putting up bamboo sea walls and raised boardwalks.) You can head out for a day of fishing, diving, sea kayaking, or snorkeling, then enjoy a delicious meal in the thatched-roof dining room, sip an ice-cold drink and surf the web on the free wi-fi in the bar before heading to your seaside or over-the-water cabaña where you'll be lulled asleep by the trade winds. Nightly all-inclusive rates, including lodging, all meals, drinks, marine reserve fees and use of non-motorized water sports equipment and round-trip transportation from Dangriga, are US$595 double per night for both island cabañas or over-the-water bungalows. Taxes aren't included, and rates are higher during holidays. Diving, fishing and wedding packages are also available.

Thatch Caye strives for sustainability, with solar and wind power, and discourages the use of air-conditioning.

Coco Plum Island Resort. Cocoplum Caye, 800-763-7360 in U.S./Canada; www.cocoplumcay.com. Coco Plum Island Resort is an adults-only all-inclusive on a 16-acre island, a short distance from Thatch Caye. It has 14 cottages, all air-conditioned and painted in bright tropical colors. The larger cottages have kitchenettes. A four-night package with all meals, drinks, boat transfers from Dangriga, two snorkeling tours and use of snorkeling equipment and kayak is US$2,720 in-season, US$2,440 off-season. Taxes but not gratuities are included in packages. Some more-expensive packages include flights from Belize City and a number of mainland and other tours. The snorkeling off the shore is only so-so, but most packages include snorkel trips to the reef a few miles farther out. Diving, fishing and romance packages also available. It may be better now, but on one of our stays here we were eaten alive by sandflies.

Yak Ha Resort. Water Foot Caye, (office is at 1211 North Riverside Street, Dangriga), 501-630-7870; www.yakhabelizeresort.com. Yak Ha is on a small, 3-acre island about 8 miles from Dangriga. The resort has three types of cabañas, all with air-conditioning. Rates including lodging and all meals are US$410 to $535 double in-season and US$350 to $475 June to November. If you prefer a full all-inclusive, including drinks, add US$100 per day. Dive packages start at US$1,500 per person for a four-night package in-season and US$1,340 per person off-season, including two dives a day, all meals and park fees. All rates are plus 9% hotel tax and 5% service charge. The top pick among the five accommodation options here is the Loa cottage, which has its own private deck, a small beach and an outdoor shower as well as an indoor bath.

OFF PLACENCIA

Hatchet Caye Resort. Hatchet Caye, 501-523-3337; www.hatchetcaye.com. On this small private island (you can walk the length of it in five minutes) about 17 miles off Placencia, Hatchet Caye Resort could be what you're seeking, especially if you want snorkeling from shore, good food and relaxation. Hatchet Caye Resort has seafront rooms in the main house and seaside cabañas spread out around the island. Rates for three nights including lodging, three meals a day, all taxes and service charges, boat transfer from Placencia to the island and use of paddle boards, kayaks, pedal boats and snorkel gear are US$1,100 in a room or $1,200 in a cabaña, per person. Longer stay rates are an additional US$250 to $275 per night per person. These rates don't include drinks, diving, fishing or the marine reserve fee of US$10 when taking a snorkel trip to Turtle Spot (no fee for snorkeling at Hatchet Caye). The Lionfish Grill restaurant is good, although as often in Belize service may take a little time. This is a popular stopping spot for boaters and The Moorings chartered sailboats, so occasionally the restaurant and bar fill up.

Ranguana Caye. 501-674-7264; www.ranguanacaye.com. Ranguana Caye is an idyllic little 2-acre caye with a couple of cabins, a private beach bar, a nice beach and snorkeling and bonefishing off the shore. Rates are around US$500 for two persons, plus 9% tax and include transportation to and from the island from Placencia, lodging in a seaside cabaña, use of kayaks and paddleboards and all meals. If you just want to visit for the day, excursions from Placencia including a beach barbecue are US$125 per person. It's about an hour's boat ride from the new Placencia Municipal Pier. This is also a good place for boaters to moor for the night, get ice and enjoy a delicious meal. Contact the caye in advance on VHF Channel 68.

Reef CI. Tom Owens Caye, (Office: Mile 18, Placencia), 501-626-1428; www.reefci.com. Founded by Polly Alford, originally on Hunting Caye in the Sapodillas off Punta Gorda, Reef CI offers diving conservation holidays from their new home at Tom Owens Caye about 25 miles off Placencia. In 2015, Reef CI also moved its office from PG to Placencia. Reef CI offers recreational dives, marine survey dives and PADI dive training and qualification. The conservation emphasis focuses on spiny lobster and queen conch preservation and reduction of the threat by the invasive lionfish. All-inclusive Monday-Friday marine conservation SCUBA packages are for four nights and five days and include transportation to the island, all meals and three dives daily. The price is US$1,330 per person, with additional four-night packages US$995. Non-diver four-night/five-day packages are $1,025 per person. Rates don't include marine reserve fees or gratuities. A PADI open water dive course is $100, and an advanced open water course is $150. Reef CI also offers four-week internship programs and special courses such as underwater photography. On the tiny 1½-acre island, the lodge has rooms in a main building and in stone cabañas.

Whipray Caye, about 11 miles off Placencia, is a spot for anglers, as you can wade out about 50 yards in the flats and fish for tarpon, permit and other game fish. Julian Cabral, a well known Placencia fishing guide, owns the island and with American wife Beverly Montgomery-Cabral operates **Whipray Lodge** and the **Sea Urchin** bar and restaurant (501-610-1068, www.whipraycayelodge.com.) The three basic cabins can accommodate up to eight people. There's also good snorkeling here.

OFF PUNTA GORDA

Off Punta Gorda in Toledo are the Port Honduras Marine Reserve and, farther out, the Sapodilla Cayes Marine Reserve. The Port Honduras reserve, known for its great fishing, has about 135 mangrove islands including Frenchman Caye and the Snakes Caye. It is home to the protected West Indian manatees and saltwater and Morelet's crocodiles. The Sapodillas, a 90-minute boat ride from PG, has some of the most beautiful cayes in Belize. For diving, including night dives, you'll find gradual wall declines and spur and grooves. Hunting Caye is a hawksbill turtle nesting site, and Lime Caye has a lovely white sand beach.

Garbutt's Fishing Lodge. Lime Caye (main office, Joe Taylor Creek, Punta Gorda), 501-604-3548; www.garbuttsfishinglodge.com. Lime Caye is owned by three Garbutt brothers, Dennis, Scully and Oliver. The brothers grew up Punta Negra, spending holidays at the Sapodilla Cayes where their father was the lighthouse keeper. Garbutt's Marine has its main fishing lodge, run by the brothers, a cousin and an uncle, in PG but has primitive bunkhouse cabins on the small island (toilets and showers are outside, about 100 yards from the bunkhouse). You eat at Sandy's Cool Spot, a snack shack on the island. Packages are US$350 to $700 per person including transportation, lodging, meals, snorkeling, fishing and park fees (US$10 per person per day).

University of Belize. www.ub.edu.bz/. Hunting Caye is the site of one of the University of Belize's small satellite campuses, and it sometimes rents out its basic rooms to visitors (around US$40 per person). The Belize Coast Guard is also stationed here, and there's a lighthouse. The island has nesting grounds for hawksbill turtles. Camping on the island is US$5 per person.

THE ATOLLS LODGING AND DINING

Atolls are characterized by a large lagoon surrounded by coral reefs. While atolls are common in the South Pacific, they are rare in the Western Hemisphere. Of the four known atolls in the Western Hemisphere, three are in Belize – Glover's, Turneffe and Lighthouse. The fourth, Chinchorra, is in southern Mexico.

GLOVER'S ATOLL

Glover's Atoll (also spelled Glovers) is the smallest of the three atolls in Belize, with an area of about 140 square miles. Some 45 miles from the mainland, Glover's offers some of the best diving and snorkeling in the Caribbean. The atoll, named after a pirate, John Glover, has some 800 coral patches in the lagoon. It, with the Belize Barrier Reef, is a UNESCO World Heritage Site. Around the atoll are 50 miles of walls dropping from

40 to 2,500 feet or more. There's a US$30 marine reserve fee. Fishing is restricted in parts of this reserve – if you are fishing, reserve rangers will collect a weekly license fee of US$25 per person.

Isla Marisol. (P.O. Box 10, Dangriga), 501-610-4204 or 855-350-1569; www.islamarisol.com. Southwest Caye, where Isla Marisol is located, is owned by a Belizean family, which obtained the island in the 1940s. Lodging at this resort is in 12 wood cabins with air-conditioning and zinc roofs and two suites in a house. There's a restaurant and bar. Four-night packages, including lodging, meals and transport from Dangriga, start at about US$2,150 per couple. Fishing and dive charges are extra (for example, one-tank dives are US$56 plus 12.5% tax per person). Isla Marisol's sister resort on the mainland is Fantasy Island Eco-Resort.

Off the Wall Dive Center and Resort. Long Caye, 501-532-2929; www.offthewallbelize.com. Off the Wall, run by Jim and Kendra Schofield, focuses on diving, but there's excellent snorkeling and fishing as well. Facilities are rustic — five small wood cabins, composting toilets and outdoor rainwater showers. Meals are served in a beachfront thatch palapa with sand floor. There is no a/c, no room phone, no room TV, with solar-powered lights and candles, which many find just about perfect. Great snorkeling is available from shore, and you can also fish for bonefish, permit, grouper and jack right from the lodge's pier. Rates US$1,495 plus tax per person weekly for lodging and meals; gratuities and rum and beer are additional. Boat transfers from Dangriga, leaving on Saturday, are included. Dives are extra –a 12-dive package is US$450 plus 12.5% GST. Any needed dive and fishing equipment rental also is extra.

Glover's Atoll Resort. Northeast Caye (P.O. Box 563, Belize City), 501-520-5016; www.glovers.com.bz. Don't let the name mislead you – this isn't your typical resort. The Lamont family, who came to Belize in the 1960s, offer very basic accommodations on Northeast Caye, about 45 miles out in the Caribbean at a reasonable price in a beautiful setting. You won't get running water or electricity here, but you can enjoy one of the most stunning parts of the Caribbean Sea. Around the 9-acre island you can dive or snorkel right from the shore. Weekly per-person rates year-round: Simple palmetto thatch cabañas are US$249 and those built over the water are US$299; thatch cabañas on beach, US$249; dorm room is US$149, camping, US$99. Children under 12 are half price. Rates include transportation by boat to and from Sittee River near Hopkins but not 9% hotel tax. The weekly boat from Sittee River leaves Sundays. If you can't make the Sunday boat, charters are expensive: One-way US$350 for up to six passengers from Sittee River Village or Dangriga, and it takes 1½ to 2 hours to island. From Placencia the charter is US$400, and from Belize

City, US$800. You'll need to bring most everything you need, including toilet paper, food, beer, cooler with ice and other supplies. Bottled water (US$1.50 a gallon) and kerosene (US$1 a pint) and a few grocery items are usually available on the island. Simple meals are offered, but they're fairly expensive. You can rent kayaks, canoes, and dive and snorkel gear. Glover's Atoll Resort is quite a remarkable place, but not for everyone.

Also check out the **Slickrock Adventures** lodge on Long Caye (800-390-5715 from U.S./Canada, www.slickrock.com), with rates around US$1,500 per person for a five-night trip. Another good option is **Island Expeditions** (800-667-1630 from U.S./Canada, www.islandexpeditions.com), which has a tent camp on Southwest Caye. Three-day packages cost from around US$640 per person.

LIGHTHOUSE REEF ATOLL

Lighthouse Atoll is about 45 to 50 miles off the mainland coast, east of Belize City. The atoll is famous (thanks to Jacques Cousteau) for the Blue Hole inside the lagoon. The Blue Hole, an underwater sinkhole or cenote, is about one-quarter mile across and about 500 feet deep. Divers usually find the Blue Hole less interesting than they expected it would be, with very little sea life other than some sharks, but it's worth doing once. Several divers have died here, and it is not for novices. Half Moon Caye, a 45-acre coral island, is one of the most beautiful of all the Belize cayes, and it was part of Belize's first marine reserve. There's a daily fee of US$40 per person to visit the marine reserve and caye.

Lodging at Lighthouse Reef Atoll has a checkered history, in part because of its remote location and the difficulty of getting guests and supplies to the main atoll island, the 650-acre Long Caye. Note that there are several Long Cayes in Belize, which can cause confusion.

Huracan Diving. Long Caye, Lighthouse Reef Atoll; www.huracandiving.com. Huracan has a four-room guesthouse and a dive operation on Long Caye. The guesthouse is less than 15 minutes by boat to the Blue Hole. Huracan offers dive packages that include accommodations, all meals, dives and transportation (Wednesday and Saturday only) from the Ramada Princess Hotel Marina in Belize City, generally at 2 p.m. Three-, four- and seven-night packages are available, starting at US$935 per person double occupancy for a three-night package with five dives off-season (June 30-October 30) and US$1,045 per person the rest of the year. Seven-night packages with 14 dives are US$1,880 to $2,095 per person double occupancy. Snorkel and fishing packages also available. Rates do not include taxes, tips, a 3% fee for using a credit card, bar charges or marine park fees. Rooms in the guesthouse have king beds, fans and electrical outlets for charging cell phones, computers, etc. but not air-conditioning. Huracan has complimentary satellite internet wi-fi.

Itza Lodge. Long Caye, Lighthouse Reef Atoll (P.O. Box 2050, Belize City), U.S. phone 305-600-2585; www.itzalodge.com. Itza Lodge is about 50 miles offshore from Belize City. Transportation to Itza is by boat from the Ramada Princess Hotel in Belize City, a trip of 1½ to 2 hours, depending on weather. The lodge's boat runs on Wednesdays and Saturdays. If you'd rather fly, helicopter transfers by Astrum Helicopter are around US$2,000 one-way for up to four persons. The lodge has 24 rooms, 12 in the main lodge building and 12 in the Sea Wing. Rooms in the main lodge have private baths while those in the Sea Wing have shared baths. Rooms have fans but no air-conditioning. There is a restaurant, bar and swimming pool. Diving is the big reason to come here. The lodge is only 6 miles from the Blue Hole and is near several other excellent dive areas including Half Moon Wall. Three- to seven-night dive packages including dives, meals and boat transport from Belize City range from US$893 to $2,173 per person, plus hotel and sales taxes, tips, equipment rental and US$40 per-person park fees. Also available are snorkeling and fishing packages.

TURNEFFE ATOLL

Turneffe Atoll is about 25 miles from the mainland, to the east of Belize City. The central lagoon, which has some 200 small mangrove islands, is about 240 square miles in area. There is also a smaller northern lagoon. Like Belize's other atolls, Turneffe offers magnificent diving and great fishing. The eastern and southern side of the atoll offers the best diving. Probably the most famous site is The Elbow, on the southern tip. Spur and groove diving is here only for experienced divers.

Turneffe Flats. U.S. office: P.O. Box 10670, Bozeman, MT 59719, 501-232-9032 or 888-512-8812 in U.S./Canada; www.tflats.com. It's remote, it's beautiful and it's air-conditioned. The lodge, on the northeast side of the atoll, provides boat transport from Belize City to Turneffe on Saturdays. The trip takes about 90 minutes. Dive packages are around US$2,750 in-season and US$2,550 off-season per person for a week, inclusive of lodging, meals, three dives a day and transport to the island but not booze, tips, park fees or taxes. Weekly fishing packages are more, around US$3,780 to $4,280 per person. Three- and four-night packages also are available, as are many other packages.

Blackbird Caye Resort. 866-909-7333; www.blackbirdresort.com. Now under new management, Blackbird Caye Resort is about 25 miles from Belize City, with about 4,000 acres and some two miles of beachfront on Blackbird Caye at Turneffe Atoll. Accommodations are in duplex and triplex cabañas, a beach house, a beachfront suite and in three levels of rooms. Dinner is served in a large thatch palapa, and there's a pool with bar. All-inclusive packages that include transfers by air to the caye (Blackbird has an airstrip), lodging in an oceanfront suite, meals, diving and more, for US$4,000 per person for a week and US$3,200 for four nights. Rates do not include a resort fee, tips or drinks. There are myriad other packages and rates.

Turneffe Island Resort. 501-532-2990 or 800-760-0241 in U.S./Canada; www.turnefferesort.com. Accommodations are in eight private cabañas or in 12 superior-level or deluxe-level rooms on Big Caye Bokel at the southern end of the central lagoon. Weekly packages range from US$2,090 to $4,590 per person, depending on type of activities, the time of year and other factors. Three- and four-night packages also available, starting at US$1,340 per person. Rates include boat transport to the island but not taxes, tips or alcohol.

LIVE ABOARD DIVE BOATS

Another option for visiting Belize's atolls is the live aboard dive boat. These are mini-cruise ships whose focus is on diving. They provide comfortable cabins, good food and the opportunity for up to five dives daily including one night dive.

Belize Aggressor Fleet. 209 Hudson Trace, Augusta, GA 30907, 706-993-2531 or 800-348-2628; www.aggressor.com.

The Belize Aggressor Fleet has two yachts that are in Belize. One is the *Belize Aggressor III*, a 110-foot yacht that has been in the fleet since 1987. It has a capacity of up to 18 passengers in nine staterooms, with six crew. The other is *Belize Aggressor IV*, formerly the Sundancer II. Its length is 138 feet with a beam of 26 feet. It carries up to 20 passengers in 10 staterooms, with a crew of seven.

Both boats do seven-day trips, Saturday to Saturday, year-round departing from the marina at the Radisson Fort George Hotel in Belize City. The usual itinerary includes stops at Turneffe Atoll and at Lighthouse Reef Atoll including Halfmoon Caye and the Blue Hole. Current rates range from US$2,795 to US$2,995 per person, double occupancy. Rates include all dives, airport transfers, meals and snacks and local beer and wine; they do not include air fare to Belize, $95 port fees, marine reserve fees, Belize exit tax, equipment rentals, Nitrox or gratuities.

SOUTHERN BELIZE

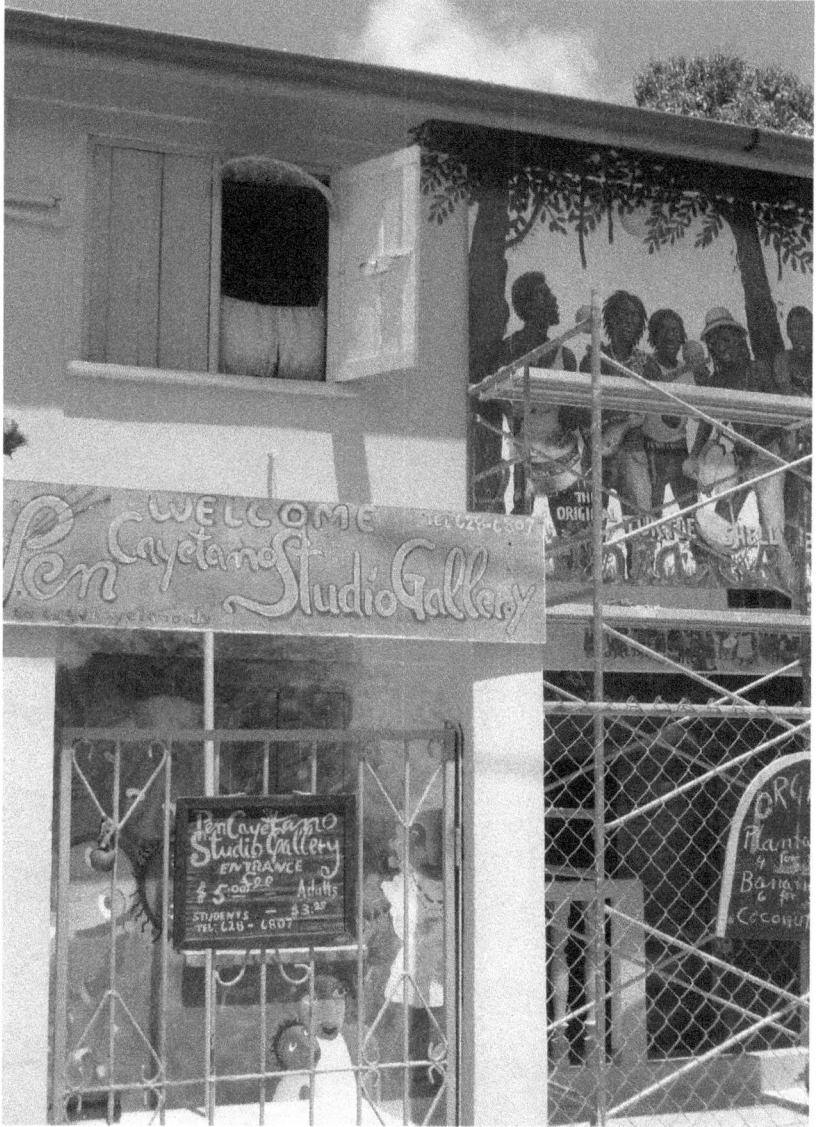

Pen Cayetano's studio in Dangriga

Southern Belize begins on the southern part of the Hummingbird Highway near Dangriga, leaving behind the scenic green Maya Mountains and transitioning to citrus and banana plantations. Dangriga may not be a tourist magnet, but it is a Garifuna cultural and art center.

A short distance farther off the Southern Highway is the friendly and fast-changing coastal village of Hopkins and the wild inland expanses of the Cockscomb Basin Wildlife Sanctuary, with its roaming jaguars, and Mayflower Bocawina National Park.

A little farther south is the Placencia peninsula, a rival to Ambergris Caye and Caye Caulker for beach vacation popularity. Development has changed the peninsula already, and it may change more with the scheduled opening in late 2016 of a controversial Norwegian Cruise Line cruise port off Placencia village. There's an unfinished international airport here whose future no one seems to know.

Going farther still into the Deep South, you reach Toledo District, with lush, rain-soaked rainforests, ancient Maya ruins and contemporary Maya villages. Then, you come to the end of the road, Punta Gorda, a friendly ends- of-the-earth little bayside town. PG is also an exit point for boats to the Caribbean Coast of Guatemala and, perhaps sometime soon, by land to Guatemala and Honduras via the newly built and paved San Antonio Road, where a second Guatemala border crossing (the first being near Benque Viejo in Cayo District) is expected to open near Jalacte village.

By the time you get to southern Toledo District, coastal beaches are not easily accessible and the tail end of the Belize Barrier Reef is a good ways out from shore. But the sea and reefs are pristine, and the fishing is fine. Dangriga, Hopkins, Placencia and PG are jumping off points for visiting the offshore cayes and atolls, although the distances involved make some of the boat rides long and sometimes rough.

DANGRIGA AND HOPKINS

DANGRIGA AND HOPKINS RATINGS

Ratings are on an A to F scale, just like your old high school report card. A is the top grade; F is failing.

Popularity with Visitors	C (B for Hopkins)
Popularity with Expats	C- (B- for Hopkins)
Cost Level	B-
Safety	B
Scenic Beauty	C+
Lodging	B-
Dining	C+
Nightlife	C
Outdoor Activities	A
Water Activities	B
Cultural Activities	B-
Museums/Galleries	C-

Maya Sites   B
Historical Sites   C
Tourism Infrastructure   B-
Transportation   C+
Medical Care   C+
Shopping   C+ (B- for Dangriga)
Overall Visitor Rating B-

DANGRIGA AND HOPKINS OVERVIEW

ADVANTAGES OF HOPKINS/DANGRIGA AREA: •
Fascinating, exotic Garifuna culture • Excellent opportunities for water
sports – boating, fishing, diving, snorkeling • Proximity to Cockscomb
Basin Wildlife Sanctuary and other natural areas • Jumping off point for
some offshore cayes and atolls

This part of Stann Creek District is Belize at its most exotic, with
Garifuna settlements that may remind you more of a coastal village in
Senegal than Central America. Rural Maya villages look much as they
did hundreds, or thousands, of years ago. A few miles inland are a wild
jaguar preserve and the highest mountains in Belize. The Cockscomb
Basin Preserve west of Hopkins is real rainforest jungle, and the tallest
peaks in Belize, Doyle's Delight at 3,688 feet and Victoria Peak at 3,675
feet, are in the mountains above.

Unlike much of the rest of Belize's mainland coast, the Hopkins area
has real beaches. The beaches here are similar to those in Placencia *(see
below)* — ribbons of khaki-colored sand, with a good deal of seagrass in
the water off the beach. Swimming is possible, especially in areas where
the seagrass has been removed, as at the end of a dock. The snorkeling off
the shore usually is not very good, although you can see some fish and
possibly even a stray manatee.

The barrier reef is about 12 to 15 miles offshore from Hopkins and
Dangriga, so it takes a while to get out to the reef for diving.

The Garifuna (usually pronounced Gah-RIF-u-nah) people who
settled in this area have a fascinating history. Before the time of
Columbus, Indians from the South American mainland came by boat to
the island of St. Vincent in the southeast Caribbean. They conquered,
and then intermarried with, Arawak Indians, adopting much of the
Indian language. They went by the name Kwaib, from which the
names Carib and Garifuna, meaning cassava-eaters, probably evolved.

Then, in the 17th century, slaves from Nigeria were shipwrecked off
St. Vincent. They too mixed with the Caribs or Garifuna. For years,

Britain tried to subdue these free people of color, but the Garifuna, with the support of the French, fought back until the late 1700s, when the French and Garifuna finally surrendered to the British. In 1797, several thousand surviving Garifuna were taken by ship to Roatán in Honduras. Over the next 150 years or so, many Garifuna moved from Roatán up the coast of Central America to Belize, where they worked in logging. The largest migration to Belize took place in 1823, and today that is commemorated nationally on November 19 as Garifuna Settlement Day.

Many ended up in what is now called Dangriga. Hopkins, Seine Bight and, in Toledo, Punta Gorda Town and Barranco village also have sizable Garifuna populations. Initially, Dangriga was called Black Carib Town and then Stann Creek.

The Garinagu in Belize are working hard to continue their language and culture. They have a complex system of religious beliefs, combining African and South American elements as well as Catholicism. Dugu or "Feasting of the Dead" is one of the ancestral rites practiced by the Garifuna. There is a good small museum near Dangriga, Gulisi Garifuna Museum, with displays on the Garifuna people, their culture and their art.

Dangriga itself is not a very popular area for visitors, but the Hopkins/Sittee Point area south of Dangriga is attracting a lot of attention.

Hopkins is a delightfully friendly and still mostly unspoiled village, though it is changing fast. In Hopkins and nearby are several excellent beach resorts, notably Hamanasi, along with many smaller, less expensive lodging options. You'll find some good spots for dining as well.

The Sittee River and the Caribbean waters offer some of Belize's best fishing. The barrier reef isn't close to shore here, but once you get to the reef there's good diving. There's also good diving in the Southwater Caye Marine Reserve. Inland you're only a few miles from the world's first jaguar preserve, Cockscomb. Also within a short drive are Maya ruins and waterfalls at Mayflower, along with a revitalized jungle lodge, formerly Mama Noots, with the country's longest zipline.

In Dangriga you'll find some shopping and a regional hospital for medical care. The access road from the Southern Highway to Sittee village and the coast is mostly paved, and the road to Hopkins village from the Southern Highway has been rebuilt and surfaced. If there's a rub to this paradise, it's the sand fleas, which can be fierce in this area.

Dangriga/Hopkins Practicalities

Dangriga is the hub of this area, and for medical care, shopping and other services this is where you will need to go. Hopkins has only a few small shops.

Banks: Belize Bank, Heritage Bank and ScotiaBank have branches and ATMs in or near Dangriga. There are no banks in Hopkins, but there is a Belize Bank ATM, but we've heard that fairly frequently it is either out of order or out of cash.

Groceries: There are several sizeable groceries in Dangriga. Try the one near Pen Cayetano's home and studio.

Restaurants: The restaurant at Pelican Beach Resort is the best Dangriga has to offer, but there are other options including Riverside Café. Hopkins has several small restaurants owned and operated by local ladies, including Innie's that serve good local food and low prices. Chef Rob's, now at Parrot Cove Resort, is one of the top restaurants in the south. The restaurant at Beaches and Dreams is very good, too.

Vehicle Rental: As of this writing, Hopkins has one small car rental agency, Hopkins Auto Rental (South Side, Hopkins village, 501-669-8102). Dangriga Auto Rental & Tours (Michael Evans, Sabal's Community, Dangriga, 501-607-0435) may have a few cars for rent from around US$80 to $180 a day, plus GST.

Medical: The Southern Regional Hospital (501-522-2078) at Mile 1½ of the Stann Creek Valley Highway opened in 1999. Dangriga is a regional medical center for Southern Belize, including Placencia.

Infrastructure: Dangriga and Hopkins have municipal water and in most areas sewerage systems. These areas as well as most villages are on the electrical grid. Cable TV, DSL and cellular internet are available. More remote areas are not on the grid and must depend on their own resources for water, sewerage and satellite internet. Many Maya villages have homes with no running water or electricity.

For More Information: The website Visit Hopkins Village (www.visithopkinsvillage.com) has some tourist information.

GETTING TO DANGRIGA AND HOPKINS

Dangriga is connected with the north by the Hummingbird Highway and by the Coastal Highway, which is also known as the Manatee Highway. Running south from Dangriga to Punta Gorda, a distance of about 100 miles, is the Southern Highway. Once this was widely considered the worst "main" road in Belize, with cars and big trucks raising thick clouds of dust in dry weather and bogging down in the mud in wet.

Things have improved a lot. The Southern Highway is now completely paved and one of the best roads in the country. **James Bus Line** (www.jamesbusline.com) buses connect Dangriga with Belize City (around US$8). Dangriga has an airstrip, with regular service on **Maya Island Air** (www.mayaislandair.com) and **Tropic Air** (www.tropicair.com) from Belize

City. One-way fares from the international airport are around US$92, and from municipal about US$61. There also are shuttle services from Belize City, San Ignacio and elsewhere that will take you in a van to Dangriga or Hopkins. *See the section on Placencia for more information on shuttles.*

The road into Dangriga is completely paved. The access road to Hopkins from the Southern Highway also is now paved, and that to Sittee River is paved as well, but the paving ends around Sittee village before you get to Hopkins.

WHAT TO SEE AND DO IN DANGRIGA AND HOPKINS

Few visitors stay for long in Dangriga. In many ways that's a shame, because Dangriga is home to a unique culture, the Garifuna. It is also home to a number of nationally and internationally known artists, musicians and drum makers. The town, scruffy at first look, is actually quite photogenic. Physically, it slightly resembles the older sections of Belize City, although it is much smaller.

Dangriga, with a population of around 9,000, is the largest town in Belize south of Belize City. Until the 1980s it was known as Stann Creek, when it was renamed Dangriga, meaning "sweet waters" in the Garifuna language.

One interesting attraction in Dangriga is the **Gulisi Garifuna Museum** (George Price Drive, 501-669-0539, open 10 to 5 Monday-Friday and 8 to noon Saturday, admission US$5). It has excellent displays on Garifuna culture, art and history.

Another must-see near Dangriga is the **Marie Sharp's Factory** (Melinda Road, off Stann Creek Valley Road, 501-532-2087, www.mariesharps-bz.com.) It's open 9-4 Monday-Friday. You can usually take a brief tour, or at least a look, at the small factory that produces the famous hot sauce and other condiments. You can also buy all the Marie Sharp's products at a shop there. Marie Sharp herself is often there. There is another Marie Sharp's store in Dangriga (near Stann Creek Bridge, 501-522-2370, open 8-5 Monday-Friday.)

Dangriga is also something of an art center, with **Pen Cayetano's Studio Gallery** (3 Aranda Crescent, Dangriga, 501-628-6807, www.cayetano.de). Pen Cayetano painted an impressive mural for the Dangriga Town Hall in 2012. Cayetano himself now spends most of his time in Germany. **Austin Rodriquez's drum workshop** is here, too. Artist Benjamin Nicholas and doll-maker Mercy Sabal also do their work in Dangriga.

The biggest event of the year here is **Garifuna Settlement Day,** celebrated on November 19 and the days around that date. There's a reenactment of the Garingu landing in British Honduras, along with drumming concerts, dancing, music concerts, art exhibits and more.

Dangriga is also a **departure point for many offshore cayes**, including Southwater Caye, Tobacco Caye, Cocoplum Caye and Thatch Caye, all with resorts. It's also a good place for departures to the wonders and the several resorts on Glover's Reef Atoll.

A little farther south, the **village of Hopkins** offers Garifuna culture is an easier-to-absorb form, and the beaches, restaurants, dive resorts and small guesthouses are draws here. Hopkins bills itself as being midway between the reef and the rainforest. You can go diving one day, and the next tour the jungles of **Mayflower Bocawina National Park** and **Cockscomb Basin Wildlife Sanctuary**.

Mayflower Bocawina National Park

Mayflower Bocawina National Park (admission US$5) is off Mile 6 of the Southern Highway near Silkgrass village. You then go about 4½ miles west on an unpaved road to the entrance of the park, which has a small visitor center staffed by a park ranger. Mayflower Bocawina comprises about 7,000 acres of broadleaf rainforest.

In the park are five waterfalls and three small Maya sites. Getting to the waterfalls requires a fairly strenuous hike.

Also in the park is a jungle lodge, **Bocawina Rainforest Resort and Adventures,** (501-670-8019, www.mamanootsbocawina.com) formerly Mama Noots Eco-Lodge. Bocawina Rainforest Resort has a variety of accommodations, from rooms to suites to cottages, for US$120 to $225 in-season and US$99 to $185 off-season. Rates plus 9% hotel tax and 9% service. There's also a restaurant and bar at the resort and what is billed as the longest zipline in Belize. The 2½-mile zipline costs around US$65 plus 12.5% tax for daytime tours and US$75 plus tax for a night zip.

Cockscomb Basin Wildlife Sanctuary

You'll probably get wet and get eaten up by mosquitoes, but you'll get to experience the "real jungle" at **Cockscomb Basin Wildlife Sanctuary**. This preserve covers nearly 150 square miles of broadleaf rainforest. Much of it has been selectively logged for mahogany and other valuable trees, and some of it was affected by hurricanes, but to the novice bushwalker the rainforest canopy, up to 130 feet high, and the exotic plants and trees are nothing at all like back home. Parts of the preserve get up to 180 inches of rain a year. The preserve is the starting point for expeditions to Victoria Peak, the second-highest point in Belize at 3,675 feet, behind Doyle's Delight at 3,688 feet.

Take the entrance road to Cockscomb at Maya Center, about 14 miles south of the intersection of the Stann Creek District Highway (aka Hummingbird Highway) and the Southern Highway. A roadside women's co-operative, **Maya Center Crafts Co-Operative** (open daily 8-5, admission free) sells Maya and other local crafts. There's also a small private museum nearby, **Maya Center Maya Museum** (admission US$7.50), with a small chocolate maker, **Che'il Chocolate Factory.**

Cockscomb Basin Wildlife Sanctuary admission is US$5 per person, collected at Maya Center. If you don't have your own transport, you can hire a taxi at Maya Center for around US$15 to take you to the visitor center in the park, or you can hang out at the crafts co-op and perhaps hitch a ride.

Cockscomb has the most extensive trail network of any park in Belize. Trails at the preserve vary from short self-guided hikes near the visitor center to the 17-mile multi-day trek to Victoria Peak, only for the physically fit and best done with a local guide during the dry season. While it's unlikely that you will see one of the 200 or so jaguars in the preserve, you may well see tracks or scat, as the jaguars do frequent the trails and entrance road at night. If you hike long enough, however, you will run into quite a few other wild creatures. The preserve is home to some 300 species of birds, along with all five types of Belize's wild cats, black howler monkeys, peccaries and snakes of all types and biting abilities. The best time to see wildlife is at the start of the rainy season, usually mid-June to early August, although with luck you will see wild creatures anytime you are in the preserve. Animals are most active on cooler, cloudy days.

Near the visitor center at the sanctuary is a tent campground (US$10 per person per night) and rustic cabins and a dorm from around US$20 to $55. Reservations can be made through the **Belize Audubon Society** (www.belizeaudubon.org.) Bring your own food and water.

DANGRIGA AND HOPKINS LODGING
Dangriga Lodging
Pelican Beach Resort. Scotchman Town, on the sea near the airstrip, 501-522-2044; www.pelicanbeachbelize.com. The rambling white wood-frame main building at Pelican Beach, reportedly once a dance hall, always reminds us of boarding houses of our youth in Florida; others say it reminds them of old hotels on the coast of Maine. Inside, though, it's vintage Belize, with simple wood paneling and furniture that wasn't selected by any interior designer. There are about a dozen rooms in the main building and others in a separate structure. All rooms have fans, and some have air conditioning. In any event, this is the best hotel in Dangriga. It's on

the water at the north edge of town, and there's a beach area and a breeze-swept pier. Some people swim here, but it's not exactly Cane Garden Beach in the British Virgin Islands. The Coconuts Grill & Bar is quite good, if a bit expensive (US$18 to $35 for dinner). Originally opened in 1971 by retired citrus farmer William Bowman Sr. Later, Tony and Therese Rath, granddaughter of the resort's founder, joined the Pelican Beach team. Therese's family, the Bowmans, was prominent in colonial days. Tony, a noted photographer, is among Belize's internet entrepreneurs, running the Belize by Naturalight web sites and doing web design for many Belize businesses. Rates: Doubles range from around US$135 to $147 double in-season (mid-November thru mid-May) and US$106 to $105 off-season. Prices are plus 9% hotel tax and 8.5% service. Packages are available. Pelican Beach Dangriga is associated with the delightful Pelican Beach cottages on Southwater Caye.

Chaleanor Hotel. 35 Magoon Street, 501-522-2587; e-mail chaleanor@btl.net. This is a decent budget/low moderate choice in Dangriga. It's well run and a good value. The 18 rooms in this tall, three-story hotel are larger than at many budget hotels, and all have private baths. Some rooms with TV and air-conditioning. Rates around US$22 to $75, plus tax. Another budget spot nearby is the recently upgraded, 16-room **Pal's Guesthouse** (868 Magoon Street, 501-660-1282) with rooms from around US$45 to $60.

Hopkins Lodging

A seaside Garifuna village of about 1,500 people living in simple frame houses, Hopkins was first settled in 1942 after a hurricane devastated New Town, a Garifuna community just north of present-day Hopkins. The village gets its name from Frederick Charles Hopkins, a Catholic bishop of the early part of the 20th century. Hopkins was itself leveled by Hurricane Hattie in 1961. The village only got electricity and telephones in the mid-1990s. If "poor but proud" fits anywhere, it fits here. Villagers have gotten by on subsistence fishing and farming, and some are now earning cash money from tourism. You'll find most folks friendly. Many are eager to share their thoughts with visitors, and it's safe to walk around the village. The beach is nice, though many coco palms have died from lethal yellowing. Just south of Hopkins is the Sittee Point and False Sittee Point area, where hotel and real estate development are taking off. Many lots have been sold to expats looking for their little piece of the Caribbean, though only a few homes have so far been built.

You may have heard about the ferocious sand flies in this area, and, yes, they can be pretty bad. At other times, they're hardly to be noticed.

Sorry, but we're not able to predict exactly when they are at their worst. The hotels here do their best to control the little devils, without resorting to hydrogen bombs, but at times the sandflies can be a pain in the neck, and also the foot, leg and everywhere else. An oily lotion such as baby oil or Avon Skin-So-Soft helps.

Hamanasi Adventure & Dive Resort. Sittee Point, Stann Creek District, 844-235-4930 or 877-552-3483; www.hamanasi.com. The resort was opened in 2000 by Americans Dana and David Krauskopf who quickly made Hamanasi one of the top beach and dive resorts in southern Belize. It has been named "Hotel of the Year" by the Belize Tourism Board and gets high ratings on TripAdvisor.com and other social media sites. On about 22 acres with 400 feet of beach frontage, the resort is south of Hopkins village. The restaurant and lobby are attractive, graced with local art, the grounds well kept and the pool, with a "zero effect," one of the nicest in Belize. There are several types of accommodations — 10 rooms and two suites in beachfront buildings and five deluxe and eight regular "tree houses" (actually just units raised on stilts and set in the trees in the back). All the accommodations are attractive, though we like the beachfront suites best. Hamanasi's dive operation provides full diving services. Hamanasi has three dive boats, including a big 45-footer with three 200-horsepower Suzuki outboard engines. A two-tank dive on the southern barrier reef is US$115 and a three-tank, full-day dive trip to Turneffe Atoll is US$185, and to Glover's Atoll US$195. A half-day reef snorkeling trip is US$75. Prices don't include dive or snorkel equipment rental. The resort also offers inland trips. Tours to Cockscomb are US$75. Room rates are way up there: US$398 to $690 in high season (Christmas and mid-February until Easter), US$333 to $608 in shoulder season and US$251 to $462 in low season (early June to mid-December, excepting U.S. Thanksgiving). Rates plus 9% hotel tax and 8% service charge. A continental breakfast is included in room rates. The hotel's restaurant is good, if very expensive, with a fixed-price dinner at US$50. There are usually minimum-stay requirements of three to five days, depending on the season. Packages are available: Three-night packages including a beachfront standard room, meals, taxes and service fees, air and ground transfers from Belize City and one tour (such as a half-day dive trip or tour of Cockscomb) start at US$1,161 per person in high season, based on double occupancy, a little lower the rest of the year. A top end high-season seven-night package in a beachfront suite is US$3,091 per person.

Jaguar Reef Lodge & Spa. Sittee Point, Stann Creek District, 501-523-7365, or 866-910-7373 in the U.S. and Canada; www.jaguarreef.com. Jaguar Reef is now jointly operated with **Almond Beach** next door. These two Hopkins properties are part of the Viva Belize group that also includes

La Beliza on North Ambergris, Sleeping Giant Lodge on the Hummingbird Highway and the treehouses at Ian Anderson's Caves Branch Lodge. The resort has many different types of accommodations. The attractive main lodge building houses the beachfront restaurant, bar, gift shop and front desk. The sandy beach here is nice. Jaguar Reef runs a variety of tours, both on land and sea. Rates for cottage rooms start at around US$130 off-season and go up to over twice that in-season. Rates are plus 19% for tax and service. Packages and specials are available. The Viva website is a little confusing and really hypes the discounts – call and see what they tell you.

Belizean Dreams. Hopkins, 501-523-7272 or 800-456-7150; www.belizeandreams.com. This condo colony just north of Jaguar Reef is among the most upscale accommodation choices in the area. All villas have the same floor plans and furnishings, but some are directly on the beach, and the others have sea views. The units can be reserved as a complete three-bedroom villa, or choose a single bedroom or two-bedroom suite. The bedrooms have vaulted ceilings with exposed beams and four-poster king beds. Rates: US$295 to $675 in high season, US$225 to $575 in summer. Rates include taxes and service. All-inclusive packages available.

Parrot Cove Lodge. Hopkins (P.O. Box 212, Hopkins), 501-523-7225; www.parrotcovelodge.com. Just to the south of Hopkins village, Parrot Cove has rooms and suites around a pool in the main building and also rooms and suites next door in the Blue Parrot beach house. There's a nice stretch of beach, and the lodge is home to Chef Rob and his great food at Chef Rob's Gourmet Café and the beachfront Love on the Rocks. Complimentary use of bikes and kayaks. Rates are US$169 to $300 double year-round (US$400 for the entire beach house for four persons), plus 9% hotel tax and 5% service. There's usually a four-night minimum stay in-season.

Beaches and Dreams Seafront Inn and Barracuda Bar & Grill. Sittee Point, 501-523-7259; www.beachesanddreams.com. Owners Tony and Angela Marsico traded running a restaurant in Alaska for operating a beachside inn and restaurant in Belize. They spruced up the inn's two octagonal cottages, each with two units with vaulted ceilings and rattan furniture, totally redid the main building, adding a couple of rooms, plus a treehouse that sleeps up to five. They also turned the restaurant into one of the better eateries on the southern coast. Rates US$125 to $215 in-season, US$99 to $169 mid-April to mid-November, plus 9% hotel tax and 9% service fee.

Coconut Row. Beachfront, Hopkins village, 501-670-3000; www.coconutrowbelize.com. This is a collection of rooms, cabins and houses, all on the beach in the heart of Hopkins village. The main guesthouse has three rooms and two suites. Next door, under the same management, the upgraded Palm Cove Cabins has three beachfront cabins and a two-bedroom house. A third property, Buttonwood Guesthouse, is a little north, also on the beach with attractive rooms. All accommodations have air conditioning, wi-fi and fridges. Rates range from around US$100 to $150 double, plus tax, depending on the type of room and time of year.

Jungle Jeanie by the Sea. Hopkins, 501-533-7047; www.junglejeanie.com. These cabañas are on a nicely shaded stretch of beach a little south of Hopkins village. Founders "Jungle Jeanie" Barkman and husband, John, Canadians who lived in Belize for years, made this into one of the nicest little moderate range beach resorts in southern Belize. Rates for cabañas are US$60 to $120 double, plus hotel tax. Jeanie is now putting an emphasis on yoga here.

Hopkins Inn. Hopkins (P.O. Box 121, Dangriga), 501-665-0411; www.hopkinsinn.com. With attractive cottages on the beach, with fridge, fan and private verandah overlooking the sea, the Hopkins Inn is well run by Greg and Rita Duke, who are knowledgeable about the area. Rates US$59 to $109 double, including continental breakfast, plus tax. German spoken.

Tipple Tree Beya Inn. Hopkins, 501-533-7006; www.tippletree.com. If you're looking for an affordable, simple little place on the beach, this is a great choice. The hotel is popular, so reserve in advance. Beachside room and cabin rates range from US$40 to $98 double, plus tax. There's also a two-bedroom apartment with air-conditioning sleeping up to four person for US$175. All rates plus 9% tax. German spoken.

DANGRIGA AND HOPKINS DINING
Dining in Dangriga
Your best option in Dangriga is the **Coconuts Grill** restaurant (Expensive) at **Pelican Beach Hotel.** It has a nice setting with a sea view. For something more local, try the **Riverside Café** (Inexpensive), a good choice for breakfast, or **King's Burger** (Inexpensive), which does have good beefburgers along with standard Belizean dishes such as stew chicken.

Dining in Hopkins
Price ranges shown are for typical meals for one (usually dinner), not including tip, tax or alcoholic drinks. Price ranges:

Inexpensive: Under US$7
Moderate: US$8-$19
Expensive: US$20-$39

Very Expensive: Over US$40

Restaurants at the larger resorts, including **Hamanasi** and **Jaguar Reef,** are attractive if expensive, but you don't need to limit yourself just to hotel dining. There are several excellent chefs and cooks in Hopkins, and a number of new eateries have opened in the past couple of years.

Restaurants here are listed alphabetically.

Barracuda Bar and Grill. Beaches and Dreams, south of Hopkins village at Sittee Point, 501-523-7259. This waterfront restaurant has a long-time reputation for tasty seafood and interesting takes on Belizean dishes, along with good pizza. Closed Monday. Expensive.

Chef Rob's sign at Parrot Cove Lodge uses part of an old Peugeot

Chef Rob's Gourmet Grill. Parrot's Cove Lodge, south of Hopkins village at Sittee Point, 501-670-0445. For upscale dining, Chef Rob Pronk's place is the top restaurant in Hopkins and one of the best in southern Belize. Nice seaside setting at Parrot's Cove Lodge. Chef Rob also has Love on the Rocks, his cook-your-own concept where you grill your seafood or meat on 700-degree lava slabs. Expensive.

Driftwood Beach Bar and Pizza Shack. Beachfront at north end of village, 501-667-4872. Popular seaside place for drinks and wood-fired pizza. Open for lunch and dinner. Closed Wednesday. Moderate to Expensive.

Gecko's. 101 North Road, north Hopkins, 501-629-5411. This is a laidback spot for a good meal. Check the blackboard for what's cooking -- dishes like jerk chicken, a huge pork chop and fish tacos. Open for lunch and dinner. Closed Sunday and sometimes Tuesday. Moderate to Expensive.

Innie's. Main Street, Hopkins, 501-503-7333. Not as cheap as it used to be, Innie's still serves authentic local Garifuna dishes, such as *hudut* (fish in a coconut broth with plantains) and seafood at moderate prices. Open daily for breakfast, lunch and dinner. Moderate.

Loggerheads Pub & Grill. Sittee Village Road, south of Hopkins, 501-667-4872. This second-story bar and grill is a good choice for a beefburger or seafood sandwich and a cold beer. Moderate.

Thongs Café. Main Street, 501-662-0110. European-owned, this little café is popular for morning coffee and breakfast − it's open 8-2 Wednesday-Sunday. Inexpensive to Moderate.

PLACENCIA PENINSULA

Cottage on beach on Placencia peninsula   Photo by Adam Stocker

PLACENCIA RATINGS

Ratings are on an A to F scale, just like your old high school report card. A is the top grade; F is failing. Grades are relative compared to other areas in Belize.

Popularity with Visitors	B+
Popularity with Expats	B
Cost Level	C-
Safety	B
Scenic Beauty	C+
Lodging	B
Dining	B
Nightlife	B-
Outdoor Activities	B
Water Activities	A-
Cultural Activities	D
Museums/Galleries	C+
Maya Sites	B
Historical Sites	D
Tourism Infrastructure	B

Transportation   C+
Medical Care   C-
Shopping   C
Overall Visitor Rating B+

PLACENCIA OVERVIEW

ADVANTAGES OF PLACENCIA: • 16 miles of Caribbean beaches on the peninsula • Growing tourism industry including new hotels and restaurants • Excellent fishing and water sports • May eventually give Ambergris Caye competition for the most popular beach destination in Belize • New cruise port on island off the peninsula

Placencia's boosters boast that it has the best beaches on mainland Belize. The 16 miles or so of beaches on the peninsula indeed are a beautiful resource, a narrow, long loaf of toast-colored sand. Like most beaches in Belize, these are only fair for swimming, as there's a good deal of seagrass except where hotels have removed it around piers. You can snorkel here and there, but for world-class snorkeling you'll have to take a boat out to the reef or to one of the small offshore cayes with patch reefs, a 10- to 20-mile boat trip. There is closer snorkeling at False Caye off Maya Beach and in a couple of other areas.

Several marine national parks and reserves are within an hour or two by boat, including Laughing Bird Caye, Southwater and Port Honduras. The Caribbean is incredibly beautiful, above and below the surface. Above, the crystal clear water sparkles in the sun. Poke your head below, and you find a whole new universe of color and activity, from tiny tropical fish to dolphins, manatees and whale sharks.

You can also visit the Cockscomb Basin Wildlife Sanctuary and Mayflower Bocawina National Park from Placencia. You can even visit the Maya sites near Punta Gorda, or go north to the Belize Zoo and attractions around Belmopan and San Ignacio, but those are long full-day trips.

The peninsula is beginning to take off in development, but contradictions abound. Unpainted wood shacks stand next door to luxury resorts, where a week's stay costs more than a local worker might earn in a year. Local families who a few years ago fished for a living have opened restaurants, bars and hotels, and they don't always have all the management skills down pat. There's a modern water system, and most of the peninsula is on the power grid, yet local schools have few books and, until a Cuban volunteer medical team came to the peninsula, locals had to go to Independence or Dangriga to see a doctor.

The biggest change is that after years of promises the road from the Southern Highway to Riversdale and then down the peninsula was finally paved. What formerly was a series of mud holes is now one of the best roads in Belize, with its main disadvantage being the annoying speed bumps, locally referred to as speed humps. Another development: a new international airport, funded by private interests on the peninsula and elsewhere in Belize, was partially built in the area just northwest of Riversdale. It remains incomplete and unopen. Whether this airport actually will open and handle international flights is still, well, up in the air.

Another BIG change is the Norwegian Cruise Lines cruise port at Harvest Caye off Placencia. After a series of delays the latest projection is that it is set to open at the end of 2016.

In October 2001, Hurricane Iris did extensive damage to the southern part of the peninsula. The peninsula is back to normal now. The area is attracting a mix of expats: Those with cash and a dream have opened resorts. Some are middle-class baby boomers that are buying lots and hope to build a vacation or retirement home. A few are marginalized escapees from the North American rat race, who live hand-to-mouth and seem to spend most of their time boozing.

Hundreds of condo units were under construction or planned, and then the Great Recession hit. Several major projects were cancelled or postponed. At least one large project closed. Since 2012, however, the peninsula has made another comeback, with new restaurants and condo developments opening.

However, tourism is still a hit-and-miss seasonal thing on the Placencia peninsula. Except for a few well-marketed properties, annual occupancy percentage at peninsula hotels averages in the mid-30s%. During the winter, especially around holidays, and around Easter, hotels fill up and it can be tough to find a decent room, or any room at all. But, off-season, the peninsula slows down, some hotels and restaurants close and most of the peninsula reverts to its sleepy self.

Land on the peninsula is low-lying and flat. The Maya Mountains are visible to the west. Placencia, a Creole village, with a population of about 1,200, is at the southern tip of the peninsula. A long concrete sidewalk runs up the center of the village. A stroll up and down the sidewalk will give you a good introduction to life in the village. A Garifuna village, Seine Bight (population over 1,000), is a little farther north. Maya Beach, not a village but a collection of houses and small resorts, is known for its good beaches. The Placencia Hotel & Residences, the overblown hotel and housing development above Maya Beach near the top of the peninsula looks out of scale with the rest of the peninsula.

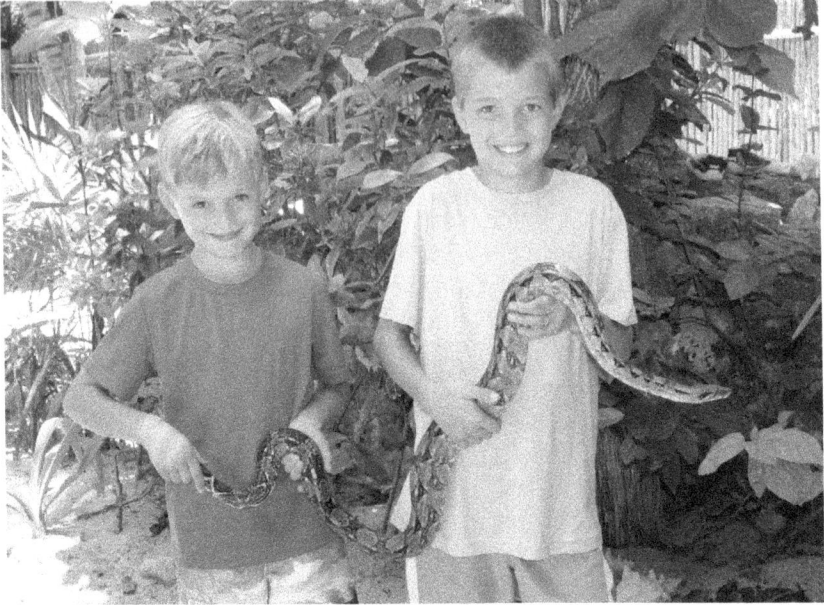

Kids discover a pal, a boa constrictor (and, yes, we've seen a boa in the thatch roof of a resort in Placencia)   Photo by Matt Jeppson/Shutterstock

Placencia Practicalities

Shops and services mostly are clustered in Placencia village, though a few are located in Seine Bight and in Maya Beach.

Banks: Atlantic Bank, Belize Bank and ScotiaBank have branches and ATMs in Placencia. Heritage Bank has a branch across the lagoon in Independence.

Groceries: There are several small groceries on the peninsula. Wallen's Market (on the main road in Placencia village, across from the soccer field), is one of the oldest, but there are other choices in the village, including Ming's and Everyday. A newish, modern grocery, Top Value, opened farther up the peninsula, on the main road just north of Placencia village, and there are small groceries in Seine Bight and Maya Beach. Placencia village also has several small bakeries. John the Baker Man has long been making pastries and breads in his home in the village. For a bigger selection of groceries and better prices, you may want to go to Dangriga, Belmopan or Belize City. A truck from Dangriga makes deliveries selling fresh fruit and vegetables, and there are small fruit and vegetables stands in Placencia village.

Restaurants: The dining scene on the peninsula has greatly improved in recent years. The Bistro at Maya Beach Hotel is one of the best restaurants in Belize. Rumfish y Vino in Placencia village is a nice spot for drinks and small plates, and there are other good choices including La Dolce Vita and The Secret Garden. Several of the hotels, including Turtle Inn, Singing Sands and Laru Beya, do a good job with food and beverage. Among the more modest spots, Dawn's Grill 'n Go, De Tatch, Yoli's, The Shak and Omar's offer good local food and reasonable value. The highly notable Tutti Frutti has authentic Italian gelati, by far the best we've tasted anywhere in Central America. Heck, maybe anywhere.

Vehicle Rentals: There are several companies on the peninsula that rent vehicles, including these: Barefoot Services (Main Road, Placencia village, 501-523-3066, www.barefootservicesbelize.com) has car, golf cart and scooter rentals, with car rentals from US$69 a day plus 12.5% GST and 2.5% service fee; Budget, (Live Oak Plaza, Placencia village, 501-523-3068, www.locations.budget.com) is a branch of Budget Belize in Belize City, the rental company we used with good results for many years; Placencia Car Rental (Placencia Road 1½ miles north of Placencia air strip, 501-523-3284, www.placenciacarrental.com), associated with AQ Car Rental in Belize City, has older cars at lower than average rates starting at around US$40 a day off-season and US$50 in-season, plus GST and CDW if you do not rent with an American Express card). Hertz (www.carsbelize.com) may also have a rental location in Placencia when you arrive. Captain Jak's (www.captainjaks.com), Barefoot Services and others on the peninsula also rent scooters, golf carts and bicycles. Expect to pay around US$40 a day for a scooter rental, US$65 a day for golf cart rental and US$10 for a bike, all plus GST.

Other Services: There is a gas station in Placencia village, another a little north of the village, fairly well equipped building supplies stores and a number of gift shops.

Medical: A small medical clinic is located near the school in Placencia village, and another clinic is in Seine Bight. Cuban doctors, on loan from Fidel and Raul, may still be in residence when you are there. Otherwise, for medical attention you may need to go to Dangriga or across the lagoon to Independence.

Infrastructure: The Placencia peninsula is now on the power grid, has good water straight from the Maya Mountains and in most areas a sewerage system. The peninsula has cable TV and DSL and cellular internet.

For More Information: The Placencia BTIA has a helpful website, www.placencia.com. Mary Toy's private company, Destinations Belize, has a website with much information about lodging, fishing and other details at www.destinationsbelize.com.

GETTING TO PLACENCIA

By Car

From Belize City (the Goldson International Airport) to Placencia village by road is a trip of about 140 miles, via the George Price Highway, Hummingbird Highway, Southern Highway and Placencia Road. All these roads are paved and in good to excellent condition. However, with speed bumps and road conditions, it will take you at least three hours non-stop and likely a little longer. It is shorter by about 30 miles to take the Coastal Highway (aka Manatee Highway) from the village of Democracia on the George Price Highway to near the start of the Southern Highway, but as the Coastal Highway is unpaved it is usually smarter, and certainly more scenic, to go via the Hummingbird.

Glory be! Paving of the road to Placencia is completed, and it is now one of the best roads in Belize, although in some sections you have to watch out for jumbo speed bumps or "speed humps."

From the intersection of the Hummingbird Highway (also known at this point as the Stann Creek Valley Highway) and the Southern Highway, it is about 22 miles to the turn-off to Placencia. The left turn is well marked. Then, from the Southern Highway, it is about 9 miles to near Riversdale, the elbow point at which you may begin to see the blue Caribbean to your left. From here, it is another 16 miles or so to the south end of Placencia village.

Air

Maya Island Air (www.mayaislandair.com) and **Tropic Air** (www.tropicair.com) each have seven or eight flights daily from Belize City. Fares from the international airport are about US$133 one-way and from the municipal airport, about US$112.

Bus

As of early 2016 **James Bus Line, Ritchie's, G-Line** and **Williams** are the bus lines licensed to go to the Southern Zone from Belize City. Several other bus lines operate from Dangriga south to Punta Gorda. This could change.

Ritchie's Bus Service (501-523-3806, www.ritchiesbusservice.com). is the only bus line that offers one-line – that is, no change of bus line – service from Belize City (the Novelo's station) to Placencia. Ritchie's has only one departure a day to Placencia from Belize City, currently at 3:30 p.m. It is regular service, not express, with scheduled stops at Belmopan and

Dangriga plus pick-ups en route on demand. Cost from Belize City is US$10.

James Bus Line (7 King Street, Punta Gorda, 501-664-2185, www.jamesbusline.com) is the largest and best (all things being relative) of the lines and has the most daily service to the south. As of early 2016, James has 10 daily departures (nine on Sunday) from Belize City's Novelo's bus terminal to Punta Gorda, beginning at 5:30 a.m. (this express bus doesn't operate on Sunday), with the last departure at 3:45 p.m. Although these buses don't go to Placencia, they do make a stop in Independence, across the lagoon from Placencia. The cost from Belize City to Independence is about US$8. From Independence/Mango Creek you can take the little pedestrian-only water ferry, the *Hokey Pokey* (501-622-3213, www.aguallos.com/hokeypokey), across the lagoon to Placencia. This boat has nine daily crossings (eight on Sunday) from Independence to Placencia, starting at 6:30 a.m. and the last at 5:30 p.m. (4:30 p.m. on Sunday). Cost is US$5 per person one-way.

G-Line, RDS and A-Jays bus lines also offer service from Dangriga to Independence.

Otherwise, you can take James or another bus line from Belize City, Belmopan or San Ignacio, or by flagging down a bus anywhere on those routes, to Dangriga and change to a Ritchie's bus there. Ritchie's at present has at four departures daily, currently at 11 a.m. and 2, 4:30 and 6:15 p.m., from Dangriga direct to Placencia village. Cost from Dangriga to Placencia is US$5. As always, schedules and prices are subject to frequent change. Service may be reduced seasonally and on some holidays.

Shuttles

Several shuttle services will take you between Belize City or San Ignacio, or elsewhere, and Placencia. Tour companies such as PACZ Tours in San Ignacio also provide shuttle services. Rates vary depending on several factors including the number in the party, whether it is a private shuttle or a group shuttle and whether you go on a pre-arranged pick-up schedule or on a custom schedule. Expect to pay about US$50 to $125 per person between Belize City and Placencia and around US$40 to $110 between San Ignacio and Placencia. Check with the services and compare prices and schedules:

Discounted Belize Shuttles and Tours (Philip S. W. Goldson International Airport, Ladyville, 501-620-1474, www.discountedbelizeshuttlesandtours.com)

William's Shuttle Belize (501-620-3055, www.williamshuttlebelize.com)

Belize Shuttles and Transfers (Belize City, 501-610-2258, www.belizeshuttlesandtransfers.com)

Mayan Heart World (29 Burns Avenue, San Ignacio, 501-824-3328, www.mayanheartworld.net)

PACZ Tours (30 Burns Avenue, San Ignacio, 501-824-0536, www.pacztours.net)

WHAT TO SEE AND DO IN PLACENCIA

Some of the same destinations that you can reach from Hopkins and Dangriga are also possible from Placencia, especially now that the paved Placencia Road makes it easier and faster to get back to the Southern Highway. You can drive yourself or take a tour to **Cockscomb Basin Wildlife Sanctuary** and **Mayflower Bocawina National Park** *(see above in the Dangriga/Hopkins section for information.)* Daytrips to Hopkins and Dangriga are another option. A destination closer to Placencia than to other places in the area is **Red Bank** village, known for its scarlet macaws, especially from January to March, when the annatto fruit that the macaws feed on are ripe.

Consider a tour to **Monkey River Town**. While often still called a town, Monkey River has shrunk in size from 2,500 people engaged in logging, fishing and banana production in the early 20th century to only a few hundred and is no longer classified by the Belize government as a town. The almost entirely Creole village, hard hit by Hurricane Iris in 2001, is south of Placencia peninsula in Toledo District, at the mouth of the Monkey River. From Placencia, popular day tours usually go by boat, but most of the year it is also possible to drive on an unpaved road off the Southern Highway to near the village by road. You'll have to cross the river by boat to get to the village proper. Monkey River does indeed have howler monkeys, and on boat tours from Placencia you'll likely also see crocodiles and manatees. Tours, which cost US$90 to $150 per person from Placencia, include a Belizean lunch at a home in the village. A fresh-water lake near the village, Punta Negra Lagoon, has good fishing.

You can also make day trips to the **Lubaantun** and **Nim Li Punit** Maya sites near Punta Gorda. *For more information, see the Punta Gorda/Toledo section of this book.*

A main reason to come to Placencia is for activities on the water, primarily fishing, diving and snorkeling. There are plenty of tour operators and dive shops on the peninsula that will take you snorkeling or diving on the Belize Barrier Reef, about 20 miles out, or on patch reefs, sometimes called the inner reef, closer in around **Laughing Bird Caye National Park** (www.laughingbird.org), about 11 miles from Placencia village.

Activities also are available at other marine locations such as the **Silk Cayes** or **Southwater Caye Marine Reserve.**

Placencia Dive/Snorkel Shops and Tour Operators

Among the better-known dive shops on the peninsula are **Seahorse Dive Shop** (near pier in Placencia village, 501-523-3166, www.belizescuba.com) and **Splash Dive Center** (Chabil Mar Villas, 501-523-3080, www.splashbelize.com).

Altogether, the Placencia area has about 80 licensed tour guides and many tour operators, so you will have no trouble finding someone to take you on trips and tours. Here is just a sampling:

Ocean Motion (in the village, on the sidewalk near the pier, 501-523-3363, www.oceanmotionplacencia.com) arranges snorkeling trips and also does land tours. **Pirates Point Adventure Tours** (on the sidewalk, Placencia village, 501-632-8399, www.tourbelize.org) has, among others, snorkeling tours from US$45 to $85, a horseback riding and waterfall tour for US$130, cave tubing at Caves Branch/Jaguar Paw near Belmopan for US$140 and visit to Nim Li Punit and a cacao farm in Toledo from US$110 per person. In some cases, taxes and equipment rentals are extra. **Cayequest Private Tours** (Placencia village, 501-633-6330, http://cayequestadventures.blogspot.com), run by Mark Leslie, a fourth-generation Placencia resident and a licensed boat captain, specializes in marine tours, especially fishing and snorkeling. **Belize Experts** (www.belizeexperts.com), run by a French woman who has lived in Belize for almost two decades, is a tour operator that offers a variety of land and sea tours.

Several of the larger hotels, including Turtle Inn, Chabil Mar, Inn at Robert's Grove have their own dive operations and also arrange land and sea tours of all kinds.

Whether with a hotel or an independent tour/dive operator, you'll pay around US$65 to $90 a person for a Laughing Bird snorkel trip and around US$130 to $150 for a two-tank dive, depending on whether marine reserve fees, tax and equipment rental are included; to Southwater Caye snorkeling is around US$90 to $100 and diving US$150-$190. A full day of snorkeling at Glover's Reef starts at around US$100 per person. Dive trips to Glover's Reef are around US$180 to $250 depending on the number of dives. Equipment rental is extra, as may be taxes and marine reserve fees.

If you want to see fish without getting wet, **Sea n' Belize's glass bottom boat** (based at Inn at Robert's Grove Marina, 501-610-1012) is a very nice way to do it. The boat has a mahogany interior and 24 square feet of glass for viewing underwater. A half-day trip is around US$80 per person.

Bunches of Fun (Mile 8, Placencia Road, 501-624-4297, www.bunchesoffuntours.com) offers an interesting **tour of a local banana plantation.** Currently, group tours are scheduled three times a day on Monday, Thursday, Friday and Saturday. A field tour is US$10 per person, and a full tour including video and demonstrations is US$15. It's bunches of fun!

Taste Belize (501-664-8699, www.tastebelize.com), run by Lyra Spang, who grew up in Toledo and has a PhD in anthropology, does chocolate and other food tours in Southern Belize, along with snorkeling and other tours.

Among the more unusual marine attractions near Placencia are **whale sharks.** These gentle giants – they are sharks, but they eat only plankton and other small things, not humans – show up at Gladden Spit and elsewhere in late spring and early summer. The whale shark is the largest fish on earth, although it is smaller than some whales, which of course are mammals. You're mostly likely to see a whale shark about three days before and after a full moon during the months of March, April, May and June. But spawning dates vary from year to year, so sighting dates may change, and there are no guarantees, especially since whale sharks are mostly night feeders. Dive and snorkel shops in Placencia often book up well in advance for the limited number of available spaces. Talk with the dive shops and tour operators listed above for information and advance reservations.

Sport fishing is big here. Bonefish and permit are the main targets for fly anglers on the flats inside the barrier reef. Add tarpon and you've got a "grand slam." Bones, permit and tarpon can be caught year-round off Placencia. A day of fly-fishing on nearby flats costs around US$300 to $400 for two persons including boat, guide and lunch and refreshments. You'll need a Belize saltwater fishing license (US$10 a day or $25 a week). Ideally you should bring your own equipment and flies. According to local guides, flies should be unweighted and tied on a #6 hook. The best colors are orange, white, brown and pink.

Spin casting and trolling trips, using live bat or artificial lures, inside and around the barrier reef also are an option. Fishing for jacks and king fish is usually good. You'll pay about the same for a trolling/spin casting trip as for a fly fishing trip, around US$300-$400 for two persons, including boat, guide and refreshments.

Long-time Placencia resident Mary Toy at **Destinations Belize** (Placencia village, 501-523-4018, www.destinationsbelize.com) can help with fishing and local tours, or she can do your entire Belize trip, including lodging. Leon "Gas" Leslie, a fourth-generation local fisherman, and his

On the Hook tour company (Placencia village, 501-628-8817, www.hookedonplacencia.com) does fishing, snorkeling and other sea trips.

Day sailing on a catamaran (check with **Daytripper Catamaran Charters**, 501-666-3117, www.daytripperbelize.com), **canoeing or kayaking** in the lagoon on the back side of the peninsula or **paddlesports** are other recreational options.

The Moorings, (844-573-7936, www.themoorings.com), based at Laru Beya's marina, **charters monohull sailboats and catamarans,** starting at around US$4,000 a week. Bareboat charters must stay inside the barrier reef. A licensed captain is required for visiting the barrier reef or going to the atolls.

Jaguar Lane bowling alley in Maya Beach

Believe it or not, there's a bowling alley on the Placencia peninsula – **Jaguar Lanes and Jungle Bar** (501-601-4434) in Maya Beach.

To get to know Placencia village, take a stroll on the narrow concrete **sidewalk** that runs for more than a mile north-south through the village. Along the sidewalk there are little gift shops, a few eateries and bars and access to small guesthouses. The sidewalk is a lot quieter than the main road (Placencia Road) through the village, which is often gridlocked with vehicles.

279

The jam-up may get worse when the new **Norwegian Cruise Line Port** opens in late 2016 on **Harvest Caye.** NCL ships carrying 2,400 to 4,500 passengers are scheduled to dock here, mostly skipping Belize City. The US$100 million cruise port has been controversial. Many local people on the Placencia peninsula strongly opposed cruise tourism. Construction has been delayed several times.

Easter weekend in Placencia is always busy, as is the Placencia Lobsterfest the third week of June.

PLACENCIA LODGING

You have a choice to make about where to stay on the Placencia peninsula. You have to decide whether you want to stay in Placencia village, the main "population center" for the area, or farther up the peninsula. Placencia village is a Creole village at the southern tip of the peninsula. It's a bit funky, and nearly all of the lodging choices here are in the budget or moderate categories, but the village is the focus for dining and for shopping (such as it is).

By contrast, the area north of Placencia village has most of the peninsula's upmarket resorts. It's less jammed up, and the beaches are generally prettier, with softer sand. If you're a budget traveler, or if you don't have a car (and don't want to bike or take a taxi back and forth between your hotel and the village) you may want to stay in or near Placencia village. If you decide you want something more upscale and with fewer people around, then your decision becomes: Where north of Placencia village do you want to stay?

There are two "addresses" north of Placencia village: Seine Bight, a Garifuna village about 5 miles north of Placencia village, and Maya Beach, about 7 miles north of Placencia village. Maya Beach isn't a village but a small collection of houses and hotels.

Another collection of houses, condos and a hotel, most very expensive, is farther north, between Maya Beach and Riversdale, the elbow point where the Placencia Road from the Southern Highway comes near the Caribbean Sea and turns south down the peninsula. This area is dominated by the controversial The Placencia Hotel & Residences.

A primary consideration is how far north of the "action" in Placencia village you want to be. Unless you have a car, you're at the mercy of your hotel shuttle, if there is one, taxis (which cost as much as US$20 one-way to go between Placencia village and the north end of Maya Beach). Some hotels do offer guests the complimentary use of bicycles, which is another option for getting back and forth, though not a very good one after dark.

On the peninsula, you can rent a car, a golf cart or a scooter. *See Practicalities above for a list of rental companies.*

There are many other options for lodging on the peninsula than just the ones listed here. For information on other places, visit the Belize Tourist Industry Association's Placencia site, www.placencia.com, or the Belize Tourism Board's site, www.travelbelize.org.

Properties listed here are arranged roughly by cost, from highest to lowest.

Turtle Inn. Placencia, 501-523-3150 or 800-746-3743 in U.S./Canada; www.thefamilycoppolaresorts.com. The original Turtle Inn was a fixture for many years in Placencia, when the late Skip White ran it as an inexpensive barefoot beach spot. It was bought by Francis Ford Coppola and reopened as Blancaneaux's Turtle Inn. Not long after the purchase a nasty lady named Iris paid a visit to Placencia in October 2001, and Turtle Inn was virtually blown away. After a complete rebuild, Turtle Inn reopened in early 2003. It has since grown to a total of 25 units, all located just a short drive (or a long hike) north of Placencia village.

Our experience staying at Turtle Inn has been somewhat mixed. On one stay, we had a two-bedroom sea front villa, and you couldn't ask for anything nicer or more stylish. The villas and some of the single cabañas sit just feet from the sea, so the gentle lap-lap of the Caribbean soothes you, and the prevailing offshore breeze keeps you cool. There is no air-conditioning, so on a calm summer day it can get pretty warm. Our villa was a pure delight: The bay-thatch ceiling soars high, there's a wide screened porch across the front and the main living area has comfy seating and a fridge. The two bathrooms are in the Japanese-style, with both showers and tiled square tubs (there also are private outdoor showers, which are more fun than you'd think.) The villas and cabañas at Turtle Inn are Balinese in inspiration, with wonderful art and furnishing. Even the doors were picked out personally in Indonesia by Mr. Coppola and his wife.

However, on another stay we had a cabaña at the back of the resort, away from the breeze and with no view of the sea. It was hot! The cabaña, especially the bath, also needed some TLC. You may find improvements.

In any case, you'll be happy with the resort's grounds. The pools include a large turtle-shaped, zero-effect pool between the restaurant and the attractive sandy beach, and another infinity pool in the triangular shape of the Coppola Resorts logo. There's also a private pool at Mr. Coppola's personal villa. The beach here is pretty good for Belize, but not as good as the beaches farther north on the peninsula at Maya Beach. Turtle Inn has a small marina on the lagoon side, and one lodging unit is on that side.

The main restaurant at Turtle Inn is Mare, open to the breeze with a thatch roof, bar and a tropical atmosphere. It features Italian and seafood dishes. Like Blancaneaux, Turtle Inn has a wood-burning pizza oven and serves excellent wines from the Niebaum-Coppola winery. Prices aren't cheap. There are two other dining options for dinner, the Gauguin Grill and Auntie Luba's, which purports to serve Belizean food, along with the delightful Laughing Fish beach bar. We found the food, drink, service, amenities and staff responsiveness all very accommodating. At the prices you pay here, you would expect them to be.

Rates at Turtle Inn range up into the stratospheric category. Cabañas not on the water are US$319 to $829 double, depending on the time of year. Seafront cabañas are US$529 to $1,019. Two-bedroom villas and the three cottages/bungalows are US$649 to $1,469 double. Coppola's Pavilion, Sofia's Cottage, Ramon's Lagoon Bungalow and the Starfish Cottage range from US$859 to $4,519, with occupancy of up to eight persons in some cases. Rates are plus 9% hotel tax and 10% service. From January through April there is a three- to four-night minimum stay, seven-day minimum at Christmas. Off-season, May 1 to mid-December, provides the lowest rates. A continental breakfast of fresh-baked breads and fruits is included in the room rate.

Chabil Mar Villas. Placencia, 501-523-3606 or 866-417-2377 in U.S./Canada; www.chabilmarvillas.com. This gated condotel resort, a 10-minute stroll on the beach from the north end of Placencia village, is one of the most upscale places to stay on the peninsula. Chabil Mar means "beautiful sea" in the Kekchi Maya language, and the sea and 400 feet of beach here are indeed beautiful. The 19 one- and two-bedroom deluxe villas and one suite are tastefully designed and luxuriously furnished, down to wine corkscrews and service for eight. They have stylish features such as marble floors, original art and four-poster king beds. Every comfort is at hand, from wi-fi to cable TV to DVD players to washers and dryers in each unit. There's a private pier with al fresco dining and a beach bar, plus two infinity swimming pools. Room-only rates are around US$375 to $525 double per night, depending on the time of year and the unit, plus 9% tax and 10% service. A four-night package that includes air transfer from Belize City, lodging, all meals, one full-day snorkeling tour and two other tours, use of golf cart for two days, all taxes and service (but not drinks) is US$1,631 to $2,023 per person in summer, based on double occupancy, and US$1,762 to US$2,226 in winter, higher during peak holidays. You'll need to call or email to reserve your villas, as Chabil Mar doesn't have online booking.

Inn at Robert's Grove. Seine Bight, 501-523-3565; www.robertsgrove.com. This large property on 22 acres just south of Seine Bight, opened in 1997, raising the standard on what visitors to this part of Belize could expect in a beach resort. It was developed by New Yorkers

Robert and Risa Frackman. When they owned it, it was our favorite place to stay on the Placencia peninsula, but all things change. They sold it and now only visit occasionally. It's still a good lodging choice, but somehow, at least for us, it's not the same.

Inn at Robert's Grove has a big variety of lodging choices, from standard rooms to one- to three-bedroom seafront suites to new lagoon-side one- to four-bedroom villas. Some of the units are available for sale as condos. Our favorites always have the deluxe one- and two-bedroom seafront suites. Each has a large, strikingly decorated living room — a happy mélange of Mexican tile, Guatemalan fabrics and African art nicely put together by Risa Frackman — with cable TV, veranda with a sea view, bedrooms with king-size bed with a luxuriously firm new U.S.-made mattress and jumbo bathroom, with big, tiled combination bath and shower. However, the marina/lagoon-side villas are the newest accommodations at the resort, developed by the new owner.

The resort has three swimming pools, a fitness room, private pier and small sailboats, kayaks, canoes, windsurfers, bikes and other equipment for guest use. The main restaurant, Seaside, has sea views. A casual restaurant on the lagoon side, Habanero Mexican Café at the marina and near the dive shop, and a Belizean-style spot, Sweet Mama's, located where the tennis courts used to be, are open at times. There's a small bakery and deli, a tour desk, PADI dive center and, on the sea side a sandy beach where you can actually swim.

In-season, rates are from US$195 for a double in standard garden view rooms to $655 for three-bedroom seafront suites, while the marina villas are US$395 to $910 depending on the number of bedrooms and number of people. Maximum occupancy in the four-bedroom villas is eight persons. Off-season, rates range from US$170 to $695, again depending on the size and location of the accommodation and the number of people. All rates plus 9% tax and 10% service. Robert's Grove also offers all-inclusive lodging, meal and drinks packages at a private island, tiny Robert's Caye. Weekly package rates start at US$1,903 in-season and US$1,608 off-season.

Belize Ocean Club. Placencia Road, Maya Beach, 800-997-1289, www.belizeoceanclub.com. The Ocean Club is a mid-size condo resort at the north end of Maya Beach. It formerly was Bella Maya, a partially completed condo project and timeshare that closed in 2010 during the Great Recession, to the likely distress of the people who had bought there. It reopened, having completed the 60 units, with some improvements and somewhat higher prices. In-season two-bedroom units sleeping four are around US$400 to $580 per night, and one-bedroom units are $200 to $250 double, with lower prices off-season. Rates are plus 9% tax and a service charge. Rather unusually for the peninsula, the resort is on both sides of the road, with 30 units on the sea side and 30 on the lagoon side. The two-bedroom, two-bath condos here are now being offered for sale for prices from US$425,000 to $550,000.

The Placencia Hotel & Residences. Placencia Road, at the north end of the peninsula, 501-533-4117; www.theplacencia.com. This controversial 3,000-acre project, still in development, has grandiose plans that include a large condotel, villas and a boutique hotel on a private island, a marina with nearly 300 slips including 25 for super yachts, a yacht club, gun club, 18-hole Robert Trent golf course, an international airport and private McMansion homes on the lagoon side of the peninsula. The golf course, yacht club, marina, gun club and private island are still just mostly on paper, while the airport northwest of the peninsula sits unfinished. The related high-rise Copal Beach Resort has million-dollar condos for sale. The completed Placencia Hotel has about 100 condo apartments in a gated area north of Maya Beach. Apartments are offered as nightly rentals when owners are not in residence. There is a nice stretch of private beach, a long pier with palapa, three restaurants, tennis courts and what is claimed to be the country's largest swimming pool. Rates are US$188 to $312 double, plus 9% tax and 10% service. Optional meal plans are US$97 per person per day plus 22.5% tax and service. Due to its location, you'll probably want a rental car to go into Placencia village, or pay high taxi rates. We have stayed at and visited this large property a number of times and usually found very few guests.

Laru Beya. Placencia Road, Seine Bight, 501-523-3476 or 800-890-8010 in U.S./Canada; www.larubeya.com. This upscale resort on a nice beach just south of Seine Bight village, next door to Inn at Robert's Grove, offers deluxe seaside accommodations at somewhat lower rates than the competition. It has a good restaurant, the Quarterdeck, and bar on-site. In-season rates for seafront rooms US$170, seafront suites, US$250 to $390 (a three-bedroom seafront penthouse is US$520); off-season rooms US$140, suites US$180 to $300 (penthouse US$400). Rates plus 9% hotel tax and 10% service. Complimentary use of sea kayaks, small sailboats, bikes and wi-fi. There's a fresh-water infinity pool and a small mini-golf course.

Belizean Nirvana. Westby Way, Placencia village, 501-523-3331; www.belizeanirvana.com. If you're looking for a smaller, personality place, this new five-suite property on the beach may be it. Enjoy scenic views east and west from the rooftop deck. In-season rates are US$185 to $275 (higher at Christmas), and from June to mid-December US$150 to $225, all plus 9% tax and 5% service. A continental breakfast is included. Evan and Barbara Hall are friendly, helpful owner-hosts.

Author at work, diligently researching beer at
Maya Beach Hotel and Bistro   Photo by Sheila M. Lambert

Maya Beach Hotel and Bistro. Maya Beach, 501-533-8040; www.mayabeachhotel.com. Before ending up here, owners John and Ellen Lee (he's Australian, she's American) traveled and worked in 20 countries. They must have figured out what travelers like, because their little hotel is a classic beachy inn and their seaside Bistro *(see below)* is one of the best restaurants in Belize. A swimming pool is beside the restaurant, steps from a lovely stretch of beach. In addition to the five simple but pleasant and reasonably priced hotel rooms with views of False Caye and the sea, the hotel rents seven apartments and houses nearby. Hotel room rates: US$109 to $159 in-season, US$104 to $139 off-season. Rates plus 9% tax and 10% service charge. Highly recommended.

Maine Stay. Seine Bight, 207-512-2381 in the U.S.; www.traversbelize.com. This is a good spot for families to stay for a week or longer. The suites have a pair of wooden cabañas, connected by a covered breezeway and deck, with two bedrooms and two baths. Both units have a kitchen, washer and dryer and wi-fi. There's 400 feet of beach and a 100-foot pier. Rates in-season (November–May) for four persons is US$1,895 per week and US$1,295 off-season, plus tax (no service charge). Owners, from Maine of course, live across the street. It can be booked through Vacation Rentals By Owner (www.vrbo.com).

Miramar Apartments. Beachfront, Placencia village, 501-523-3658; www.miramarbelize.com. This relatively new and appealing option has seven apartments/suites in Placencia village, just a coconut toss from the water. You're within a short walk of a bunch of restaurants and watering holes. Miramar has two studio suites, four one-bedroom units and a three-bedroom, two-bath family apartment. All units have air conditioning, flat-screen TV with cable, wi-fi and kitchen or kitchenette. Rates in high season are US$110 for the studios, US$200 for the one-bedrooms and US$275 for the three-bedroom unit; off-season, they're US$90, $185 and $235. All rates plus 9% tax.

Barnacle Bill's. Maya Beach, 501-523-8110; www.barnaclebills-belize.com. American owners Barnacle Bill (known as the wit of Maya Beach) and Adriane Taylor have two one-bedroom Mennonite cottages about 60 feet from the beach. The bungalows are on stilts, cooled by fans and sea breezes, and each has a full kitchen with fridge, microwave, two-burner stove and cooking utensils. They'll sleep up to three. The bedroom has a queen bed, and there's a sofa sleeper in the living/dining area. For groceries, a small market is not far away, and there are several restaurants and bars nearby. Doubles are US$115 Nov.-May, US$100 rest of year, plus hotel tax. Minimum-stay five nights, seven at Christmas.

The Village Inn. North end of Placencia village, 501-223-0992; www.thevillageinnbelize.com. This spot at the northern end of Placencia village has four small wood cabins, two directly on the water and two near. Rates in-season are US$85 to $135 a night, off-season US$75 to $115, plus tax, with lower weekly rates available. All cabins have kitchenettes, cable TV, wi-fi, fans and "nature's air-conditioning."

Tradewinds. Placencia village, 501-523-3122. If you want a beachfront cottage but don't want to pay the higher prices north of the village, Tradewinds is a decent bet. The nine pastel-colored cabins right on the beach at the south end of Placencia village are cute as a bug's ear. They're not large and could stand some maintenance and improvements but starting at around US$75, they're an okay value. Fridges, fans and two double beds are standard. The beach sand here is a little rough on your naked feet.

Sea Glass Inn. Garden Grove, Placencia village, 501-523-3098; www.seaglassinnbelize.com. Formerly Dianni's, new owners have updated this affordable six-room inn at the south end of Placencia village. Sea Glass has nice sea views, although this part of the beach isn't that great for swimming, in our opinion. It's far enough away from the popular bars not to get much noise and is near the new Municipal Pier. Sea Glass has air-conditioning if you need it and free wi-fi. Rates are US$79 double plus tax in-season and only US$59 plus tax off-season.

Seaspray. Placencia village. 501-523-3148; www.seasprayhotel.com. This oldie goldie (it was the first hotel in Placencia, opened in 1964) has seaside and non-seaside rooms, plus one cabaña on the beach, located in the heart of the village. Not fancy, but okay if you're not too picky. Fans, no A/C, cable TV and small fridges. Some rooms with kitchenettes. Rates US$27 to $70 in-season, plus tax.

Deb & Dave's Last Resort. North end of Placencia village, 501-523-3207. Budget travelers will enjoy one of the four rooms with shared bath at Deb & Dave's. It's in a shaded area of the village but not on the water. Fans, no A/C, free wi-fi. The owners are helpful and knowledgeable. Rates around US$25 plus tax.

Lydia's Guest House. Placencia village; tel. 501-523-3117; e-mail lydias@btl.net. This is a top backpacker's choice in the village. It offers eight basic but clean rooms, with fans, shared bath, shared kitchen, refrigerators and, on the second floor of the wood-frame house, a veranda with hammocks. Rates around US$25 double plus tax.

PLACENCIA DINING

Mare at **Turtle Inn** and **Quarterdeck** at **Laru Beya**, both in the Expensive/Very Expensive category, are worthy hotel restaurants. In addition, try the following local places, listed alphabetically.

Price ranges shown are for typical meals for one (usually dinner), not including tip, tax or alcoholic drinks. Price ranges:

Inexpensive: Under US$7
Moderate: US$8-$19
Expensive: US$20-$39
Very Expensive: Over US$40

Brewed Awakenings. Placencia Road, Placencia village, 501-668-1715. Popular place to get your latte or other fresh-brewed coffee. Open from 6:30 a.m. to 5 p.m. Closed Sunday, Inexpensive. For fresh-baked goodies to go with your coffee, look for signs to **John the Bakerman's** house in the village.

Dawn's Grill 'n Go. Placencia Road, Placencia village, 501-602-9302. This little spot by the main road cooks up tasty Belizean and American food. The fried chicken is excellent. Open for breakfast, lunch and dinner. Closed Sunday. Moderate. Recommended.

De Tatch. Laidback and tropical, De Tatch is popular for its beer and simple but pretty good food. In the village at the Sea Spray Hotel. Inexpensive to Moderate.

La Dolce Vita. Placencia Road in Placencia village, 501-523-3115. Located upstairs next to Wallen's grocery, La Dolce Vita is our long-time fave for good Italian in Placencia. The chef-owner makes his own pasta, sauces and breads. Moderate to Expensive.

Maya Beach Hotel Bistro. Maya Beach, 501-520-8040. The restaurant at this small inn is probably the best restaurant in Southern Belize and one of the top three or four in the country. The seaside setting is wonderful, service is very friendly and virtually anything you order you will love. The Bistro has a selection of small plates and appetizers including fish cakes, a shrimp corn dog and honey-coconut ribs, along with regular entrees, creatively presented, such as cocoa-dusted pork chop on risotto, prosciutto-wrapped grouper and lobster grilled cheese. The Bistro bakes its own breads, breakfast cinnamon rolls (huge) and other pastries. Open daily for breakfast, lunch and dinner. Reservations for dinner suggested. Moderate to Very Expensive. Highly, highly recommended.

Rumfish y Vino. Placencia village, 501-523-3293. Run by expat New Yorkers, in a breezy second-story location in Placencia village, Rumfish y Vino is a good spot to have drinks and interesting food. Try the lionfish sashimi or blackened lionfish (great way to help get rid of this alien intruder that is messing up the Caribbean ecosystem), lobster pizza or one of the ceviches. Nice selection of Italian wines. Lunch and dinner daily. Expensive.

Tiger Beach Club. Seine Bight, 501-628-1250. This is *the* spot for authentic Indian food in southern Belize. The chef, from Mumbai, works his wonders with naan, samosas and curries in an open kitchen in the middle of the restaurant. Tiger Beach Club is open to the breezes. Closed Tuesday. Expensive.

Secret Garden. Placencia village, 501-523-3617. Pleasant spot to have dinner in a garden patio setting. The menu has been revamped, offering Argentine-style steak, seafood gumbo, pasta and other dishes. Open for dinner. Closed Sunday. Moderate to Expensive.

Tranquilo. Placencia Caye, 501-620-7763. Hop on a free shuttle boat at the Placencia pier for a short ride to this new restaurant on Placencia Caye. Open for dinner daily except Tuesday. The setting is marvelous and the food, mostly seafood dishes, is pretty good. In-season, reservations suggested. Moderate to Expensive.

Tutti-Frutti. Placencia Road, Placencia village. Great place for amazingly delicious and authentic Italian gelati in a variety of tropical fruit and other flavors. Inexpensive. Highly, highly recommended!

Other places for inexpensive local food in Placencia village include **Omar's, The Shak** and **BJ's Bellyful.**

Where to Party in Placencia

Barefoot Beach Bar relocated from the main road to the beach in Placencia village. It is a very popular spot to drink and eat. There's often live music, and you can dance your heart out. Next door, also on the beach, is another party place, **Tipsy Tuna.** Rum drinks are just US$1.50 at happy hour. **Yoli's** on a pier at the south tip of the peninsula has the most tropical setting in the village to sip your Belikins. Good food, too. **Pickled Parrot,** in the middle of the village, is under new ownership. Come here for the beer, drinks and TV.

PUNTA GORDA

Fruit and vegetable vendors at the old market in Punta Gorda

PUNTA GORDA AND TOLEDO RATINGS

Ratings are on an A to F scale, just like your old high school report card. A is the top grade; F is failing. Grades are relative compared to other areas in Belize.

Popularity with Visitors	D+
Popularity with Expats	C-
Cost Level	B
Safety	B+
Scenic Beauty	B+
Lodging	C
Dining	C
Nightlife	C-
Outdoor Activities	B+
Water Activities	B+
Cultural Activities	C-
Museums/Galleries	C
Maya Sites	B
Historical Sites	C-
Tourism Infrastructure	C

Transportation   C+
Medical Care   C-
Shopping   C-
Overall Visitor Rating B-

PUNTA GORDA AND TOLEDO OVERVIEW

ADVANTAGES TO PUNTA GORDA AREA: • Lush, beautiful tropical scenery • Excellent fishing • Good diving and snorkeling, though trips out can be long and fairly expensive • Diverse mix of Maya, Garifuna, East Indian and other cultures • Moderate hotel and food prices (the exception is Belcampo Belize) • Proximity to Rio Dulce area of Guatemala • You can enjoy this off-the-beaten path destination before interest in area before others find it, due to completion of Southern Highway and construction of new road to Guatemala with border crossing

You've probably heard stories about Punta Gorda being the end of the earth and all that. You may be surprised, then, at how inviting a town it is. With about 6,000 people, it has a mix of Mopan and Kekchi Maya, Garifuna and a dollop of Creoles, Lebanese and Chinese, plus a few American expats, missionaries and dreamers.

PG, as it's known in Belize, is colorful and friendly. There's usually a breeze blowing from the Bay of Honduras. The renovated downtown market draws Maya from surrounding villages. PG's waterside setting is, like that of Corozal Town, truly pleasant.

Business activity in the town is not exactly hot and hopping. Hotels in and around PG almost always have rooms available, although several new ones have opened -- hope springs eternal. The hotel occupancy rate is under 30%, with government officials and missionaries occupying many of the rooms.

As yet, only a few tourists make it all the way down the Southern Highway from Belize City or Placencia. Some backpackers do pass through on their way to cheaper towns in Guatemala and Honduras. With the completion of the paving of the Southern Highway, and the planned completion of a new paved road to Guatemala, conventional wisdom is that PG could soon explode with new hotels, real estate developments and other businesses. We're not so sure that will happen to any great extent, but certainly things will get a bit busier.

Outside of PG, the land in Toledo District is lush, wild and wet, fed by 160 inches or more of rain each year — the only "dry" months are February through May. Emerald green valleys lay between low peaks of the southern end of the Maya Mountains. Rice grows in flooded fields, and giant bromeliads line the roads. There are no beaches to speak of around PG, but the rocky shorelines are cooled by near constant breezes from the Bay of Honduras. Offshore are isolated cayes and the straggling end of the barrier reef.

The Maya have lived in this part of Belize for millennia. Among the Maya ruins here are Lubaantun ("Place of the Fallen Stones"). Lubaantun was occupied only from around 700 to 900 CE. The famous, or infamous, "crystal skull" was supposedly discovered here in 1926 by F.A. Mitchell-Hedges, on assignment from the British Museum, though most experts believe the skull is a hoax. Nim Li Punit ("Big Hat") was occupied about the same time as Lubaantun, in the Late Classic period. At its height, several thousand people may have lived there. Among other notable Maya sites in the area is Uxbenka (pronounced Ush-ben-ka and meaning "Ancient Place").

The Maya were joined in the early 19th century by Garifuna from the Bay Islands of Honduras and, after the American Civil War, by a group of former Confederate soldiers and their families who attempted to settle here, with relatively little success. In modern times, Punta Gorda has held an attraction for missionary groups, mostly fundamentalists from the U.S.

Who knows? You may find PG is precisely your kind of place, too.

Punta Gorda Practicalities

Banks: Belize Bank and ScotiaBank have branches and ATMs in PG.

Groceries: All of the groceries in Punta Gorda are small. Try Mel's Mart or one of the several Supaul Stores (usually referred to by color, "green Supaul's," "white Supaul's," etc.) The old PG market on Front Street, where vendors sell fruit, vegetables and other items, has been upgraded. Market days in PG are Monday, Wednesday, Friday and Saturday, with Wednesday and Saturday the most active.

Restaurants: Asha's Culture Kitchen, Mangrove Inn, Marian's Bayview, The Snack Shack, Gomier's and Grace's are good local choices. At the lodges, the restaurant at the luxurious Belcampo Lodge is lovely but expensive, and the Farm Inn on the San Antonio Road has a Belizean-South African restaurant.

Vehicle Rentals: Sun Creek Lodge used to rent cars but last time we checked no longer does. Barefoot Services in Placencia (see Placencia Practicalities) will deliver rental cars to PG, for a fee. Some hotels and lodges offer the use of bikes for free. Gomier's restaurant rents bicycles. Ask around to see if anyone has a car for rent.

Medical: Punta Gorda Hospital (south end of Main Street) can provide basic emergency care; for more serious issues, you may want to upgrade to the Southern Regional Hospital in Dangriga or to hospitals in Belize City.

Infrastructure: Punta Gorda has power, municipal water and a sewerage system. Cable TV, DSL and cellular internet are available also. Many remote areas of Toledo District are not on the grid, and residents must depend on their own resources for water, sewerage and, if they can afford it, cellular or satellite internet. Maya villages have many homes with no running water and no power.

For More Information: Southern Belize's website, www.southernbelize.com, is useful but some information is outdated. Hickatee Cottages' site, www.hickatee.com, provides useful information on buses and other facts about PG and Toledo. *The Toledo Howler* is a more or less quarterly print publication on Toledo tourism. Google it to find the current edition online.

GETTING TO PUNTA GORDA
Car

Via the Southern Highway, Punta Gorda is about 100 miles by car from the junction with the Hummingbird/Stann Creek Valley Highway near Dangriga. It is about the same distance from Placencia village, due to the 25-mile drive back to the Southern Highway. Since the Southern Highway is now fully paved, if you push it a little you can make the trip in about two hours. From Belize City by car, figure on about five hours.

If and when the new Guatemala border crossing at Jalacte village at the end of the new San Antonio Road opens, you will be able to travel into Guatemala and then, if you, on to Honduras by road. You can even connect with the Pan-American Highway that, in a patchwork of roads, connects the north of Alaska with the tip of South America, the world's longest road trip, broken only by a 50-mile missing link, the Darien, between Panama and Colombia, which must be traversed by air or sea.

Bus

By bus from Belize City -- **James Line** (www.jamesbuslines.com) is your best choice -- figure about six hours minimum. Besides seven or eight regular buses a day, James has two daily express buses that are a little faster. Fare from the Novelo's bus station in Belize City to PG is around US$6-8.

Air

Both **Tropic Air** (www.tropicair.com) and **Maya Island Air** (www.mayaislandair.com) each have about four or five flights a day from

Belize City to PG. From the international airport to Punta Gorda, the fare is around US$175 one-way and from municipal, US$148.

Shuttle service by van is also available to Punta Gorda. *See the Placencia section for information on shuttles.* A shuttle from Belize City to PG is at least US$200 for up to two or three people.

Sea

Moving on from PG, or getting here from Guatemala, there is regularly scheduled pedestrian water taxi service between PG and Puerto Barrios, Guatemala. Currently, there are four boats daily to Puerto Barrios – Requena's, Tek-Dat, Pichilingo and Sharkboy -- at 9:30 a.m. and 1, 2 and 4 p.m. respectively. The trip takes about an hour and the one-way fare is US$20 to $25. There's one boat daily to Livingston, Guatemala, Memos, at 1 p.m. Fare depends on the number of people going.

WHAT TO SEE AND DO IN TOLEDO

The Deep South of Belize offers a lot to do on land and sea. It's too bad that so few visitors make it here. Unfortunately, prices for sea and land tours tend to be high, due to lack of volume and the distances involved.

Punta Gorda Town has an attractive waterfront location. However, there are no real beaches in or near PG. The town, with its mix of Garifuna, Creole, Maya, Guatemalans and quite a few expat Americans, is generally safe. There's not much to see or do in town, except for a few small shops along Front Street and elsewhere in town. There's a market primarily selling fruits and vegetables on Front Street. At Central Park, near a large clock tower, is a market with shops and stalls selling used clothing and other miscellaneous junque. **Fajina Women's Group Craft Center** (Front Street near the pier) is a small co-op selling Maya crafts.

Cacao growing is big business (but with a lot of small cacao farmers) in Toledo. The Toledo Cacao Growers Association (www.tcgabelize.com) has some more than 900 members. Most grow their cacao organically and bring it to a central facility for processing. A small chocolate factory, **Cotton Tree Chocolate Shop** (2 Front Street, Punta Gorda, 501-621-8772, www.cottontreechocolate.com), is in town. Other chocolate making operations include the **Ixcacao Maya Belizean Chocolate** (San Felipe village, Toledo, 501-742-4050, www.ixcacaomayabelizechocolate.com). Ixcacao also offers a cacao farm tour.

Near Mafredi village is the **Maya House of Cacao** (San Antonio Road, 501-722-2992, open daily 8-5), which opened in late 2015. It has exhibits on the cacao tree, chocolate making and a gift shop.

The **Chocolate Festival** (www.chocolatefestivalofbelize.com), held the third week in May) is a growing annual event held downtown and in other venues in Toledo.

PG has a couple of Garifuna drumming schools, including Ray Mcdonald's **Warasa Drum School** (501-632-7701, www.warasadrumschool.com), an excellent musical and cultural experience, and **Maroon Creole Drum School** (501-632-7841) run by noted drummer and drum-maker Emmeth Young. Mr. Young's drums are sold at the Driftwood Café at 9 Front Street in PG.

In rural Toledo, you'll see **true rainforests,** lush and green, **Maya villages** that are little changed from 1,000 years ago and several interesting **Maya sites,** including Lubaantun and Nim Li Punit. You can also hike in the national parks and forest reserves and go caving.

While you're here you must visit the rural areas where there are a number of Mayan villages, both Mopan and Kekchi. **San Pedro Columbia** and **San Antonio,** Kekchi villages, are two of the largest. San Pedro Columbia is home to **Eladio Pop's Cacao Trail.** Mr. Pop will take you on a tour of his cacao farm and demonstrate how the ancient Maya made chocolate.

Other interesting villages include **Blue Creek** (Kekchi and Mopan), home to **Blue Creek Cave (Hokeb Ha).** You'll need a guide to explore the cave, although you can swim a few hundred feet into the cave on your own. The **Tumul K'in Center of Learning** (501-608-1070, www.tumukinbelize.org), dedicated to preserving Maya heritage and practices, is also in Blue Creek. **International Zoological Expeditions** (IZE, 501-532-2404, www.izebelize.com), which runs educational and research programs in several parts of Belize, has a small lodge and research station at Blue Creek with a couple of treehouse cabins and a dorm. Rates for lodging, meals and a couple of tours are around US$115 per person per night.

At **Santa Cruz** village is **Río Blanco National Park,** a small (105-acre) park with a waterfall, small lake and a cave. Near **San Miguel** village is **Tiger Cave.**

Near **Big Falls** village is the **Living Maya Experience** (501-627-7408), which provides visitors with an immersion experience in Kekchi Maya culture, including farming, making tortillas and basket weaving. You visit two Maya families. Living Maya Experience is a part of the **Toledo Cultural Trail,** being developed to showcase Maya, Garifuna, Mestizo, Creole and East Indian cultures in the district.

Not associated with the Living Maya Experience but in the same general area is a zip line operated by **Big Falls Extreme Adventures** (www.bigfallsextremeadventures.com). Doing the zip line costs US$40 per person. A half-day combination zip line, river tubing and Lubaantun tour is US$110.

Near **Golden Stream** village about 30 miles north of PG is the **Belize Spice Farm & Botanical Gardens** (501-732-4014, www.belizespicefarm.com). Owned by an American couple of East Indian descent, this is one of the largest vanilla and black pepper farms in Belize. Tour the farm, US$10 per person, in a trailer pulled by a tractor. Pepper and vanilla make good souvenirs of Belize.

Ya'axché Ranger Program (www.yaaxche.org) allows you to experience a day with a ranger in the rainforest. You'll call with a Ya'axché ranger as he travels around trying to find illegal hunting. You might track a jaguar or tapir. The program starts at Golden Stream Field Center. There's no fixed charge, but a donation to Ya'axché of US$35 to $50 is requested.

Payne's Creek National Park, north of PG, covers more than 37,000 acres of mixed saltwater, freshwater and savannah land habitat. It has manatees, yellow-headed parrots, howler monkeys and all five species of Belize's wild cats including jaguars. The park is co-administered by the Forest Department and Toledo Institute for Development and Environment (TIDE).

Barranco is a Garifuna fishing village of about 600 people near the Sarstoon-Temash National Park. It was the home of Andy Palacio and a number of other well-known musicians and artists. There is a dügü, a Garifuna temple, here along with the **Barranco House of Culture.** A tour of Barranco from PG is around US$100 for two people.

Monkey River is a Creole village in northern Toledo on the coast, about 30 minutes south of Placencia by boat. *For information on Monkey River village, see the Placencia section.* Although Monkey River is in Toledo District, it is most easily visited by boat from Placencia, or in good weather on a road from the Southern Highway. You park your car and take a small boat to the village itself.

Another small, remote coastal village in Toledo, about half an hour south of Monkey River by boat, is **Punta Negra**. Punta Negra, accessible by boat from PG or Placencia, is nestled between the Port of Honduras Marine Reserve to the front and the Payne's Creek National Park to the rear. The closest thing to a hotel here is **Sabal Beach** (501-732-2324, www.sabalbeach.com), about 1¼ miles north of the village. It has two self-catering cabañas with kitchens for US$85 each or US$145 for the two together, plus 9% tax. Bring your own food from PG or Placencia, or the owners can provide provisions for a US$75 fee plus the cost of the food and drink. Lodging may also be available in rental cottages and in local homes (check Airbnb). Meals are offered at **Punta Negra Grill and Tavern** (open only when there are customers). About 5 minutes south of Punta Negra village is **Punta Negra Lagoon.** The shallow lagoon, with depths of 4 to 9 feet, offers great fishing for tarpon and snook.

For a more complete immersion in Maya life, consider a **homestay** or **guesthouse stay** in a Maya village. Several different programs are available in Toledo.

One is the **Toledo Ecotourism Association** program (501-633-9954, www.teabelize.org.) TEA offers stays in guesthouses (not individual homes) in five villages: Laguna, San Antonio, Santa Elena, San Jose and San Miguel starting at US$28 per person. A one-day, one-night program including guesthouse stay, three meals and various activities is US$100 per person. TEA also offers farm, village, cave, chocolate making and other day tours, most from about US$10 to $30 per person.

Another is the **Aguacate Belize Homestay Program** (501-633-9954, www.aguacatebelize.com). Stays in a Maya home in Aguacate village, a Kekchi community, are around US$8 per person per night, plus US$3.50 per meal, plus a one-time US$5 registration fee. Keep in mind you will stay in a Maya thatch home with dirt floor that will not have electricity or running water. You'll sleep in a hammock, bathe in a creek and eat simple meals of tortillas, beans and eggs that the family eats.

Maya Sites

Nim Li Punit, near Indian Creek village off Mile 75 of the Southern Highway, 501-665-5126, open 8 to 5 daily, admission US$5, is a late Classic period site noted for its stelae. More than two dozen large stelae have been found at the site. Some of the stelae and other artifacts are on display at the informative visitor center. Nim Li Punit is on a hilltop with good views of the surrounding rainforest. Maya women and children from Indian Creek set up tables near the exit area, selling their Maya crafts.

Lubaantun, near San Pedro Columbia village off the San Antonio road, is a late Classic period site. The site is open daily from 8 to 5. Admission is US$5. There is a visitor center. Lubaantun was at its peak from around 730 to 900 CE. The site has 18 plazas. From the tallest structure in the plaza, about 50 feet high, you can see the sea. Lubaantun was first rediscovered in 1875 and has been excavated by a number of different archeologists, including Thomas Gann and Norman Hammond. The so-called "Crystal Skull" allegedly was discovered here in 1924 by Anna Mitchell-Hedges, the daughter of the adventurer F. A. Mitchell-Hedges. In fact, tests suggest the skull is of modern origin.

Pusilhá and **Uxbenka** are two other Maya sites in Toledo. Neither is much excavated. Both are difficult to visit except on a tour (around US$100 for two people). *See Archeological Sites in Belize in More Depth section for additional information.*

Offshore Cayes

Off the coast of Toledo are some of Belize's most pristine cayes and excellent diving, snorkeling and fishing.

Closest to PG are the **Snakes Cayes** in the **Port Honduras Marine Reserve.** These cayes offer good snorkeling, diving and swimming about a 30-minute boat ride from town. There are **East, South, West and Middle Snake** cayes. The best beach is on West Snake Caye. South Snake Caye has abundant sea life on view for snorkelers and divers. East Snake Caye has a lighthouse. Middle Snake Caye is for researchers only, off limits to regular visitors. There is a US$5 per person per day reserve fee for visiting Port Honduras Reserve.

Farther out are the **Sapodilla Cayes** in the **Sapodilla Cayes Marine Reserve.** It's about a 90-minute boat ride from PG, and when the weather is bad it's a rough ride. Hunting Caye and Lime Caye both have good swimming and snorkeling. **Lime Caye** is owned by the Garbutt brothers of PG. Garbutt's Marine (501-604-3548, www.garbuttsfishinglodge.com) has its main fishing lodge in PG and has primitive bunkhouse cabins on Lime Caye (toilets are outside), with packages costing US$350 to $700 per person including transportation, lodging, meals, snorkeling, fishing and park fees. The marine reserve has a US$10 per person per day reserve fee. **Hunting Caye** is the site of one of the University of Belize's small satellite campuses, and it sometimes rents out its basic rooms for visitors (around US$40 per person). The Belize Coast Guard is also stationed here. Camping on the island is US$5 per person.

Maya Villages

Within an hour or so of PG are some two dozen small Maya villages. Some are Mopan Maya, some Kekchi and some a mix. Getting to the Maya villages areas is easiest done with your own transportation, but you can also go on a tour or take a bus. A bunch of local buses leave from the clock tower area of Central Park to go to various Maya villages and to Barranco in Toledo. Usually there are just one or two buses a day to each village. Ask locally for current schedules, or look in the local tourist newspaper, *The Toledo Howler.*

Punta Gorda Tour Operators and Guides

There are about a dozen registered and licensed tour operators in Toledo, including the ones below. They can arrange land and marine tours. The larger lodging properties also run tours. Full-day land tours range from about US$100 to $150 per person. These tours include guide, transportation from PG and lunch. Full-day private snorkel and swimming tours to the Snake Cayes cost around US$250 for two persons. If you can join a group, the rate may be lower.

Garbutt's Marine, Joe Taylor Creek, Punta Gorda, 501-722-0070, www.garbuttsfishinglodge.com. Garbutt's Marine has cottages to rent in PG, primitive bunkhouses on Lime Caye in the Sapodilla Cayes Marine Reserve and does a full range of fishing dive and snorkel trips. The three Garbutt brothers, Dennis, Scully and Oliver, were born in the tiny Toledo coastal village of Punta Negra and have spent much of their lives in the waters off PG.

PG Tours, 501-629-4266, Punta Gorda, www.pgtours.com.

TIDE Tours, Mile 1, San Antonio Road, 501-722-2129, www.tidebelize.org.

Toledo Cave & Adventure (Bruno Kuppinger), 501-604-2124, Sun Creek, www.tcatours.com. Bruno Kuppinger, a German who is now a Belizean citizen, specializes in adventure and extreme adventure tours, including a 10-day Maya Divide trip into the Central and Southern Maya Mountains. Kuppinger says this trip may be the hardest 10 days of your life.

For more information on tours and about the Toledo area in general, visit the Belize Tourism Industry Association (BTIA) office on Main Street, 501-722-2531. Pick up a copy of *The Toledo Howler* tabloid, published several times a year.

TOLEDO LODGING

Lodging choices in the PG area and elsewhere in Toledo are listed roughly by cost, from high to low.

Belcampo Lodge. Wilson Road, 5 miles north of PG, 800-299-9940 in U.S. and Canada; www.belcampobz.com. Formerly the fishing lodge known as El Pescador PG, and then Machaca Hill, Belcampo Belize now focuses on more traditional jungle lodge activities, such as trips and tours in the Laughing Falcon Reserve, a 12,000-acre private nature reserve. The owner has taken the lodge far upscale, redoing the main lodge and adding a gorgeous spa. Rates with meals are among the highest of any lodge in Belize. The lodge is set on a steep hill, called Big Hill for the farm that was originally here, on 470 acres above the Rio Grande. A small tram takes guests down to the boats docked on the river at the base of the hill. It's really cool! Up top, on a clear day, you have views of the Gulf of Honduras, with Guatemala and Honduras in the distance. Troops of howler monkeys come by frequently. After a day exploring the Toledo rain forest, dive into the pool, then dine on fish and fresh vegetables from the lodge's organic garden. The 16 renovated cottage suites have vaulted ceilings, tile floors and air-conditioning. Room rates start at US$380 to $455 per night, plus tax and 10% service. An eight-night package including lodging, all meals, air transfers from Belize City, taxes, service and several tours and activities is a whopping US$4,320 per person based on double occupancy.

Cotton Tree Lodge. San Felipe village; 501-670-0557 or U.S. number 212-529-8622; www.cottontreelodge.com. Named after the silk cotton tree, aka kapok or ceiba, a giant example of which stands near the main lodge building, Cotton Tree Lodge sits on 100 acres beside the Moho River about 15 miles from Punta Gorda. Cotton Tree accommodations include rooms, one- and two-bedroom cabañas and even a river cabaña anchored in the middle of the Moho River. The lodge has raised wooden walkways; in the summer rainy season the Moho sometimes floods, and at times the lodge grounds become a shallow pond. Good meals are served in a huge thatch palapa. Room rates are US$196-$350 double in-season, US$162 to $306 off-season. All-inclusive rates with all meals and daily guided tour are US$459 to $614. All rates are plus 9% hotel tax and 12% service.

Garbutt Fishing Lodge. Joe Taylor Creek, Punta Gorda, 501-722-0070 or 501-604-3548; www.garbuttsfishinglodge.com. The lodge is on a small point of land on the Joe Taylor Creek, overlooking the creek on the back and the Gulf of Honduras to the front. Nearby are wood cabins with private baths, air conditioning, cable TV and wi-fi. One deck hangs over the open sea, and another overlooks the creek. Upstairs at the main lodge building is the Grand Slam bar and restaurant. As noted above, the Garbutt brothers, along with a cousin and uncle, offer a full array of fishing, dive and snorkel trips to the Port Honduras and Sapodilla Cayes marine reserves. They also have primitive lodgings and a tiny restaurant on Lime Caye in the Sapodilla range. Many guests here are on fishing trips. One-week (six-night, seven-day) all-inclusive fishing packages including boat, guide, lodging, all meals, taxes, marine reserve fees and local drinks and beer are around US$2,900 per person. Shorter packages are also offered.

Lodge at Big Falls. Big Falls (P.O. Box 103, Punta Gorda), 501-732-4444; www.thelodgeatbigfalls. This lodge, on about 30 acres on the banks of the Rio Grande River near the village of Big Falls, is an attractive option for birders, nature lovers and outdoor lovers. The owners are Rob and Marta Hirons. They've done a good job developing the lodge property. The accommodations are what most visitors are looking for in a lodge — there are thatch cabañas, nice ones, with tile floors and private baths. In addition, the lodge has three newer cabins with air-conditioning. There's a swimming pool, and you also can swim in the river. The main lodge building has a restaurant and library. Current rates: high season (November to May), US$206 to $225 double; May to October, US$161 to $181 double. Rates are plus 9% tax and are higher Christmas/New Year's. Breakfast is an additional US$14, packed lunch US$12 and dinner US$40 per person, plus 12.5% tax.

Tranquility Lodge. San Felipe Road, Jacintoville, 501-677-9921; www.tranquility-lodge.com. This lodge just off the Southern Highway has gone through several changes of ownership over the last 10 or 15 years. It has rooms, thatch cabañas and a restaurant on about 20 acres on the Jacinto River. Rates are US$125 to $145 double, in season and US$105 to $125 off-season, all plus 9%tax and 10% service charge.

Sirmoor Hill Farm B&B. Mile 3, New Road, Punta Gorda, 501-722-0052; www.sirmoorhillfarm.com. This bed and breakfast inn isn't for everyone, but we think it has one of the most beautiful settings in Southern Belize, on a 775-acre cattle ranch and farm. (We use a photo of the farm and an old Massey-Ferguson tractor as one of the screen savers on our MacBook Pro.) You enter the farm on a winding driveway lined with royal palms. The white frame colonial house, more than 100 years old, is set on in four acres of lawn and gardens on a low hill to catch the breezes and provide views of the rolling farm land and lush jungle. There's a beautiful infinity swimming pool and patio out back. Sirmoor has just two bedrooms, with a shared bath. The rooms have comfortable beds, fans and 12-foot ceilings. Year-round rate for one room is US$110 and for both US$190, plus 9% tax. Marty and Richard are knowledgeable, charming hosts.

The Farm Inn. San Antonio-Santa Cruz Road, Toledo, 501-732-4781; www.thefarminnbelize.com. The Farm Inn is a small lodge on 52 acres just off the newly paved San Antonio Road. The managers are from South Africa. The Farm Inn has three rooms in a two-story building near a small creek, plus two other rooms closer to the lodge office. All rooms have private baths and fans, no air-conditioning (power at the lodge is solar). Rates are US$107 to $162 double year-round, including tax and breakfast. The restaurant serves Belizean and South African dishes, with many items from the lodge's own garden. Guinea fowl and other creatures scamper around the grounds.

Coral House Inn. 151 Main Street, (P.O. Box 43, Punta Gorda), 501-722-2878; www.coralhouseinn.net. Americans Rick and Darla Mallory bought and renovated a 1938 colonial-era house and turned it into one of the coolest guesthouses in Belize. You'll recognize it by the coral color and the vintage red and white VW van parked in front. There's a small swimming pool and use of bikes is complimentary. Nearby are Confederate graves in a cemetery, a legacy of the Confederate immigration to Toledo after the U.S. Civil War. The five guest rooms and one suite -- US$96 to

$108 double year-round, plus tax -- have tile floors, good beds, air-conditioning and free wi-fi. Highly recommended.

The signature VW bus at Coral House Inn in PG

Blue Belize Guest House. 139 Front Street, Punta Gorda, 501-722-2678; www.bluebelize.com. This pleasant, well-located guesthouse is owned by marine biologist Rachel Graham, though last we heard Dr. Graham was in San Pedro. You can do your own thing in one of the five attractive self-catering flats, with kitchenettes, large bedrooms and verandas with hammocks. The guesthouse is set on a bluff overlooking the water, within a short stroll of everything in town. A continental breakfast is included. Bikes are complimentary. Rates US$75 to $135 plus 9% tax. Recommended.

Hickatee Cottages Lodge. Mile 1.5, Ex-Servicemen Road, Punta Gorda, 501-662-4475; www.hickatee.com. This charming and down-to-earth lodge on 20 acres just south of Punta Gorda was created by a British couple, Ian and Kate Morton. It opened in late 2005 and quickly became one of the best little inns in Belize. The Caribbean-style cottages, with zinc roofs and private porches, are nestled in lush foliage. Rates for the six rooms are an affordable US$65 to $130 double, including continental breakfast. There's a small but well-stocked bar with free wi-fi. On certain days, the lodge offers guests free visits to Fallen Stones butterfly farms. A hickatee, by the way, is a river turtle, *Dermatemys mawii*. Recommended.

Sun Creek Lodge. Mile 12, Southern Highway, 501-607-6363; www.suncreeklodge.de. This small lodge, on a dirt road to the east of the Southern Highway about 12 miles north of PG, has four rustic thatched cabañas with outdoor showers, plus two larger "villas" scattered around the tropical grounds. Formerly operated by well-known Toledo adventure guide Bruno Kuppinger and wife Melissa, the lodge is now run by Germans Marisa Holtz and Thomas Schreck. They can set you up with tours, too. Cabaña rates are US$40 to $70, year-round. Two larger units are US$90 to US$120. All rates plus 9% hotel tax.

Tate's Guest House. 34 José Maria Nuñez Street, Punta Gorda, 501-722-0147. Run by William Tate, a long-time post office worker in PG, and his family, this guesthouse on a quiet residential street is a good value. The rooms are clean, and the atmosphere friendly. There's a small common kitchen with refrigerator and microwave for guest use. Rates around US$20 to $45.

Nature's Way Guesthouse. 65 Front Street, Punta Gorda, 501-702-2119; e-mail natureswayguesthouse@hotmail.com. This rambling, funky old guesthouse/hostel appeals to the hippy backpacker in us. Run by long-time expat Chet Schmidt, it has a nice location, on the water toward the south end of town. Guests here are often well traveled, with stories to tell. There are nine basic rooms, three with private baths. At these prices — at around US$19-$25 — don't expect a Hampton Inn.

PUNTA GORDA/TOLEDO DINING

In addition to the restaurants listed below, **Belcampo Lodge** (Expensive to Very Expensive) has an excellent restaurant, open to the public by reservation. **The Farm Inn** restaurant, (Moderate) serves an unusual combination of Belizean and African dishes. The South African dishes are cooked in a three-legged cast iron pot.

Price ranges shown are for typical meals for one (usually dinner), not including tip, tax or alcoholic drinks. Price ranges:

Inexpensive: Under US$7
Moderate: US$8-$19
Expensive: US$20-$39
Very Expensive: Over US$40
Restaurants are listed alphabetically.

Asha's Culture Kitchen. 80 Front Street, Punta Gorda, 501-632-8025. This is usually our first stop for dinner in PG. The setting is great: Asha's is in a wooden building over the water, with a breezy deck with views of the sea. For another, it serves tasty seafood and other dishes in large portions at modest prices. It's one of the few restaurants in town that draws a crowd – as the evening wears on, the availability of the day's dishes is checked off on a chalkboard. Dinner daily except Tuesday. Inexpensive to Moderate.

Coleman's Café. Big Falls village, near the rice mill, 501-720-2017. This Big Falls village spot serves simple, tasty Belizean dishes such as stew chicken with beans and rice. Sit at tables under a covered patio, open to the breezes, and enjoy real Belizean hospitality. Inexpensive to Moderate.

Gomier's Restaurant and Soy Centre. 5 Alejandro Vernon Street, Punta Gorda, 501-722-2929. This restaurant opens only if the St. Lucia-born owner, Ignatius "Gomier" Longville, feels like cooking. When open Gomier's does excellent vegetarian meals, from organic ingredients. Closed Sunday and some other days. Inexpensive to Moderate.

Grace's. Main Street, Punta Gorda, 501-702-2414. This long-established local place is especially good for breakfast. Open for breakfast, lunch and dinner daily. Inexpensive to Moderate.

Mangrove Inn at Casa Bonita. Front Street in Cattle Landing area, Punta Gorda, 501-722-2270. The cook and co-owner of this little restaurant, Iconie Williams, formerly operated one of PG's best eateries, also called Mangrove Inn, and she reopened it here in the B&B in her home. Iconie cooks different dishes every evening, but you'll usually have a choice of seafood (snapper, snook or shrimp) or hearty fare like roasted chicken. Open daily for dinner only. Inexpensive to Moderate.

Marian's Bayview. 76 Front Street, Punta Gorda, 501-722-0129. Here you choose from a couple of dishes owner Marian prepares for the day, perhaps local fish or an East Indian dish. The restaurant is on the third floor of a concrete building, with views of the water. It has bare light bulbs and rough cement floors, but you come here for the food, not the atmosphere. Open daily for lunch and dinner. Inexpensive to Moderate.

Snack Shack. Main Street, Punta Gorda, at Belize Telemedia Ltd. parking lot, 501-702-0020. This is PG's version of fast food – build-your-own burritos, freshly made flavored tortillas, pancakes, fruit smoothies and such. Try the papaya shake. Open Monday-Saturday for breakfast and lunch. Inexpensive.

Where to Party in PG

There's not much action after dark in PG. You can get a cold one and a snack at **Waluca's Bar & Grill** across from the water a little north of the main part of town or at **D'Thatch** on Front Street.

APPENDIXES

BEST BELIZE WEBSITES

Here are some of our favorite web sites about Belize:

Destination and General Websites

www.ambergriscaye.com Impressive site by Oregonian Marty Casado with a massive amount of material about Ambergris Caye. Good links to other sites, including most hotels, dive shops, real estate firms and other businesses on the island. Active message board.

www.sanpedrosun.com News about Ambergris Caye by its leading weekly newspaper (published in print as well as online).

www.ambergristoday.com Another excellent source of news and information on Ambergris Caye.

www.corozal.com Pretty good information about Corozal District. A sister site, www.corozal.bz, has business listings and information.

www.hopkinsbelize.com Information on Hopkins village.

www.placencia.com Good tourist information on the Placencia peninsula from the BTIA.

www.destinationsbelize.com A privately owned site by a Placencia resident and travel agent with all kinds of news and information about Placencia.

www.cayecaulkervacation.com Official site of BTIA in Caulker.

www.puntagordabelize.com The official web site of the town of Punta Gorda.

www.southernbelize.com Lots of information for visitors on PG and Toledo District.

www.belmopanbelize.com Information on Belize's capital city.

www.travelbelize.org Recently revised version of the official site of the Belize Tourism Board, with tons of information on hotels and sightseeing.

www.nichbelize.org is the website of the Belize National Institute of Culture and History (NICH), devoted to archeological, cultural and historical sites in the country.

www.btia.org The official site of the Belize Travel Industry Association, a public-private partnership for the promotion of tourism in Belize.

www.belizehotels.org. Site run by members of the Belize Hotel Association.

www.belizefirst.com On-line magazine about Belize (Lan Sluder, editor and publisher) with dozens of articles on travel, life and retirement in Belize. It also offers free listings of real estate for sale and real estate wanted.

www.belize.gov.bz Official site of the Government of Belize – not always up-to-date, unfortunately.

www.belizeinvest.org.bz Site of Beltraide, which is charged with attracting business investment to Belize.

www.belizenet.com Well-done site on Belize travel and other information, by folks who provide a lot of web design services in Belize. Associated with an active message board, Belize Forums at www.belizeforum.com.

www.belize.com is a site with extensive information on Belize, although in places it repeats information from other sources. It claims it was the first website completely devoted to Belize.

www.belizean.com has news updates and other information on Belize.

www.channel5belize.com This Belize City TV station provides the most definitive and reliable source of news on Belize. The weekday evening news broadcast is provided in transcript form and also in video.

www.7newsbelize.com Another good Belize City TV station with transcripts of the evening news broadcasts.

www.breakingbelizenews.com An aggressive site that provides breaking news reports on Belize. The owners say that 2 million people visited its website in 2015, that it received more than 10 million page views on Facebook and that Google ranks it the number 1 source of news about Belize.

www.belizenews.com This site has links to most newspapers, TV and radio stations, magazines and other media in Belize.

www.stonetreerecords.com Stonetree has been making Belize music since 1995.

www.cubola.com Site of publisher of books and maps on Belize.

www.fodors.com Some guidebooks authored or co-authored by Lan Sluder, including *Fodor's Belize, Fodor's The Carolinas and Georgia,* and *InFocus Great Smoky Mountains National Park* are published by this Random House division, and parts of these books are available on-line.

www.belizeembassy.gov Official site of the U.S. Embassy in Belize.

www.expatexchange.com This site has a fairly active forum section on moving to and living in Belize.

www.nationalkriolcouncil.org Information about the B*ileez Kriol* language.

www.ngcbelize.org Information about the Garinagu people of Belize.

www.belizebirding.com Put together by The Lodge at Big Falls, this is a commercial site, but it has good information on birding in Southern Belize.

Best Belize Blogs

http://belizebus.wordpress.com Excellent site with up-to-date information on bus, water taxi, air and other transportation options in Belize.

www.tacogirl.com Perhaps the best of all the personal blogs about Belize. Tacogirl covers the country although it is mostly focused on Ambergris Caye, where the author lives.

http://winjama.blogspot.com Run by a man who moved to Corozal, this very helpful blog focuses on living in Belize.

http://tropicat.wordpress.com This blog is about living in the Belize bush.

http://bubbasbirdblog.blogspot.com Elbert Greer's blog on birding in Belize.

http://exploringbelizecontinues.blogspot.com Adventures of two expat women in San Pedro.

http://barnaclesbelize.blogspot.com Great Belize photos on this blog by Barnacle Bill Taylor in Maya Beach.

http://latitudesbelize.blogspot.com Put together by the owners of Changes in Latitudes B&B in San Pedro.

http://moonracerfarmbelize.blogspot.com A couple with a small lodge in Cayo near the Mountain Pine Ridge blog on living and running a hotel in Belize.

www.caribbean-colors.blogspot.com Lee Vanderwalker of Caye Caulker blogs about her life and art.

Kriol & Spanish Phrases

English is the official language of Belize, the primary language used in government, in schools, on signs and in most media. However, Spanish is now the first language of more Belizeans than any other. Garifuna is spoken in some areas in Southern Belize, and three modern Maya languages (Yucatec, Kekchi and Mopan) are in use in Maya villages. You'll also hear a version of German spoken by some Mennonites, Mandarin and Cantonese Chinese and some East Indian languages. Many if not most Belizeans today, regardless of their mother tongue, understand and speak Bileez Kriol (the proper spelling approved by the National Kriol Council.) Kriol is the "default" language among Belizeans, and you will hear it spoken especially in Belize City and in Creole villages. Many people interviewed on radio and television speak at least partly in Kriol.

Here are a few phrases in Kriol and Spanish that may be useful for travelers in Belize.

BASIC BILEEZ KRIOL

The various Creole languages of the Americas came out of the slave trade in West Africa. The language evolved in Jamaica and elsewhere in the Caribbean, Central America and the Southern United States where slavery was an institution well into the 19th century. It is an adaptation of the language of the slave masters, using the local language in the New World with some elements of West African languages, grammar and a unique pronunciation. In some areas the base language was French, in some areas Spanish and in Belize it was mostly English. However, a number of Kriol words were borrowed from the Spanish, Garifuna and the three modern Maya languages used in Belize (Kekchi, Mopan and Yucatec Maya).

Originally only a spoken language, in 1994 a standard orthography for Bileez Kriol was developed for written Kriol and a dictionary was published. For more information, visit the website of the National Kriol Council at www.nationalkriolcouncil.org.

GREETINGS
Gud mawnin! or *Mawning!* Good morning!
Weh di go aan? What's up? How are you?
Aarite Fine, all right
Weh yuh naym? What's your name?
Mi naym da... My name is...
Yuh da Bileez? Are you from Belize?
Si yu lata See you later
Gud nite Good evening.

USEFUL PHRASES

Humoch dis kaas? What does this cost?
Gyal Girl
Bwah Boy
Weh gaan ahn gyal? What's up, girl?
Da weh time? Or Weh taim yu gat? What time is it?
Weh paat... Where is...?
Luk paan Look at.
Evryting gud Everything's fine
Haul yo rass! Get out of here!
Fu tru? Really? (Is that right?)
Fu tru! That's the truth!
Rais ahn beenz Rice and beans
Mi laak eet rais ahn beenz I like to eat rice and beans
Dis da fi wi chikin This is our chicken (well-known slogan of Quality Poultry Products Mennonite poultry co-op in Spanish Lookout)
Betta no litta Better not litter (trash cleanup slogan seen on signs all around Belize)
Dah no so, dah naily so If it's not true, it's nearly so
Wi de da Bileez We are in Belize
Mi love Bileez! I love Belize!

SPANISH PHRASES FOR TRAVELERS

The Spanish spoken in Belize varies somewhat depending on where in the country you are. In Western or Southern Belize, Spanish speakers may be immigrants from Guatemala, so Guatemalan and Central American Spanish may predominate, with special slang and the common use of *vos* for you. In Northern Belize, Mestizos came from Mexico's Yucatán, although many Mestizos have spent generations in Belize and accents have changed due to the influence of English, Kriol and the Latin American and United States mass media But don't worry – almost any accent will be understood, and the effort to speak Spanish will be appreciated by those who have little or no English. This also goes if you make a side trip to Tikal or Chetumal.

GREETINGS
Buenos días (*bway nos dee ahs*) Good morning
Buenas tardes (*bway nahs tar days*) Good afternoon
Buenas noches (*bway nahs noh chayss*)
Hola (*oh lah*) Hello or hi (used with people you know)

¿Cómo está? *(coh moh es tah)* How are you?

Bien, gracias *(bee ayn, grah cee ahs)* Good, thanks

Por favor *(por fah vohr)* Please

Gracias *(grah cee ahs)* Thank you

Muy bien *(mwee byehn)* Very well

Mucho gusto *(moo choh goos toh)* Nice to meet you (said by both parties when introduced)

Adiós *(ah dyohss)* Goodbye

USEFUL PHRASES

¿Habla inglés? *(ahblah een glays)?* Do you speak English?

Yo quiero, Yo no quiero *(yoh kee ay roh, yoh noh kee ayr oh)* I want/I don't want

Quiero un cuarto para dos personas con baño *(kee eh roh oon kwar toh pah rah dohs pehr sohn ahs kohn bah nyoh)* I want a room for two persons with bathroom

¿Dónde está...? *(dohn des tah)* Where is...?

¿Cuánto cuesta? *(cwahn toh cways tah)* How much does it cost?

Eso es muy caro *(eh soh ehs moo ee kah roh)* That's too expensive

¿Cuándo? *(kwan doh)* When?

¿Qué? *(keh)* What?

No funciona *(noh foonk see oh nah)* It doesn't work

¿Qué hora es? *(kay orah ess)* What time is it?

¿Tiene usted...? *(tee ayn ay ooh sted)* Do you have...?

Yo tengo, Yo no tengo *(yoh tayn goh, yoh noh tayn goh)* I have, I don't have

Yo entiendo, Yo no entiendo *(yoh ayn tee ayn doh, yoh noh ayn tee ayn doh)* I understand, I don't understand

Deme *(deh mee)* Give me

¿Entiende? *(ayn tee ayn day)* Do you understand?

Sí *(see)* Yes

No *(noh)* No

Perdóneme *(pehr doh neh meh)* Excuse me (to pass by)

Disculpe *(dees kool peh)* Excuse me (to break in to ask a question)

Bueno *(bweh noh)* Good

Malo *(mah loh)* Bad

Más *(mahs)* More

No más *(noh mahs)* No more

Menos *(meh nohs)* Less

Médico *(meh dee coh)* Doctor

RESTAURANT TERMS

Desayuno *(deh sah yoo noh)* Breakfast

Almuerzo *(ahl mwehr soh)* Lunch

Cena *(seh nah)* Dinner

Una mesa para dos tres, cuatro *(oona may sah pah rah dohss, trays, kwah troh)* A table for two, three, four

Un menú *(oon may noo)* A menu

Presto? *(press toh)* Ready [to order]?

Yo quiero... *(yoh kee ay roh)* I want...

Sopa *(soh pah)* Soup

Ensalada *(ayn sah lah dah)* Salad

Hamburguesa *(ahm boor gay sah)* Hamburger

Con salsa de tomate, mostaza, tomate, lechuga *(cohn sahl sah day toh mah tay, mohs tah sah, toh mah tay, lay choo gah)* With ketchup, mustard, tomato, lettuce

Una entrada *(oona ayn trah dah)* Appetizer/starter

Bistec *(bees steck)* Beefsteak

Cerdo *(cer doh)* Pork

Jamón *(hah mohn)* Ham

Pollo *(poh yoh)* Chicken

Pollo y arroz (poh yoh ee ahr rohs) Chicken with rice

Frijoles *(free hoh lehss)* Beans

Papas *(pop pahs)* Potatoes

Papas fritas *(pop pahs free tohs)* French fries

Un postre *(oon pohs tray)* Dessert

Una bebida *(oona bay bee dah)* A drink

Agua *(ah gwah)* Water

Cerveza *(sayr vay sah)* Beer

Vino tinto *(vee noh teen toh)*, **vino blanco** *(vee noh blahn coh)* Red wine, white wine

Un café *(oon cah fay)* A coffee

¡Señor! or **¡Señorita!** *(say nyor, say nyor eetah)* To call your waiter or waitress

La cuenta *(lah cwayn tah)* The check

¿Tarjeta de credito? (tar hey tah day cray dee toh) [D you take] credit card?

DAYS OF THE WEEK

Lunes *(loo nehss)* Monday

Martes *(mahr tehss)* Tuesday

Miércoles *(myehr koh lehs)* Wednesday

Jueves *(wheh behss)* Thursday
Viernes *(byehr nehss)* Friday
Sábado *(sah bah doh)* Saturday
Domingo *(doh meen goh)* Sunday

DIRECTIONS

¿Dónde está la estación de autobuses? *(dohn des tah la ays ta see ohn day ow toe boos ehs)* Where is the bus station?

¿Dónde está un restaurante? *(dohn days tah oon rays tore rahn tay)?*

¿La calle ... ? *(lah cah yay) The street?*

¿Un banco? *(oon bahn coh) A bank?*

¿El baño? *(ayl ban yoh)* The bathroom?

Yo quiero un hotel *(yoh kee ayr oh oon oh tel)* I want a hotel

A la derecha *(ah lah day ray chah)* To the right

A la izquierda *(ah lah eez kee ayr dah)* To the left

Derecho *(day ray choh)* Straight ahead

En la esquina *(a lah ays kee nah)* At the corner

A una cuadra, a dos, tres, cuatro cuadras *(a oona dohss, trayss, cwah troh cwah drahs)* In one, two, three, four blocks

NUMBERS

1 **uno** *(oo noh)*

2 **dos** *(dohss)*

3 **tres** *(trehss)*

4 **cuatro** *(kwah troh)*

5 **cinco** *(seen koh)*

6 **seis** *(sayss)*

7 **siete** *(syeh teh)*

8 **ocho** *(oh choh)*

9 **nueve** *(nweh beh)*

10 **diez** *(dyehss)*

11 **once** *(ohn seh)*

12 **doce** *(doh seh)*

13 **trece** *(treh seh)*

14 **catorce** *(kah tohr seh)*

15 **quince** *(keen seh)*

16 **dieciséis** *(dyeh see sayss)*

17 **diecisiete** *(dyeh see syeh teh)*

18 **dieciocho** *(dyeh syoh choh)*

19 **diecinueve** *(dyeh see nweh beh)*
20 **veinte** *(bayn teh)*
21 **veinteuno** *(bayn teh oo noh)*
30 **treinta** *(trayn tah)*
40 **cuarenta** *(kwah rehn tah)*
50 **cincuenta** *(seen kwehn tah)*
60 **sesenta** *(seh sehn tah)*
70 **setenta** *(seh tehn tah)*
80 **ochenta** *(oh chehn tah)*
90 **noventa** *(noh behn tah)*
100 **cien** *(syehn)*
1,000 **mil** *(meel)*

ABOUT LAN SLUDER

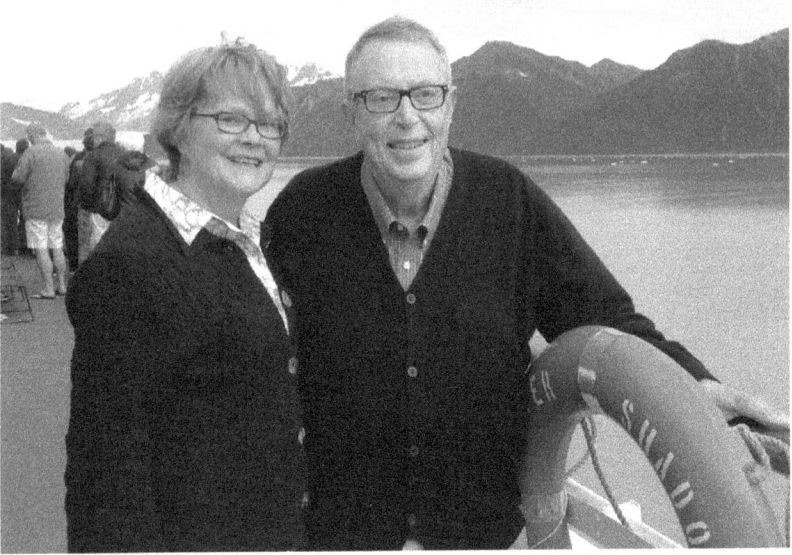

*On location off the coast of Alaska, with wife Sheila M. Lambert –
the Hubbard Glacier is in the background*

Lan Sluder has been reporting on and writing about Belize for more than a quarter century. The author of 15 books and ebooks on Belize, Sluder has helped many people plan the adventure of a lifetime in this fascinating little English-speaking country on the Caribbean Coast of Central America. Over the years, Sluder has personally stayed in more than 250 hotels, resorts, inns, guesthouses and lodges in Belize and has visited and toured hundreds more. He has eaten at most of the restaurants in Belize and has visited every corner of the country, most many times.

Among Lan Sluder's Belize books, besides this one, are *Fodor's Belize; Lan Sluder's Guide to Belize; Easy Belize: How to Live, Retire, Work and Buy Property in Belize, the English Speaking, Frost Free Paradise on the Caribbean Coast; Living Abroad in Belize; Adapter Kit: Belize; Lan Sluder's Guide to Mainland Belize; San Pedro Cool; Belize Book of Lists* and *Belize First Guide to Mainland Belize.* Sluder is also founder, editor and publisher of *Belize First Magazine* – a web edition is at www.belizefirst.com.

In addition to his books on Belize, Sluder has authored several books on Asheville and the North Carolina mountains, including *Amazing Asheville; Asheville Relocation, Retirement and Visitor Guide;* and *Moving to the Mountains.* He wrote *Frommer's Best Beach Vacations: Carolinas and Georgia, Fodor's InFocus Great*

314

Smoky Mountains National Park and co-authored *Fodor's The Carolinas & Georgia.* His Asheville website is www.amazingasheville.net. Also, he has written a book on the game of bridge, *Play Bridge Today,* and a book on vintage Rolls-Royce and Bentley motorcars, *Buy a Classic Rolls-Royce or Bentley.*

A former business newspaper editor and reporter in New Orleans, Sluder has contributed articles on travel, retirement and business subjects to media around the world, including *The New York Times, Chicago Tribune, Miami Herald, Where to Retire,* Canada's *Globe and Mail, Bangkok Post, The Tico Times, Charlotte Observer,* TravelChannel.com and *Caribbean Travel & Life.*

Sluder was educated at Duke University and in the U.S. Army in Vietnam. When not in Belize or traveling elsewhere, Sluder lives on a mountain farm near Asheville, N.C., with wife Sheila M. Lambert, an attorney.

The opinions in this book are those of Lan Sluder. Questions, complaints and rants can be sent to him at lansluder@gmail.com.

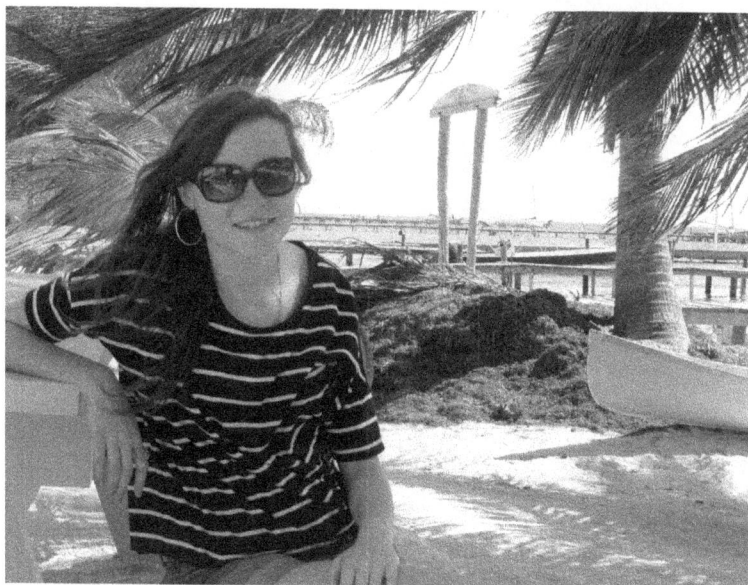

Rose Lambert-Sluder, taking a break on Caye Caulker

Rose Lambert-Sluder, who shot many of the photos for this book, has traveled extensively in North, Central and South America, Europe, Eastern Europe and Turkey. She graduated with distinction and highest honors from the University of North Carolina at Chapel Hill and now is a Graduate Teaching Fellow and a graduate student in the Master of Fine Arts program in fiction at the University of Oregon at Eugene.

www.ingramcontent.com/pod-product-compliance
Lightning Source LLC
LaVergne TN
LVHW011217080426
835509LV00005B/173